SPRITUAL AWAKENINGS

First Contacts with People in Crisis & Spiritual Emergencies

A Handbook about and for
People Experiencing Various Sorts of
Psychological, Emotional
& Spiritual Crisis,
Spiritual Emergence Processes,
Spiritual Emergencies,
with information especially
for their Carers & Therapists

2nd Edition: 2024

COURTENAY YOUNG

Copyright © 2010, 2024: Courtenay Young: Body Psychotherapy Publications.

ISBN: 979-8-89465-051-7 (sc)
ISBN: 979-8-89465-052-4 (e)

All rights are reserved. No part of this book may be reprinted or reproduced or utilised in any form or by any electronic, mechanical, or other means, now known or hereafter invented, including photocopying and recording, or in any information storage or retrieval system, without specific permission in writing from the publishers or the author. Brief passages for the purposes of quotation, illustration or criticism may be cited, but only if the proper provenance is given.

Copyright © 2010, 2024: Courtenay Young: Body Psychotherapy Publications.

The author of this book retains the sole copyright to all of his contributions to this book and has hereby asserted his moral and legal right to be identified as the author of this work in accordance with the Copyright, Design and Patents Act 1988.

Cover image supplied by Dreamstime: www.dreamstime.com under licence.
Typeset by: xxx xxxxxx

Integrity Publishing
39343 Harbor Hills Blvd Lady Lake,
FL 32159

www.integrity-publishing.com

CONTENTS

Introduction vii

PART ONE

Types of Crisis 3
Crisis or Emergency 7
Emergency Situations 9
Identifying a Person in Crisis 12
Possible Indications or Symptoms of People in Crisis 14
    1. Abuse of Drugs or Medications: 14
    2. Inability to Maintain Contact with Concensual Reality: 15
    3. Lack of Awareness of, and Responsibility for, own Process: 16
    4. Extraordinary or Inappropriate Behaviour: 17
    5. Lack of Firm Boundaries or No Adherence to Agreements: ... 19
    6. Unusual Levels of Need or Demand: 20
    7. *Continuous* - Emotional Catharsis or Withdrawal: 20
    8. Lack of Real Contact: 21
    9. Neglect of the Self: 21
Different Levels of Crisis 24
Making Contact & Staying in Contact 28
What To Do at First 32
Use of Psychotherapy 39
Appropriate Actions 43
Other Ways of Working With a Crisis 45
Forming a Crisis Group 49
Forming a Community Around a Person in Crisis 51
Some Basic Strategies 55
A "Zen" Space 57

Meditation & Mindfulness 59
Transformative Processes 67

PART TWO

Spiritual Emergence vs. Spiritual Emergency 71
The Difference Between a Spiritual Emergence and A
    Spiritual Emergency 74
Criteria to Help Define a Spiritual Emergency and
    Conditions Under Which it may be Appropriate to Work
    With Someone as a Spiritual Emergence Process 86
Stages of Spiritual Emergence 89
Symptoms / Types of Spiritual Emergence Processes or
    Spiritual Emergencies 93
Crisis as Seen in Transformational Terms 109
Spiritual Technologies and Toolkits 111
'Madness' Seen Differently 122
Some Self-Help Exercises 133
    1. To Get Rid of Obsessive Thoughts. 133
    2. Going Crazy Safely 134
    3. The Body that Brought Me Here: Life Changes! 135
    4. The Castle of the Spirit 137
    5. Re-Building Your Aura: (Auric Boundary) 139
    6. Dynamic Meditation 141
    7. Death Fantasies and How They Stop You Living 143
    8. The Felt Sense of Self 145
    9. Descending into the Dark 151
    10. Imagine Your Family 'System' as a Chessboard 156
    11. Better Mental Health: Guided Reflections 160
    12. Better Mental Health: Yoga &/or Tai Chi 163
Basic Spiritual Principles 165
Recovery & Integration 188
The Spirit of the Body & the Body of the Spirit 195
Crucial Support Issues 199

PART THREE

Therapeutic Communities 211
The Arbours Association, North London 218
The Windhorse Community 222
Lothlorien Therapeutic Community 231
Soteria Network 243
12-Step Communities 248
Spiritual Crisis Network UK 253
Spiritual Emergence Network USA 260
Mindfreedom International... 264
Democratic Therapeutic Community (DTC) Model **270**
Some Caveats – Warnings 275
The Rainbow 283
Transformation & Enlightenment 287
Quotations 298

ADDENDA

S.E. Resource List 309
Spiritual Emergency Book List 333
Appendix 1: Spiritual Emergencies in DSM4: Internet article........343
Appendix 2: Different Facets of the Sense of Self.............350
Appendix 3: DSM-IV Classification...................................355
Appendix 4: Research Studies...357
About the Author 361
Body Psychotherapy Publications 364

INTRODUCTION

Our current Western, 21st century society does not fully acknowledge the very human process of spiritual growth and maturation, to the extent that there is hardly even a proper language for much of this material, and to the extent that people who have experienced problems with this maturational process are often seen as unstable or insane, and are thus discriminated against, or even condemned as mad.

The actual process of spiritual maturation or emergence has itself long been marginalized in the West: it has also often been removed from any 'normal' realms, either by sanctification or beatification, or by a prevailing secular, mechanical, materialistic view of so-called "reality". However, please remember – *"There are more things in Heaven and Earth than are dreamt of in your philosophy".*[1]

But, at least in the last 100 years or so, the process of emotional and psychological maturation has developed its own particular language, and many of the concepts from these processes have become relatively well accepted, if little understood, by society at large.

C.G. Jung's concept of 'individuation', for example, is the concept whereby an 'individuated' person has worked through most of their childhood dependencies and neurotic attachments and has emerged as a reasonably functioning adult individual. However, in the arena of spiritual maturation, we are unfortunately still pretty much in the Dark Ages. We either cross our fingers and ring for the men in white coats.

There has been more credence given recently to different cultural or esoteric practices: the prevalence of Yoga and Tai Chi; shamanistic rites; the Gaia movement; multi-cultural values, etc. have all impacted

---

1   Shakespeare, *Hamlet,* Act 1, Scene 5.

somewhat on our consciousness. But nowadays few people plant crops at the right phase of the moon, or celebrate the Celtic fire festivals, or watch the stars for heavenly signs.

Many of the symptoms of a spiritual maturational process often happen unnoticed: a gradual loss of interest in the 'religion' of one's family of origin, followed by a growing interest, as a teenager or adult, in something that feels more meaningful. This may, or may not, be another established religion, or a different belief system, or joining a political or social movement, or developing an esoteric perspective. For some, however, the changes can be much more dramatic. Their symptoms may become similar to a psychotic episode, or it may take a major crisis for us to understand that the old familiar ways of doing and being are becoming increasingly dysfunctional; or the person may suddenly make significant changes in their whole lifestyle. This handbook is written for these people, and their families and friends.

More primitive societies more readily acknowledge that when a young man or woman has a "big dream" for the tribe, or falls into a coma and then awakens with wonderful tales of what has happened to them whilst asleep, or shows particular aptitudes for divination or healing, that these 'symptoms' are indications that their "spiritual maturational" process is starting (i.e. their spirit is growing and emerging) and they are then given the appropriate training from the elders, shamans, priests and priestesses, and so forth. If the societal structure has been destroyed, or the society is now largely secular, then these symptoms are often not recognised as such, and so they can be misinterpreted as aberrations or pathologies.

That is the cultural background to this book. The majority of people in a country or a nation – and there is another aberration as we may be 'ruled' by people of a very different ilk – who may (unconsciously) enforce cultural norms which bear no real relation to the people's individual life pathways. Just because most people do 'this' or 'that' or see things 'this' way or 'that' way, does not mean that these are 'right' and thus differences can become 'aberrations' or even 'deviations'. [2] Cultural oppression is just as 'nasty' – and even more insidious – to those being oppressed by political fascism, racism, or other prejudices, all of which are similar in their effect to the minority that is being discriminated against. However, things can slowly change.

In the 1970' &1980's, a Czech psychiatrist, Stanislav Grof (who had previously worked with LSD, when it was legal to do so), working with his wife Christina at Esalen, a community in Big Sur, California, coined the phrase "Spiritual Emergency" to describe a number of (otherwise 'normal') spiritual emergence processes that seemed to be going wrong. [3] These were later defined as intense spiritual experiences that resulted in an individual having an identity crisis that disrupted their psychological, social, and operational functioning. [4]

This does not mean to say that there is (or was) something psychologically 'wrong' with the person involved; often it has been the society around the person that has not recognized what was happening with that individual. This 'not knowing' about such manifestations of spiritual, religious, or transpersonal experiences can easily become a process of 'demonization': essentially, they are not understood – and thus feared – by those around them.

Further work and research by Miller and C'de Baca (2001) [5] with people having such manifestations described these as an integrated awakening, or as a "quantum change", or conversely as *"a point of desperation, a breaking point where something has to give, and [which] does result in a new and dramatically reorganized identity"*.

Maslow referred to these as 'nadir experiences': during which, *"there is an awareness of stepping beyond the usual limitations of one's everyday state of consciousness, bringing an intensified sense of clarity about one's purpose or mission in life and transcending one's usual sense of separateness from the natural world"*.

---

2   Psychiatrists, especially those who appeared in court, were once called 'alienists'. It was the alienist's job to study, understand, care for, and assist patients in overcoming their "mental alienation" or illness.
3   See Grof, S. & Grof, C. (1990)
4   See Judah, S.S. (2022). *The Clinician's Guide to Spiritual Emergence*. Helm Counseling.
5   Miller, W.R. & C'de Baba, J. (2001). *Quantum Change: When epiphanies and sudden insights transform ordinary lives*. Guilford Press.

People going through such experiences find themselves "out of sync" or even "alienated" from those around them; the 'perfect' job that they found themselves in a few years ago, is now palling, boring, or just 'wrong' for them; their marriage or relationship has changed radically – they (or their partner) may have suddenly fallen in love with someone else and/or out of love with them; their material circumstances may have changed radically – a plane fell on the roof of their house; or someone may have 'stolen' their identity; or they may have developed a serious illness, or even faced a life-threatening one; all sorts of different circumstances may have pushed them out of their 'comfort zone', out of their 'normal' life; suddenly, essentially – their "World Has Changed"!

A spiritual emergence process is generally understood to be a normal process of deep psychological change, albeit one that might involve non-ordinary states of consciousness, intense emotions, visions and unusual thoughts. A spiritual emergency occurs when the person (or those around them) is unable to integrate the spiritual experience. When a spiritual emergency is experienced by the person, their shift in perspective has become overwhelming and the person may find themselves in a crisis state that interrupts their lives. In other words, the spiritual emergency is a mystical experience turned "upside down", which can often have the appearance of a psychosis. This 'upside-downness' is something that should be a wonderful opening or pleasant mystical experience, so it has thus become something now to be feared.

In an increasingly materialistic society, the echelons of that society, the priests and particularly the medical profession, doctors, and psychiatrists, nowadays see the signs and symptoms of these maturational (or spiritual emergence) processes, not as signs or symptoms to be recognised, but as an aberration or even as a threat to the 'stability' of their society, or to their established 'power' positions, or as an 'illness' that they don't recognise or that seems bizarre and strange.

So, these medical or religious experts 'diagnose' these manifestations (because of their ignorance of spiritual processes) either, if they are religious priests, as signs of demonic possession (needing their powers of exorcism); or, if they are psychiatrists, as symptoms of potential pathologies (requiring the enforced administration of powerful psychotropic medications). Resistance (or avoidance) by the individual is seen a further anomaly, requiring even harsher measures.

Imagine if we – as a culture – did not acknowledge the symptoms of the physical maturation process of (say) puberty and adolescence, so that ... bodily hair and growing breasts were seen as aberrations. Fashion would then demand bound chests and underarm shaving, or, in extreme cases, medical interventions would require depilation or mastectomies. Something similar quite often happens to people who are going through these processes of Spiritual Emergence. Their symptoms are not recognised by those around them and thus their processes become interrupted or interfered with: i.e., become Spiritual Emergencies.

In James Hillman's book, *The Soul's Code,* he theorizes that we all have this innate potential for spiritual development. But, if you have been brought up to be 'safe' and 'conventional', then you will probably **not** allow the symptoms to emerge, even as remote possibilities. You might worry about being 'different' and go to a conventional counsellor or psychotherapist to have this problem analysed, or to learn, cognitively, how to change your behaviour. Or, you might think you have been possessed by 'demons' or something – and therefore go and consult your priest, pastor or spiritual guide.

These are ways in which you might be able to stay 'safe' a little bit longer. But then – your 'world' changes more – beyond redemption – and nothing is ever the same again. The 'symptoms' may, can or have overwhelmed your stable / static position and the 'safe' environment that you were living in. Resisting this sort of process is a bit like damming a river, it doesn't always work. But "going with the flow" is scary, it bring the fear that one might be to be swept away by the flood.

So, how to **manage** this process? This does not mean to 'control' it; nor to 'avoid' it: nor does it mean that the process overwhelms everything. It means that we get to learn to swim in the river.

This 'handbook' was originally written, in a much shorter format, as a manual for the staff of the Findhorn Foundation, an international spiritual & educational community in Northeast Scotland, where I ended up as the (sort of, unofficial) resident psychotherapist for 17 years (1986-2003). [6] It is now 20 years since I left. It has thus been re-written, added to, and developed over more than 30 years, based on a great deal of personal, practical and professional experience, rather than being based on any abstract theory.

I have also had the experience of teaching this material many times to psychotherapists, trainees, workshop participants and community members. Generally, I try to make the material content pragmatic, and (of course) it is always changing and being added to.

The first edition of this book came out in 2011: about 8 years after I had left the Findhorn Foundation. So, the first part was somewhat retrospective. By that time, I had been working as a Counsellor and Psychological Therapist in the National Health Service in Scotland, so my perceptions had – on the one hand, become slightly more clinical. On the other hand, when teaching a workshop (mentioned later) in Lübeck in Germany where I had stayed on for a few days afterwards, I 'downloaded' a whole lot more 'spiritual' information, which was added to the latter half of the 2nd part of this book. And there it stayed until 2022.

In the 20 years since I have left the Findhorn community, the world itself has changed – or taken a few more steps – thankfully, mostly in a more liberal direction – and thought forms (and pop songs) have developed to incorporate some of the more 'shadow' sides of our culture; so … songs like *"Let's Go To San Francisco"* transmogrified into *"I'll See You on the Dark Side of the Moon"*; the traditional romantic ballad or the pop song, *"She Loves Me"* becomes *"No More 'I Love You's"*. We now have many pop songs celebrating different forms of mental health and struggles as well: *"Help!"* by the Beatles'; *"Now I'm In It"* by Haim; *"1-800-273-8255"* by Logic; *"Today"* by The Smashing Pumpkins; *"Skyscraper"* by Demi Lovato; *"Smile"* by Jay-Z; *"Head Above Water"* by Avril Lavigne; *"24/7"* by Kehlani; *"Everybody Hurts"* by REM; etc. And many films explore – and so widen and deepen – the territory between what is now considered 'sane' and what is still 'extreme'. The boundary line is ever-changing.

---

6   When I moved there in 1986, I was the only person who was a psychotherapist registered in the UK. When I left in 2003, there were several UK registered counsellors and psychotherapists living there.

In the 2024 revision to this book, I have kept – rightly or wrongly – much to the original format, but I have added bits that seem relevant to the newer perspectives and I have also added a totally new section: Part Three. Additionally, I have put a couple of words, *"Spiritual Awakenings"* into the title: reprising Oliver Sachs' poetic 1973 book and 1990 film. [7] Needless to say, this book has virtually nothing to do with psychotropic drugs and psychiatric patients. The word is used in a more psychological and spiritual (psycho-spiritual) sense. Anyway, that is what came to me when I went back to the Findhorn Community for its 60th birthday in November 2022, and when started re-writing and adding to this book.

Part One still describes & defines what is meant by a crisis, any type of crisis, and differentiates between a crisis and an emergency, and gives some ideas as to what to do if, or when, someone you know or come across or are working with goes into a type of crisis. Please remember: a crisis is not necessarily the person being overwhelmed; often, it is signalling a problem that is not being properly recognised. *"Not Waving, but Drowning"* is Stevie Smith's poetic take on this dilemma, explored further by Keith Waterhouse in 1972, in an article about Pauline Jones's treatment by the British medical and judicial system. [8] [9]

Much of this **Part One** material is fairly traditional, mainstream and pragmatic. Because of the fear of these 'unknown' areas in the general collective; because of the discrimination against mental illness; because of our lack of understanding of altered states or the world of spirit; so, people generally do not know what to do with a person in such a crisis … unless they have been specifically trained, as a clinician, or in the mental health field, or as an enlightened social worker. Therefore, we need to be diagnostically quite careful.

---

7   Oliver Sachs (1973, 1976, 1991). *Awakenings*. Duckworth & Co, Picador, Pelican. A non-fiction book recounting the life histories of those who had been victims of the 1920s encephalitis lethargica epidemic. Sacks chronicled his efforts in the late 1960s to help these patients at the Beth Abraham Hospital using the new drug, L-DOPA.
8   wordhistories.net/2020/03/17/not-waving-but-drowning/
9   *Keith Waterhouse on Monday*, published in *Daily Mirror* (London, UK) of Monday, 13th March 1972.

But, even then, people's training (decades ago) may have been overly traditional and therefore in many ways 'wrong' for people in such 'borderline' cases now. Some parts of this part of the book help to demystify these processes and can act as a sort of manual for carers, etc. However, this section is mainly "safeguarding": by that, I mean, by going through these steps – on a broad or basic level – and checking things out. This is so we don't 'jump to conclusions', or diminish by saying, *"Don't worry: things will get better"*, or glamorise the crisis by saying, *"Because it's happening at Findhorn (or Esalen), it must be a Spiritual Emergency"*. The charisma of Glamour is a dangerous one and, as a result, many have gone astray. [10]

Part Two tries to go much deeper into the concept of Spiritual Emergence processes and some of their different manifestations and ramifications. I have separated the two aspects out in this way as … if someone is in a crisis, psychological, relationship, financial, spiritual or otherwise … then the pragmatic material in Part One is probably necessary, but only first and foremost.

However, many people will be more interested in starting to read the slightly more theoretical, or possibly attractive, aspects that are contained in Part Two. But, please, please, please don't do any direct, hands-on work with someone… until you have read through Part One. The two parts practically hang together and complement each other.

As Spiritual Emergence facilitators, we become midwives, helping to birth this new 'being' that we really know nothing about. We 'follow' – repeat the '**follow**' – the person's emergence process; we don't lead or dictate. Our diagnoses (hopefully) get left behind. We explore – with them – or are led by this person's unique and often weird development – until such time that their 'extreme' energy levels quieten down; or that external 'things' in their lives start to stabilise; or that there is a sense of integration and cohesion within themselves; or that our clinical expertise, or 'guardianship', becomes less necessary, or even starts to get in *their* way.

---

10   *Charisma*: In its original, and strongest, meaning, it is not just stage presence (Glamour), but a spiritual gift that draws followers to share a leader's commitment and calling.

Their "process" – of having a mid-life crisis, or a spiritual development process (now no longer a 'Spiritual Emergency') continues – without us: which then frees us up to ... go sailing, or do the dishes, or work in the garden, or 'take on' the next client who arrives: Etcetera, *und so weiter*, and so on ...

It is so very inspiring to work in this field in these different ways. It is also an incredible privilege and opportunity to be, in some ways, both selected as a channel for this sort of ... exceptional material. Their extraordinary process triggers a different process in you: as an electrician, prepare to be shocked; as a chef, you also have to taste the food. And, hopefully, I have also discovered a way of making it more ... ordinary and 'normal'.

I believe this material, and the whole process of Spiritual Emergence, is our normal human birth-right, our spiritual heritage, and is not limited to any particular religion, sect, community, or to people who go into crisis. It should become part of normal and healthy development **for everyone** to open up into these realms, even though, in the moment, sometimes we have to have a bit of a crisis in order to drive out any old and redundant material that the world requires us to "know" or "do" - in order to "be" who we think we should "be" at that moment in time: and so, we can allow in the new, very personal, and unique material that allows us to "be" *different* and also truly Ourselves.

Some of this material forms the basis for training modules that I have given, internationally, mainly to psychotherapy trainees, on Spiritual Emergencies and crisis work, and in seminars and workshops that I have given at psychotherapy conferences. Some of it is very newly written material, and deals with basic spiritual principles, many of which are very old and fundamental truths. My wife, Laura Steckler, a Clinical Psychologist and Body-Oriented Psychotherapist, as well as being a dancer & performance artist, and I together developed some of this material into a residential workshop format for members of the public, which we called *"The Spirit of the Body"*. We gave this in Forres (a town close to Findhorn) and in Lübeck in Germany – and we have also now both moved on from that as well.

And so, we now come to **Part Three.** There are several and very different therapeutic and spiritual communities all over the world:

some are relatively well-known – like the Findhorn Foundation, Esalen, Sotoria, Khiron, Windhorse, Samye Ling, Lothlorian, the Arbours Association, the Philadelphia Association, etc. – that also work with some of this material, or with these (sort of) ways of thinking, and with people with problems, similar material, albeit in their own particular methods of spiritual practice and as part of their fairly well-defined spiritual and educational path. [11] Whilst such communities can provide a somewhat more welcoming environment for someone going through their own Spiritual Emergency, they can also have problems with that person, if that person's process is in a very different format from their own: e.g., if a person is having a Shamanic Journey (where they are howling like a wolf) in a community or culture that is very different, as for example in a Tibetan Buddhist community.

However, we all know that there is no "One Way" and yet – amazingly – people in such Spiritual Emergence processes often find themselves with the 'right' person, in the 'right' place, at the 'right' time, for 'them': until (possibly) something or someone comes in from outside and starts to interfere. The person then has to reconnect – in some way – with their own "Guardian Angel" (or "Guide") – as we all do – who is there all the time, working for them, in one form or another, often through another person, who is just 'there' for Them at that place, or that moment in time. And so, it goes!

I believe in and thus whole-heartedly support this (sort of) broadband perspective, mythology and practical methodology, and thus the whole process of 'normalization' of this 'spiritual' material.

Therefore, I give some information in Part Three about some of these "communities" – mostly abstracted from their websites. Anyone who really wants to can contact them and – maybe – do a programme, or work alongside members of this or that community, and see and (more importantly) **feel** how this material can be applied with them, by them, on a day-to-day basis. Perhaps, we should see it as something like learning how to farm 'organically'. It may / will take a while, but – by sticking with it – you will nearly always get very good results.

---

[11] Spiritual Communities in the UK: www.diggersanddreamers.org.uk/communities/spiritual-communities/ New Age Communities: en.wikipedia.org/wiki/New_Age_communities

Whether you are recycling your glass and cardboard, or eating organic food, or trying to save the world, or working with someone in crisis, or whether you are in a crisis or an emergency yourself, the spiritual principles and processes are hopefully still very relevant.

But, for some people, either it is important or necessary, or maybe it just happens, that they are on a different 'life path', or they jumped the "Spiritual Maturation 101" course and found themselves in the wrong grade, and so they need a "crash course" to catch up; or maybe they are just in the wrong school, or they feel that they are even on the wrong planet. There is a nice Sufi story to that effect, where the Sufi master gets rid of a student, who is in the wrong place. [12]

People are – often unexpectedly – experiencing a crisis, instead of the regular steady developmental programme of a gently unfolding spiritual emergence process. And so, they are in a different process– their World has Changed – and the process of change can sometimes be dramatic and painful, as well as being incredibly beautiful. It is nearly always very, very powerful and occasionally (seemingly) out-of-control. This is what we tend to call a Spiritual Emergency.

There are no particular rules of "how" to go through these processes; we – as practitioners – just have to work with each individual situation as we find it. More and more, people are having these situations at home, and in their own environments, without coming to Findhorn, or Esalen, or going to India, or taking drugs, and also (hopefully – thankfully) without getting taken off to their local psychiatric ward. Equally hopefully and thankfully, these Spiritual Emergence processesarenow becoming much more "normal", and this is the new way that we must, I think, **all** begin to look at all these processes.

One of my colleagues who helped established the first Spiritual Emergence Network (in Menlo Park, San Francisco), told this story:

One evening, a little old lady from Texas rang up and said, 'Can you help me?' 'God came and sat in my head last Christmas.' 'I know what people are thinking as they come towards me.' 'But – my Pastor says I am of the Devil; my women's group think I am a witch; and my husband just doesn't want to know.'

---

[12] One of the stories from Idris Shah's (1964) book: *The Sufis*. and (1968) *The Way of the Sufi*. ISF Publishing.

Her crisis was that the other people around her couldn't accept her (possibly) new telepathic abilities that she was able to frame as 'God sitting in her head'.

This sort of reactive rejection – all too common in the late Middle Ages when they still burnt female herbalists as witches – is still met with today, though usually with incarceration in a psychiatric hospital or by numbing the process by the use of psychotropic drugs. Some people swing the other way and glamourize what is a small 'opening' into a wonderful cavern into which only a Select Few can enter.

Unfortunately, there are still tendencies to hang on to the feelings of 'specialness', the mystery, the glamour, the mystique, or to consider oneself as blessed, privileged or, in some way, 'Special', or superior by having access to – or experiencing – this sort of material, and thus it seems appropriate or justified to charge large amounts of money for a particular form of initiation or 'transformative' experience: Bullshit! Just go out; open your Self out; and say, *"Now I Am Ready!"* Then, just wait and see what happens!

In the past, people have made a 'mystery' out of finding their "spiritual path", or 'their' Guru, and only certain people have been 'initiated' into these mysteries ('Mysteries'). This should not be the case any longer, even if it was appropriate – or legitimate – in some earlier times. We have to make this material, this 'stuff', much more normal and accessible and 'down-to-earth'. It is our spiritual 'birth-right'.

Everyone has this capacity, built-into their Psyche. You just have to want to go there – and then surrender to these dynamic forces.

Our Western materialistic society also – desperately – needs these particular energies in order for **it** to change; in order for **it** to mature; in order for **it** to redress the balance between "doing" or "having" and "being"; being polarized into: 'right' or 'wrong'; 'good' or 'bad'; 'light' or 'dark'; is all a nonsense. All is One.

All of this material is in order to decrease the individual's sense of 'rightness' or to have what they want 'right now', and, instead, to get pleasure and satisfaction about working together, with others, for the greater good. We all need to find better the balance between hatred and acceptance; the balance between war and peace; the balance between hopes for sanity and acts of insanity; between materialism and planetary stability.

7 billion people just cannot **all** have cars, TVs and washing machines – there are just not the available material resources and – in our short-sightedness, we risk 'swamping the boat' and creating a global catastrophe that will really change our human lives – a different type of transformation, if you will. The planet Gaia will still exist after we have gone: she will just evolve a different 'animal' in our place. I wrote a poem about some of that once: I called it, *"Mother's Anger".* [13]

Instead, we can all start – now – to lead "good" – socially, creatively, environmentally, spiritually – lives, and this will – in time – redress the imbalance and the divisory, materialistic components will settle down: we just **have** to put Spirit first. That is enough!

We need to disseminate the essential spirituality embedded in ourselves and how we deal with these emergent processes, and to find these processes being reflected in our social lives, as we try to cope with these new spiritual technologies and a new world order, especially as a result of the processes of increasing globalization and the more recent events of … September 11, 2001, the Gulf Wars, global warming, annihilation of species, increased weather events, and a resultant desertification of much of the planet … etc.

This sort of esoteric material needs to become more of the 'norm', rather than the exception. Archbishop Desmond Tutu once said: *"The wonderful thing is that God has placed in each of us a hunger, a hunger for transcendence: a hunger for the thing your heart is restless for until you find it."*

The increasing acceptance of 'spiritual' and influential people into mainstream society like: Carl Gustav Jung, Rudolf Steiner, the Dalai Lama, Mother Theresa, Desmond Tutu, Eckhart Tolle, Louise Hay, Paulo Coelho, Deepak Chopra, Thich Nhat Hanh, A.H. Almaas, Ravi Shankar, Pope Francis, Greta Thunberg (the Swedish teenage environmental activist), David Attenborough, Alice Walker, Sadhguru, Oprah Winfrey, and even Eileen Caddy (one of the founders of the Findhorn Foundation, recently awarded the MBE for "services to spirit"), can give us all some degree of hope. [14]

---

13 Mother's Anger: www.courtenay-young.co.uk/courtenay/poetry/Mothers_Anger.pdf
14 For other names, see: www.watkinsmagazine.com/watkins-spiritual-list-for-2021

There are many things wrong with the present, conventional society – and with the New Age movement – that seems to epitomize this 'search' for spirit, but it also reflects a growing need for pragmatic down-to-earth material, which is relevant today, rather than (perhaps) a religion that became codified many hundreds of years ago, or a cult or sect that leads people astray.

These spiritually-based processes also have great power – the power for good, the power to change, the power to awaken one's inner spirit, the power to transcend, the power to directly experience the magical and mystical, or … indeed … the power to wreck other people's lives.

There are also plenty of false gurus, or leaders of sects: like Jim (James Warren) Jones, Bhagwan Shri Rajneesh, L. Ron Hubbard, Charles Manson, David Koresh, and (most recently) Woo May Hoe, etc. There is also the insidious power of materialism – leaking into our lives through advertising, and Amazon, and philosophies like, *"Have it now, pay for it later"*, etc. There are also many, many Paths that lead … precisely nowhere.

In the 'guidance' section in this **Part Two**, there are a number of aphorisms, not meant as rules, nor are they mandates, nor formulae: they are mostly just open descriptions, suggestions, and possibilities. Each person will find their own spiritual pathway. Our job – as practitioners, helpers and guides – is just to help them to find that! That then helps us to find out what we need. Thus, we come Full Circle!

The spiritual, transformative power of this sort of Path can be awesome. But then, so is electricity, and nowadays we think nothing of turning on a light switch, when (in the past) to have this facility, this instant power, would have been considered a miracle to our cave-dwelling ancestors. Maybe, it is all to do with how we perceive the light, or how we relate to the Light that casts those Shadows that dance on the wall. Often, these shadows are just problems within ourselves, and we are facing the wrong way: we are just not looking at "The Light", or it scares us, or blinds us. Instead, we focus on the Shadows: the 'wrongness'. We can always see it more clearly in Others: they are 'good', 'bad', 'right', 'wrong', 'nice', 'nasty', etc. – nearly always polarised. We have much more difficulty in working with it within ourselves: sifting through and sorting out this material. Working more with a variable spectrum, than with a polarity.

Please also don't make the mistake of thinking that this is all to do with someone else – to do with *their* crisis. Yes, *they* may be having a crisis, and maybe it is even a spiritual one, however it will almost inevitably affect *you* as well, and thus some of *their* material will become part of *your* process, *your* life, and ultimately become part of *your* transformational process.

We are not islands: we are all connected – even though those connections may not be visible, may not be clear, or may not even be understood– yet. There was a recent example given in an eco-lecture about how all trees and plants are connected via mycorrhizal connections under the ground. This may also be true for our psychic connections with others – above the ground, on many different etheric levels.

Your internal reactions and processes will also reverberate on to other people and their processes and may even facilitate – or hinder – their process; and all of these processes will also affect any others involved, or close by. Walk into a room where two people had just ended an argument and you will notice the 'thick' atmosphere: it will affect you. The psychic ripples spread wide once a stone has been dropped into the pond.

And how we use all this material – this increased awareness – is also very important. We can choose to react positively, or we can be scared of these processes. We can either view our glass as half-full, or as half-empty. Any particular crisis can therefore become an opportunity, a side-track, a stuckness, or a disaster. Here is a Hebrew story about *Four Rabbinim*:

One night, four Rabbinim were visited by an angel who awakened them and carried them up to the Seventh Vault of the Seventh Heaven. There, they beheld the sacred Wheel of Ezekiel. Somewhere in the descent from Pardes (Paradise) to Earth, one Rabbi, having seen such splendour, lost his mind and wandered frothing and foaming until the end of his days. The second Rabbi was extremely cynical: *"Oh, I just dreamed of Ezekiel's Wheel. That was all! Nothing really happened."* The third Rabbi carried on and on and on about what he had seen, for he became totally obsessed. He believed that he had been especially 'Chosen'. Thinking he was particularly special, he talked and lectured, and would not stop proselytising his theories about how everything was connected, how it was all constructed, and what it all meant ...and, in this way, he also went astray and betrayed his true faith. The fourth Rabbi, who was a poet, took a paper and a reed-pen into his hand, and sat near the window writing song after song praising the evening dove, his daughter in her cradle, and all the stars in the firmament. And thus, he lived his life better than before.

In **Part Three**, which forms most of the new material in this 2nd Edition, my basic intention was to have been to ask for contributions from other Spiritual Emergence practitioners, 'guides-from-behind', 'Path-Work' practitioners, gatekeepers and guardians, what *their* way of working is now, and to ask other Spiritual Communities how *they* work with people having these issues nowadays. However, as there were no responses, I have relied on publicly available information. There is now even a University that deals with many aspects of spiritual emergence processes: the Integrative Medical Health University (IMHU). [15]

I have also included some information about the DSM-IV category that covers Spiritual Emergencies and about a few of the research papers that support this category.

These additions are also because – over the several years since I first published this book (in 2011) – many spiritual communities have closed or collapsed (especially since the CoVid pandemic); others have started up; many Spiritual Emergence practitioners have dropped out, or burnt out, or passed away, or moved into other areas of working; and others are working differently in their particular own ways; and – of course – there are new opportunities that have opened up to other peoples' pathways and processes. There is also more research. So, hopefully, we shall see!

In this new-found landscape of people going through their Spiritual journey, I can therefore only wish again that you can all – **"Travel Well!"**

Courtenay Young
Findhorn & Edinburgh
2011; (revised 2024)

---

[15] IMHU: www.imhu.org

PART ONE

TYPES OF CRISIS

A crisis is defined as occurring: "... *when a person faces an obstacle to important life goals that is, for a time, insurmountable through the utilization of (their) customary methods of problem solving. A period of disorganization ensues, a period of upset, during which many abortive attempts at solution are made.*"

Caplan: An approach to community mental health.

This is a description of the **process** of a crisis. A crisis is also an internal process where we feel that we are out of our control. However, there are many different forms of 'triggers' for such a crisis process. These triggers include some of the following:

Different types of crisis:

There are many different types of crisis and they affect people differently:

- Death of a parent, a child or close family member (this can also include a pet animal); deep grief at such; not being able to 'complete' the grief process
- Sudden loss: ... of job, home, role, status, finance, marriage/relationship, security, integrity, self-image, world view, faith or trust
- A serious physical illness (possibly life-threatening, like cancer, heart attack, diabetes, etc), major operations, chronic conditions, serious disability

- A substantive change in mental/emotional stability: depression, schizophrenia, bi-polar, character disorder, episodic psychosis, borderline cases, repressed memories
- A serious upset to one's emotional, financial or material equilibrium: triggered by redundancy, burn-out, premature events, loss of expectations, or with feelings of malfunctioning or powerlessness
- A series of continuing stressful life situations or events, none of them being crises in themselves, but that collectively accumulate to exceed one's (anyone's) normal capacity to cope
- Maturational crises: adolescence, menopause, retirement, old age – often creating forms of isolation: often a crisis to a 'social animal'
- A substantive change in one's life circumstances: loss of job; economic or financial crisis; imprisonment; onset of severe illness; marriage ending; partner's infidelity; serious legal case; an (often unfair) accusation or dispute with neighbours or employers or co-workers, traumatization
- Accidents and/or disasters: people experiencing disasters now commonly receive help in the form of counselling, but that does not mean that this always happens and that some people almost inevitably slip through the cracks
- Physical abuse: rape, domestic violence, mugging, childhood sexual abuse and/or recovered memories of such
- Substance abuse: drugs, alcohol, cigarettes, other (often psychotropic) substances
- Suicide attempts or patterns of self-harming
- Social upsets: economic depression, war, riots, political crises
- Western society is in a crisis: enforced need for continuing economic growth; being flooded with (often negative) news; informational overload; increasing materialism; social alienation; isolation
- Environmental changes: increasing desertification, global warming
- Acts of God: fire, flood, earthquake, storm, famine, plague
- Family (systemic) crisis: child abuse, death in family, divorce, breaking of co-dependencies, uncovering of secrets

- A build-up of different factors: moving house *and* having a new baby *and* losing one's job *and* a parent dying – all in a relatively short period of time
- A culmination point of an increasingly dramatic process, where often a point of 'no return' has been reached and unwanted change seems inevitable and yet there is no clarity about one's next step(s)
- Existential crisis – an often quite sudden loss of sense of self; finding no raison d'être; loss of any meta-perspective or sense of 'knowing'; or having a spiritual emergency – often as a result of one or more of the above

Please remember that some sort of a "mild" crisis is probably both necessary and essential to any form of substantive developmental change or growth. We sometimes need a kick-start to get us out of a rut. This can help us lift ourselves up out of the rut that we've gotten ourselves into and inspire us to develop further or in a somewhat different direction. Remember the old maxim: *What doesn't kill one, makes one stronger!* (Friedrich Nietzsche).

Growth involves change: if the caterpillar gets 'stuck' into its present form, it will not metamorphose into a butterfly, but it cannot necessarily imagine the change that is about to happen and what its new form will be. It might be that one feels that one is in a crisis, which might not be able to be imagined. There is thus a whole "unknown" aspect to any substantive change process, and this is – of course – very, very scary. We do not 'know' what is round the next corner, or what lies ahead of us, or what might be the result of such a change. This is why we see tend to see these change processes as a crisis: the change is substantive, often quite sudden, and often contains an 'unknown' element. Once we 'know' – or understand – that this is a "change process", the critical (crisis) component – and thus the accompanying fear – often diminishes.

Thus, the most helpful thing that can happen is for the 'crisis' to have become identified as an (as yet unknown) 'process of change' as early as possible. This allows our "normal" coping strategies (which will not be able to cope) to cease; the natural fear to diminish a little, and whatever "coping strategies" that exist to come into play, and thus the negative effects of the crisis are less likely to be to be compounded, and then the appropriate support systems can be identified and mobilized. As the crisis begins to diminish, more normal support systems become ready to be activated again. The 'crisis' is over, the change process can continue.

All these things can happen to any one of us: at any time; and many of these things will actually happen, one way or another. Life is essentially a change process, and it is also sometimes difficult. Sometimes, we will have to cope with one of these change events, or even some of these, reasonably well, but then something else will come along, seemingly out of the blue, and throw us totally 'off-base' and wham: the World has Changed! It seems as if nothing will ever be the same again. Do we go under; or act (like Job in *The Bible*) and just bemoan our woes; or do we face the challenge, see where it will take us, and start to grow?

At a psychotherapy conference several years ago, the 17th EAP Congress, in 2010 in Bucharest, Romania on *"Crisis: Change or Challenge"*, I found myself writing a little comment, perhaps even a sort of 'koan' on the title of the conference:

> *I expect to be challenged **and** to be forced to change:*
> *I fear to be changed, as this is often a challenge:*
> *I also – somewhat surprisingly – look forward to both.*

This is not an epitaph, nor is it a road map; it is – perhaps – a road sign, or a way-post, or a marker, saying:

"You Are Now On The Road Towards A Transformation."

CRISIS OR EMERGENCY

It may be worth noting here, before we go any further, the traditional definitions of – or distinctions between –**a crisis** and **an emergency**:

- An **emergency** should be able to be resolved within about 36 hours – that is to say the person should be able – by then – to cope more by themselves, or get into a situation where they can cope with 'normal' methods of support and (possibly) with some recuperative care, within that sort of time period. Or that other responsible people (doctors, first attenders, professionals, etc.) will have – in effect – taken over.

- A **crisis** may still be occurring after 36 hours and will probably not end until the person can start to cope with various aspects of their life situation, as well as, or better than, before they went into the crisis.

It is more than possible to have both going at the same time. An ongoing crisis can suddenly become escalated into an emergency situation. The emergency can then be resolved and be got through, and yet there is – as yet – no resolution to the ongoing crisis situation.

There is another definition, which uses these concepts of crisis and emergency, and which will be dealt with later in the second part of the book: that of a "Spiritual Emergence" process that happens to go astray and then becomes a **"Spiritual Emergency"**. But more about that later.

A crisis can happen to anyone at any time. The chances are that we will have several in our lifetime. They can be seen as something almost natural, inevitable even (like Mid-Life Crises); something that we might have contributed to (a Personal Crisis); something to overcome (an Environmental Crisis or Disaster); something to learn from (an Educational Crisis); or something to endure and survive an Existential Crisis). It has become a crisis because our "normal" (i.e. habitual) survival techniques are not working any longer. We may thus survive, but things may not (almost certainly, will not) be the same.

An emergency is when there is – quite suddenly – a severe risk that we might not survive; or that things might never be the same again; or that someone (including ourselves) may get hurt. In an emergency situation, you will almost certainly, absolutely and definitely, need some form of external or specialized help. Do not even try to 'cope' – recognise as soon as possible that it is an emergency and say, "Help".

There is a lovely new book that has come out recently: *"The Boy, the Mole, the Fox, and the Horse: An animated story"* by Charlie Mackesy (Ebury Press, Nov. 2022). In it, there is a quote:

> *"What's the bravest thing you ever said?" asked the boy.*
> *"Help" said the horse.*
> *"Asking for help isn't giving up," said the horse,*
> *"It is refusing to give up."*

It is really good to get some help if or when you are in a crisis: mainly because it is not easy to get through a crisis all by yourself. However, it may just be possible to get through a crisis by yourself, but you will really have to face your difficulties alone, which is not easy by itself: so, it is not easy by yourself. This is another distinction between a crisis and emergency.

That is also when some form of outside help often suddenly – miraculously – appears. But, more about that later.

Remember – another good indicator of a crisis is whether or not the person can stay in reasonable contact with other people around them. If they can't, then that person is almost certainly in a crisis.

In an emergency situation, the person involved (in crisis) may not be able to do anything to help themselves, and they also may be, in some way, totally out of touch. There is no proper contact. This then also differentiates a crisis from an emergency: they are out of touch. They need external help!

EMERGENCY SITUATIONS

It is very important to be able to differentiate between someone being in a crisis and/or someone being in an emergency situation. There are certain things that **you** (or anyone without very specialized training) ***cannot*** and ***should not*** and ***must not*** try to cope with. These are real **EMERGENCY** situations & include:

OVERDOSE OF DRUGS or MEDICATION
PHYSICAL VIOLENCE
DESTRUCTION OF PROPERTY
SELF-INFLICTED INJURIES or SUICIDE ATTEMPTS
RESCUE SITUATIONS

As soon as you come across one of the above – **IMMEDIATELY** –call, or have someone call, the police, ambulance, rescue services or a doctor. These people are the proper people to deal with such emergencies. Don't try to emulate their training and experience. Don't try to 'rescue' the person. That is someone else's job. It does not matter if it seems only a very minor incident, just call. It does not matter if the person seems just out of reach. The person involved is in an emergency, is likely to be unpredictable, cannot cope, may even cause *you* to become involved in *their* emergency, and/or might even repeat this behaviour (try again) in a moment, or just as soon as your back is turned.

You can still help the person in the emergency situation: (a) by calling the emergency services; (b) by staying in contact; and (c) by 'being there' after the emergency is over – as the responses of the emergency services will be often limited only to the emergency situation.

You can help by giving the emergency services a balanced account of the situation; by going with the person to the hospital or police station; by having access to a mobile phone or a credit card; or just being there to act as an advocate or a caring person (maybe only holding their hand, whilst others do what is necessary).

In addition, all the after-care, and lots of it, will probably be needed from someone like yourself – not necessarily directly, but by helping the person get the right sort of after-care. By calling the Emergency Services, it does not mean that you are surrendering your ability to help, or that they will cut you out of their web of support. In fact, as a family member, or a friend, or a passer-by (a Good Samaritan), you will probably be indispensable – once the emergency is over.

Your choice … to call for emergency assistance … ensures access, at the right time, to the right type of trained people with the right level of skills and awareness, to cope with this very specialized, and potentially dangerous situation.

In an EMERGENCY SITUATION:

- **Do not leave the person alone, if possible, even for a moment.** Try to have other people present and in attendance at all times, until the Emergency Services arrive.
- There is a very high probability that – if not responded to now – the emergency situation can then re-occur, or even get worse, within the very near future / a very short time. That is why it is an emergency. So, make the call as soon as possible.
- **It is absolutely *your* responsibility to make sure the Emergency Services are called.** Don't assume someone else will make the call. Act now! Make the call yourself, or instruct someone else to make the call, whilst you stay with the person in an emergency. The Emergency Services do not mind being called out: that is their function! They are then doing their job. Your job is to call them.
- Even if the person in crisis begs and pleads with you not to tell anybody, as difficult as this might be, still make the call. Part of their crisis may be that they don't fully realize that this is an emergency (and not a crisis), which is a very dangerous

situation. They are still trying to 'control' a situation that has got out of control. If there has already been evidence of one of the above crisis situations: then it may re-occur at any moment, despite their protestations. So, make the call.
- If you are not sure if any the above conditions are happening, just make the call anyway. The emergency services themselves would prefer you to get it wrong, and it proving <u>not</u> to be an emergency, rather than <u>not</u> making the call and it proving to be a **real** emergency. So, make the call.
- If it has been a very minor incident of one of the five situations above, make the call anyway. One of these situations can reoccur in a moment; maybe, even worse the next time. So, call now!
- There is a poem by Stevie Smith called *"Not Waving, but Drowning"* – that (sort of) says it all! [16]

---

[16] www.poetryfoundation.org/poems/46479/not-waving-but-drowning

IDENTIFYING A PERSON IN CRISIS

Once we have identified the situation facing us in not an emergency situation, we can consider it as a crisis: - but what sort of crisis?

There are a number of indications, which can inform you that someone is in or is approaching a crisis. These are mainly emotional/psychological aspects. It may not be particularly significant if only one type is apparent (as we all have our odd moments); however, the more types or indications that are apparent, or that can be identified, can be an indication of the extent – or the depth – of the person's crisis.

The 9 main categories to watch out for are:

1. ABUSE OF DRUGS OR MEDICATIONS
2. INABILITY TO MAINTAIN CONTACT WITH CONSENSUS REALITY
3. LACK OF AWARENESS OF & RESPONSIBILITY FOR OWN PROCESS
4. EXTRAORDINARY OR INAPPROPRIATE BEHAVIOUR
5. LACK OF FIRM BOUNDARIES OR ADHERANCE TO AGREEMENTS
6. UNUSUAL LEVELS OF NEED OR DEMAND
7. CONTINUED EMOTIONAL CATHARSIS or CONTINUED WITHDRAWAL
8. LACK OF REAL CONTACT
9. NEGLECT OF THE SELF

(For fuller explanations of these, please see next pages.)

The First Rule that accompanies an emotional or physical crisis is that the person in crisis in increasingly unable to maintain normal emotional or relational contact.

A Second Rule is that, if someone else experiences the same, or a similar, reaction, on a different occasion, with **that person**, both your reactions are possibly / probably correct and that person is in, or is approaching, a crisis.

A Third Rule is that, if the person is getting into crisis and being increasingly less able to cope, then the situation is more than likely to get worse than to get better.

A Fourth Rule is that the person in crisis often feels that their signals (sometimes unconscious, often a 'cry for help') are not being responded to properly, so they end up having to exaggerate them. They themselves are not sure what is happening. They don't know how to cope. And they may not know how to ask for help properly or directly.

Therefore, calling in a professional to help them is <u>not</u> an indication of failure, but is possibly a means to a successful intervention and a beneficial outcome. It is impossible to overemphasize the importance of a timely intervention. An early intervention often does NOT result in a significant period of time in a psychiatric hospital. Later interventions sometimes do, and then the person in crisis has to get over the effects of that as well.

So Please, Please, Please Do Something Sooner Rather Than Later!

POSSIBLE INDICATIONS OR SYMPTOMS OF PEOPLE IN CRISIS

Please remember – *the following examples are only examples. This is not an exclusive list. It is not a diagnostic. Also, anyone behaving in any one of these categories may just be having a bit of a hard time. Check it out. Just ask. Many times, people will appreciate your awareness and concern.*

*Often the person is perfectly aware of what is happening, or what has just happened, and are in reasonable control, and can give you a very clear, appropriate and satisfactory response. This is then possibly **not** a crisis. This sort of response has a very different feeling to it than some form of a justification, evasion, defensiveness, or something like an attempt to cover-up what is actually a crisis situation*

1. ABUSE OF DRUGS OR MEDICATIONS:

Examples of abusive (or lack of self-care) behaviours in this category include:

- **a)** Going off (psychotropic) medications without proper safeguards, or supervision, or suddenly and without the full agreement of a medical practitioner. This sort of behaviour can even precipitate a psychosis. e.g., Lithium, Valium, some anti-depressants, some psychotropic medications.
- **b)** Mixing homeopathic, herbal or alternative remedies **and** pharmaceutical medications, without consent from, or consultation with, qualified practitioners or a doctor. Sometimes these remedies DO NOT mix well: e.g., St John's Wort and anti-depressants.

c) A seeming carelessness about taking (or not taking) medication, or about dosages, or mixing medications (as above), especially combined with some of the more socially approved drugs such as alcohol, which again can potentiate some psychotropic medications.
d) An over-indulgence of drugs, or medications, or remedies, *or alcohol* - "over-dose" is the classic extreme; drunkenness is also a very common example. Heavy or addictive smoking may be indicative of a latent crisis: pill-popping is another.

2. INABILITY TO MAINTAIN CONTACT WITH CONCENSUAL REALITY:

Examples of this type of behaviour include:

a) 'Spacing out' and not being able to "space back in" or "come back to earth" when requested, or when directly addressed.
b) Having delusions, visions, altered states, etc. ... without a lot of control and without really realizing that they are delusional or altered states, or without being able to 'integrate' these into a coherent picture.
c) A very exaggerated viewpoint, often about the significance of themselves, another person, or other events, that bears very little relation to the views of many other people around them. These points can include suddenly falling in 'love' totally inappropriately, or becoming obsessed with someone, positively or negatively, and giving up their normal lifestyle without any preparation, like joining a sect, or fanatical fan-club, or becoming a 'stalker'.
d) If someone gets very angry (or fearful), or if their latent anger (or fear) from their past experiences, which has not been dealt with properly – is triggered by a present situation, then they may be unable to see that their present anger (or fear) is inappropriate to the existing "fault" (or "threat"). They are

"out of touch". "Road rage" is a good example: sometimes also categorised as Intermittent Explosive Disorder. [17]

e) Classical paranoia is an obvious example of not being in touch with 'consensual reality' – but it is rarely found. What is much more common is a form of continual blaming of situations and events onto other people; or being (behaving as) a continual victim; and/or a holding onto this blame, despite reassurances or evidence to the contrary; and/or a seeming inability to accept any sort of responsibility for one's own actions or perceptions. [18]

This can link to …

3. LACK OF AWARENESS OF, AND RESPONSIBILITY FOR, OWN PROCESS:

Examples of this type of behaviour include:

a) Constant blaming: The person cannot or will not accept responsibility for their part in their own process. It is always someone else's fault.

b) The classic victim statement: *"This happened to me – and it was terrible. Then this happened to me – and that was even worse."* This pattern is often repeated without the sort of "owning" statement: *"I did this and then that"* or *"Then, I made this mistake … again".*

c) The repetition syndrome: *"Everywhere I go, this happens.",* or *"This is the fourth time this month…",* or *"Nobody ever…",* etc.

d) There is a very significant difference between responsibility for, and responsibility to (also see later). People need to be responsible *for* their own actions: and they also need to be responsible *to* everyone else … for their own actions. 'Freedom

---

[17] DSM-IV to DSM-5: www.ncbi.nlm.nih.gov/books/NBK519704/table/ch3.t18/
[18] In extreme situations, this can be a symptom of 'Compulsive Narcissism': Narcissistic Personality Disorder: see DSM-5: www.ncbi.nlm.nih.gov/books/NBK556001/

to act' does **not** mean that your free actions then prevent other peoples' freedoms: viz. A.S. Neill *(Summerhill)*, who used to say: *"Freedom, not licence."* [19] [20]

e) A seemingly total indifference towards the effects of their actions, or inactions, on other people, or of their 'normal' responsibilities to friends, family, commitments, etc. The person seems to be increasingly totally "cut off" from others. They may seem callous or indifferent; they may intimidate or manipulate; they may even lie, if confronted about something. These sorts of behaviours can even be an indication of potentially sociopathic behaviour. [21] This does not – at this stage – mean they have a mental disorder: they may just be going through a temporary bad phase, whereby this type of behaviour is increasingly frequent. If not addressed, this may result in a mental disorder.

4. EXTRAORDINARY OR INAPPROPRIATE BEHAVIOUR:

Examples of inappropriate behaviour, like all of these classifications, are not significant in themselves, as they occur quite often in most people on occasions. They are only significant if found in conjunction with other examples. We all have our moments!!!

Examples of this type of behaviour include:

a) A person sharing deeply confidential or intimate details at a first meeting, transcending normal acquaintanceship, or made in a non-intimate or public situation.

b) A person offering to involve themselves much too much, often with one's private life, and from a relatively casual acquaintanceship: almost like a boundary invasion.

---

[19] en.wikipedia.org/wiki/Summerhill_(book)
[20] archive.org/stream/FreedomNotLicence-A.S.Neill/freedom-neill_djvu.txt
[21] www.mayoclinic.org/diseases-conditions/antisocial-personality-disorder.

c) A person suddenly doing something bizarre: like, coming down to breakfast in a hotel, semi-naked; giving a lot of money away to a relative stranger; not sleeping for more than 36 hours and then acting very strangely; suddenly shop-lifting an item; doing something impulsively that has considerable potential consequences, etc. This is – possibly / probably – a symptom of an underlying, as yet unaddressed, crisis. It is not to be judged: just noticed. *"Waving, signalling, 'Hey: I need help', but I don't know how to ask for it."*

d) A person under- or over-reacting emotionally to a situation that naturally involves such emotions as anger, sadness, enthusiasm, defensiveness, grief, anger, etc. where the emotion may be appropriate to the event, but *their* 'level' of emotion is not; or perhaps where the length of time of their emotional reaction is not appropriate (either too little or too long) …

e) A person not doing (or doing) something that the rest of the group / office / community, etc. are doing (or not) without disclosing their intent, reasons or any information about their emotional state, or the extent of their deviation.

f) An excessive or prolonged activity in a person (sleeping, drinking, fasting, dancing, spending money, meditating, etc.) with a reluctance or resistance to stop, and often with a defensiveness or inability to explain why they are over-indulging in this way.

g) An experience of a sense of confusion or wariness that one has when in contact with a person that seems to be engendered by their behaviour <u>and</u> that this feeling is also experienced by others on different occasions with that person. 'You are not alone in thinking that person is out-of-order.'

h) The absence of any emotion, affect, or a sense of withdrawal by a person from other people, or life, especially if the reason for this is not properly communicated. Again, the person 'removes' their 'self' from others, or from normal activities, and becomes often quite suddenly very 'cold', 'impersonal', 'withdrawn'.

Again, just by itself, this is not a sign of a crisis or a psychopathy: their pet, or a family member, may have just died suddenly – tragically – and they have problems in grieving. However, if this symptom becomes linked in with other symptoms, this may indicate a person is entering into some sort of crisis.

5. LACK OF FIRM BOUNDARIES OR NO ADHERENCE TO AGREEMENTS:

Examples of this type of behaviour include:

a) A person increasingly breaking rules, boundaries, rhythms, constraints or agreements. They may attempt to involve others in this, or may get increasingly vehement, aggressive or defensive about their rights or justifications. They may react strongly against guidelines or 'norms'.

b) Alternatively, they might be very apologetic or continuously make promises (i.e., *"Oh, I'm so sorry, I'll never to do that again"*; *"I'll stop gambling or drinking"*, etc.) that are just not kept. They may not pay the mortgage or a direct debit, if they are short that month, but won't tell anybody. They may always be late – with a different excuse.

c) An unwillingness or an inability to maintain or to form an agreement so that there seems no hope of resolution unless someone (you) has to compromise their (your) own position or make an exception for that person. (You need to have a good level of objectivity for this category.)

d) A sense of when one is with the person, of them being scattered, or uncontained, or unbounded, or overly emphatic, or over-euphoric, or hyper-manic … something 'different' … that is also experienced by others, on different occasions, with that person.

6. UNUSUAL LEVELS OF NEED OR DEMAND:

Examples of this category can include:

a) Spending an inordinate amount of time with a person or giving them lots of attention and getting no feeling of resolution with or satisfaction from them.
b) A person who makes out a special case for themselves in nearly every circumstance. This is often accompanied by a heightened sense that it is they or their need that matters and that no-one else's is really important. (Selfish)
c) A sense of being drained whenever one is in close contact with the person that is also experienced by others on different occasions with that person.
d) A person is increasingly involved in a frenzied or continuous level of activity over time without let-up and usually within a particular sphere or project, but can also apply to work. This is sometimes called "manic".
e) A person who has been "window-shopping" through all the available therapies; trying the "smorgasbord" approach (a little of everything) and yet never seeming to stick with one thing or be properly satisfied. Their reasons for their dissatisfaction may, or may not, be significant.

7. *CONTINUOUS* - EMOTIONAL CATHARSIS OR WITHDRAWAL:

Behaviour in this category is really only significant when the first word "Continuous" is applied.

a) Someone who breaks into an emotional state - old memories etc. - and starts crying, abreacting, getting angry or depressed etc. and then cannot seem to get out of this or stop that pattern. It is good that it is coming out. It is not so good if they cannot stop and leave it.
b) It is fine for someone to be withdrawn - especially if they can say they feel a bit withdrawn and perhaps give a clear, simple

reason. It is possible indicative of something else if they stay withdrawn.

c) Someone who is out of contact, may just be spacing out, withdrawn, wholly or unable to express themselves clearly and, God knows, that sometimes happens or is necessary and/or helpful. If they are staying out of contact, that can indicate a problem.

8. LACK OF REAL CONTACT:

Examples of this category can include (also see below):

a) A person who is avoiding issues which are obvious to those around them, and yet refuses to respond to their concerns or questions.
b) A sense that this person is not making proper contact on a day-to-day basis, only going through the motions, and that there is not really anyone there when talking about 'real' issues.
c) A regularity of a withdrawal situation so that there is a disassociation with any degree of continuity.
d) Someone who continually shifts into somewhat disassociated topics, or who talks about issues in a very disassociated way.
e) Someone who talks continually from one particular perspective (eg: work), or on one particular level (eg: social) and never seems to be able to, or willing to, talk about anything else or on any other level.
f) A person who is very self-absorbed and it seems as if you, the other, don't really exist for them, so there is no contact from them to you.

9. NEGLECT OF THE SELF:

Examples of this category can include:

a) A person not washing, sleeping, eating, being tidy, having clean clothes with this behaviour becoming prolonged and seemingly on the increase.

b) An increasing withdrawal, often rationalised by the person as "I don't feel like it", from their usual activities and very often accompanied by statements indicating a lack of self-worth.

c) Excessive or prolonged activity in one confined area with a reluctance or a resistance to stop, and that activity seems to be increasingly detrimental for that person.

d) A sense of depression or sadness or neglect coming from that person that is also experienced by others with that person on different occasions.

e) An increasing use of escapes like T.V., meditation, studying, leisure activities, hobbies, or drugs like alcohol, tobacco or tranquillisers etc. where the usage level is becoming seemingly detrimental and with either promises to reform that do not materialise or a strong resistance towards admitting that there is any problem.

f) Someone working too hard and getting increasingly irritable or explosive and unable to stop or find a way out of their dilemma - the neglect comes in putting the work before the person themselves. This is a classic burnout syndrome.

N.B. The symptoms of burnout are: being exhausted all the time, not matter how long you spend in bed; a sense of isolation from other people, to the extent of becoming a recluse; low self-esteem; ineffectual, no matter how many hours of work put in; a feeling of emotional deadness, or of being trapped; chronic or sudden bursts of anger; loss of empathy for other people's problems; an increase in sarcasm, cynicism or general disparagement; loss of sense of humour; loss of sex drive in a relationship, but an increase in casual sex and/or other addictive behaviours; an increase in physical problems including back and heart pain, headaches, frozen shoulder, chronic fatigue, adrenal or thyroid problems, irritable bowel syndrome, post-viral illnesses, and other illnesses, sometimes major like heart attacks brought on essentially by stress.

It must be re-emphasized that you can probably classify everyone you know into one of these categories at any one time or another. So, they may only really be significant as an indicator of a person in crisis under the following sets of circumstances:

a) **if you (and others) experience a person as being in more than just one category,**

or

b) **that the category of behaviour they seem to be exhibiting is fairly continuous and also escalating.**

CAVEAT - Beware of significant cultural differences. What is appropriate in one culture is often not appropriate in another, and visa versa. Many cultures have certain rules of behaviour, and not abiding by these rules could be a significant indicator for a member of that culture; whereas, in another parallel culture, nothing significant could be drawn from this. So, in a multi-cultural society, whose standards are <u>you</u> judging <u>them</u> by?

DIFFERENT LEVELS OF CRISIS

There are also different levels of crisis: so far, I have mainly been referring to an individual in crisis, but it is also important to recognise that the individual (supposedly identified as being in crisis) has often been deeply affected by crises at other levels that that individual is involved with.

A crisis can obviously happen within the couple relationship, or within the family; or at work (in the team, department, company, sector); or in the social environment (where there might be discrimination, degradation, isolation, or victimization); or in other organizations in which the individual is involved (i.e. being treasurer of a voluntary organisation with its funding suddenly cut); or in societies and political systems (like Soviet communism, or the Arab Spring); and in kingdoms or nations (like Zimbabwe, Syria, Ukraine, Yemen or Eritrea). These crises can then impact on the individual to create and/or add to his or her own personal crisis.

There are also crises in economic systems (as in the world financial crashes of 1929-30 and 2008); and in weather and ecological systems (like desertification, earthquakes, tsunamis, deforestation (in Brazil, the Philippines, and in other rain forests), flooding or global warming (and we may soon see many cities in crisis with rising sea levels); or crises pollution (as with BP in the Gulf of Mexico). Individuals affected by these crises can suddenly find themselves in crisis, through no fault of their own.

There are crises in belief systems and religions (like the relative demise of Christianity in 20th century, or in the wave of paedophilia and child abuse being exposed involving members of the Catholic church). We have also had numerous religious wars and persecutions throughout the last 2,000 years (as with the Cathars in France). These crises also impact on individuals and can trigger their own personal – or even spiritual – crisis.

The industrial revolution (starting in the mid-19th century) created different levels of crises with people streaming away from the countryside and into the cities – with the result that there was a crisis in agriculture (with not enough people on the land) and a crisis in the towns and cities with the number of incomers outstripped the provision of housing and basic services (power, water, sewage, transport, etc.). This is still happening in Shanghai and Beihai in China, Dubai in Saudi Arabia, and in many other cities worldwide (like Sao Paulo in Brazil) with a massive growth of slums surrounding the city and the attendant features of crime, disease and social unrest.

The Western world went into a sort of crisis in the 1960s with the advent of the contraceptive pill; and with freely available (though illegal) drugs; with the post-WW2 economies booming; and the whole 'pop' and 'hippy' culture of the 1960's contradicting traditional values.

The whole human world is currently facing another set of crises: that of global warming, 8 billion people, rising sea levels, and increased weather events. We have also recently had several minor pandemics (including the 1918, 1957 & 1968 influenza outbreaks, SARS (2002-4), & Covid-19 (2020-22) – to name just a very recent few out of a total of the 249 recorded since 1,200 BCE, with (perhaps / probably) another one just around the corner.

All these levels of crisis inevitably affect those individuals involved deeply, both those within the direct affect of these socio-political and environmental crises, but there are also considerable 'knock-on' effects to the individuals around those directly affected.

An economic crisis can create a sudden loss of jobs, with rising inflation, increased taxes, decreasing property values, and the loss of capital, pension funds, etc. There are increasing numbers of unemployed, poor, or homeless people, and a growing gap between rich and poor. Richer countries give 'aid' to poorer countries (often in the form of loans, which the poorer countries have difficulty repaying) but the rich get richer and the poor continue to suffer.

There are other types or levels of crisis: wars, both as aggressors and as victims, create massive levels of crisis, both socially and individually.

Some of these are territorial: some of these are ideological (as in the Korean War and the Vietnam War): some of these wars are based on different belief systems: Christians v. Muslims (Crusades); Catholics v. Protestants; Christian v. (so-called) heathen (British Empire in Africa, India, etc.); Jewish v. Muslim (recently in Israel); Sunni v. Shia (in Iraq); some of these are racial (as in Hutu v. Tutsi in Rwanda); some genocidal (as with the Spanish v. South American Indians), with the North American Indians, the Australian aboriginals, and so forth.

We have seen many wars to do with territory throughout the ages, and some to do with trade (e.g. Opium Wars); soon we may see wars in space, or wars about water. There are also the armed polarizations between one orthodox and another orthodox (as in Northern Ireland) or, (hopefully less warlike) between orthodox and liberal (as within the world-wide Anglican church over homosexuality).

These are all crises in systems: and all of these systemic crises deeply affect individuals. Coping with a crisis cannot therefore focus totally on the individual involved and their personal dynamics, but may also need to deal with (or minimally acknowledge) the issues on some of these different levels.

As therapists, we might therefore even have to become partly 'political' – supporting the individual (patient / client) against the system, which may also be in crisis. The social and political responsibilities of a psychotherapist could or should perhaps be revised in the light of some of these issues:

- We are a significant part of the social and political system, and we cannot avoid this responsibility
- We are amongst the professional specialists that really know about individual suffering
- We are – perhaps more than most – professionals that are aware of the effects of the sufferings and malfunctions of society and the prevailing cultural and political systems
- We can use our professional positions and contacts to influence our social and political systems, so that they can become more human

- As professionals in professional associations, we can make public statements, or host debates, or make these issues into themes for conferences and publish the results
- We have **not** done much of this to date; so, perhaps we need to change our professional attitudes, as well as our work with clients.

These different 'levels' of crisis – and thus of crisis working – should all be taken into account as we work with people in crisis. It is relatively pointless trying to patch up an individual if the rest of the family is homeless and starving.

People experiencing crisis are often likely to be traumatized. This may not be apparent initially, but may appear subsequently. This book is not designed to deal with all the aspects of traumatization: there is now a mass of literature and educational programmes doing that. Perhaps this is an additional sign that our whole society is in crisis. We are all becoming increasingly traumatized.

Finally, please remember: the more sudden or violent is the crisis, the higher is the risk of traumatization. The more abstract (or further removed from the individual) the crisis is, the more powerless the individual is to cope with it.

Some of the material on these last 2 pages was gratefully adapted from a presentation by **Peter Schulthess** at 17th EAP Congress, *"Psychotherapy in Times of Crisis"*, Bucharest, Romania, July 2010.

MAKING CONTACT & STAYING IN CONTACT

In defining this concept, I am trying to give a feeling of how contact is often **not** made, without reference to any particular situation, time, place, or type of crisis.

Any of these 'lack of contact' states might also affect you: after a while of being in contact with the person in crisis, you may feel as if you are (also) out of contact with the person in crisis, rather than they being out of contact with you, or those around you. We resonate with these people – that is how we work.

Types of situations in which there is a definite lack of contact may include:

A. The person is seeming very distant, or not really present, possibly with their mind drifting, or possibly very spacey, or with a sense of fuzziness, or vagueness about them, and what they are saying, and you are not quite sure if there is or there isn't, or not being sure about exactly what has happened. **Action Point:** In this instance, you may have to wait and piece things together later; the person may disclose 'this' to this person and 'that' to that person.

B. The person is being quite disjointed, or is not keeping to the point, or telling long, complicated stories of doubtful significance, or continually changing the subject, or playing with words (rhymes or puns), so that you only get little glimpses of where they are and not a clear, coherent & comprehensive picture from them. **Action Point:** In this instance, the person may be somewhat schizoid and might need some gentle medication (tranquilizers) to 'come down', or may need some help 'grounding' (work or aerobic exercise).

C. The person is claiming to be someone else[22], or to have special knowledge about the way that someone else thinks; or to have direct and absolute contact with some mystic being.

What makes this different from a healthy spiritual revelation (which sometimes also happens) is that you are unable to manage to keep a sense of the person in front of you <u>as well as</u> a sense of what the special knowledge, information or channelling is all about. Being in receipt of this sort of information does not mean that *you* (as an individual) disappear: sometimes it feels that you do. **Action Point:** In this instance, the person may seem to be 'taken over' or 'possessed' – please don't react against them/. This may just be the beginning of a psychic opening and they may take some time to integrate this with their 'normal' persona.

D. The person may be very depressed and/or diminutive about themselves, coming out with statements like *"I don't really matter"* or *"It's not important how I think"*, to the extent that you get the feeling that you are hardly with a person at all, just a shell, or a blob, or something pretty amorphous. You may find yourself encouraging them, or trying to talk them out of this state. This is also a form of lack of contact. **Action Point:** In this instance, they may need some help to 're-frame' their perception to a more positive perspective. They might need a reality check. If they don't respond, they might need medical help from a low-level anti-depressant.

E. The person is being very obsessive about a particular event, incident, or topic and continually comes back to that particular subject whatever the situation or topic is at present so that contact with them is very limited in terms of content.

---

[22] This is unlikely to be in the form of someone thinking that they are Julius Caesar or Napoleon – more likely that they are Jesus, or a reincarnation of an Egyptian Priestess of Isis!

F. The person that you are with is expressing emotions that are valid, given the set of circumstances, but the level of emotion is considerably over the top (or denied) and there is a seeming lack of contact with this exaggerated (or underplayed) reaction. Their level of emotion is taken as "normal" in the circumstances by them, and is obviously not normal.

G. The person is seemingly very coherent on a moment to moment basis, but a few minutes later will either totally contradict themselves, or will have "forgotten" that something was said or agreed so that there is no real continuity over time. People in the early stages of Alzheimer's have this as an increasingly chronic condition. For people in crisis, it is slightly different and comes and goes more frequently.

H. There is contact with one aspect of the person's personality, but there is virtually no contact with another aspect, or any other aspect: and then it changes. It is almost as if two people or two different personas, are inhabiting the same body (which may actually be the case). Sometimes the lack of contact is between these two personas: i.e., you may be able to relate to both, but they are not relating to each other. Confusing? = Lack of contact.

I. There is a lack of contact with "consensual reality" (mentioned earlier). What they might be saying sounds wonderful, except that the world just doesn't work that way. They may have grandiose ideas that Nelson Mandela will be interested in their ideas for a "peace plan" or something, and they have just faxed him these ideas, and are now awaiting a response (viz: "and they have done it from your machine and have to stay in your office till he replies").

J. They have just now decided to… make a significant change in their life: divorce their partner: leave their job: stop the medication they have been on: - immediately, despite having no contact with their partner, or boss, or despite what has been said by their doctor, who "doesn't know anything", or "who just doesn't understand" or whatever. And all this is on the basis of a Tarot reading, or because they had a dream, or came to Findhorn for the weekend, or whatever. Out of touch!

K. They may have suddenly ceased all contact with a particular member of their family, friends or workmates. However, contact with this person may be essential or necessary, at least for the moment, and some form of contact must be restored (it could be for a parental, logistic, or financial reason).

Make sure you don't get caught up as a go-between – because of their particular form of crisis: advocate or negotiator is perhaps a better role, albeit relatively skilled, and it demands a quid-pro-quo and being in contact with consensual reality and degrees of reason and rationality.

L. The person is – for some reason – in a fairly chronic regression that makes them more likely to be susceptible to groups that offer a "home", a "new family", some form of "relief" or "salvation" etc. These groups can be genuine, or they can be esoteric sects, cults (with charismatic leaders), or political, religious & ideological movements, that may also be radical and possibly even terrorist. These groups retain power over the members by isolating them from others, and thus there is enforced lack of contact.

Once you have identified that the person is – really and truly – in a crisis, the next section follows on directly:

WHAT TO DO AT FIRST

If you find yourself with a person in a situation such as described, and you do <u>not</u> have any sort of therapeutic contract with them, and you do <u>not</u> have a lot of experience in this field, then you <u>MUST</u> try to get in someone who can help therapeutically. This is your first "appropriate action". Please read the whole section.

<u>Getting the Person in Crisis to a Point of a Successful Intervention</u>

A. You Should or Must Inform:

(i) someone who <u>is</u> in direct contact with that person (i.e. a member of their family, flatmate, etc.) <u>and</u>, if this is appropriate,

(ii) someone in their place of work or organisation. Ideally one of these people, or you, will then get in contact with:

(iii) someone who has experience of working with people in crisis. (Also see the "Resources" List)

As the person is possibly demanding some sort of a response by this type of extraordinary behaviour, they will often continue in this type of behaviour (or worse) until an appropriate response is made. The person's extraordinary behaviour may even exaggerate itself until an appropriate response is made.

An appropriate response can usually only be made by someone who is relatively skilled at, or trained in, crisis intervention. Your task now, having identified someone in crisis, is to find this person and get them involved. The rest of this section centres around this point. So:-

B. **The Sooner an Appropriate Response can be Made, the Easier and Better the Resolution will Be for All People Concerned.**

This particularly applies if there has been any disclosure about previous mental illness, breakdowns, psychoses, psychiatric treatment, or if the person has been prescribed any of the psychiatric drugs.

Sometimes people try to deny that a crisis is really happening. They are trying to hold it off. A slight escalation of their situation may bring on the crisis, but the person's character pattern or whatever is determined not to admit this. This aspect may have to be confronted, and as soon as this is done, they will then be able to 'have their crisis'. Though this may also mean that they might also try to run away from it, or you, as you have confronted them.

<u>An appropriate response is for the person in crisis to be 'met' by a person with some experience or skill in these matters.</u> This could be almost anyone, and it is quite dependent on the type of crisis.

Sometimes the person in crisis cannot help himself or herself easily, it is therefore up to the people around them to get them the appropriate help. Getting help is essential. Getting the right help is desirable. Don't delay too long trying to get the exact 'right' person.

*** **Now**, please check out the note at the bottom of this section to see if you are the appropriate person to continue, and, if you are, then continue: otherwise, **stop here, now!** Wait with them till the appropriate person arrives.

C. **Confront Them Gently, especially if you have any position of authority or responsibility, or if you have any special relationship with them, and try to get some more detailed information – then check this information out.**

Good accurate information is really vital at this point. It may help determine who makes the successful intervention, how, when, and where.

- Is it going to be a psychiatrist; a social worker; a psychotherapist; a priest; a counsellor; someone from the SEN Network, or what?
- Is it better for them to stay where they are, or at their home, or in another special place (yet to be identified)?
- What resources have they got? – money, credit cards, available shelter, belongings, tickets, support, friends, family, etc.

It may be necessary to ask specifically about some of the points mentioned above, and about the history of their crisis, especially if any suspicions have been aroused that it might actually be an emergency situation, rather than a crisis. Hints about aspects of their history, medication, damage, etc, are often dropped gently, or picked up from other sources. Disclosures are often made subtly – but not necessarily to you! Ask the person, and then ask others, to see if the stories tally and complement each other, or are contradictive.

D. Find Out More Information from those people around the person in crisis, and from the person themselves, and try to build up a bigger picture.

Ask their flat-mates, partners & others in their work group/department or whatever event or programme they are on. It is always worth trying to pick up bits of information in odd moments.

You sometimes do need to meet and sit with the person in crisis – they need to be present, and see you are working for them; you should not do of this all from another office. The person who is in crisis is often quite desperate to talk about himself or herself. Anything they say (because of their exaggerated emotional state) is probably very relevant, but it may not be complete, or it may be distorted a bit. It helps to build trust if you listen properly. When chatting, the person often relaxes and is less guarded and when being "interrogated" their defences are up and stronger.

E. Now Make the Call!

At some point shortly after you have got as much of the necessary information as you can get within a reasonable time frame, it is then the time to make the call, or calls. You are trying to get specialist help for this person. You are not a specialist; you do not have the available resources. They're out there somewhere. It is now your job to try to find them and get the person in crisis the appropriate assessment or referral. At this point you may need someone else to sit with the person in crisis, as it is quite difficult to speak about someone to someone else in front of them. You may need to make several calls. Be as factual and succinct as possible. Take notes of whom you call, their number, and what they say. Always ask the person you are speaking to on the phone if they have any other ideas about referrals to who could be a suitable person for a crisis intervention. Try to establish an idea of times, availability, contracts, payments, etc. Don't be in a position where you have to wait to long; get someone here now, as soon as is reasonably possible. It is a crisis! You are also just making a call about someone who is in crisis. You are not becoming responsible for saving their life; or their soul. You should not commit yourself to anything that you are not prepared to do or unable to do with this third party. They (the people you are calling) are some sort of relevant professionals. They carry a certain degree of authority, responsibility and hopefully also a degree of "respondability". Check their referral criteria: does the person in crisis fit?

F. Report Back.

Tell the person in crisis what is happening: what you have done: what you think might happen now. That means you are being as honest as possible with them. You don't have to justify anything, but expressions like: *"I think that you are having a crisis and that means that we should get in some specialized help: so, I have called So-&-so."* This may be sufficient. The person may have a reaction: that's OK. You have made a decision that, given the circumstances, you think is the correct decision: and that's OK as well. These are differences of opinion and will get sorted out eventually.

Tell the other people involved on a "need-to-know" basis: who and how much. Some people just need to know you have called someone and that someone is coming to help. Others may need more detailed or specific information. Do not necessarily feel bound by any confidentiality. You are not a professional. This does not apply to you. You need to get the person professional help. They need to be informed about the full situation – all the details.

G. Then Stay in Contact.

The person in crisis will sometimes move in and out of contact with you, and in and out of contact with consensual reality. This is quite normal for someone in a crisis. Gently plot this movement. Notice when it happens and what triggers any changes. Just try to make sure that you are in contact with them, and stay in contact with them, even if they are not totally in contact with you.

Please read the section about "Staying in Contact".

Make sure, if you have to leave and someone else takes over, that they have all the relevant information. This is part of you "staying in contact". Write down all important information, before you leave.

H. Create as much of a relaxed situation as possible. Defuse any panic.

Get rid of the kids and any other anxious people around. Just chat. Get someone else to make a cup of tea for everyone. Act pretty normally. There is nothing to do now except to wait.

Remember it is often YOUR fear or anxiety that can escalate a situation. The person in crisis will (inevitably) sense it and may also re-act to it. So, just wait for whom-so-ever you have called to arrive, or for the time of the appointment, and until then, make sure that the person in crisis doesn't go off alone somewhere by himself or herself. <u>Always</u> go with them; you can wait just as well walking along the streets, or sitting in the park. Take a mobile phone with you so that you are still in contact and contactable.

I. It is nearly always worthwhile making some case notes.

FIRSTLY, this helps you keep things reasonably clear. SECONDLY, you may not overlook or forget things if you keep such notes. THIRDLY, you may have to make a summary to someone else and these notes could help you do this. FOURTHLY, you may have a degree of responsibility or accountability, either for others or in respect of this person, and the notes can help you should how you exercised that responsibility. FIFTHLY, you may have to write up the situation. SIXTHLY, it helps you review the situation, by yourself or with others, especially if you make a mistake you want to learn from. SEVENTHLY, as mentioned, you may have to leave and 'hand over' to someone else. So, Make the Notes!

*** **NOTE:** From point C. onwards, you should be fairly committed to and available for the first stage of this unfolding process:

Getting the person in crisis to a point of a successful intervention.

If you aren't committed, or you can't so commit yourself to continuing with the person in crisis, then get someone else in who can. You may be just about to go on holiday, or you have kids that need to be picked up from school, or you need to lead a workshop now, or have to get a contract signed, or whatever. So get in someone else, anyone else, and then go and do what you have to do. Tell them what has happened, give them this handbook (if this feels appropriate), and ensure that you "hand over" properly.

You can ask the person in crisis who they would to come like in, to be with, or to make these arrangements with, for a while: you may be pleasantly surprised. They often have resources that you are unaware of. They may already have a therapist or counsellor, or they may have an affinity with someone else.

Tell them why you have to leave and that you will/may be able to come back later. You may be freer then, and have more space and time, and can come back in and help out later without any conflict.

The person in crisis should be able to understand this. Be clear about your parameters, and do not promise to do anything that you cannot commit to happily.

There are also different roles to take in a Crisis Group (see later) and you may well fit into one of these roles: a role that is more appropriate for yourself.

Consider thanking the person for the privileged of becoming involved (so far) in their process.

USE OF PSYCHOTHERAPY

The Basic Steps & Goals To Resolve A Crisis

The aim of this book (and of a Crisis Group) is to attempt to help you (or someone) to provide an **appropriate** set of responses as quickly as possible to someone in a psychological, emotional, or spiritual, crisis. It must then be the ultimate aim to assist that person to regain their normal functioning to a level <u>as good as</u> or <u>better than</u> their pre-crisis level as soon as is reasonably possible.

However, this must not necessarily be taken to be understood as restoring the situation back to what it was before: as this could be to deny the value of a crisis, or not to follow the process of a crisis.

There may also be a psychological component that can really only be worked with by somebody with some training in psychotherapy. This does not necessarily mean a psychiatrist or psychologist. The 'medical' or 'treatment' model that is often part of their training can sometimes make these professions unsuitable to work with a crisis in a 'process-oriented' way.

There are several basic steps to resolve a crisis: so far, we have been looking at various aspects of the first three points:

1. Gain the rapport & trust of the person in crisis & of the people around:
2. Formulate a clear definition of problem.
3. Clarify your own involvement.

There are several other steps to follow.

4. Establish what has already been tried: by the person; by others (friends / family); bythe medical profession; by other therapists, skilled helpers, etc.?
5. Focus on different perceptions of reality – how do they differ?
6. What is the person's own perception or dynamic?
7. What are possible goals for treatment, or jointly achievable aims.

A crisis also has three distinct phases:

A. The 'preparation' or escalation phase
B. The 'critical' phase
C. The 'post-crisis' or de-escalation phase.

Different Phases

A. Psychotherapy can be very useful in a number of different ways with the prevention of any further escalation, especially in the first phase. These ways can be:
- Degrees of support, mediation and process skills for any possible conflict resolution to try to prevent further problems
- Awareness of growing tension and thus suitable responses made, or appropriate action taken earlier, again to aid prevention of the crisis
- Training and awareness for the client / patient and other possible supporters
- Empowerment and self-help techniques used more conscientiously to increase potential and use of resources
- Support of self-responsibility and ego-functions.

B. Psychotherapy can also be very useful, as has been and will be described, in the full crisis phase:
- Calming the person in crisis down
- Establishing a constructive therapeutic relationship

- Helping them connect with their body (grounding)
- Collecting information: what has happened; what are the available resources?
- Organising a crisis group (see later) to 'hold' the person's process
- Exploring issues within the process; occasionally challenging or confronting inappropriate behaviour
- Examining and discussing what has been irrevocably broken or damaged and what might be repaired or resorted to and what is still functioning
- Examining what resources the individual has to overcome or cope with the crisis
- Ensuring that all basic needs are satisfied and managed on a day-to-day basis (more the work of the 'Carers' – see Forming a Crisis Group).

C. Psychotherapy can furthermore be very appropriate after the crisis has 'peaked' in the post-crisis or 'de-escalation' stage:
- A continuation of the support (and rapport) in working through the crisis process
- Helping to mourn the loss of aspects, status or items from previous to the crisis
- Expressing emotions connected with the crisis in the safe space of the therapy room
- Experimenting with new possibilities, attitudes, perceptions and behaviour
- Looking forward, with new orientations
- And very importantly – helping with the integration of the crisis at lots of different levels
- Finally, to encourage the person's abilities to experiment with these changes and assimilate these, in order to find creative adjustments to their new life circumstances.

There is an oft-quoted maxim possibly relevant here:

"God, grant me the serenity to accept the things that I cannot change; the courage to change the things that I can; and the wisdom to know the difference." Reinhold Niebuhr, American theologian, 1892-1971

The material on these last 2 pages was gratefully adapted from a presentation by **Peter Schulthess** at 17th EAP Congress, *"Psychotherapy in Times of Crisis"* Bucharest, Romania, July 2010.

APPROPRIATE ACTIONS

So, as we have mentioned, if someone has been identified as being a person in such a state, contact should be made with somebody who has definite experience of crisis work (ideally a psychotherapist or similar), and who can come and help assess the situation, quickly and discretely. This is essential.

If there is no way of a professional being able to get to the person in crisis easily, another or an additional course of appropriate action is to help the person in crisis to set up a crisis group around them: to create (or re-create) a sort of community around that person in crisis. Sometimes, someone who is aware of the parameters of a crisis group can offer this sort of organisational help very successfully over the phone. The parameters of a Crisis Group are dealt with below (page 49). This sort of 'holding situation' may be what is appropriate in such cases, or it may be that it is decided that it is appropriate to form a crisis group.

Much of what is called "appropriate action" here revolves around having a much more 'useful' or supportive perspective of the person who is in crisis and what it is all about for them. This is what is "appropriate" to them; and they are the ones having the crisis.

If you see the person as dysfunctional, this will not help them – or you. If you can identify with those times when you might have been in crisis yourself, and then try to empathize with their position, you may be of more use. You will only really be able to help them from a position where you are supporting their "process", rather than telling them they are "wrong" and what they "should" be doing is what is "right". This is very much more of a developmental "process-oriented" type of work, rather than a black-white, right-wrong, polarized situation. So, how can we help you move to a slightly better state?

This is not to say that, at relevant points, you cannot help them cognitively understand their situation better, if that is what they indicate is needed: nor is this contradictory in assisting them to work step-by-step towards a better way of doing things, if that is what they decide that they would like to, or need to do. There may also be systems of thought or well-defined perspectives, that it might be appropriate for them to consider whether they fit into these categories or not. Occasionally it is helpful for people to identify themselves into a category like "alcoholic", or "co-dependent", or "addictive", or "abused", or "psychic", or whatever. Rarely is it appropriate for you to do so.

I have already suggested how psychotherapy can effectively address some of the issue in the preparation phase: now I would like to start to look at what is generally considered as some more "appropriate actions", prior to deciding whether to form a crisis group and what that might look like.

OTHER WAYS OF WORKING WITH A CRISIS

Often these crisis states can also be a cry for help. One of the better responses is to react as soon as possible to the basic need, rather than to the symptoms of the crisis (which may actually be self-defeating). It may be that someone can help with the identification of this basic need through their experience or training, so please use the talents that exist around. To establish some of these basic needs with the person in crisis, some counselling or psychotherapy is probably an essential prerequisite

Teamwork is paramount in any form of crisis intervention. It may be that the most appropriate response will be to continue your contact with the person, but (<u>and this is absolutely essential</u>) only with proper back-up and support from several others. It is highly unlikely that you, or any other single person, can provide the person in crisis with everything that they need to regain their functioning, or to get out of, or through their particular crisis.

Alternatively, they may possibly some help need to get out of their present situation (with you?) into a more appropriate situation (for them) and the crisis symptoms are a cry for help and a (sort of) method of achieving that end. Either way, teamwork is very important, and if you are a part of their crisis, or represent a part of their crisis, you (and they) will need some outside help to sort it all out.

A crisis situation can sometimes run for 36-72 hours non-stop. How long can you stay awake? How useful are you three-quarters of the way through that period. We therefore recommend the structure of the "Crisis Group" (page 49).

However, there are also some organic conditions, such as certain mineral deficiencies, withdrawal from certain drugs, or certain types of epilepsy, that can imitate psychiatric symptoms, or those of extreme emotional distress. As it may be important to distinguish these organic and medical situations from true psychological, emotional or spiritual crisis symptoms, some level of medical or psychiatric assessment sometimes has a very important role to play in helping to identify what is the most appropriate response. A person skilled in crisis work will usually know when to call upon medical diagnostic skills and at what point –whether or not medical (psychotropic) treatment is eventually used. Please suspend any (possible) biases of your own against any members of the medical or psychiatric profession: these contain many kind, very knowledgeable, and dedicated people. They also have access to many resources, and a medical cabinet is just one of these.

Contact someone: Whenever the question arises around a person in crisis, *"Shall we contact a psychiatrist, psychotherapist, a member of the Spiritual Emergence Network, or whatever?"*, **always, always, always** try to veer towards actually doing so. The thought itself usually means that either a crisis is precipitating and that you are beginning to recognise it, or the thought can be a part of your deep wisdom and intuition working to solve the problem which your cognitive mind is having a difficulty with. The contact you are seeking might be to get supervision, support, and advice for what you (and the others with you) are doing reasonably adequately at the moment.

Situations like These <u>often</u> get Worse before They get Better: A timely intervention and appropriate action can often really help the person and even defuse the crisis, as the message to the person is that they are being taken seriously and thus do not have to develop a full crisis to get the attention or aid needed. Alternatively, to delay can mean that the situation gets a lot worse and the "appropriate action" then is often much more costly or traumatic (emotionally, time-wise and financially). Sometimes, the appropriate action is to do nothing: but this must be determined specifically, and most other possibilities eliminated first.

As a Rule of Thumb, Always Inform the Person in Crisis what is Happening: why you have decided to take this action and what is going to happen next – even though they might not like it. There is no reason to treat them as anything less of a person just because they are in crisis. Crisis can often include a level of paranoia, which is not helped by whispered conversations and strange people suddenly appearing and asking a lot of questions. If needed, refer to "authority/ regulations/ procedures etc." as a justification for calling someone else in, even though there may be some resistance to this – even though there may be some resistance to this. It also gives them an opportunity to say "No" and suggest an alternative that seems appropriate to you (and others) as well.

Always have Someone Stay with the Person: It is not good, for them or generally, to leave someone who is in or near a crisis alone, even for a moment. If possible, always have someone else present and in attendance as well (or on immediate call) at all times. A person in crisis can do sudden and weird things without any previous warning. Unfortunately, one usually only learns this by experience. Bathroom doors should stay ajar: privacy, but also accessibility: there are many things in a bathroom that a person in crisis can use to abuse. Anyway, I hope I have made the point!

Be Clear and Direct: It might be necessary to be quite firm and matter-of-fact at times and to tell the people around you just how it is. *"This is what is happening; this is what has happened and it is important that you (the person) stay here until such & such else happens. There seems to be a crisis and I have taken charge for the moment. I have also called [the police/ambulance/for a psychotherapist/or whatever]. I may be wrong, but it's probably best to be on the safe side, and anyway it's my job/or the clinic's policy to do this ... etc."*

Try to Work with the Person's Process: Try to speak to them in their language, and in their terms. Try to ensure that you are genuinely on their side and working for their benefit. If there are conflicts of interest, then maybe you can take a different 'role' and still support them in some way, whilst being also true to your other interests. "Working with the person's process" is not a license for them to do anything they want and you all to run around trying to support and facilitate them; it is a deep and sincere attempt to help them expiate themselves out of their crisis situation, which may be a significant and meaningful point in their lives if given this respect and opportunity. It is respect for the person; the factors that brought them there; the environment they are in (and the people around them; and for your own part in their process. For more fundamental components of working with people's processes, please consult the reading list: Arnold Mindell's work is particularly good in this respect.

Crisis States in Others Can, Will and Do Affect You Emotionally Too: This effect is also one of the indicators of a crisis. You are (hopefully) monitoring your own emotional reactions all the time. However, when you are eventually clear of the situation, take some time to "get clear" yourself; a shower will help; or talking it over with a friend & crying on their shoulder; getting angry or whatever you need to do. You must look after yourself – as well. No-one else will do that for you. <u>Do this before you go and do anything else significant.</u>

Use Cleansing Techniques Liberally: Light a candle. Use incense. Have a long shower. Plants are good and help absorb energy; do a bit of gardening. Walk on the beach or by the river, if you can. Sunlight, wind and rain are really good cleansing agents. Watch a bad or funny movie. Get a support person for yourself. You can also cleanse yourself by catharting a bit: shout or scream, bash cushions, laugh, cry. And/or you can also cleanse yourself by whatever form of meditation you find appropriate for yourself.

Get as full a history as possible: At some point – though this is not a major priority – it is important to get as full a history of the person's crisis and their background as possible. You do not have to do this: sometimes the carers or support people can do this. Have it recorded flexibly and so that others can add to it. It can also be therapeutic: to have someone recount back to you (the person in crisis) the narrative of your crisis, especially if there have been altered states or even periods of dissociation, can really help understanding, and the 'owning' of your (the person's) process.

FORMING A CRISIS GROUP

Components of a Crisis Group:

There are four main components or 'roles' within a crisis group and these are usually mutually exclusive in that these roles just do not mix. This is a very important "caveat" – something to 'beware' or be aware of: stay in one role only. Don't 'cross over' to being in a different role.

The Companion(s) or Carer(s) - a person in crisis needs extra help and support – at differing levels according to their need – sometimes 24 hours a day – sometimes for a half-hour chat, twice a day. The people in this role are not (necessarily) therapists– the role is more to be a companion or friend or a process observer. They need to be present, coming from the heart, purely and simply. A lot of helpful therapeutic work can be done – but only from the positive reinforcement side. This can be an unskilled role –though a very loving and caring one.

The Facilitator or Therapist – this role can also be positive but at times the person in this role may need to challenge the person in crisis's attitude or process. It is difficult or even impossible in extreme cases both to support and challenge. It is much easier to separate the roles. The facilitator has an overview of the person's process and may also help direct the crisis group. There is a fair degree of training and experience implied here to fulfil this role. Hopefully, there is also a reasonably democratic process as well. It is the person's process after all. Other people have to agree whole-heartedly as they may be doing the work.

Both these first two roles are centred around the dynamic of the person in crisis. The people should stay centred with that person and limit all contact to anyone else with the family etc, as far as is humanly possible. This role is taken by:

The Gatekeeper or Guardian– whose job it is to protect the person's process and see that it can happen undisturbed. A safe space is thus created. This role can be an administrator (of a clinic) who will also negotiate finances and placements. It can also be the person who organises rotas etc. Information to the outside should be channelled in and out through this person. This can bequite a hard role.

The Process Supporter(s)–are the people who back up the process, who support the supporters, who give supervision to the therapist, and who work with the rest of the family to create a different and better environment for the person in crisis to emerge into. This work with doctors (perhaps), family & friends is most important as this group can and should take over from the crisis group, if they are not involved as such already. The "supporting the supporters" aspect is also very important as the carers (particularly) can get very drained.

We have also found it very useful for the crisis group to keep a journal/diary/log book of the crisis process with everyone (crisis person as well as helpers) writing in anything: dreams, events, impressions, feelings, times, freak-outs, medication etc. This is really useful for the person afterwards to help integrate their crisis and get the full picture of what happened.

Acknowledgements to Joseph Berke: Arbours Association

FORMING A COMMUNITY AROUND A PERSON IN CRISIS

It is also sometimes impossible to work with a person as a therapist alone. The person needs or declares their need for a wider 'community' in which to have their crisis. An example might be of a person still living at home who has an emotional breakdown. In this instance, probably staying at home – the environment that they had their crisis in, might not be the best solution; they may need some time and space away from the home in order to discover what their next steps are: yet it needs to be a relatively safe space. One client who I had worked with by telephone consultation in this situation 'remembered' that a cousin, living in a nearby town had a spare room in their flat. I encouraged them to follow up this idea, and also suggested that they explain to the cousin some of the things we had talked about, so there would be a context to their situation and a support for that person in crisis. I also encouraged them to take this opportunity to follow up another idea they had had: of taking up art classes; an idea that their parents had disapproved of. I felt the extra support that they might gain in this situation, and the new people they would meet, and the widening of their boundaries, and the 'fresh start', and the personal interest, all justified supporting their suggestion. In effect, I was encouraging them to create a sort of 'community' around themselves in their crisis situation: a more supportive community than their home environment.

In another instance, a member of our extended (Findhorn) community came into crisis when s/he was living on the West Coast of Scotland. In this instance, s/he felt that s/he needed much more support and a much closer "family" feeling in order to get through their crisis: this was again working with them initially over the phone. So, we agreed that this person should come over to the main community, and, since, in this instance, they were very shaky and almost borderline, I actually drove across Scotland to meet them off the ferry and brought them back to the community where we 'commandeered' an empty bungalow and set up a daily support rota with those people who s/he had nominated, and who had agreed to help. For three weeks, we all worked with this person as s/he went much deeper into their crisis; the darkest fears and the blackest moments. We all wrote down, in a sort of logbook, what we had done, and what we had perceived and felt whilst we were with this person: whatever the role: carer, therapist, supporter, friend, etc. This log turned into a record of this person's crisis that was very useful to them later on in their integrative process. No-one got over-loaded; no-one got stressed out; and yet there was a continuity and a level of support that allowed a depth of working that I have experienced rarely in my 20 or so years of work as a psychotherapist.

At one point in this particular person's therapy work, s/he mentioned that s/he was worried that s/he couldn't make enough noise, even though the bungalow was relatively private, as s/he felt there were still people around who might be disturbed. So, we went into the sound-proofed recording studio and there s/he explored the noises that s/he wanted to make. The finding of her 'voice' also allowed him/herself to regress to the point at which their deeper self could emerge and start to be recognised more fully. This was a break-through point for his/her crisis.

There are other ways in which one can consider creating a sort of community around a person in crisis. Sometime the support and personnel are there, but the understanding isn't. So, the task here might be to educate the people around the person in crisis in the concepts of crisis work and process work and to encourage them to adopt some of these roles, and constraints. This coming-together for a common purpose with an educative input has often been sufficient to create a sort of community – or support group – around the person in crisis, so that they can feel that the contact and support they receive is helpful and constructive; and with that, and with the emphasis on self-directed strategies and process, they have been able to have their crisis successfully.

Sometimes, it is necessary just to slow down a person's spiritual emergence process, rather than stop it. It is often much too difficult to put everything back into its box. But, slowing down enables the process to find its own energy and its own speed.

I emphasise, again and again, that when working with a person in crisis, it is really important to really listen to **their** story, and what lies behind **their** story. If they report, or it is reported that, that they spent three hours with a person in (say) the kitchen or the pottery: firstly, *"Hey, That's great! You must have really enjoyed being with them."* And secondly ask, *"What did you get from being with them?"* You are trying to find what aspect of their process is it that took them there and kept them there? This will often be the really significant material.

In a community setting, it may also be possible to find out from the other person (in the kitchen or pottery) what their experience was of the person in crisis for that three-hour period (Here you are in the Guardian Role). This can be very helpful if part of 'creating their community' can in future include the person in some role or other. It may be necessary to encourage the person in crisis (in Therapist's Role) to discover from the person in crisis, whether they can go again; or discourage them from going again to that person, if it transpires that the Guardian's report is negative.

Maybe it is possible to get the 'something' that they got from that person, from another person in the future; or in some other appropriate way; and so we come back continually into the therapeutic exploration of the person's process; what the person needs and how they might achieve it.

Sometimes, though fairly rarely, the person in crisis has not been able to cope with the 'expansion', or break-through components that they have come to in their crisis; instead, they have wanted to back-off from the crisis and restore the elements that existed previously. Whilst one can never completely turn the clock back, the therapist's role here would be (still) to support their process, and thus help them to restore relationships that have been broken, either prior to, or possibly even contribute to the crisis, or which have been broken or disrupted by the extremities of the crisis. Working with others – as well as the person in crisis – is sometimes needed. (See "Forming a Crisis Group")

Finally, as I was reminded in a seminar I gave on this topic, sometimes the sanctuary of the therapeutic, one-on-one, intimate, dispassionate, and confidential space that can exist in the therapy room, is what is really necessary to help the person through their crisis. This point is picked-up again in the 'Zen Space' section that follows later. But it helps proves the point that one strategy doesn't fit all, and sometimes just 'being' with a person is what is needed: sometimes, you don't have to 'do' anything: sometimes, something just happens when two people spend some time together.

SOME BASIC STRATEGIES

There are various basic strategies sometimes useful for defusing emergencies and helping someone in a crisis:

1. **Try to incorporate the person's world-view into any design.** Their language, fears, values, perceptions of themselves and others make up their world. If you can communicate with them in these terms – or in their native language – it can really help. A crisis often increases a person's rigidity of viewpoint and their alienation from others – a form of bridge helps.

2. **Try to re-frame.** If you can help them adjust their perceptions into something slightly closer to mainstream reality, then they can get more in contact with you, others and themselves. This should not distort their own perceptions.

3. **Accept their defensiveness & incorporate their resistance into any intervention.** You are intervening, in some way, in their process. They can get defensive. Avoid the headlong collision. Try to keep yourself (seemingly at least) on their side, not against them. Go *with* their resistance, but in your direction.

4. **The "illusion of alternatives"** – is where you offer a seeming choice, but both involve change. *"Do you want to go to the hospital in my car or in an ambulance?"* is a little gross, but sometimes the situation gets to this point.

5. **Negotiate change.** See if you can offer a "quid pro quo" or get some concessions from both sides. Their strategies are not working. Yours might, but they don't know that. Make them an offer that seems attractive, *"Let's try this"* rather than an ultimatum, *"You do this or we'll do that"*.

6. **Delay the final decision.** Anything that is final seems like the end... of something. People are very scared of endings – death, parting, separation, abandonment, giving-up. Don't force one – unless you have to: delay it, if possible. Their process will continue anyway.

7. **Focus on their process.** It is imperative for a successful outcome that the person involved in the crisis is able to see their part in their own process. By focussing on their overall or deeper process, the intermediate ups-&-downs or the symptoms can be overcome more easily.

8. **If it works, use it**- as long as this doesn't mean lying or abuse. Tactics like: Distracting with trivia if an escalation is being threatened; Appearing confused – playing on a person's desire to be understood; Re-framing crisis behaviour in a more positive light, which can help remove some fear & shame; Limited medication; Giving them the control (but not perhaps the choice); Paradoxical interventions; 'Stealing' the person's process – instead of them smashing up a chair, you do it, as it's safer – or substitute a cup for a chair, as it's cheaper; Cautious use of humour; etc. are all reasonably pragmatic strategies that can be used – with caution, if they seem to have a chance of success.

9. **Alternative strategies may be better**– not only for them. They have inner wisdom - access it! Listen to your own intuition. Check it out, if possible. What has not been addressed yet, and why? What is 'left field'? Could this be better?

A "ZEN" SPACE

Sometimes, or often, it is necessary to allow the person to be in a "Zen" space. They may want it, or need it, or ask for it – in some way. And it is absolutely O.K. if they do. And there are just the normal safeguards that need to be taken to ensure that they are not going to be abusing the space, or abusing themselves within this space. By a "Zen" space, we are meaning the voluntary, unique and especially designed equivalent of a sanctuary, a retreat space, or a padded cell, or something in between. A "Zen" space is a quiet, safe space where the person in crisis can go to just "be".

When someone is going through deep and powerful traumatic change, there are a number of factors that need to be considered from the perspective of what this person is experiencing. Consider the caterpillar metamorphosing into a butterfly. They absolutely need the cocoon in order to do this. This is not just an unnecessary invention; nature doesn't work that way. Similarly, as John, or Mary, is transforming into their new, more spiritual, potential, they may well need something of a safe space, a cocoon, in which to do this.

If there have been quite traumatic experiences: Kundalini, Life-Death-Rebirth, etc., (see Section 2) then a fair amount of time is needed to just experience the effects of "being changed" by this process. What is it like to be in this new body? What effect have all these changes had on me? Who am I now? What do I do next?

A "Zen" space should be comfortable and quiet. There should be a clear rule about entry, or non-entry, for other persons. No-one should be able to come in at their own volition, or without specific permission, except in certain emergency conditions. Maybe there should be set times of the day when the "Zen" space is dissolved and freer entry, exit, and communication is resumed. These things must be carefully negotiated, built-up or "tweaked" until they are right. Just knowing that such a space exists can aid the person in crisis to get through some of the other 'bad' times.

Contact with nature can be excellent: like a shack in the woods or a caravan somewhere. The ability to paint, draw and write can be important, so these facilities can be provided. Some people like having their own music: others like the enforced silence without any distractions available. TVs and radios are probably not a good idea. Books can be good (see Reading List). Simple food and drink should be provided by the carers at regular (agreed) intervals, maybe by being left in an agreed spot, with an understanding that if it is not consumed after x hours, that constitutes a warning signal for the carers.

The ability to get up in the night and paint, draw, or write or whatever without disturbing anyone else, and then to sleep, almost endlessly, and all at one's own rhythm, is often prized by "Zen" space users. It is very healing. One-on-one therapeutic contact with someone who is totally uninvolved and absolutely neutral, in a room that has no other connections, can also be a form of "zen space."

MEDITATION & MINDFULNESS

A quiet physical space is not the only thing that is needed: a quiet mind is sometimes essential. The regular practice of meditation has many different advantages. Meditation is a very powerful form of relaxation. Meditation does not have to be religious or based on any particular faith. Essentially, it is sitting still, breathing regularly, and quietening your mind. When you do this, your body slows down and you shift more into the parasympathetic part of the Autonomic Nervous System (that's a good thing). Eventually your mind will slow down as well and you will become more peaceful and relaxed. This is extremely good for many medical conditions, like hypertension (high blood pressure), and also many psychological ones. We often need to reduce the stress caused by everyday living and then the extra stress caused by extraordinary events.

Meditation Position: Make sure that you are not going to be disturbed; switch off the ringer on the phone; turn off the mobile; hang a note on the bedroom door; tell the others in the house that you are going to meditate for (say) 20 minutes (they will get used to the idea soon). Settle in a comfortable sitting position, either on a straight-backed chair, with your feet flat on the floor, or on a soft surface on the floor, sitting cross-legged. Your spine should be vertical; your body relaxed; your weight supported and balanced.

Check your Body and Breathing: Bring your awareness to how your body is feeling. Spend a minute or two checking yourself out, doing a body scan. Become aware of how your body feels; warm or cold; comfortable or uncomfortable; the feel of your clothes against your skin; whether your belt or neck feels constrained; the feel of any jewellery or watches on your body. Make any adjustments necessary to be comfortable.

Then become aware of your breathing; is it shallow or light; is it only in the chest or belly; are you holding your breath at all, or is it flowing in and out fairly freely. Become aware of which parts of your body move when you breathe. Maybe there is a slight pause at the top of the in-breath or the bottom of the out-breath. Maybe you are breathing in and out only through your nose, or only through your mouth. Don't try to control your breathing, just allow the breath to flow in and out. Simply let the breath breathe itself. This is very peaceful. You do not have to do anything else, just keep on doing this.

Either Empty your Mind or Focus your Mind: Sooner or later your mind will start to wander, or thoughts will come into your mind to distract your awareness and your 'peace of mind'. This is very common, especially in the early 'learning' stages. It is not a mistake or failure: it is just what the mind does. Congratulations for noticing that your attention is not on your breath. Just empty your mind of all thoughts, and/or focus your mind back on your breathing. This will happen over and over again. Just keep on emptying your mind of thoughts and re-focussing your awareness on your breathing.

Sometimes you might wish to focus or meditate on a particular topic, like 'world peace' or 'healing'. As you breathe in, focus on these qualities within you; as you breathe out, send out these qualities into the world. Again, your attention may wander at times, or thoughts may cascade through your mind. This is normal: just refocus your attention and awareness. Make each moment count. Keep coming back to the topic or focus of the meditations.

All thoughts have equal value: there are no 'good' thoughts or 'bad' thoughts. Thinking is not 'bad' and an empty mind 'good'. Don't get distracted by content and don't get into judgement: do not try to eliminate or suppress certain types of thoughts or topics or feelings. What matters most is the awareness – of your thoughts and when you are thinking; and try to balance this with an empty mind and a sense of peace, as much as you can. If you hang onto thoughts, or find yourself judging them (or you), just let it all go and re-focus on your breathing, or on the topic again.

Continue like this for about 15 - 20 minutes (or longer, if you wish). 15 – 20 minutes is probably the minimum time to get the maximum benefit. Try doing this once or twice a day – regularly, every day. The effect is cumulative, so you may not notice a huge difference after the first few times. The effect is usually quite subtle and – over time – can also be quite powerful. After a while, you may notice when you miss out on doing it. Just find a few moments and do it again.

Practice, practice and more practice: You are gradually training your mind to become less reactive and calmer. You will find that this has other, wider benefits. Your stress levels will diminish; you will be able to concentrate more, and for longer; you will feel more centred; you will have greater patience; you may become less judgemental. Try to keep on doing it regularly and the benefits will accumulate.

Different meditations: There is no one way each meditation is different, even if it follows the same pattern. Meditations vary considerably. Some meditations can be dramatic, visionary, or life-changing; however, these are fairly rare. In some meditations you may fall asleep. Just observe the differences. Don't get caught up in the 'glamour' of a powerful meditation.

There are hundreds of specific types of meditation. People have been meditating in different cultures and different religions (including Christianity) for hundreds and even thousands of years. Here are some Questions that can arise from such a Meditation:

(thanks to Vadivu Govind for these [23])

If reflecting with others, listen and hold space with appreciation and compassion. The honouring through your response is just as important as the sharing, so people feel truly Seen, Heard and Held. May your Presence be a Gift.

---

[23] www.linkedin.com/feed/update/urn:li:activity:7146810219098955776

1. When did you feel most alive?
2. When did you feel at home?
3. What took your breath away?
4. When were you most out of your comfort zone? What did you find there?
5. Which belief of yours was most challenged?
6. What broke your heart? What put it back?
7. What was unexpected? What emerged as a result?
8. Whose love and wisdom inspired you deeply?
9. When did you give and receive unconditional love?
10. What service did you render that especially lit you up?
11. What self-discovery feels particularly precious?
12. What do you celebrate in your growth?
13. What golden threads emerged as themes?
14. What life lessons emerged?
15. Looking at how your 2023 days went, if you could design one tiny improvement into your days in 2024, what would it be?
16. What seeds planted this year would love to be nurtured in the next?
17. What's the most precious gift (in any form) you received this year?
18. What unanswered questions from this year are to be lived through in the next?
19. What's your soundtrack for the year?
20. What's your photo of the year?
21. What's your word for the year?
22. What, from 2023 or this reflection exercise, could enrich your service to others next year?

Before Another Year Ends…

23. As another war broke out this year, what peace-making could you cultivate in your life?
24. Who would you like to express gratitude to?
25. What act of love would stretch your heart to new dimensions?
26. Where could you surrender?

27. What is one thing you could do for yourself that would be truly restorative?
28. What would you regret not doing?
29. What is awaiting your self-mercy?
30. If 2024 were your last year to live, what calls you?

A Timeless Question …

31. Who are you without all your roles? What are you here to experience, receive and offer?

Your Question …

32. What question do you offer yourself and others?

Mindfulness Practice

When we are stressed, we often become absent-minded; or we may be doing something (like reading a book) and we realise that we are not fully aware of what we are doing; or we may indulge in some 'mindless' activity (like watching afternoon TV, or playing Sudoku) as an escape from our day-to-day life and problems: our mind becomes distracted: we are 'mind**less**'. When we are on 'automatic pilot' like this, our body is doing one thing and our mind is doing another. Accidents and mistakes can happen. Negative thoughts can build up and coalesce. We are trying to find better solutions, but we are constantly monitoring (and judging) how we are doing – and probably repeating old patterns (because we don't know anything else): this is ultimately counterproductive. On a day-to-day basis, mind**less**ness is not very productive and is often quite harmful.

Mind**ful**ness means – paying attention – in a particular way – on purpose – in the present moment – non-judgementally – with all your senses. As a practice, it can be very useful for anxiety, depression, better pain control, anger management, obsessive-compulsive tendencies, and self-healing, as well as for stress. The core skills of mindfulness are – Be Aware and Let Go. Be Fully Present, with All your Senses, in the Present Moment!

Mindfulness practice is part of the practice of Buddhism, and has therefore been around for about 2,500 years. Recently, it has been accepted as a valuable therapeutic asset within Cognitive Behavioural Therapy in the NHS.

"What goes around, comes around." Socrates also once said, *"The unexamined life is not worth living for a human being."* He also said, *"As for me, all I know is that I know nothing."* This is – perhaps – saying something similar.

Being Aware – is literally just that: being aware that you have a pain here; or that you find this or that activity stressful; that you don't have the energy for 'this' any longer; or you are irritated by 'that' person – or rather when that person does 'that'.

Letting Go – is literally just that: letting go of your irritation, your pain, your stress, your boredom and fatigue; freeing yourself from any attachments or fixed ideas.

Practicing Mindfulness: You can start practicing mindfulness by introducing 'mindful' meditations into your regular routine of meditation. Let mindfulness (or awareness of something) become the 'focus' of your meditation. In the meditation, done as before, become aware of every feeling or sensation in your body; every thought and every noise outside – the ticking of a clock, the distant traffic, bird song. And then let these perceptions – or the thoughts attached to the perceptions – go! Expand and extend your awareness – and then just let any thoughts or perceptions go: there is a continual process of gentle emptying. Try to stay in the moment: what am I aware of now? What now? And then let go and move on to the next moment.

Then you can extend your mindfulness practice into other things that you are doing. How am I doing this? How interesting! What am I feeling now? How interesting! And now let this go. The moment passes: you are doing something else: How interesting! And now move on again to the next moment.

You can also go much deeper into what you are doing at this precise moment. When eating a tangerine, become aware of the texture of the outside of the crinkly orange skin compared to the smooth white texture of the inside. Be aware of the tiny spurt of juice and scent as you peel the tangerine; the separation of the segments and the peeling off of any pith; the explosion of taste as you bite into a juicy segment; the tangy, sweet smell; the discarded peel. You can become aware of the tree on which it grew in some foreign country; the water and sunshine necessary for it to grow; all the people who grew it, picked it, transported it and sold it; the number of hours worked and miles it has travelled to get into your hand. What a depth and miracle of mindfulness there is in this one action of eating a tangerine. And now you can move on to the next action, but you will move on feeling differently (hopefully more pleasant and peaceful) because you have done this action differently, mindfully.

When you are doing the washing up, standing at the kitchen sink, don't do it thinking about this, or worrying about that, try doing it mindfully. Just 'do' the washing up: become aware of the feel of the warm water on your hands; or the scent of the soap liquid; the feel of the action of the mop as it travels around the plate, getting the food off; the way some bits stick and some bits of food don't; the change in the appearance of the plate; the sight of the water running freely across the plate as you put it under the tap to rinse; and the satisfying clunk as it goes into the rack. You may then become aware of the sunshine (or weather) outside the kitchen; the bird song or street noises; other people in the house – these are all part of the mindful experience of doing the washing up (or whatever you are doing).

If you catch yourself thinking about tomorrow's shopping list, or what you are going to have to say to this person at work, stop doing the washing up and write the shopping list, or makes some notes in your Filofax, then return to doing the washing up mindfully. Stay in the moment as much as possible. If you don't like doing the washing up and want to finish it quickly or jump to the next moment (so as to watch TV or eat dessert), you may be equally incapable of fully being in that moment and enjoying the TV or the dessert: your mind may be jumping to the next action and then to the next, so that you are never at peace with yourself and what you are doing. Focus on this one, just this one, and you may find that you quite enjoy the process of doing the washing up mindfully.

The Deepening Process of Mindfulness: There is really no end to this process. Each meditation, each mindful action builds and grows. The further you go in (into the territory of mindfulness, into yourself), the bigger the territory gets. You will possibly slow down a little; you may well become calmer and less reactive; you will probably look more at the wider picture and may become more thoughtful.

Mindfulness is so simple – and it is not, for a moment, very easy! This is definitely 'the road less travelled' – yet it is a very rich journey in itself. We are not trying to get anywhere; we are making every moment count; we are enhancing every moment of experience; we are enriching the journey itself and travelling well. We can even make each step that we take (literally) mind**fully**: this then becomes a walking meditation.

Start listening to those little whispers of thoughts at the edge of your consciousness. These can even start guiding you. They can enhance and deepen your perception; they can even start to lead you. In some cultures, this could be described asan "Opening the Third Eye".

Parts of this section have been adapted from
Thich Nhat Hahn: *'Peace is Every Step'*.

Another good source of 'wisdom' about Mindfulness Practice is Ram Dass' (1971) book "Be, Here, Now."

TRANSFORMATIVE PROCESSES

There can – of course – also be 'transformative' elements or 'transcendental' components involved in a person's crisis process. If this is the case, people with some experience of these transformative processes should become involved at some point as well, (and this does **not** necessarily require a priest, shaman or a guru); such persons can also be psychotherapists or experienced counsellors, who are familiar with these more spiritual processes.

Psychotherapists often have training in, and understanding of, intrapersonal, interpersonal and transpersonal and other types of changes and how these can all be interconnected. They can help empower the person to use their personal resources, promote self-responsibility and develop better cognitive functions, as well as keeping the doors open to the transpersonal, possibly through meditation, mindfulness practice, Yoga, Tai Chi, or similar..

Please be aware that these transformative components may take some time to work through or achieve, but there should be a sense of what might be a good direction or outcome at a reasonably early phase in the intervention process. Hopefully the actual crisis will be over relatively quickly, but the transformative process can continue, sometimes gently, sometimes powerfully, sometimes gradually, even for years.

Please be very careful here: in transformation (as opposed to change) much of the new type of process, or thestrangeness of the symptoms, require a sort of re-assessment or re-integration depending upon these new perspectives, and which help 'expand the frame' of their situation. Whilst this may mean a form of re-education for the person in crisis –as well as for those around them, please ensure that you (the therapist or guide) are not forcing them into such a new particular perspective, which is more familiar to you than maybe relevant to or appropriate for them. You are "guiding from behind": following their process, not leading it.

This is especially relevant where one considers whether the person is, or is not, fitting into the Spiritual Crisis or Spiritual Emergency category (see later). What has also been mentioned, and now is re-iterated, is that there are sometimes significant cultural differences, which can affect these processes: weird and wonderful in one culture, might be scary in another, and normal in a third: and all of these cultures may co-exist in the same city or country. It is important to try to accept the transformative process exactly and precisely for what it is and how it manifests itself at any one moment.

What follows now – in the next section – are some very different sets of ideas that may help change some of the more fixed or conservative attitudes that tend not to be so helpful for a person in crisis: from themselves and from others. Doctors and psychiatrists may be helped in such changes by assuring them that "Spiritual Crisis" is now a category in DSM IV (see Appendix 3).

PART TWO

SPIRITUAL EMERGENCE VS. SPIRITUAL EMERGENCY

There is a lot more material around nowadays about: what the definition of a Spiritual Emergence process is; and what a Spiritual Emergency actually is; how to identify a person in a spiritual crisis; the different types of Spiritual Emergencies; psycho-spiritual process-oriented work; and useful strategies in dealing with Spiritual Emergencies; etc. There is now even a 'university' founded by Emma Bragdon, one of the early SE pioneers: the Integrative Mental Health University (www.imhu.org).

For the purposes of this book, Iam using the terminology of "Spiritual Emergence" processes and a "Spiritual Emergency" to refer to a sudden break, or an involuntary change in a person's fundamental systems of intellectual belief, spiritual activity and psychic behaviour, often accompanied by or immediately following a crisis, or a seemingly psychotic episode, or a period of extraordinary behaviour or life-work stress.

A Spiritual Emergence process is an experience whereby an individual self-identifies with a process of spiritual emergence (i.e., a transcendental and transformative process, characterized by one's conscious awareness expanding or awakening beyond the ordinary level of waking consciousness), that includes a state of psychological crisis, involving perceived trauma, and perceived inability to cope.[24]

Sometimes, the next sentence reads:

---

[24] Adapted from: Harris, K.P., Clark, G. & Rock, A.J. (2020). Defining Spiritual Emergency: A Content Validity Study. *Journal of Transpersonal Psychology, Vol. 52, No. 1, 113-141.*

However, a process of a Spiritual Emergency may involve a state of psychological crisis (involving various degrees of self-perceived trauma, self-perceived coping difficulties, and lack of understanding by self and others), with severe cases appearing almost identical to clinical psychosis.

However, this sudden transition can also be seen (usually retrospectively and possibly with some therapeutic help) as part of a long-term developmental process that has been largely unconscious and unrecognized until that point, and thus is generally unprepared for, and often relatively unaccepted.

Stanislav Grof, MD, is a psychiatrist with more than 60 years of experience researching non-ordinary states of consciousness. He was chief of psychiatric research at the Maryland Psychiatric Research Center, assistant professor of psychiatry at Johns Hopkins University, and scholar-in-residence at Esalen. More recently (in the 1990s), he was professor of psychology at the California Institute of Integral Studies (CIIS) in San Francisco.

Essentially, Stan Grof & his wife Christina [25] initiated these concepts and terms, following their ground-breaking work with people in crisis at the Esalen Institute in Big Sur, California (see Table 1). Grof also defines a number of different manifestations of "Spiritual Emergencies" (see later), but the common denominator of all crises of transformation (according to them) is the manifestations of different aspects of the psyche that were previously unconscious. [26] In this sense, it can also be seen as a perfectly normal (psycho-spiritual) aspect of our human development – albeit a fairly unique one, as it doesn't happen to everyone.

---

[25] Grof, C. & Grof, S. (Eds.) (1989). *Spiritual Emergency: When personal transformation becomes a crisis.* Tarcher.
[26] Grof, Stan & Grof Christina (1992). *The Stormy Search for Self.* Tarcher.

SPRITUAL AWAKENINGS

Spiritual Emergence	Spiritual Emergency
Inner experiences are fluid, mild, and relatively easy to integrate.	Inner experiences are dynamic, jarring, and difficult to integrate.
New spiritual insights are welcome, desirable, expansive.	New spiritual insights are philosophically challenging and threatening.
Gradual infusion of ideas and insights into life	Overwhelming influx of experiences and insights.
Experiences of energy that are contained and easily manageable.	Experiences of jolting tremors, shaking, energy disruptive to daily life.
Easy differentiation between internal and external experiences and transition from one to the other.	Sometimes difficult to distinguish between internal and external experiences, or simultaneous occurrence of both
Ease in incorporating non-ordinary states of consciousness into daily life.	Inner experiences interrupt and disturb daily life.
Slow, gradual change in awareness of self and world.	Abrupt, rapid shift in perception of self and world,
Excitement about inner experiences as they arise; willingness and ability to cooperate with them.	Ambivalence towards inner experiences; *and yet* willingness and ability to cooperate with them using guidance.
Accepting attitudes toward change.	Resistance to, or experiencing difficulties with, change.
Ease in giving up control; going with the changes.	Need to be in control or panicking when out of control.
Trusting in your inner process.	Dislike of / mistrust in your process; or unable to manage your process.
Difficult experiences being treated as opportunities for change.	Difficult experiences are disturbing, overwhelming, or often unwelcoming,
Positive experiences accepted as gifts; welcoming new experiences.	Positive experiences are difficult to accept, seem undeserved, and can be painful.
Infrequent need to discuss experiences; calmly accepting experiences.	Frequent, urgent need to discuss one's experiences; need for overview.
Discriminating when communicating about process (when, how, with whom).	Indiscriminating communication about process (when, how, with whom).

Table 1: Adapted from Grof, S. & Grof, C. (1990). *The Stormy Search for the Self.*

THE DIFFERENCE BETWEEN A SPIRITUAL EMERGENCE AND A SPIRITUAL EMERGENCY

We all share in the search for meaning and purpose in life. A spiritual experience that makes you more aware of powerful subtle energies impacting the personal self is part of this, as is the quest to make meaning of such experiences. This is what we describe as a Spiritual Emergence process, which is a natural process that is insufficiently recognized currently in modern mental health care, particularly as research studies are showing that those who prioritize spiritual practices in their lives have better mental health.

When Spiritual Emergence processes are especially intense, there may be an inner demand to stop everything in order to integrate the event(s) at a deeper level. Sometimes this demand makes it hard to function as usual in work or in relationships. You may become very self-absorbed and even have difficulty finding words for the experience(s). This is when the process turns into a Spiritual Emergency. Although these terms were coined and elaborated by Dr. Stanislav Grof and Christina Grof in the early 1980s, most healthcare providers today still cannot discern the differences between varieties of mental illness and Spiritual Emergency without special training beyond their conventional knowledge bases.

In transpersonal psychology, the term "Spiritual Emergency" defines a critical turning point in human development, which can lead to an increase in interest in the spiritual aspects of life. It can be a marker of growth, in which a person expands their sense of self and their understanding of the world, giving more peace of mind and self-acceptance.

Spiritual Emergency and the process of Spiritual Emergence in general may be catalysed as a result of stress, loss, grief, psychedelic experiences, a sexual experience, spiritual practices like meditation or yoga, or evolution itself. A person in Spiritual Emergency needs a particular kind of care which is typically not available in conventional hospitals or clinics. The individual needs understanding and a sense of safety, i.e. someone to affirm their experience, maintain positive expectation about its ultimate conclusion, interrupt the sense of isolation that may be present, and encourage connection to human community without unnecessary pathologizing. Table 1 on the previous page contrasts the process of Spiritual Emergence with the kind of difficulties a person might have when they are in Spiritual Emergency.

Please note that it is not always clear whether someone is in a Spiritual Emergence or a Spiritual Emergency. To better understand how the distinction between them impacts you, or someone you care for, it might be worthwhile for you take one of IMHU's [27] longer courses, like 'How to Effectively Support Someone in Spiritual Emergency', and 'Differentiating Spiritual Emergency from Pathology'.

The first four books written about Spiritual Emergency in English are:

1. Bragdon, E. (1988). *A Sourcebook for Helping People in Spiritual Emergency.*
2. Grof, S. & Grof, C. (eds) (1989). *Spiritual Emergency.*
3. Bragdon, E. (1990). *The Call of Spiritual Emergency.*
4. Grof, S. & Grof, C. (1990). *The Stormy Search for the Self.*

These books help to discern the difference between a Spiritual Emergence process, Spiritual Emergency and emotional disturbances categorized as "illnesses" or "disorders". There is a good deal of overlap between these four texts–so, consider choosing one to dip into first.

Much more is being written nowadays about these aspects of spiritual development that is more within 'mainstream' thought: C.J. Jung referred to the process of the emerging spirit as a "moral

---

[27] IMHU: Integrative Mental Health University: www.imhu.org/

obligation" to live out and express what one learns when one has had contact with other aspects of oneself.

Whilst there has been a long tradition of writings about spiritual development, these have often been pushed to one side and denigrated as 'esoteric' or 'mystic' because materialism and the need to "make a buck" or "get on" with one's career or to deal with day-to-day, common-sense issues, have been considered as priorities.

For example, some of Jalāl al-Din Muhammad Rumi's writings and poetry also speak about this sort of (spiritual emergence) process directly. He was a mystic writing in the 13th century (1219-1273 CE), originally from Balkh in the Middle East (but he lived in Anatolia, Afghanistan, Samarkand, Tajikistan, & Iran). [28]

The work of similar, more modern visionaries, Joseph Campbell ['*The Hero with a Thousand Faces*' (1949), the four-volume *The Masks of God* (1959-68), *The Power of Myth* (1988)] along with books like Robert Bly's *Iron John* and Clarissa Pinkola Estes' (1996) *Women Who Run with the Wolves*, or the work of Jungian analyst, Robert Johnson (see Reading List) are also helping to chart the spiritual path in more modern terms.

Harris *et al.* [29] have established an empirical validation of the definition is an important step towards the validation of instruments designed to measure the phenomenon, as well as appropriate clinical diagnoses and further research.

In answer to the frequently asked question: *"What is the difference between a Spiritual Emergency and a psychotic episode?"*, part of the problem of differentiation is also cultural one. Nowadays, most of us live in such a very materially and medically orientated culture that it is sometimes very difficult to step outside of these paradigms and the parameters that usually bind us and blind us. When we do so, voluntarily or involuntarily, we have no positive images or support to reinforce our journey, nor any routes or maps for our process. We thus

---

28 Rumi: A biographical account of him is described in Shams ud-Din Ahmad Āflākī's *Manāqib ul-Ārifīn*. See also: Lewis, Franklin (2008). *Rumi: Past and Present, East and West*. One world Publications.

29 Harris, K.P., Clark, G. & Rock, A.J. (2020). Defining Spiritual Emergency: A Content Validity Study. *Journal of Transpersonal Psychology, Vol. 52, No. 1*, 113-141.

resort to the (culturally 'normal') negative images of people in crisis – either as being sick, mentally ill, or just crazy – and this ('normally') means that we need to separate ourselves from such people, and such cultural limitations, exclude them from us, or even protect ourselves from them. Nowadays, we may also think that we also need to protect them from materialistic swamping!

Lukoff *et al.* (1992, 1998) [30]a&b][30a&b] proposed a category – *Religious or Spiritual Problem* – for inclusion in the DSM, which appears DSM-5 (APA, 2013) as a v-code (V62.89) [31], which identifies additional issues that notes:

> This category can be used when the focus of clinical attention is a religious or spiritual problem. Examples include distressing experiences that involve loss or questioning of faith, problems associated with conversion to a new faith, or questioning other spiritual values that may not necessarily be related to an organized church or religious institution. (p. 725)

Just to suggest that we could perhaps re-frame these extra-ordinary processes into a much more positive light is pretty radical – even without actually trying to do so. To suggest that we might perhaps actually involve ourselves in these peoples' psychic processes and possibly even interact with them, or maybe even learn something from them, is seen by some very well-established (and thus conventional) professional people as totally "off-the-wall". If one goes a step further and actually does something, there can sometimes even be an accusation of acting unprofessionally to ensure that other miscreants are kept in line.

[30a] Lukoff, D., Lu, F. & Turner, R. (1992). Toward a more culturally sensitive DSM-IV: Psycho-religious and psycho-spiritual problems. *The Journal of Nervous and Mental Disorders, 180,* 673-682.

[30b] Lukoff, D., Lu, F. & Turner, R. (1998). From spiritual emergency to spiritual problem: The transpersonal roots of the new DSM-IV category. *Journal of Humanistic Psychology, 38,* 21-50.

[31] See also: Prusak, J. (2016). Differential diagnosis of "Religious or Spiritual Problem" – possibilities and imitations implied by the V-code 62.89 in DSM-5 (in English). *Psychiatria Polska 50(1), 175-186.* www.pubmed.ncbi.nlm.nih.gov/27086337

But 'off-the-wall' and 'out-of-line' is sometimes where people actually are when they are in their crisis, or in a Spiritual Emergency, or whatever you like to call it, and maybe we (the slightly more enlightened professionals) need to be able to explore and reconnoitre these areas in order to be able to interact with these pathfinders, and to find out more about what the territory is like, and what conditions and rules exist there, so as in order to help them better.

> Although the classical medical model does not consider the broader contextual and developmental factors necessary to make such a distinction, a holistic approach incorporating both developmental psychopathology and transpersonal psychology takes these numerous dynamics into account. As such, this expanded framework may offer enhanced differential accuracy by providing clinicians greater nuance in their interpretive maps, thus helping them conceptualize why an individual presenting with seemingly psychotic symptoms may not necessarily be experiencing a psychotic disorder. [32]

However, there is also now quite a body of respectable research work that helps to establish the validity and effectiveness of the Grofs' (and others') concepts of Spiritual Emergence and Emergency, especially if one extends the remit to include issues of 'cultural diversity', in which spirituality and the transpersonal becomes a matter of an added cultural competence for psychotherapists. [33] [34] [35]

Instead of "poo-pooing" such fanciful concepts, denying the experience of thousands of eminent 'Seekers of Truth', and relegating such concepts into some materialistic waste-bin, the psychiatric

---

[32] St. Arnaud, K.O. & Cormier, D.C. (2017). Psychosis or Spiritual Emergency: The potential of developmental psychopathology for differential diagnosis. *International Journal of Transpersonal Studies, 36(2), 44-59.*

[33] Viggiano, D.B., & Krippner, S. (2010). The Grofs' model of spiritual emergency in retrospect: Has it stood the test of time? *International Journal of Transpersonal Studies, 29(1), 118–127.*

[34] Fukuyama, M.A. & Sevig, T.D. (1999). *Integrating spirituality into multicultural counseling.* Thousand Oaks, CA: Sage.

[35] Johnson, C. & Friedman, H. (2008). Enlightened or delusional? Differentiating religious, spiritual, and transpersonal experience from psychopathology. *Journal of Humanistic Psychology, 48(4), 505-527.*

profession and mental health professionals should – perhaps – be encouraged to take off their blinkers and acknowledge that – perhaps – *"there are more things in heaven and earth than are dreamt of in their philosophy"*.

Some different (possibly earlier or more primitive) cultures go so far as to elevate those amongst them who have had such spiritual experiences themselves by allowing or elevating them to become their shamans, priests & priestesses, visionary leaders, or even gurus. Whereas, in contrast, we in the Western World, as being immersed in a more secular and materialistic culture, usually discriminate actively against those who claim to have had such experiences. We treat them with suspicion, discriminate against them, dismiss or ignore them, or just think that they are crazy; we medicalise them (at best); we sometimes even take away their citizen's rights and incarcerate them (as well); or *"re-arrange them till they are sane"* [36], chemically, electrically or surgically (at worst).

Someone [37] – a music Ph.D. student – once wrote an interesting article analysing the *"socially, politically and spiritually transformative potential of progressive rock [music], through facilitating "re-enchantment" in the listener's perspective"* using *"an autoethnographic account of a listening relationship, both analytical and numinous"*, with that iconic album from Pink Floyd. [38]

It is amazing what can trigger such a Spiritual Emergency experience: you don't need magic mushrooms or peyote (as supposedly used in Carlos Casteneda's books) in order to have a shamanic experience – or something similar. There are more real-life reports of triggering events such as: major accidental damage or illness (leading towards Near-Death Experiences); withdrawing from psychotropic medications; mediating, withdrawing (and sometimes fasting), such as

---

[36] Pink Floyd "Brain Damage" track on *The Dark Side of the Moon* album: Pulse Concert, Earls Court Concert, London, 2013. www.youtube.com/watch?v=WPxJIS744M0

[37] Kimberley Anderson: www.itia.wp.st-andrews.ac.uk/people/students/kimberley-anderson/

[38] Kimberley Jane Anderson (2020). "Re-Arrange Me 'Till I'm Sane": Utopian and Spiritual Experience, Encountering *'The Dark Side of the Moon'*. Rock Music Studies, 7:1, 82-94.

in Tibetan Buddhist practices; traumatic experiences (such as in wars); being exposed to radically different social and cultural influences; etc.

How a particular culture treats its children, the poor, the criminal and the insane is often an indication or a reflection of its intrinsic nature (see, for example, the work of Michel Foucault [39]). How these *"sad, bad and mad"* people are treated often does not show the essential goodness or civilized sophistication of that society. Those different, more primitive, cultures have either learnt, over time– or have never lost the fact – that their society can actually benefit from such peoples' transcendental processes; or it even needs such people to have such experiences, and it cannot survive healthily, lor make major existential decisions, without them. So, just maybe, many of us all have quite a lot of work to do, turning some of our cultural prejudices around.

Just for a moment – imagine a culture, where normal teenage puberty and adolescence is essentially denied, and variations of this process are seen as illnesses needing treatment. Instead of saying: *"Oh, dizzy spells and puppy fat are perfectly normal: they will pass as you get older"*, we would be exposed a situation where the growth of breasts would result in a mastectomy; and beards, pubic hair and underarm hair would mean extensive depilation, or chemical treatments to inhibit the growth of hair; and the pre-pubertal (almost anorexic) body would be seen as desirable (as with modern fashion models).

This is actually how we react, as a society (not to the physical symptoms of a denied process of adolescence) but to the psychological symptoms of a denied spiritual maturation process. We often treat the symptoms of this process as a pathology and often medicalize the treatment of the person. *"They are hearing voices; they must be psychotic!"*

By the way, it is perfectly possible, and quite common, for someone to have a Spiritual Emergence process **and** a psychotic episode, or a major trauma or illness **and** a Spiritual Emergence process. These are not necessarily mutually exclusive.

However, here and now, we are concerned with aspects involved in the going through, and the recovery from, such events, and we will delve more into these aspects in this second part of the book.

---

[39] Foucault, M. (1961). *Madness and Civilization: A history of insanity in the age of reason*. Routledge.

A 'healing' implies that things are restored, a 'recovery' implies things are back to normal; neither may be appropriate in a transformational process, which implies significant change. In the Reading List, there is a mention of a book by Podvoll (2003), who speaks about recovery from mental illness. He claims that the principles of healing and recovery are very similar, even though these two things, mental illness and spiritual emergency, can be very different. I think it is more a process of 'going through': you will be changed by this process, and things can become 'normal' again, but they will also be very different. Nietzsche spoke of *"What doesn't kill you, makes you stronger"*, and there is often some truth in that. However, going through this sort of transformational process can mean that you realize that the shallow and materialistic life that you might have led previously is the one that now seems crazy, so we could say instead, *"By going crazy, you become sane."* [40]

Anyway, what follows now is a relatively brief synopsis of the various different types of Spiritual Emergency. The first ten or twelve types (or categories) of symptoms are listed by Grof. [41] However, coming from my own clinical experiences, I have added several more categories to these. The descriptions of these different types might help you to discern what is happening, or has already happened, to the person who is having, or who has had, a crisis. Was it just a major illness, or a mental illness, or were other more spiritual components present? If they were these other elements present, then physical recovery, gentle exercise, good food, etc., which are all components of physical recovery, need to be incorporated as well as the other components necessary for a healthy spiritual emergence process, many of which are mentioned here.

It is unfortunately necessary to state this very clearly; nowhere, at no time, do we advocate someone coming off medication, prescribed by a doctor, without that doctor being informed. Dealing with someone in crisis as a Spiritual Emergency is NOT an alternative to any form of medical treatment: it is a perspective which is an adjunct to

---

40   Vonnegut, M. (1975). *The Eden Express: A memoir of insanity*. Bantam.
41   Grof, Christina & Grof, Stanislav (1991). *The Stormy Search for the Self: Understanding & Living with Spiritual Emergency*. Thorsons.

whatever is happening with them - physically, medically, emotionally, psychologically, or generally in their life at this moment in time.

The crisis, however traumatic it was, *can* often be converted into something ultimately beneficial, by treating it as a process of the emerging spirit. This connects with the "acorn" theory of James Hillman [42], where our *genius,* our *daimon*, or our *guardian angel*, motivates our growth in particular ways uniquely designed for that particular person at that particular moment. The crisis just happens to be taking this form, in this person, at this time. There are a few exceptions, of course. But spiritual strength can emerge from such a crisis, and a new determination to lead a much 'better' life. This is often accompanied by an increase in wisdom, gained through the crisis events, which is part of the essential transformational process. Then crisis itself can just be a trigger for these events and have no further bearing on the actual transformational process. The crisis can also contain very significant components that shape the later spiritual development. Everyone is unique.

Eventually there develops a better 'practice' or lifestyle, one component of which regularly acknowledges that "Something" which is greater than all of us – you can call it God, Allah, Yahweh, Vishnu, Gaia, one's Higher Power, or whatever. We move into new territories of the mind, and beyond the mind, into new realms of existence, sometimes only previously accessible through the use of drugs (which also distort perception of these spaces). This is the maturational process into full spiritual emergence; and it happens all the time to ordinary people all over the planet through normal processes like falling in love, being hurt, having babies, working, burying parents, etc. Most of the time that it happens, it is within normal levels of tolerance and is just not fully recognised, and so it is unfortunate that we have to point a finger at aspects of such a normal, healthy development: So, we now have to call it "Spiritual Emergence" so that people, who are going through some of the more extreme forms of it, can be put into a similar context, and not be treated as aberrant or abnormal.

Most of the time, the "Spiritual Emergency" – the 'emergency" part of it - has been created, not by the processes of the person involved,

---

42 Hillman, James (1997). *The Soul's Code*. Bantam.

but by the inability of the environment around that person to contain that person's particular process of Spiritual Emergence at this moment in time. In many ways, the environment of the Findhorn Foundation, or other similar spiritual communities, has allowed many people to have their process there, relatively un-traumatically, surrounded by others in a caring and supportive environment. I have seen notices on a Foundation member's bedroom door, *"Do Not Disturb! Having a Spiritual Emergency!"* This is great; they are acknowledging it themselves! But. we have also sometimes been called out in the middle of the night because someone is having a real emergency situation, spiritual or otherwise, and urgent appropriate action is needed. The energies of some of these places are very powerful, can affect people unused to them, and they do need handling properly.

In the 1970s and 1980s, Stan Grof and his helpers categorised a number of different types, or channels, through which people experienced their "Spiritual Emergencies". This is not theoretical categorisation; it is empirical research. They did not invent these categories: they just collected different types from their experience, and then described them. This sort of categorisation was somewhat ahead of its time. As mentioned, some more categories have been added to this list since then; some by me, some by colleagues; again, not from theory but from direct experience. These are what Spiritual Emergence processes can really look like.

However, we first have to do a little check, to ensure that we are not misinterpreting something for what we might like it to be. We have to ensure that the person is really **only** having a Spiritual Emergence process, and that there is no pathology, or other circumstance, that might otherwise be covered up or ignored by categorising this process improperly.

A Spiritual Emergency, which might be more suitable to be treated by alternative responses, can be similar to, but very different from, pathological psychoses or aspects of mental illnesses or conditions, which are often more suitably contained (but not necessarily cured as of now) by more traditional methods like hospitalization & psychotropic medication. What follows next are those conditions which might indicate whether it is appropriate or possible to work with a person from the perspective of a Spiritual Emergence process. These criteria can also be used as contra-indications. If some of these criteria are present, then it may not be possible to work with this person on their Spiritual Emergence process – at this moment in time.

However, there is an increasing awareness that a spiritual crisis can be part of the transition between any stages of faith (as put forward by developmental theories, such as those of Piaget [43] or Kohlberg [44]). These transitions from one stage to another are often difficult and can also include other manifestations, as well as often acknowledged "meditation-related problems" and "illnesses seen as a punishment". This is also true of spiritual and cognitive developmental phenomena, as more advanced levels of human growth transform consciousness in the direction of increasing selflessness and spirituality, rather than simply toward greater intelligence.

It may also be worth noting that there are now various measures – Spiritual Emergency Scales and Subscales (Goretzki *et al.*, 2014; Bronn & McIlwain, 2015; Cooper *et al.*, 2015; Harris *et al.*, 2015; Storm & Goretzki, 2016) [45a,b,c,d&e] – that can assist in the clinical diagnosis of this phenomenon: attempting to differentiate between a Spiritual Emergence and a Spiritual Emergency, though this test is not really valid for differentiating a Spiritual Emergence process:

---

[43] See: Dale, E.J. (2014). Spiritual Consciousness and the Age of Quality: The strange case of Jean Piaget's mysticism. *Journal of Consciousness Studies, 21*, 5–6, 97–119.

[44] Motet, D. (1978). Kohlberg's Theory of Moral Development and the Christian Faith. *Journal of Psychology and Theology, 6(1)*, 18-21.

[45a] Goretzki, M., Thalbourne, M.A. & Storm, L. (2013). Development of a Spiritual Emergency Scale. *Journal of Transpersonal Psychology, 45(2)*, 105-117.

[45b] Bronn, G. & McIlwain, D. (2015). Assessing spiritual crises: Peeling off another layer of a seemingly endless onion. *Journal of Humanistic Psychology, 55(3)*, 346-382.

[445c] Cooper, E.J., Rock, A.J., Harris, K.P. & Clark, G.I. (2015). The factor analytic structure and personality correlates of 'spiritual emergency'. *Journal of Transpersonal Psychology, 47(2)*, 242-262.

[45d] Harris, K.P., Rock, A.J. & Clark, G.I. (2015). Spiritual emergency, psychosis and personality: A quantitative investigation. *Journal of Transpersonal Psychology, 47(2)*, 263-285.

[45e] Storm, L. & Goretzki, M. (2016). A Defense of the Spiritual Emergency Scale: Emergency vs Emergence. *Journal of Transpersonal Psychology, 48(2)*, 190-209.

Scores on the 30-item SES may indicate, to varying degrees, spiritual crises and spiritual emergency, but only hint at spiritual emergence. We find no case to class the Spiritual Emergency Scale as a scale that measures spiritual emergence. ...

... On the one hand, to really know if emergence has taken place, other devices would be needed in the SES aimed at getting various forms of confirmation from the respondent that a state of emergence is underway, or has transpired. On the other hand, in the case of emergency, we have already argued that the association between crisis and emergency is proved by definition, by theory, and by statistical findings. [40e]

However, it should be noted that, depending on which test or scale is used, and also from which culture one comes and therefore which parameters operate, different results can be obtained.

CRITERIA TO HELP DEFINE A SPIRITUAL EMERGENCY AND CONDITIONS UNDER WHICH IT MAY BE APPROPRIATE TO WORK WITH SOMEONE AS A SPIRITUAL EMERGENCE PROCESS

Criteria:

a) There are episodes or experiences which involve changes in consciousness (altered states) or significant changes in perceptual / emotional / cognitive or psychological functioning that incorporate a psycho-spiritual perspective.

b) There is an absence of organic brain disorders underlying the abnormal mental / emotional functioning of the psyche (i.e.: the symptoms of some types of epilepsy (temporal lobe) can be mistaken for psychoses, but are easily curable with a non-reactive pill: changes in the production of dopamine / serotonin in the brain can also significantly affect the person's mental and emotional state.

c) There is an absence of a physical disease in another organ system, which will permit the person to undergo safely the physical and emotional stresses that can accompany the working through of a transpersonal crisis - AND there is sufficient ego and physical strength available in order to go through such a (possibly powerful) transformative process.

Such an illness or organic condition does not mean that it is impossible to work from an S.E. perspective, but it makes things more difficult; other factors need to be taken into account; or the working with or treatment of the illness / organic condition becomes more relevant.

- d) **(This is an essential condition.)** There exists in the person the ability to see their condition as an inner psychological process and approach it in an internalized way with the capacity to form working co-operative relationships with people around them. This thus often excludes people in severe paranoid states, persecutory delusions and hallucinations, socio-pathic or violent behaviour, and cases where there is a lot of projection, exteriorization and acting out; or it excludes normal working with these people when these conditions are present, as one then may be working with them to get back within the 'comfort zone' of a normal therapeutic relationship.
- e) There is an absence of a long history of conventional psychiatric treatment and hospitalization which tend to make the working out of a transpersonal crisis much more difficult, or sometimes even impossible, due to the physical /emotional / mental damage to the psyche from the medical or psychiatric treatments and institutionalization to date.
- f) Since the line between a Spiritual Emergency and a Psychosis is unclear, any decision made should involve clear and maintainable agreements. If these cannot be maintained, therapeutic work stops, until they are restored firm and final diagnoses or decisions are inappropriate. This implies that there must be a continual assessment and supervisory process paralleling the personal (or transpersonal) process.
- g) **(This is an essential condition.)** There exists a safe, supportive environment in which the person can go through some of the more dramatic or demanding stages with people available to assist their process, if needed, who have had similar experiences, and/or professional training, and/or who are very good for that person.

This last condition (of a safe and supportive environment) implies either special residential facilities and /or a special 'crisis' group essentially formed around the person in crisis. There therefore has to be a special place, a special crisis group, special agreements, and people specially assigned. If these criteria can be met, then – and only then – treating the crisis as a transpersonal process or a Spiritual Emergency **might** be more appropriate than a traditional psycho-therapeutic or a psychiatric approach.

There is sometimes a dichotomy between:

1. Taking the person out of their environment into a much more specialized environment (a Crisis Centre, a Retreat House, a Sanctuary, etc.) where the person can have their crisis more safely, and with more resources to hand; and
2. Forming a crisis group around that person, in their own environment, using a 'grass-roots' approach with some specialized input.

These are not mutually exclusive. Sometimes one is more appropriate than the other; other times first one, then the other, are appropriate. However, if the crisis centre approach is used, great care and preparation must be taken when the person is eventually re-introduced back into their previous environment (see Crucial Support Issues).

Further reading on the concepts of a Spiritual Emergency can be had from the Grof's book, *The Stormy Search for Self* (Tarcher) and other specific Spiritual Emergency books in the Reading List. There are also some Internet articles by David Lukoff (and others) added as an Appendix to this book, on this precise subject.

The definition of a Spiritual Emergency, as a "religious or spiritual problem", has now been included into DSM-IV. [46]

---

[46] DSM IV is the Diagnostic & Statistical Manual of Mental Disorders, Fourth Edition, of the American Psychiatric Association. It uses a multi-axial classification.

STAGES OF SPIRITUAL EMERGENCE

In an excellent book, *The Clinician's Guide to Spiritual Emergence*, Stacy Judah proposes 5 stages of Spiritual Emergence:

Stages of Spiritual Emergence

1. **Dark Night of the Soul:** Feeling lost / hopeless / confused.
2. **Disillusionment:** Complacency with life is replaced by dissatisfaction with how things are.
3. **Seeking:** Seeking deeper meanings and experiencing breakthroughs.
4. **Inner Work:** Mindfulness, shadow work, inner child work, deep introspection.
5. **Unity:** rebirth, connection with the Divine, deep alignment with life, community inspiration.

She then describes a set of categories, similar to those of Grof, starting with:

Peak Experiences, described as altered states of consciousness that may be experienced as dissolution of personal boundaries, a sense of becoming one with other people, one with nature or the Universe, transcending time and space, a sense of sacredness or numinosity, and / or strong positive emotions.

Kundalini awakening, also known as the "awakening of serpent power" as it is described within indigenous cultures around the world, is believed to be a creative force of energy residing in latent form at the base of the human spine. When the kundalini energy is "awakened," individuals may experience intense involuntary, nervous system hypersensitivity; visual and tactile sensitivity; sensitivity to violence on television, social media, etc.; startled response to loud noises; visual disturbances; intense heat, vibrations, or electricity surging through the body; and a struggle to distinguish what is real from what is imagined.

Near-Death Experience (NDE) is when an individual 'dies', for example, after an accident, and has an experience in the spirit realm before being returned to their bodies – usually vastly changed. Those who have a near-death experience have reported feeling detached from their body, at peace and feeling unconditional love, passing through a dark tunnel, seeing a brilliant white light, seeing loved ones (including pets) who have died, having the opportunity to "review" their lives, and receiving profound lessons about life and universal laws.

The Emergence of Past-life Memories may consist of a non-ordinary state of consciousness that presents information and visions from other lifetimes, including being in another country, having a particular skill, or interacting with people they may or may not know in their present incarnation. These are often accompanied by powerful emotions, physical sensations, and a sense of "remembering".

Psychological Renewal may present as a feeling of returning to one's centre and the blissful state of merging with something greater than oneself. It is sometimes associated with a preoccupation with death, or wanting to "return" to that blissful state.

A Shamanic Crisis is a transformative crisis similar to the initiatory processes to which shamans within indigenous cultures worldwide are subject. There may be a loss of contact with the environment, inner experiences such as journeys to the underworld, a celestial region, a vision quest, a period of exclusion, or dramatically improved physical and psychological well-being upon completion. There is often an association with a spirit bird or animal.

Awakening of Extrasensory Perception (ESP) or a psychic opening may present with increased intuitive abilities; knowledge of paranormal phenomena such as mediumship or telepathic abilities; or the ability to have a spirit speak through them, speaking in 'tongues,' or speaking in 'light language'.

Communication with Spirit Guides and channelling may be experienced as a message from the 'Source,' the angelic realm, or a star family. The information may be a message for all of humankind, or for a group (like a tribe).

Close Encounters with Extra-terrestrials (ETs): There have been many reports of close encounters with ETs or encounters with unidentified flying objects (UFOs). These reports may include memories of seeing craft, full or partial memories of the encounter, or being abducted (then returned) by what appeared to be beings from other planets.

Possession States include a feeling that one's psyche and body have been invaded and controlled by an entity or energy with personality characteristics that are not under one's control. The entity or energy has personality characteristics that are not one's own. The experience of the possession may feel hostile or benevolent. This has also been called "a walk-in" experience. When a walk-in happens, an individual may feel as though another soul has "switched places" with them. This could be part of a pre-incarnation contract. The client often knows who they are and have the same memories but feel a disconnect from their lives and families. Often, this leads to divorce, a career change, or major move.

Synchronistic Events are significant and hold meaning for the individual but may seem random for others. An individual may believe the synchronicity is a bridge between the Earthy and the Divine – a message from the Universe.

The Dark Night of the Soul may look pathological, resulting in delusions about meeting death, fear of loss of control, sense of helplessness, anxiety and nihilistic despair, lack of a sense of boundaries, depersonalization, and a loss of sense of meaning is a period of time in which a crisis in faith or profound spiritual concerns cause distress.

Next, there is displayed a table of the different types of EHE categories, with descriptions and examples:

Exceptional Human Experiences (EHE)– A taxonomic scheme of EHE types, with description and examples found below (based on Tassel-Matamua & Frewin, 2020) [47].

EHE Types	Description	Examples
Psychical	Involve perceiving knowledge or information outside of the usual sensory modalities, about events that have or are about to occur.	Stigmata Glossolalia Kundalini Telepathy Precognition Déjà vu Extrasensory perception Intuition
Encounters	Involves meeting or engaging with realms, beings or entities	UFO encounter Divine encounter Inner guide
Unusual death-related	Occur in association with the actual death or a close brush with death of another or self	Deathbed experience After-death communication Near-death experiences (NDE)
Peak Experiences	An intense moment of self-actualization and/or potential is experienced	Flow Inspiration
Exceptional human performance / Feats	Typified by individuals extending themselves beyond their usual behavioural limits	Unusual strength or stamina Athletic performances Musical performances
Healing	Contravene Western medical and/or psychological expectations about recovery or prognosis	Spontaneous recovery Healing of physical and/or psychological ailments
Desolation	Intense feelings that serve as catalysts for peak experiences	Meaning Satisfaction Loss Isolation
Dissociation	Typified by feelings of detachment or disconnection from usual sense of identity or stream of consciousness	Out-of-body states

---

47   Tassel-Matamau, N. & Frewin K. (2020). Psycho-spiritual transformation after an exceptional human experience. *Journal of Spirituality in Mental Health, 21, 237-258.*

SYMPTOMS / TYPES OF SPIRITUAL EMERGENCE PROCESSES OR SPIRITUAL EMERGENCIES

The common denominator of all crises of transformation is the manifestations of different aspects of the psyche that were previously unconscious.

S. & C. Grof: "The Stormy Search for Self"

The following list does not mean that these types or forms of process appear by themselves or are neatly differentiated. Neither are the following examples completely inclusive. The psyche is a continuum with few boundaries, many levels, and very many different dimensions. Often aspects can appear together, or in succession, or cyclically. Categorising actual case histories and then creating an observable differentiation between them originally created this very empiricallist. From my own clinical experiences, I have added to Grof"s original list (the items marked by a •). This list of manifestations is not necessarily complete. Spiritual openings and phenomena can take many different forms and manifestations.

An Opening to Life Myths or Archetypes

Where one perceives one's environment and one's own process in terms and symbolic images relating to much larger perspectives. Issues of power thus become Dreams of Kingship; a cave can represent an Entrance to the Underworld: decision-making becomes the struggle between Good and Evil. Other examples include: Communing with Nature; that one has a Mission in Life, etc. All these sorts or any sort of these experiences can fall into this category; and you can almost hear the 'capitalisation' of the words.

A Shamanic Journey

Where elements of the person's transformational process relate to similar experiences that are often found in earlier, tribal, or more primitive societies; like perhaps the native American-Indian, or such as those described by Carlos Casteneda. Experiences such as 'vision quests'; the appearance of 'spirit guides' or 'allies'; preparations involving fasting & purification; journeys to the spirit world, the 'crisis' often involves a feeling of total annihilation (or death), followed by resurrection and re-birth to celestial realms or contact with ancestors, or the Great Spirit; special connections with natural elements or an identification with particular type of animal; development of different healing powers and certain types of spiritual illness; can all form a part of this classification.

Communication with Spirit Guides or Channelling

Where someone is both getting and giving out informational material that seems quite disconnected from their normal self, and has a strong consistent spiritual quality and often is couched in teaching or guiding terms, either for the individual concerned or often for people in general. Sometimes the 'channel' is in a trance (more like a medium) and unaware of this material, or sometimes they are acting more consciously. The information can be relayed by speech, in trance, or by automatic writing, telepathic transfer, visions, etc. Well-known examples include: the works of Alice Bailey, Eileen Caddy & Dorothy McLean (Findhorn Foundation); the Hindu Vedas & Upanishads, Christian Science's *'Science & Health with Key to the Scriptures'*, *'The Book of Mormon'*, *'The Course of Miracles'*, the Seth Material, *'Seth Speaks'* and other books by Jane Roberts, etc.

Near-Death Experiences

People's experiences of being close to death or even of dying and then coming back to life can (nearly always) lead to a form of spiritual opening and a transformational process. One's consciousness can detach from the body and float around an accident scene or a hospital surgery or distant locations (often to see a loved one); or where there is an experience of a passage through a tunnel to a brilliant & beautiful source of light and there is a presence of love, as well, then with a message that one needs to return. These elements are the most common ones and are not confined to people from any particular religion. All these elements can (often) result in a profound subsequent shift in perspective and a new determination for the individual to live their life in a much more congruent way, often dedicated to the service of others.

Kundalini Awakening

Where powerful energy is flowing, often in episodes, sometimes quite surprisingly through the body. This can take the form of cycles of jerking, shaking or sweating; spontaneous movement into yogic positions; rushes of energy, often up the spine; hypersensitivity to stimuli; powerful waves of accompanying emotion; a decreased ability to control their body voluntarily; sensory manifestations - seeing bright lights, hearing inner sounds, smelling fragrances; sometimes intense sexual or orgiastic feelings; what is sometimes called "sartori"; or an experience of the powerful opening the chakras (energy centres) of the body; and, more worryingly, possible simulation of, or stimulation of, severe medical problems. It can also be seen as a spiritual purification of your body as this powerful 'body' energy sweeps (or blasts) away, cell by cell, the detritus that has accumulated over the years in a transformative spiritual experience.

Episodes of Unitive Consciousness or Peak Experiences

Where the person experiences being 'at one' with other people; or other things; or the whole world; or the cosmos; or merging with

God. There is a sense of transcending space & time and there can be an experience of infinity or eternity. *"The emotions associated with this state range from profound peace and serenity to exuberant joy and ecstatic rapture."(Grof: Spiritual Emergency).* Abraham Maslow described these states in depth, calling them 'Peak Experiences'. They are not a hallucination or form of mental disease. Eastern philosophers refer to something like this as "kensho", "satori" or "samadhi", and these type of enlightenment experiences typically lead to better functioning, a more laid-back way of life and the goal of "self-actualisation".

Emergence of a Karmic pattern or "past-life" memories

Where experiential sequences occur of what seem to be 'past-life' situations or encounters (often connected with partners, parents or experiences of death). Beliefs in reincarnation exist in nearly all major religions, except Muslim and Christian (post 553 AD). There are however quite definite experiences or sensations for many people (of all religions) in this category. They frequently have a powerful transformative or therapeutic result and can often "explain" otherwise incomprehensible difficulties in their life up to this point. They can intrude quite powerfully and cause considerable confusion unless integrated.

Psychic Opening or the Awakening of Extra-Sensory Perceptions (ESP)

The emergence of certain paranormal abilities is quite common and quite powerful, and thus is also potentially quite difficult to deal with. It is easy to get "hooked into the symptom" and forget that this is just one aspect of a much deeper spiritual awakening process. And this is also where power can easily be abused. Out-of-body experiences, telepathic or empathic abilities, spiritual or psychic healing powers, pre-cognition, communication with other dimensions (nature spirits, devas, etc.), mediumistic identification, synchronicitous experiences and many more, all form quite common aspects of this category. Sometimes, these abilities are feared and thus rejected, either by the person or by those around them. Alternatively, they can become

"Glamorous Powers"[48] and be abused by the recipient. When they are not abused, they lead one further into one's spiritual development: they are not a end in themselves.

Experience or Close-encounters with UFO's:

Irrespective of whether or not this type of experience has actually happened, or whether alien spaceships actually exist, and irrespective of whether or not the person is judged by others as being insane or not – peoples' descriptions of these types of experiences, and their attitudes to these experiences, and the way these experiences are subsequently incorporated into their lives, and the resulting transformational changes that occur as a result, allow these experiences to be included with the other transformational experiences: examples also include 'experiences' of alien abduction, or alien insemination.

Psychological Renewal through a Return to the Centre:

The deep "renewal process" is where the psyche appears to be involved in a battlefield where the archetypes of Good & Evil, Light & Dark fight it out: *Lord of the Rings* stuff. There is a pre-occupation with themes of cosmic struggle and death; there is a fascination with opposites and polarities. People who are having these experiences:

> "... experience themselves as the centre of fantastic events that have cosmic relevance and are important for the future of the world. Their visionary states take them farther & farther back - through their own history and the history of humanity, all the way to the creation of the world and the original ideal state of paradise. In this process, they seem to strive for perfection, trying to correct the things that went wrong in the past." (Grof: Spiritual Emergency)

Things can then start to get a bit better. Quite often people having such experiences might get involved in a form of "sacred marriage"; either in imagery or even in reality – possibly even projected onto

---

[48] viz: the series of novels by Susan Howarth about the Anglo-Catholic church, one of which has this title.

someone else – and then things become fantasized as "ideal". They have supposedly now integrated their masculine & feminine. However, the crisis is by no means over, even though everything now seems wonderful. Nothing has been really integrated or worked through, just experienced. Some of these attitudes can be found around in certain "New Age" therapies, like "Soul Renewal" or Re-birthing.

Possession:

This is where the individual seems to take on the characteristics of a totally different personality or becomes 'possessed' with an interest in a particular field. Sometimes, there is a 'shadow' element in this: it can also be seen as 'evil': it can be compulsive: it can also be someone who is dominated by their environment or surroundings. e.g. the Army martinet who will only ever do things by the "book".

There has been a lot of work being done with Multiple Personality Disorders – called work with "possession states" though I might disagree as MPDs could equally well be the splitting up of the personality into fragments under situations of intolerable psychic stress in order to preserve aspects of the Self and then creating a personality around that fragment as one is unable to integrate otherwise.

Integration work could centre around the topics of respecting the personality, validating it and dis-empowering the process or the need to maintain the separation. *'The remedy is always inside the experience itself.'* Wilhelm Reich said: *"The way we got in (to the trap) is also the way out."*

Another description of possession is, *"that we can distinguish it from mental illness because the sufferer is sane; he feels he's periodically being invaded by a malign force, but this isn't a delusion stemming from paranoia. However, the condition is extremely rare and the resemblance to some forms of mental illness makes it difficult to diagnose. ... The classical exorcism of a possessed person requires extensive preparation and an army of helpers - ... a psychiatrist, a psychotherapist and possibly a social worker in attendance along with at least three strong men, all of whom, ideally, should be priests."* [49]

---

[49] Howatch, Susan (1992). *Mystical Paths*. (pp. 457-8)

Unfortunately, some 'cases' of (what might be) possession are treated very badly by 'priests' or 'ministers' within the various religions: there have been some cases of some people really suffering badly or even dying as a result of an extreme exorcism process. I am also sure that some people have been 'saved' by proper exorcists.

Synthesis of Forms: Several of the above experienced simultaneously or serially. Remember this accumulation of events, in itself, can push someone into a crisis: one can cope with one of these situations; by two or maybe three might cause the lid to blow, or a psychotic depression to set in if your psychic boundaries cannot expand to incorporate these, your limits have been overwhelmed, or your sense of yourself flooded.

This is the end of the Grof's list: Other possible clusters of symptoms follow:

• **Addictions, drug and alcohol dependency:** Christina Grof also lists dependencies as a possible form of spiritual emergency, from her own experiences, and from others, and devotes a whole chapter to it in their book, *Spiritual Emergency* (see Book List). She states that the craving for the drug, or whatever, is often a craving for transcendence, the Higher Self, or God, but in a lost and inappropriate form. The Grofs also state that addictions can be developed during spiritual emergencies as a way of easing the stress. Many addicts have highly developed intuitive senses, or visionary and precognitive capacities, and this has given them many troubles and even contributed to their addictive behaviour as they try to avoid difficulties with their psyche. It is worth noting that the AA '12 Step' programme is a spiritual programme.

• **Social Forces:** Alternatively, these sorts of processes can be 'acted out' on a sociological level involving us all. William Wilberforce 'took on' the issue of slavery and eventually managed to have it made illegal. He changed as a result of the process: from a philanthropic Member of Parliament via a "conversion experience" to a committed

Christian, resulting in major changes to his lifestyle and a lifelong concern for reform.

There is the current sociological phenomenon with childhood sexual abuse. For many, the emergence of childhood sexual abuse out of the closet into open discussion and eventual acceptance was like a revelation: we did not now have to struggle against the disbelief of society that "this sort of thing just couldn't happen in our family": but it often did. Now it is part of the mainstream fabric of society and we are realising that most abusers were themselves abused. Something similar might also be applied to the current fascination with serial killers.

With the advent of globalization, such social forces have an exaggerated effect on the whole planet. We need to consider the wider aspects. Now we are seeing again the renewal of the demonization of the 'enemy': Saddam Hussein has been called "The Butcher of Baghdad" and there is "an Axis of Evil" and a "War against Terrorism". The tabloid newspapers and Hollywood often fuel such perspectives, and maybe occasionally even help us on towards a collective form of Spiritual Emergence process whereby the exotic lives of their "stars" become more normal and accepted. They can also work the other way and demonize. Films portray subjects like contact with the dead; star gates; the development of psychic phenomena; possession; shape-changing; etc. and so begin (in a perverse way) to normalize some of these processes. Such imagery is very powerful and works on the collective. We can even see whole groups caught up in such processes, where literally hundreds of cases of child abuse with satanic rituals are diagnosed mostly erroneously. To the individuals caught up in such social forces, these can trigger off a Spiritual Emergence process.

Another form of spiritual emergence process, in the social field, could be the Olympic Games: the 'winner' is crowned with laurel leaves, is treated like a God (on Mount Olympus) and has achieved "gold" status (gold often being a synonym for spiritual transcendence. Sportsmen and women often describe the process of 'going through the pain barrier', working with their inner self, facing their fear of failure (daemon), and other experiences in terms very similar to descriptions of a spiritual journey.

- **A psychotic episode:** This experience can be an extraordinary shake-up to the whole person's psychic system. Sometimes, the person involved cannot contain their increasing spiritual energy within the bounds of their own psyche, so their psyche overloads, or floods, and they have what is essentially a psychotic episode: a real one, not a misdiagnosed spiritual emergency. But this psychotic episode can, in itself, also be a very significant part of their spiritual journey. In the episode itself, there is almost no meta-communication; but there is often a significant period of isolation away from work, family and friends. There is quite often a sense of ego-destruction and a realization that you don't really know yourself at all. You may not also have realized significant aspects of the society you lived in and the people around you, and how their attitudes to you changed dramatically when you changed. Pain can be caused and damage can be done, by the process itself, and also according to the type of 'treatment' and the length and severity of the psychotic episode. Once the episode is over and the person has recovered and is restored back into their society, their spiritual emergence process can then proceed more or less unhindered. They will have to integrate this psychotic experience and also work against the 'shock', the 'shame' and the 'black-listing' of having become psychotic; any damage that may have been caused by psychotropic medication; or guilt caused by them causing others distress. This is also a type of spiritual emergence process that it is not advisable to repeat.

- **Major illnesses and accidents:** These often result in an enforced period of reflection, a dramatic change of behaviour, and an extended process of recovery that can be cumulatively transformative, and they sometimes also have a profound spiritual component. Often, for the first time we are faced with the very real & immanent possibility of our death. Of course, not all of the people suffering from these illnesses and accidents are having a spiritual emergency, but it is often a significant life crisis, and the opportunity to develop spiritually is there, as ever. The essential parameters all exist and it is often 'used' as such. People sometimes pray seriously for the first time in their life; they confront their mortality and their belief systems about a life after death, a larger cosmology, or the purpose and value of their life to date. If we are to normalize this process of Spiritual Emergence, then we must include the ways most 'normal' people actually change their lives. These experiences happen to very normal people and many of them happen; just read the *Reader's Digest* regularly and find out what 'normal' people write about their serious illnesses.

• **Direct religious experience or conversion:** This is a form of experience where, quite naturally, and well within socially accepted formats, people have these sorts of direct experiences, usually connected to an established religion. Leonard Cheshire, a famous war-time RAF flying officer, read the Bible one night, had a religious experience, converted to Roman Catholicism, and went and founded the Cheshire Homes: a number of charitable nursing homes for ex-service men and women. Saul of Tarsus on the road to Damascus had a vision of Christ, whose followers up to then he had been persecuting. He then converted to Christianity, became the Apostle Paul and wrote a number of books (of the Bible) and many letters to other people, becoming a major force in the early Christian church – though not always for its ultimate good. Joan of Arc, a French peasant girl, heard angelic voices, which told her to save France, and so she goes and does the unthinkable – for a girl then – guided by her voices. She puts on male clothing, goes on a journey to see the king, and then raises an army, which defeats the English. There are many examples of this type of religious or spiritual emergence process. The hundreds of thousands of other men and women who have been struck by a direct religious experience, or who have received a vision, and have been transformed by such an experience, have changed their lives and have devoted their energies to the service of others: dare we really say these experiences were <u>not</u> aspects of their spiritual emergence process?

• **Ritual Initiation:** In some cultures and societies, every person is still seen as a potential initiate. At some point in their development, often around puberty, they are removed from their normal society (parents, village, etc.) and put into the hands of others: (the men, women, elders or priests). They are given a prolonged experience of teaching, often frugal feeding, nearly always extended isolation, the experience of personal surrender, isolation, and often an experience involving a high degree of pain. There may be a form of circumcision, breaking the hymen, or ritual scarring. They are also encouraged to share their dreams or visions. They are sometimes given a new name. This is the way they become an adult: in that society, and thereafter – if they pass through the ritual successfully – they are able to hunt, fight, heal, or bear children. The formats differ from tribe to tribe, but the basic pattern is nearly always there. This process is specifically designed as a transformative and initiatory experience. It is not just developmental or sociological; it is also often personally developmental <u>and</u> deeply spiritual. In our culture, this type of initiatory ritual is found often still in some private secondary schools, military academies or 'boot camp', the priesthood (of course), and medical doctors also go through something similar in their training.

• **Culture shock:** For some people it is the direct experience of being projected into another culture that is the essential trigger. This can also be a culture within their own culture, a sub-culture, that they had not experienced before: someone who is suddenly arrested and put into prison; the shock of being a new parent and realising that 'mothers' are a sub-class of society; of becoming retired, or fired and unemployed and being devalued as a person because one is not in 'productive' work; or one is just doing something different, but unacceptable to the rest. These shocks to the system, the life style, have the effect of shattering many previously held assumptions, and this can be enough to trigger such a spiritual emergence process. Of course, in many cases it doesn't, and we just have to cope with the experience of feeling that you are suddenly living on an alien planet. For other people, it is sometimes the impact of experiencing, for the first time, something like grinding poverty. Many missionaries did not get their true conversion until well into their tour of duty in the depths of another continent. The different smells, climate, food, mores, and customs are all a shock to our systems – often a much greater one than we could possibly realise. Sometimes, something in this new medley of impressions then gets through to us, and our spiritual emergence process starts.

• **Burn-out:** This is a later addition to the list, even though it has been implicit for a long time. There is a book by Dina Glouberman, a psychotherapist and founder of the Skyros Centre, called *The Joy of*

Burnout, where she writes that often we ignore our 'soul-whispering' against an unhealthy job or relationship. *"Your heart has gone out of something but fear, often of the loss of your sense of identity, drives you to work even harder or give even more."* Recently surveys by the UN International Labour Organisation in Britain, the US, Germany, Finland and Poland discovered that workplace stress, burnout and depression "are spiralling out of control" and affecting, on average, one in every ten workers. In the UK, it is three out of ten employees that suffer mental health problems. And 100 million workdays are lost each year due to stress, at a cost of £5.3 billion.

Burn-out is often not publicly or socially acknowledged because of the various associations with a mental breakdown. Society also seems to encourage this form of process by (almost deliberately) not educating people in simple stress reduction techniques: the Protestant work ethic reigns supreme! The sort of crisis situation that arises here can become a transcendent opportunity to break out into a different pattern of work, or of newly creative work, or as a breakthrough into a different way of being.

- **An intense course of study, especially if transpersonally oriented:** Starting a Ph.D. can change your life! So, can studying to enter the priesthood, or become a Buddhist monk – though there might have been an initial conversion experience first to start you on that particular path of growth and change. Many students at university either crack up or drop out, leading to further transformative changes. Since self-examination is an intense course of study, entering into psychotherapy can also precipitate a process of growth and change, even though you might have entered into it to save your marriage or your job.

- **Other crisis events:** For many others, there were experiences in the most extreme of situations; in concentration camps; when facing death on a mountain; during war time; in a shipwreck, a car accident, an earthquake; or some such similar event, where they have a direct religious or spiritual experience: it becomes an apotheosis. Their fear of death goes. They experience, at that moment, often a deep sense of peace. There is often a sense of contact with *"something much bigger* *than themselves".* They are uplifted and transformed by this experience. They now know, or have had, direct experience that there is something "other" than themselves. The horror or danger around them is then viewed totally differently. Their future life is also often changed radically. By all accounts, they are calmer, less angry, and more open, at least. They may also do more good deeds, kind work, and showing a dedication and caring for others. I believe that these types of events should be included as well in the list of Spiritual Emergency symptoms.

• **Normality:** Finally, as mentioned before, there are the hundreds of thousands of people who evolve naturally and easily through their own life experiences, the joys and the sorrows of normal existence, and develop their own form of a deep and lasting spirituality. Sometimes, this is within their established religion and culture, and sometimes they gently change it, or move into a new society, or marry into a new culture and find themselves opening up that way. There are perhaps no epiphanies, no visions, no psychotic episodes, no dramatic changes. These people vastly outweigh the ones we are writing about, but they don't talk about this much; it has been a natural process for them. They go to church; they pray; they help others; they give to charity; they contribute in many unseen ways to the betterment of their society; they are dedicated to this way of life. And they lead a truly natural spiritual life. They (maybe) don't need a 'Spiritual Emergence process.

ADDENDA:

As mentioned, there can be a succession of these events or symptoms, leading up to a crisis, or a synthesis of a number of these different forms all in one package.

Example 1: I worked with one person who just did not understand what was happening to them, and was somewhat hyper-manic as a result and as part of their process. At one point, I gave them a copy of Emma Bragdon's book, *The Call to Spiritual Emergency* (see booklist). Then they said, *"Oh, so that is what is happening to me. I have this* *symptom, and this one, and some of that one. Now I know more of what is happening, I can cope.*" Their crisis was essentially over with their expanded understanding and they were then back 'in control'. We had taken them to go to a doctor to get some mild sleeping tablets to overcome their lack of sleep and curb the hyper-activity they had been going through. Thereafter they were fine, we started the integration work, and they caught their plane back home on schedule. When that person got home, over the next 18 months, he wrote nine small handbooks for people in such crisis situations.

Example 2: Another person phoned up a Spiritual Emergency Network help-line (in the USA) and asked, *"Can you help me. God came and sat in my head last Christmas."* When asked what she meant by this, she said, *"Oh, I just know what people are thinking about when they come close to me. But my pastor says, 'I am of the Devil'; my women's group think I am a witch; and my husband does not want to know about any of this stuff."* She was essentially OK within herself with the symptoms of her Spiritual Emergence process in that she had experienced *"God sitting in her head"* and the extra-sensory perception, and these things did not frighten her, but she was having a 'Spiritual Emergency' because the people around her were uncomfortable with it – so whose crisis was it?

The Surrounding Environment:

Therefore, the environment around the person having a Spiritual Emergency is very, very important.

There is an archetypal story of a psychiatric patient coming out of an asylum who happens to see a guru, sitting naked under a tree with lots of people listening to him. He asks the guru, *"What are you doing that is different? When I did that, they locked me up in there."* The guru said, *"It all depends on who you talk to?"*

David Lukoff (see Appendix) says: *"Not talking to anyone can drive you crazy."* So, it is a matter of finding the right people to talk to, or being in the right place, at the right time, in order to go through your Spiritual Emergence process successfully. All this forms part of the surrounding environment.

Location, Location:

I first met Stanislav Grof and Arnold Mindell (see Reading List) at a conference on "Spiritual Emergencies" in Monterey, CA in 1990 where they, or Grof particularly, was promoting the formation of a crisis centre, a special place – like Esalen [50] perhaps – where you could go to have your Spiritual Emergency. I surprised myself by disagreeing with him/them, feeling from my own experience, based on my clinical work in the Findhorn Foundation community, that it is actually better to create or re-educate the people around the person in crisis, their personal 'community', rather than remove them from their friends and family, in order to have their crisis properly. And then they have to re-integrate themselves (hopefully the "New Self") back into their original 'community'. It doesn't make a lot of sense and it costs a lot less.

Like everything else, there is not really a pre-determined 'right' way or 'wrong' way for people to go through their processes. Both models have their valid moments and I have mentioned this before and I also recommended a "Zen" space for people earlier on. Many times, alcoholics or addicts may need go to a very structured detox. centre or rehab. unit in order to:

(i) go through their crisis of withdrawal, with its special medical components, and also
(ii) go through the necessary process of education and re-education, and also
(iii) have a safe, contained and tested structure with clear sets of rules in order to 'contain' them as they 'come off' their addictive substance or behaviour.

Leaving the safety of that sort of space and coming back into their community often brings on a secondary crisis. Sometimes, 'crisis centres' can be used a little bit like dustbins, especially if the crisis is not handled properly and their family and friends are not integrated into the process. Therefore I, as a single private practitioner without the access to or resources of such a crisis centre, tend to want to work really

---

[50] Esalen: www.esalen.org

hard with the person's family and friends in order to help to change the environment around that person in a Spiritual Emergency, or to help to create a supportive community around the person in crisis, before I would even consider removing them to a different location (NB: Notes on Forming a Crisis Group are in Section 1).

CRISIS AS SEEN IN TRANSFORMATIONAL TERMS

A friend of mine said to me once that often, if someone in crisis can really open their eyes, there is always help just there, ready & waiting, help which is actually perfect for them. This is nearly always true. However, this perspective involves a level of trust in the "reality" of a crisis being a real and significant part of a person's transformational process, or part of a "Greater Plan", or perhaps a new step in their "Path," or whatever.

Often, a crisis seems quite differently. I have absolutely no wish whatsoever myself (and I deplore those who do) to try to stick a label of "this is just a difficulty in your personal Path of Transformation" onto someone: e.g., whose child has just died or who is experiencing a lot of pain or fear. One client of mine came into therapy after being, and because of being, 'busted' for drugs and it was the eventual rejection of these drugs (and that lifestyle) that eventually brought about a significant change for him, his wife, and his child.

It is not just a matter of re-framing the crisis perspective from something negative towards something more positive. It usually involves a gradual change towards a whole new set of beliefs – which, if it is to be effective, has to be based more on actual experience and not just on 'nice' New Age or Zen thought forms or affirmations – however actually true or useful they may be. It is insulting to the person otherwise, especially if they are in crisis to put out these thought forms or believe systems, however strongly you may believe in them yourself, especially if they are not ready for them. However, your belief can be helpful too. The fact that you believe in this process may be very helpful, if not essential, but timing is also very important, and that is why I am mentioning it here.

You must also allow the person to become different, to transform (if that is what they are doing), - and this is very, very important – at their own pace and in their own direction. You must recognize their pain and crisis (which has to be worked through) and by so doing, perhaps help them to recognize it and fully experience it, and thus to find and re-formulate their own belief systems if they are to transform this experience. Often, new belief systems are used as an escape from some of these more painful issues. The fact that, or belief that, "God Is Love", can help one when working through the deep pain and issues of abandonment when a marriage breaks down: but it should not be used to avoid working through these issues.

Traditional priests and ministers are quite well trained in maintaining this sort of differentiation and helping people through their process – albeit along fairly traditional paths. Psychotherapy and counselling is also the "new religion" and psychotherapists are usually sufficiently well trained as well in helping people with their processes. Psychologists, counsellors, and life coaches are sometimes not quite so well trained in helping people with their deep emotions and persisting with them in working through all aspects of these: but maybe this is my bias speaking.

> Just remember – it is <u>their</u> transformation, <u>their</u> journey,
> and they may not know where they are going with it.

SPIRITUAL TECHNOLOGIES AND TOOLKITS

If you can imagine having the most wonderful super-duper screwdriver with all the fancy bits and bobs, which is able to undo every possible type of screw, but what you are actually faced with is a recalcitrant 8mm hexagonal nut, then you have got a problem, if the screwdriveris all that you have. Similarly, the most comprehensive spanner set, with all the different sizes of spanners, sockets and ratchet handles, is useless when dealing with different sizes and types of screws. To help with these processes, we need a reasonably versatile 'spiritual' "toolkit" and we also need to understand some of the "technologies" of the transformational process. Most of the "tools" and "technologies" fall into number of simple categories or precepts:

Feel the experience – Most of us have developed or learnt very good strategies to avoid feelings, especially painful ones, but also sometimes intimate ones, powerful ones, aggressive ones etc. Nothing can really happen in your transformational process unless you allow your feelings – whatever they are – to emerge. Then they can be looked at, worked with, and possibly changed. But they have to come out first. So, please, allow yourself to feel. Having done so, as fully as possible, there is often an element of grace or change that comes afterwards. This can be seen as the transformational gift: but it can't be searched for. There are also some strong connections here with some of the neo-Reichian bodywork concepts to do with helping to release deeply suppressed feelings and so some psychotherapeutic help may be helpful initially. But, "feeling the experience" is also a moment-to-moment process as well, and you are going to have to learn how to do it for yourself.

Trust that there is help – Sometimes one feels terribly alone. A friend of mine said to me once that often if someone in crisis can really open their eyes, there is always help just there, ready & waiting, which is actually perfect for them. This is sometimes true. However this perspective or belief system involves a level of trust in the "reality" of a crisis being part of a person's transformational process, or a "Greater Plan", or a new step in their "Path", or whatever. Often it seems very differently: our life is in a mess and it seems as if there is no-one there who cares or understands. Don't trust that thought! Ask for help.

You're sometimes better off not alone – In the growth movement we have often have the privilege, and know the value, of having someone else there – sometimes just to witness – sometimes to facilitate, especially in cases of emotional expression and especially those emotions that we have difficulty with. Sometimes we even need do it in groups, as the range and quality of people's experience is multiplied and thus increasingly validating. You also get wider perspectives. Sometimes, you are better off not being alone.

You are sometimes better off alone – A "Zen" space can be very useful in order to go through some of these issues by yourself has already been mentioned. Sometimes, and initially, this can be difficult; but the more that you can manage to do it, the more attractive it can become. However this might not be your path. You may need a "community" around you, or need to create a "community" around you for you to go through your 'stuff' or develop your process. Both of these can also change and be more appropriate for you at different times.

Cry if you can – The strangest thing about crying (perhaps this is a carry-over from infancy) is that we can often never cry wholeheartedly without a listener - or at least a potential listener. We often don't let ourselves cry as desperately as we might. Maybe we are afraid to sink under the surface of the tears for fear that there will be no one to save us. Or maybe tears are a form of communication - like speech - and require a listener. There is a lovely moment in a film, *Three Colours Blue* with Juliette Binoche, where someone is crying and she asks, *"Why?"* The answer was *"Because you are not."* Crying is sometimes necessary.

Stay flexible – You are dealing with a dynamic situation, which can change in a moment in directions that you cannot imagine. If you are to be any use at all to yourself, or another person, it will mean staying very flexible, being able to change as the person's process changes, and yet also maintain an underlying level of consistency. Practice this with your own process before you practice it on others. Good luck!

Develop an overview – This follows on from the last comment. The type of transformative process people go through is often very confusing and frightening. They can easily get lost in it, hence the crisis. Your job, as a supporter or family member, is to help them also have an overview - almost a view of the process itself. What is it that is changing? This understanding is also somewhat instinctual and partially archetypal; you need to develop a sense of the core of the process. In some ways it is quite visceral, almost an underview, not a 'mind view' or a head-trip.

Just be in the moment – Again, most of us are looking back to the past, or looking forward at future possibilities, or just thinking of something else. The more one can "be in the moment" and "feel the experience" the richer and fuller life becomes. You also stop punishing yourself for what has happened, or not happened, in the past and setting up expectations of the future which have little bearing on reality (when it happens) and can thus cause disappointments. This is approaching something of a Buddhist or Zen perspective.

Discover the lesson – Be aware of the process and try to extrapolate as to what the lesson is (or might be) because the sooner you get to learn the lesson, the less painful everything then becomes and so you can start to reap the benefits as you go onto the next lesson. Sometimes, the lesson is to learn to stop doing something: like hitting your head against a brick wall & hurting yourself; or giving up an addictive behaviour. You will really have to feel the pain of that type of behaviour before you will begin to learn to stop. This maxim should only really be applied to situations that re-occur. We can get into a lot of masochistic introspection otherwise.

There are No Short-cuts – That is it! "Life is Difficult." "There Ain't No Such Thing As A Free Lunch" either. "Nothing Good Ever Comes Easy". "No Gain Without Pain". "Magic Wands Only Exist in Fairy Stories." "Do the Time." Whatever! You do need to 'get' this. Any guru or New Age practitioner or someone with an Indian or mystic name who tells you that you can change you life in a weekend workshop (or whatever) is talking b***s***!

Some experiences have no obvious lesson – I have absolutely no wish whatsoever to try to stick a label of, "This is just a difficulty in your personal Path of Transformation" onto someone (say) whose child has just died. (and I would deplore anyone who would do so). Some experiences may eventually turn out to be a Spiritual Emergency, but any premature 'diagnosis' can be insensitive to the point of crassness. Similarly someone may be genuinely mentally ill and experiencing the horrors of a schizophrenic episode – and again, to say this is a Spiritual Emergency is insensitive and crass.

The picture is probably wider or deeper than you think – We, as therapists, over the last few years, have all had to include the realistic possibility of child sexual abuse and incest in a client's history, as it is considerably more prevalent than anyone previously thought. As therapists particularly, therefore, we may have had to adapt from our original views and training perspectives and, as we listen to client's stories, allow our awareness to be triggered by certain stimuli that may indicate a deeper story. Similarly, with increasing evidence and acceptability of (say) … psychosomatic connections; the power of breath work; traumas locked up somatically in the body; birth & pre-birth experiences; near-death experiences; psychic experiences; and past-life events; we have to consider whether these need to be included in our tool-kit. How these can influence present continuums? As we grow, can we expand our consciousness to include these as possibilities?

Go Higher: Go Deeper – Sometimes the problem is that the real issue is not being dealt with properly: it may be more fundamental than you think; or it may be more archetypal than you think. What is the real truth? Keep asking yourself this question; go as deep as you can; widen your perspective! What is the greatest goal, the highest good? Keep asking. You'll get there.

Go *With* the Process – This is absolutely fundamental. If you are swimming in a river or the sea, and therefore very wet and tired of swimming, but you can't for the moment get out of that situation, then it is easier to swim with the current rather than against it (trying to get back where you came from). You are just as wet either way. Accept the process of transformation and change. Accept where you are, right now = even if it is not a very nice place. Work *from* these places, rather than trying to get back to where you were before, and then try to make things better from there. Try not to guess where you are going: you may only set up expectations that will not necessarily be fulfilled. Try to keep to the fundamentals of staying 'in the moment' and 'with the process' – right now. What do you need to do – for yourself – right now! There are lots more examples of this principle running all though this Handbook.

The Symptoms are NOT the Process – They may be indicative of the process; they may be irrelevant to the process; they may even hinder the process. Don't get hooked into what is called "symptomatology". Some people (less understanding of their process) latch onto the symptoms – *"What else is there?"* The symptoms may be indicative of the process, but they are not the process. [51]

Many attempts are made to "read meaning" into a person's symptoms: Louise Hay does this in her books, *"You can heal your Life"*

---

[51] Example: Sometimes – not always – a person with anorexia is scared of her developing womanhood. She may feel that it seems unsafe for her to become sexual – she may fear becoming a sexual object or be exploited as a sexual person. If she doesn't eat, then she won't develop the breasts and hips that define her as sexual. Her periods may even stop. In this example, the symptoms (anorexia – not eating) are indicative of an underlying process (fear of sexuality). It must be emphasised that this example does not apply for all women with anorexia.

and *"Heal Your Body"*; Or statements like, *"Because the car that I was in crashed on the way to the church wedding, it meant that I should not get married."* This is a very seductive rationale. It may lead one to realising one's ambivalence about the proposed wedding. But the symptom (of the car crash) is not necessarily indicative of the process – because someone else in the same situation might have got out, left the car, hitched a lift and made it to the church on time. It is the process, what you do with it; that is important.

One might just have easily used a frown on someone's face in the church to "realise" any latent ambivalence. The two events are phenomenologically unconnected. Whereas the person who develops psychic powers as part of their spiritual awakening and transformational process may be caught by the glamour of the powers and take up a "mind-reading" act in show-business and this could hinder their transformational process, rather than (say) developing these gifts as a tool of intuitive medical diagnosis which could help a lot of people and lead one to need to understand more and more, in order to help people better. You need to choose the path you walk: ensure it is the right one.

Enjoy the Process – Using the image of the Transformational Process as a journey, and where the purpose of the process is the journey itself - then you might as well enjoy it, rather than hating it. Maybe you can even find ways of celebrating it. There is no benefit to anyone for us living a frightened or a miserable life. There are many marvels out there: and you just need to look for them as you walk along the road. Don't forget to involve your body. Eat, drink and really savour what you eat and drink. Enjoy movement, music, dance, exercise, - whatever it is that your body is telling you that you need. Seize the moment and live as fully as you can. Not doing something now, because of whatever rationale that exists in the back of your brain, may not help you later.

Regression is sometimes necessary, but don't over do it – Psychological regressive states, where the person is essentially regressed to a younger or simpler state, can have a lot of healing potential, but the choice to go into them **has** to be a totally free one. If the regression is spontaneous and chaotic, that does not necessarily help the process. Sometimes regression is over-used by some forms of therapies (e.g.,

Re-birthing), possibly because it is dramatic and effective, and more grounded work involving long periods of working with minute detail and gentle integration is then needed to counterbalance the dramatic breakthroughs sometimes achieved under regression. One must learn to manage the process, as well as go with it and not to get flooded by it.

It's really hard to go back, and looking back doesn't help very much either – Once all the stuff is out of Pandora's box, it is very hard to put the things back. If other people are involved, or significant time has passed, it may not even be possible. It may still be just possible (like anything is) but it would take an amazing amount of hard work, and it may even not be very productive. The client sometimes says, *"I wish everything could be the way it was."* It is a legitimate desire, but not a realistic one. After all, having done so much and gone so far, is it really worth trying to undo everything done already? However it is still a legitimate choice, as well. Looking back all the time can also be very counter productive. It may be that one needs to grieve for what one has left behind, in order to leave it behind, and then move on. Beware pillars of salt!

Do you really want to change? – This is a legitimate question related to the last point. However, the question ideally should have been asked much earlier in a person's process. This is a "life choice" point, and there is a legitimate question that must be put. "Do you really want to change?" I feel a therapist is ethically obliged to say, *"Therapy can change your life."* It can possibly help you to realize that your job is boring; your partner incompatible; you need a change in life style; or to go to India for a long while, etc. This may have emerged out of the therapy and is material that you (may) have been suppressing. It is important to realize that this stuff is the process of change. It is very difficult after this point to go back. It is like a point of 'no-return'. So, there is a legitimate question here: *"Do you really want to open this can of worms up?"* Also, legitimate is: *"Do I really want to change – this way? Or now? Or this part of my self?"*

Stay Grounded – Whilst flights of fancy or fantasy, wonderful new experiences, transcendental moments, 'all tinged with gold', are marvellous and maybe even necessary to the freeing of the spirit and the creativity of the soul, nothing ultimately makes any sense or can happen with this marvellous stuff unless or until you are grounded as well. You are useless to yourself, and to others, if you stay on Cloud 17. You will need to bring it all back down to earth and use it there. Become human and mundane again, **without** losing this stuff – which is quite hard to do – and then the journey will be truly worthwhile.

Grieving is difficult – Our society doesn't know how to grieve well. An Irish wake, or something similar, allows one to let out all the emotion; the tearing of clothes, sackcloth and ashes, weeping and wailing, and then getting gloriously drunk and telling and hearing all the reminiscences from all the departed person's family and friends. Alternatively create an appropriate ceremony for yourself; weave into it all the bits and pieces that will make you feel better about letting this person, or thing, go and getting on with your new life.

There is no "right way" – We so often get caught up in issues of right & wrong; good or bad, etc. There is no right way, or not "one" right way. There is the way that you are doing things now and it may be right for you, and it may also not be right for those around you, at this moment in time. If you realize that this is so, then change it. It is your judgment-call. Alternatively, you may not like the effects of this at present, *"It doesn't feel 'right'"*, but … you may have agreed to try it this way, for the moment, because others feel that this might be better for you, and them. If it doesn't pan out right, then change it. If it feels wrong, really wrong, then change it now. It is your path, your life, and ultimately your choice.

"Both… and…" rather than "either… or…" – It can be the case that something is both difficult <u>and</u> ecstatic; or works and doesn't feel right. We so often get locked into "either… or…" situations: Black & White; Yes or No; Right or Wrong. We get caught between two polarities, and (often) neither is completely right. The world is a much bigger and more complex place than this, and there are many more than two possibilities or perspectives. Try out the difference: use "both

... and ..." instead. Take some time and hold both as true; and then (possibly) step beyond them both into a different choice.

"Should's" and "Ought's" are NOT very helpful – We are often trying to change some of the precepts, rules and parameters that we have been brought up with. These thought forms or word usage tend to reinforce these: try "can" or "may" instead. *"You should stay together for the sake of the children"* is a lot narrower and more judgmental than, *"You can try to stay together for the sake of the children"*. We are trying to expand possibilities and consider different ways.

Primary? or Secondary? – Another "caveat" is to make sure of the distinction between the primary issue and the secondary ones. Often the "crisis" appears only around the disturbances generated by secondary issues. It may be "acceptable" to change one's profession, but to create a situation where one is sacked, or in a way in which you cannot continue (eg: a psychotic episode), is the way that creates the crisis. So this is more "secondary". It is these secondary processes that need "relief" and it is also these secondary processes (the 'symptoms') that are often treated by therapists or psychiatry. Once they are relieved then some of the primary issues (the desire to change) can be looked at more clearly, as long as they are not forgotten and ignored. The relief of the secondary process is often generated by an appropriate intervention. This does not cure the problem, but it may make it possible to address the primary process. If the primary issues are exposed and faced, the secondary "crisis" can disappear, and the basic problem can then be resolved without another crisis.

Develop Healthy Discrimination – Part of the mature spiritual person's tool-kit is a better sense of discrimination or discernment. *"What works for me?"* - is a question that becomes more and more automatic the further you go along the path. *"Is this right for me, now?"* – is another good question. The more you ask yourself this type of question, and the more you listen inside of yourself for an answer, the more automatic it will become and the more refined your discrimination will be, and you can extend this and refine this endlessly. It can develop into a sense of something like intuition.

Look After Your Body – As mentioned occasionally, your body is very important. Crisis, fear, shock and stress can blow your immune system to shreds; your autonomic nervous system may be seriously out of balance; medications can be quite toxic, as can be the by-products of stress itself. Make sure that you: **(i)** drink at least two litres of water a day; **(ii)** eat healthily and variedly, using as fresh, well-cooked and healthy food as possible; **(iii)** get some aerobic exercise at least 3 times a week, so that you get sweaty for at least 30-45 minutes; **(iv)** try some progressive relaxation techniques, or a meditational tape, or listening to gentle music, or repeating a mantra, whilst lying down, for at least 20 minutes (ideally twice) a day or at least 8 times per week. All of these are pretty essential, if not mandatory, for a healthy lifestyle.

No Expectations – Expectations can really screw you up; and you can also set yourself up for a major series of disappointments. Whether this is a more of a "technology" or a "spiritual principle" (see later) doesn't really matter much, they can still screw you up and distort your perception and appreciation of the here-and-now.

A Sense of Humour – is another essential tool in your toolkit, or a technology to have. Many of the 'great' and 'good' who work in this field have an excellent sense of humour: Ram Dass; Patch Adams; Caroline Myss; the Dalai Lama; Nelson Mandela; Desmond Tutu; to name just a few. Their "sacred irreverence" is very encouraging, and very lightening.

Celebrate and utilize the "duvet day" – Sometimes we really need one, or two, or even a few extra "duvet" moments. Following your inner voice, and kicking the 'Protestant work-ethic' our of the window, can sometimes be such a relief, a liberation, and such sheer pleasure that this also has to be included into our tool-kit.

What Works For You – is just what works for you. If it doesn't work for you, change it. You do not have to explain anything, justify this, or wonder about it endlessly. It either works for you, or it doesn't. Pragmatism reigns supreme.

Better Out Than In: In relation to anger, Buddha said: *"Holding on to anger is like grasping a hot coal with the intent at throwing it at someone else: you are the one who gets burned"*. In the apocryphal gospels, Jesus told his disciples: *"If you do not bring forth what is within you, what is within you will destroy you."*

Holding on to something, be it anger, inspiration, feedback to a colleague or partner, or it being just energy, transforms the energetic impulse. It turns into something that is being repressed. This sort of repression is 'life-negative' and can become toxic over time. It also takes increasing amounts of energy to hold back on all these impulses.

Remember: *"I am wise because I know that I know nothing."* – Socrates' maxim is still valid today. There is so much that we don't know and it is wise to acknowledge this. It is also a form of defence against hubris (all too common nowadays). This does not mean that you should wallow in ignorance. "To live is to learn and to learn is to live." (Contengan Jalanan Hlovate)

The Power of Prayer: It is somewhat unfashionable nowadays to believe in the actual 'power' of prayer. However, it is perhaps a mistake not to do so. Prayer – sincere prayer – not just asking for something you want, but putting your whole being into asking something for someone else – has an actual power. You are putting your energy 'out there' and that has an effect, an impact. The result may not be exactly what you imagined, but something will shift or change.

"Who you are now, is not who you really are: it is who you have become." Who you really are is the person with all the potential that you were born with. You then had to adapt, and often reduce, this potential according to all your subsequent experiences, controls, accidents, schools and rules, experiences, pleasures and extatic experiences, etc. You had to 'fit in', or 'be quiet', whatever. That was then. This is now. You can start to reclaim your true potential; you can re-find your True Self, you can become more of the Real You."

'MADNESS' SEEN DIFFERENTLY

Crisis or Process:

There has been continual talk of the client's or the person in crisis' process. There have also been two basic views put forward:

(a) That the (so-called) spiritual crisis is essentially a break-down of that person's coping strategies and what is necessary is to re-build new and better ones and to gain an understanding of what has happened; and

(b) That the spiritual crisis offers a new potential - a break-through - to new possibilities, possibly previously unimagined.

The first is much less open-ended; it is more within mainstream thought and current psychological theories (cognitive behavioural or psychodynamic); it is better grounded and more pragmatic; it is easier to conceptualise; it is 'medicalised' in that it views the person more as a patient, or a victim of events; it is framed in ending the crisis as soon as possible – though not necessarily by reverting to the pre-crisis situation; it is more socially orientated.

> ".... the salient features of crisis intervention. It is immediate. It is brief. It includes a number of people, not just a single individual. It involves a mixture of practical and interpretive help, and it can stimulate creative developments in the life of a person or family, as well as alleviate distress." (Joseph H. Berke, *Butterfly Man*)

The second view is much more open-ended in that the crisis *is an actual part* of a person's unfolding psychological process; it is more controversial and more debatable; it comes more from within the fields of humanistic and transpersonal psychology; it is much more client-orientated; it is much more uncertain or unclear, as the outcome is not known, nor is the duration – though there are often practical limits set to this; and the crisis doesn't end, but it metamorphoses into a transition, transformation, evolution, break-through, or whatever and the eventual integration of that; it is much more demanding and difficult; and involves several paradigm shifts for the helpers and professionals.

These views are not totally mutually exclusive.

Caplan & Lindemann (pioneers of Crisis Intervention) argued that the best way to intervene is not by treating the symptoms of the tensions produced, but by helping the person (or the family) to confront and work through the crisis itself. An added 'bonus' is that the crisis can create an emergency state in which one's ability to learn and re-adapt is greater than usual. The ability to get through the crisis depends upon how realistically the person perceives the situation; the degree of interpersonal support the person has; and the depth of their experience of personal resources. The tasks of those who intervene include assisting the person and/or family to achieve an undistorted view of what's happening, mobilizing supporting relationships and acting as an auxiliary ego until the person is more able to cope. There are dangers in all these points of the practitioner/ therapist/ helper "taking over" the process and imposing their own views.

The Seduction of Madness

This is a title of a book by Dr Edward M. Podvollthat is about the recovery from psychosis and especially about recovery at home, or in a community setting. He considers that psychosis may be one of the unfortunate permutations of the human condition, rather than a rare disease. The 'medicalisation' of insanity almost means – or even requires – that the treatment must therefore be medical, and the medical profession is still very confused about treatment & cure. Podvoll states that:

> "*the overuse of medications is commonplace, and along with that has come the health-consuming battle against their enfeebling side effects...* (in which he includes poor concentration, lack of interest & boredom) .... *Electro-convulsive therapy has become fashionable to a degree that some major teaching hospitals* (in the USA) *are delivering it as the primary treatment for severe neurotic depressions. It is now used on over 30,000 patients a year. And there is a renewed interest in the use of psychosurgery based almost exclusively on the argument of cost-effectiveness. The outrageous predictions of Ivan Illich in* Medical Nemesis: The Expropriation of Health *have already come true.*"

The profession of medicine and psychotherapy (especially in the USA, but increasingly in the UK) is primarily bound up with issues of cost-effectiveness, requirements to demonstrate efficacy, insurance regulations, and fear of malpractice allegations. These issues have really nothing to do with the patient or his or her condition: but they dominate the treatment. They also ... "*promote a fear of the intimate relationships that are so precious and vital to the recovery from madness.*" Training – except in physical medicine - is grossly neglected, in his opinion, and there is a continual stream of indictments against inattention, neglect & violation. Everything seems to be centred towards looking for a biological cure: a quick fix. He advocates much more motivation towards an alternative, more natural & homelike treatment – which is more traditionally based.

Paul Eugen Bleuler, one of the pioneers of psychiatry (who 'named' schizophrenia and autism), lived with his psychotic patients in an experimental healing community for 12 years; William James, & Bruno Bettelheim also advocated similar approaches to mental healing; R.D. Laing, Joseph Berke and Morton Schatzmann did something similar at Kingsley Hall, in the Philadelphia Association and in the Arbours Association; Edward Podvell founded the Windhorse Communities; Patch Adams does it (or did it) as well at his holistic medical centre in West Virginia, 'Gesundheit'. [52]

---

[52] www.patchadams.org

Podvoll speaks a lot about the 'bewitchment'&'seduction' of the person's psychotic symptoms (something also remarkably described by an early psychiatric 'patient': John Perceval, the son of an early 19th century British Prime Minister) and the incredible effort & discipline required to overcome these symptoms in order to recover fully. And, from the therapists' perspective, much of the effort includes really listening to the patients. They tend to tell that,

> "... whatever the trigger to that (psychotic) state may be, the experience must still be related to at its subtle stirrings, during the midst of psychological anarchy, and during the fragile process of awakening. One must work directly and precisely with ongoing and seemingly bizarre mental & physical events. Failure to do so drives one deeper into madness."

Podvoll doesn't advocate "going with the flow", as so many New Age therapists and people in spiritual emergencies seem to want to do. Instead, he advocates a lot of hard work, resisting the obvious symptoms of madness, however attractive they may seem to the individual concerned, AND treating that person with kindness, respect and ultimate humanity. He is primarily looking at recovery, rather than reform (which is why I have included this synopsis) and he concentrates on –

> "perceiving and nurturing islands of clarity (moments of natural recovery), for in this way full recovery from psychosis has been accomplished and will continue to occur without aggressive or physically intrusive methods of treatment."

In the introduction he quotes Dr Manfred Bleuler, son of Paul Eugen Bleuler (mentioned earlier):

> *The need to become free from the prejudice that a person who has become insane will always be so, is extremely urgent and you (Podvell) are formulating it very well. I have been much attacked within the last years as I have seen and described the recovery of many schizophrenics who had been severely sick for long periods. The critic of my teaching and my experience consist in the following opinion: 'A schizophrenic patient can never recover - if you imagine to have*

seen recoveries of schizophrenic patients the reason is: you have made a wrong diagnosis'. (This comment was made to the son of the man who categorised schizophrenia and is continuing his father's work at Burghölzli in Zurich.) In my opinion this criticism is unrealistic & harmful to our patients.

Podvoll's work – updated in his book, *Recovering Sanity: A compassionate approach to understanding and treating psychosis*, is put into practice and carried on in the "Windhorse Project" for recovery, where a team of skilled therapists work closely with a disturbed person in his or her own home. A network of these individual treatment households, together with the staff members, has evolved into an extended therapeutic community. [53]

Attitudes to Medication:

It is worth noting that the most common or traditional psychiatric approach involves generally using psychotropic medications to control and resolve the extreme parts of the crisis. These can be very damaging: physically & emotionally (see Bentall's book, *Doctoring the Mind: Why psychiatric treatments fail*). However, sometimes such medications are necessary (if other forms of containment are not possible), so involving doctors can then become a double-edged sword.

There is little respect in traditional psychiatric treatment for the person's process and their more subtle feelings. There is now an increasing awareness of their rights as a person, but even these are often transgressed. The parameters of "getting someone over their crisis" can be disrespectful in their very nature, if the crisis 'should' be gone through instead of "got over". Sometimes, there is often panic (instead of calm) at the secondary symptoms of a person's process. Sometimes, (or often if some are to be believed) medication is taken by, or is given to, patients, as much to make the staff and the carers feel better, or make their life easier, as to help the patient recover.

A very effective approach is often to stay calm, and don't become impatient, frightened or critical. The person in crisis may, or will, then trust you with their process and a joint working together towards a

---

53   www.windhorsecommunityservices.com

better position (not necessarily a cure) becomes possible. Stay cool also with the professionals who may have a different viewpoint. One good thing is that often they want to discharge this person as soon as it is 'safe' to do so (in their terms). So, it is possible to play along with this and they will (may) bless you.

The medical or pharmaceutical approach can be extremely useful for very short-term interventions, in an emergency situation, and/or combined with other techniques to actually help understanding and integration. More enlightened psychiatrists are trying to limit such usage towards a reasonably rapid (often within a few days or a maximum of 3 weeks) return to normal life – though the medications are usually (unfortunately) maintained for a considerable while longer. An example of this is the euphemism, *"Keep taking the tablets."*

Elsewhere, [54] I have described anti-depressant medications (particularly the SSRIs) as similar to having a life jacket if you fall into the ocean. It will keep you afloat, but you will still have to learn to swim. But this is not necessarily a crisis situation, though this can sometime help to prevent such.

Medication can be quite successful for the long-term management of full-blown chronic psychoses, where other attempts have failed and (quite likely) some pathology has occurred. It must be also viewed from another perspective, as some psychotropic medications can be extremely abusive to the patient. Many, many patients report other ailments or side-effects that would not be tolerated in medications taken for any other condition (e.g. birth control tablets) or "illnesses" other than mental illness.

"Madness" treated without Medication

There have been a number of very successful psychotherapeutic treatments or approaches with people who have been diagnosed as chronically psychotic, which have been used to help the person in crisis to get off their medications, and have also seemingly helped to resolve their crisis. This is sometimes where the medication had seemed to

---

54 Young, C. (2010). *Help Yourself Towards Mental Health.* London, Karnac Books.

hold or freeze the person's situation or process in a manageable, but often quite unpleasant, condition.

A tricky course has to be negotiated between these alternatives – Scylla and Charybdis, always bearing in mind (hopefully) the best interests of the client, rather than what is common practice within the system.

The client (or patient) or person in crisis, also has a totally valid perspective of their own which **must** be tapped wherever and whenever possible. After all, it is they who are going to have to live with the effects of this treatment. If ideas are 'deliberately' floated, the client will give their input. Social Work and some hospital systems now often give clients the *right* to have an advocate present to speak for them and put their perspective forward in any type of "case conference". For a fuller description of these types of social intervention, see Loren Mosher's book on the Soteria communities: *Soteria: Through Madness to Deliverance.*

Families in Crisis

One perspective also worth noting is that, in many cases, the "person in crisis" is more correctly the person in the family who is least able to cope with the *family* crisis – i.e., the crisis is actually happening in the family, and is not really based within the individual's own process. This perspective is central to much of Family Psychotherapy, and there the whole family gets treated, rather than just the identified "patient" or person in crisis.

For these reasons, the Arbours Association (for example) finds home visits very informative, if not essential in the treatment of people in crisis. R.D. Scott postulates "identity warfare" to describe the situation whereby some people become so threatening to the psychic survival of others within the family (or community) that their continued presence in the group serves as an incitement to fantasized, if not actual, murder and mayhem. The person in crisis, or the one who having a spiritual emergence process, is therefore seen as a threat to the insecure family dynamic.

Hospitalisation, exclusion, or the identification of someone as "mentally ill" is the means by which the most threatening person (or the one with the least power) can be 'sacrificed' so that the rest of the group remains intact. This, Scott calls "cultural closure", as that person is then no longer seen as a 'proper' member of the group.

There is a lovely story about someone living in the Gurdjieff community in Fontainebleau in the early 1920s who was loathed by the rest of the community. Once, when Gurdjieff was away lecturing, things became so bad that the guy up and left. On Gurdjieff's return, he pursued the guy to Paris and tried to persuade him to return. *"You must be crazy,"* the guy said, *"they'll kill me." "I'll pay you to stay there another month,"* said Gurdjieff. The rest of the community were in uproar when they heard this, especially as they were paying to live there. *"You are here to work on yourselves,"* said Gurdjieff, *"this man is bringing out all your negativities. He is therefore your perfect teacher. That is why I asked him to return."*

Network Intervention:

Sometimes the resources of the social or family group can be utilised to help the person in crisis and this type of intervention is known as a "network intervention" or "network therapy". Networks are created with the involvement of the person in crisis to stay with the person, do the household chores, look after the kids, help out at work etc. This "crisis networking" helps overcome the acts of omission or commission that the malfunctioning unit (which contains the person in crisis) has been allowing to perpetuate and often provoke the crisis. The social network is often non-familial, and much wider than the family, including neighbours, schools, office, church, and other activity-based groups, and yet contains all the family members. The extended family is more a family by choice. The "Crisis Group" structure can be easily applied to this sort of network.

"Break-through", rather than "break-down":

Another word on the "break-through" approach: Whilst this is beset with difficulties and challenges (and not just for the person in crisis), it is the approach that offers the most favourable opportunity for the person in crisis, if it can be undertaken safely. "Going for gold," was an expression from one TV quiz game and this approach can be seen in such a way. But this choice is also beset with dangers.

It can be filled with phenomenal growth, insight, spirit, grace and beauty. It can also have, as constituent elements: all the horrors of their own personal hell for the person in the crisis; possibly deeply shocking revelations for their family and friends; and extreme fatigue, provocation and challenges for the helpers involved. It should not be undertaken lightly, nor with stars in one's eyes: nor with the assumption that everything will naturally be all right because you are doing spiritual work; that is an extreme and pernicious form of spiritual arrogance.

In his (2015) book, *Iron John: A Book about Men*, Robert Bly draws the connection between the "golden ball" that attracts the youth, the "golden" coated finger of the "transformational wound" and the "golden hair" that eventually, after wandering in the wilderness, attracts the Princess. The transformational process is "going for gold", but what is it that is getting in the way of the person's natural spiritual evolutionary process, and therefore, sometimes, it is the obstructions which need to be transformed?

The boy got hurt; had to lie and steal from is parents; had to go into exile; wandered in the woods with a very scary companion; fail at a test; got rejected and had to back out into the wilderness; had to accept a menial position; had to accept bullying, discrimination and reject; had to fight three battles; got seriously wounded; and then eventually, by chance or otherwise, "got to the gold" in this instance the princess and half a kingdom. The path may be relatively simple, but it is NEVER easy.

However, pragmatism only too often wins, and all too often this approach is too difficult for those concerned in real life. Neither is a spiritual community or somewhere like Samye Ling, or the Findhorn Foundation, necessarily the answer for you, wherever you happen to be having your crisis. These places are not, repeat NOT, open therapeutic communities. They may be helping to serve the planet, in their own way, and they may have charitable aims, but they do this in their own way, on their particular path, and at their own choice. Some of the people who live and work there may be specially trained or qualified. But please, do NOT turn up on their doorsteps and say, *"I am having a Spiritual Emergency. Please, help me!"* They are as likely to reply, "Well, *so am I – now!"* In this instance, please help them by staying away and having your crisis in your own community. Any therapeutic contact – with anyone - must, repeat MUST, be very carefully and clearly negotiated.

The Soul's Code:

James Hillman talks about his "acorn" theory; where each person, each soul, has its unique 'code', which is its potential, and there is a sort of morphogenetic impulse imbedded in the person (like the oak tree imbedded in the acorn) to develop along the lines of this code and gives them the basic motivation for their particular life development.

> *"The soul of each of us is given a unique daimon before we are born, and it has selected an image or a pattern what we live on earth. This soul-companion, the daimon, guides us here; in the process of arrival, however we forget all that took place ad believe we come empty into this world. The daimon remembers what is in your image and belongs to your pattern, and therefore your daimon is the carrier of your destiny.* [55]

The conflicts that can happen are often in our childhood (psychotherapy has got that bit right) but it is the conflict between our inbuilt nemesis and the environment around us. The call of our destiny can cause the tantrums & obstinacies, the hyper-activity, the sense of isolation, the depressions and loss of faith, that happen in our childhood and affect the rest of our lives.

Like Pierro Ferrucci, Hillman examines the biographical aspects of the lives of exceptional people. Not only does Ferrucci find that many, if not all of these people have had spiritual crises, Hillman looks for instances where the Soul's Code breaks through and the person suddenly finds the motivation needed to overcome their initial environment or makes the sudden change that comes from deep within themselves, and nowhere else.

---

[55] Hillman, James (1997). *The Soul's Code: In Search of Character and Calling.* Bantam(p.8)

Hillman also tries to explore the nature of evil, as does Scott Peck in his seminal work, *The People of the Lie*. Whereas Peck explains evil as compulsive narcissism, within the context of the Soul's Code, Hillman theorises that the person's 'daimon' becomes a "Bad Seed" and turns them towards the path of evil. He outlines eight 'types' of evil, which might explain some of the psychopaths, the serial murderers, the heartless dictators and "natural born killers". It is an interesting theory, but not totally convincing. However, it certainly gives us some alternative views on these forms of human madness.

So, I would like to never lose sight of these different perspectives as distinct possibilities and I often try to consciously reinforce some of these possibilities – to the client or person in crisis – as a potential goal, if not for any immediate work with their crisis group or therapy practitioner, then certainly as a long-term possibility for him or herself and their growth. For, if this is done, then all the trials and tribulations we go through in these situations can fit into this larger framework and can become worthwhile. One does not have to go "mad" in order to resolve a crisis. It *can* often be beautiful and graceful. It *is* part of your basic human potential; your uniqueness.

SOME SELF-HELP EXERCISES

These exercises have been devised and collected from various sources, as indicated. Please use only those that appeal to you:

EXERCISE 1

TO GET RID OF OBSESSIVE THOUGHTS.

From the Tibetan "Bon" tradition: To do by oneself, or in a group all together.

Stand in a relaxed 'Tai Chi' way – knees bent a little – back straight – sitting on air – head floating on neck – looking forward, eyes horizontal.

Take very deep in-breath and then hold.

During the time that the breath is being held, very quickly, brush down whole body – head, arms, torso, legs – seven times.

Immediately shake arms and legs violently and shout "Doe-Pack" on the out breath.

Freeze. Stand. Feel your body. Just be aware.

Obsessive thoughts have been replaced with a "Zen space".

Repeat three times, or as often as necessary.

EXERCISE 2

GOING CRAZY SAFELY

From Process Oriented Psychotherapy: To be done in triads – each person to describe or be asked:

What would you / I be like if you / I went crazy?

What are your / my deepest, most fearsome, subconscious, secondary (denied) and crazy processes?

Can you see or imagine yourself going crazy? (Take a few minutes and allow any images to come.)

Can you feel it? (Take a few minutes and allow any emotions or proprioceptive (body-centred) feelings emerge.)

Now imagine yourself using some of that energy positively as a leader or facilitator? What might that look like – feel like? (Take a few minutes.)

Describe to the others in the triad how and where you might use that sort of energy in your life - at home, at work, in creativity etc. – and then act it out for a few minutes – how you would do that?

EXERCISE 3: MEDITATION

THE BODY THAT BROUGHT ME HERE: LIFE CHANGES!

Get someone to read this out to you, with about 1-minute pauses at the end of each section.

How did your body respond to some of these life experiences that you might have had? If you did, you carry all of these changes in your body and these helped to shape your body and your spirit.

1-minute pause

Pregnancy & Birth: (Inter-uterine experiences; Caesarian-section, cord & birth traumas; post-natal isolation; your welcome into and your position in the family; early family atmosphere & feelings)

1-minute pause

First Movement Memories: (of being in the womb; being held, rocked, carried, cuddled; of early boat, plane, train, ship journeys; of falling from a tree, or out of bed, etc.)

1-minute pause

Environment: the environments you grew up in: (fields; mountains; woods; by the sea; urban; suburbs; climate; friendly or hostile; safe or not; first impressions of school)

1-minute pause

Trainings: (potty training; reading; riding a bike; swimming; horse riding; playing a musical instrument; dance/ballet; gymnastics and athletics; sports at school)

1-minute pause

Messages: (sexist ones: boys "don't cry"; girls "are pretty"; "you are ..." - clumsy, intelligent, etc; "a body is ..." - nice/nasty; what posture; safety; shame; racial; class; family fears; recurrent dreams or nightmares)

1-minute pause

Sexuality: (nakedness; bathrooms; sensuality; what whispers of incest; what types of touch; film images; teenage images/role models; one's 1st affair; experiences of sex; issues about impotence/fertility)

1-minute pause

Health: (being suckled; types of food; weight; strength; flexibility; illnesses; disability; eyesight; allergies; chronic issues; hospitalisations; operations)

1-minute pause

Traumas & Accidents: (family deaths, car accidents, abuse, fractures, hospital operations, natural disasters; near misses; ecstatic experiences)

1-minute pause

Maturation: (the growth of and changes in your body; menârche; puberty & adolescence; childbirth; chronic illness; family predispositions; menopause; aging; nearing death; parts of your body 'not working' so well)

1-minute pause

What is your Best Body Memory?

1-minute pause

What is your Worst Body Memory?

1-minute pause

What is your Best Experience of Spirit?

1-minute pause

What is your Worst Experience of Spirit?

EXERCISE 4: MEDITATION

THE CASTLE OF THE SPIRIT

Get someone to read this out to you.

Imagine you are walking through a forest or wood *[short pause]* and eventually you come to a body of water. This might be a lake or a wide river. *[short pause]* Across the water there is a wonderful castle - The Castle of the Soul. In your imagination, you make your way across the water *[short pause]*. There might be a bridge, or a boat, or you might have to make a raft, or even swim. Follow your own imagery. *[short pause]*

Once you are inside the Castle of the Soul, you climb a stairway to a large Hall. *[short pause]* Note the details; try to remember them for later. *[short pause]* This Hall is called 'The Hall of Mirrors' and all you can see are reflections of yourself. *[short pause]* Eventually you see there are four doors leading from it. One to the North, South, East, and one to the West.

The door to the North is the one that you must try first. It has a label on the door that says "Psychotic Madness". Please open the door and go into the room behind it. Stay in this room for a while and notice what images come to you. *[Long Pause]*

Now come out, back into the Hall of Mirrors, and close the door firmly behind you. Look at the reflections of yourself again. *[short pause]*

Now open the door to the South. It has a label on it that says, "Altered States of Consciousness". Please open the door and go into the room behind it. Stay in this room for a while and notice what images come to you. *[Long Pause]*

Now come out, back into the Hall of Mirrors, and close the door firmly behind you. Look at the reflections of yourself again. Have things changed a bit? *[short pause]*

Now open the door to the West. It has a label on it that says, "Spiritual Emergencies". Please open the door and go into the room behind it. Stay in this room for a while and notice what images come to you. *[Long Pause]*

Now come out, back into the Hall of Mirrors, and close the door firmly behind you. Look at the reflections of yourself again. *[short pause]*

Now open the door to the East. It has a label on it that says, "Enlightenment". Please open the door and go into the room behind it. Stay in this room for a while and notice what images come to you. *[Long Pause]*

Now come out, back into the Hall of Mirrors, and close the door firmly behind you. Look at the reflections of yourself again. *[short pause]*

Have things changed a bit? Or a lot? *[short pause]*

Please now imagine now that you are exiting the Hall, going down the stairs.

There, just as you are leaving the castle, there is a gift for you. You look at it, appreciate it, and you pick it up and take it with you. Now you are going through the doors, out the gate, and leaving the Castle of the Soul - for the moment, at least. *[short pause]*

Now you know it is there, you can always find your way back again.

You are crossing the water again, and entering the forest. *[short pause]* You are now coming back into the room where you are now lying down, in your body, in this space and time, here and now. *[short pause]*

In your own time, open your eyes and remembering all that you have seen, please take some time now to make some notes, or write something of your experiences, or do some drawings, or make whatever form you wish to record something of this experience. *[Allow ten to fifteen minutes perhaps]*

Then discuss however much of this that seems appropriate with the person who is nearest to you / or who read out this guided meditation for you.

EXERCISE 5

RE-BUILDING YOUR AURA: (Auric Boundary)

This exercise is very good for people who have been traumatised. They should be encouraged to do it about three times within 24 hours. The first time only should they do it with a therapist present. Please be very careful of personal boundaries immediately after the person has done it. The exercise goes like this:-

Imagine that you are going to build an envelope or dome around yourself at arms-length away from yourself; all around; up and over; down to the ground; something like the shape of a glass dome over Victorian dolls or stuffed birds. You are going to do this from the inside, using your breath (prana) energy. You can put whatever qualities you would like into this energy field (envelope or dome): colours, healing, peace, safety, sparkly bits, whatever.

Take a deep breath into your body, expanding your chest area. Scoop the breath (prana) energy from your chest with your hand as if you are scooping up wet clay or paint. 'Paint' this energy with your hand on the inside surface of the dome as you breathe out. Notice the area that you have 'painted'. Stay in touch with your feelings – whatever they are. Breathe in again and repeat this for the adjoining area.

Carry on doing this and extending the 'painted' area all the way around the dome; up and over; and down to the ground. It will take at least 20 minutes: maybe 30 minutes the first time, or if there is a lot of emotion. If there is emotion, feel it, allow it, breathe through it, let it flow and change; then carry on.

Once you have completed the whole exercise; take some time to notice the difference - if any. Have you just been breathing and waving your arms around; or is there a qualitative difference in the way you now feel? What is this difference? Feel it and experience it: don't try to describe it; there are often not good words; sometimes these things are beyond language.

Once you have a sense of this energy field, please imagine that you can change it. You can make it like carbon 12-point steel so that nothing and no-one can get in; or it could be like a highly charged electrical force field so that if someone tries to intrude, they'll get fried (250,000 volts). You can make it like a glorious castle, or a sacred temple. You can make it obscure so that no-one can see you. Or you can make it dissolve and welcome in a loved one, or a child, or a pet. If you don't like a rigid "dome", make it a more flexible membrane or envelope.

The first time you do this exercise, you will probably put most of your attention into making it complete: all the way up and down; all the way around; no holes. Spend a few minutes checking this.

The second time you do it, put more attention into the right physical structure for how you feel now: high voltage; invisibility; brick walls; warm insulating jacket; rigid shell or flexible envelope; multi-layered, super-strong fibre-glass; science-fiction force field; etc.

The third time, try and really personalise it - for yourself: what colours; what inside textures - soft and spongy; what sparkly-bits; psychedelic, swirling colours; what smells; what atmosphere?

Then, you can give it extra qualities like healing, or peace; just by thinking about it. This is your energy field, at your control. Just breathe in and it is solid, clear and present there; just breathe out and it expands or dissipates. Breathe in again, and it is back.

Check out how you feel having this extra layer of protection to your body / mind / spirit. Does it work for you? And in what ways?

For people who have been severely traumatised, shocked, or abused, it is likely that their 'auric' boundaries are very depleted, or have holes in them. This exercise should therefore be repeated regularly, at least 3 times within 24 hours, then maybe three time a week for a couple of weeks. It is difficult to work therapeutically with someone if they have no sense of themselves or if there is not a "safe space" for themselves. This exercise can provide that: a safe space for themselves, wherever they are. Try it out!

EXERCISE 6

DYNAMIC MEDITATION

You might wish to speak this text onto a tape, with pauses, before you do the meditation, and then play it to yourself whilst you do the meditation. Or have someone else present reading it out slowing and witnessing your movement.

You may need a large clear space in order to do this. Wear loose comfortable clothing. Try doing it first by yourself. Someone else can also be present – witnessing what you do (which means watching uncritically). This meditation is adapted from Authentic Movement. Take 15-20 minutes for this exercise.

Stand still or start sitting or lying down. Maybe, at first, keep your eyes closed.

Imagine that you have been dancing all your life, but you have always felt that you have never danced properly; you have felt that you haven't really known how; or it has always been to a different tune; or it hasn't felt that it has been *your* dance.

Now go inside. Deep inside of you there is a stirring.

Imagine that *your* dance, your movement, is there, deep inside you.

Imagine (if you want to) that someone ethereal is holding your hands and drawing that special dance of yours out of you. Or that it is stirring and rising.

Imagine that the time is now, and your real dance is beginning here and now. It is beginning to move you – from deep down inside of you.

It is a bit like puppetry in reverse. No strings - but there is a movement from within that is beginning to move out; beginning to move your arms and your legs, your head and torso.

You begin to move very gently: not to any thought, but from within.

You begin to realize, on a deep level, that *this* is your dance, and the only person who knows what it is, and how to move, is you, and, since it is *your* dance, thus whatever you do, however you move is now right – for you, right now.

Begin to move slowly. Move gently. Don't think about it. Just allow yourself to move from within.

Whatever you do, however you move, is now authentically you. You can move exactly how you want to. You can stop and you can go, as and when you want to. You can move in any way; up and down; on the floor; round and about; just as you want to. This is your dance, and you are now dancing it.

Allow yourself to just keep moving. It doesn't have to be a dance now. It is just movement, your movement.

EXERCISE 7

DEATH FANTASIES AND HOW THEY STOP YOU LIVING

Work in pairs, with someone (i) who you feel comfortable with, but (ii) that you do not know very well (eg: not a life partner). Decide who is going to 'work' first. The other person will read the questions and keep to the time frame. Take at least twenty minutes for the exercise and then change over roles. Take about twenty minutes after each person has 'worked' to discuss the exercise.

1. What is one of the central problems areas of your life, that you would like to change, but you can't as you feel blocked in some way?
2. Describe this to your partner and then put it aside for a while.
3. How do you imagine you will die? Where will you be? How old will you be? Who will be there? What will you be doing?
4. What might happen at the exact moment of your death?
5. Notice your reactions (emotional, somatic, etc.) to your fantasy.
6. Allow yourself to build up on that fantasy. Use the exact details and the material above and focus on the most salient aspect of your death.
7. Notice what it is to be like fully in that death state. Explore this as if it is a lucid dream. Expand the fantasy.
8. Now ask yourself what is death ultimately trying to bring to you. What can you benefit or learn from this death fantasy?
9. Which parts of your 'ordinary' personality would have to die if you were going to have this state of awareness? Who, or what new part of you, lives when this other part of you dies?
10. Be this part. Feel it in your body. Imagine living this way in the world.
11. Who or what, either within your or outside of you, seems to be against you being in this new state? "I'd rather die than ..." "S/he'd kill me if I was ..."

12. Can you use your death fantasy as an ally or as a pattern to deal with this 'edge figure' or this fear of retribution? Play out a scenario with your partner where you are the 'death state' and your partner is the 'edge figure'.

When this is over, allow your partner to tell you the story of your death process. S/he will 'weave' all the elements above – including the original problem, the 'death state' and the 'edge figure' – into your death story. Be sure to include death as an ally in the story.

Adapted from a Process Oriented Psychology workshop
with Robert Hall and Jan Dworkin, 2001.

EXERCISE 8

THE FELT SENSE OF SELF

If we are feeling better about ourselves, then we hold ourselves differently; we walk differently; we feel differently; and we see things differently. Then we 'feel' a whole lot better about ourselves; we 'feel' that we are again our Self; and we 'feel' a sense of our Self. So, how can we get back to this feeling? – the 'felt' sense of Self.

Exercise

This exercise is designed to help you get back towards a 'felt sense' of your Self. It is in three sections and each part has three parts. The exercise should take about 15-20 minutes. You can do it anywhere: and at any almost time; though obviously not when you are working, or driving a car. You can do it on a bus, or on the train to work. It is probably best to do it whilst sitting down, rather than lying down. You can do it whilst walking – say on your morning exercise route or with the dog. Or you can pull into a lay-by and do it in the car, before you get home. It is also best to practice this regularly until it becomes more like second-nature: until it becomes your usual, proper sense of Self. This exercise is just one way to achieve this feeling, especially if you start using it, on a regular basis. There are, of course, many other ways, but these usually involve other people or events. This one you can do for yourself, by yourself, quietly and regularly. As you do it, you will build in your own changes and modifications – so that it works for you! As you do it, you should find that you get an increasing feeling of your Sense of Self.

First Section

- **First Part:** Become more aware of your breathing. You are (obviously) breathing all the time: every moment of every day: but how often are you aware of your breathing? We breathe basically in two different ways. There is the belly-breathing method that is encouraged in Yoga. This is where your belly moves in and out and – because of your diaphragm – the movement in the belly draws air in, or pushes it out, of your lungs: so it works a little like a bicycle pump. The second basic method of breathing is a 'bellows-type' of breathing. You often do this if you have just run up a couple of flights of stairs. This is where your chest and your rib cage expands, and the air is drawn in and out of your lungs by a bellows-type of action. However, when we are very anxious or afraid, our breathing becomes quite shallow and quite 'high'; panting a little, with most of the breathing action happening in the throat. When we are anxious, we also tend to breathe in and hold; and then breathe in and hold: we take more air in, but don't breathe out very much. When the fear or stress or tension goes, then we let out the tension, breathe out a lot and then start to relax. So, how are you breathing now? How much, how often, and where? Just become aware of your pattern of breathing. Spend a couple of minutes re-connecting with your pattern of breathing. Don't try and change it, but – if it changes – allow that as well.

- **Second Part:** You are not just breath: you also have a body. So, spend a couple of minutes becoming more aware of your body. You are probably sitting on a chair: so, become aware of the chair against your back and bottom. You may be sitting in a particular position: arms folded, or not; legs crossed, or not; become aware of this position. You may be wearing a watch, or a belt, or a necklace, or something: become aware of the physical sensations of wearing these objects. Become conscious of the feeling of your clothes against your skin: your shoes may be a little tight – or whatever! We receive all of these sensations into our body all of the time: just become more aware of <u>all</u> of these sensations. Become aware of your body as a living, functioning organism: you have quite an amazing body: it mostly works very well for most of the time: 60-70 years of non-stop functioning. Appreciate it a little now: spend a couple of minutes being amazed!

- **Third Part:** So, you are now aware of your breathing and your body. Now, become aware of the environment that you are in. There are lots of things around you: sights, sounds, smells, textures, temperatures, qualities of light, noises outside the house, etc. Spend a minute or two becoming aware of your breathing body in the environment that it is in, at this moment in time. Become more aware of the sensations and affects of the environment around you: the smell of the room you are in; the hum of the computer (if there is one); the noises in the street outside; birdsong perhaps. Spend a couple of minutes 'being' in 0the environment around you. This is all part of You being You, and becoming more your Self, in this present Here and Now.

Second Section

- **First Part:** You are not just a body in the here-and-now: you also have feelings: lots of them. There are those feelings that are more on the 'surface': more easily accessible. Today, you are reasonably happy because ... (hopefully) ... the sun is shining; or not so fine because you have just had an argument with your partner or child or work colleague; or someone who you thought liked (or didn't like) you said something nasty (or nice) about you; or you are looking forward to the weekend, and so forth. Spend a little time, a couple of minutes, in just contacting and being more aware of all those different 'surface' – here-and-now – feelings.
- **Second Part:** Underneath the surface feelings, there are lots of other – often contrasting – feelings. People that we basically like, also have some irritating (possibly infuriating) habits; whilst we may love someone, we can also really dislike 'this' or 'that' about them, or dislike them when they do 'this' or 'that'; we love our children dearly, and we are also sometimes really infuriated by them; we may really want to move to another town, or the countryside, but we are also scared to lose our friends where we live. We are basically a nice person, and sometimes we can get very angry, or jealous, or we can have mean thoughts. We also have to become aware of these 'mixed' or 'secondary' feelings – they are a part of who we are – and then perhaps we can accept and work through, or with, some of these conflicts. Spend a couple of minutes just allowing your awareness of some of these conflicting emotions: you won't be able to sort them out in these few minutes, so just notice them, and hold your awareness of them. Let them bubble up, and then breathe, and let them go on out.
- **Third Part:** Below these conflicting emotions, there are our deeper, basic feelings: our 'gut' feelings. These are beyond dispute: they cover humane things like the horror of warfare; the fear of violence;

the basic desire for peace and calm; a love of gentleness and beauty; the pleasure that we get from being in nature – those things that touch us all deeply. On other levels, we may never, ever vote Conservative – or Labour: that is just <u>not</u> who we are! We are deeply religious, or we are agnostic! It probably won't change. We might have been brought up Protestant, and are now Buddhist – or something. We like cats, and not dogs – or visa versa, or neither, or both. These 'gut' feelings don't often change: they help to form something of our basic human identity. Sometimes we have had a crisis, or a near-death experience, or something – and that is when some of these feelings might change: but it might take a crisis to do that! This level is where we can feel our common humanity; and our connectedness to all things. These deep feelings go to confirm our identity, and, from here, we can also begin to feel something of our spirituality. Anyway, spend a couple of minutes at this level, just contacting some of these deeper feelings. You can come back here, anytime. However, you can't short-cut the process and omit the second part, the conflictual bit. People try to do this all the time, by joining a political party, or by following a sect, or getting a guru, or by joining a movement. Only by going *through* these emotional conflicts, can we really make sense of these things, and retain a sense of the deeper understanding.

Third Section

You are not just a body and a set of feelings. There is much more to you than that. Who you are now is who you have become. There were many influences throughout your life; you made decisions along the road, and there could have been different choices, and there were missed opportunities, and so on and so forth. You may have a frustrated musician inside of you, because you had to give up piano at age seven when your family moved house; or there may be dreams of crossing the Gobi Desert on a camel, or of climbing Kilimanjaro. What might have happened (or not happened) if you hadn't gone to *that* party? This section deals with that part of the whole 'You' that is <u>not</u> manifest at this particular point in time, but remains a potential. However, I don't want to be too precise, because otherwise I may indicate something that isn't there, or you may inhibit or overlook something that is there. You will have to 'feel' your way into this section, over time, and through repetition.

- **First Part:** This first part is to do with your conscious dreams and aspirations. You may feel you deserve to be the branch manager, or the section head: you may have fantasies about how you would do 'this' or 'that'; or you might have always wanted a child or another child – the girl that you have always longed for, or the boy to carry your name forward. These thoughts, dreams, hopes, aspirations, are absolutely fine: all of these are possible; they may (or may not) happen; whether they do or not is relatively irrelevant; all of this part of your Self is a manifestation of your present potential, of you trying to exert yourself, to move forward, or do something more in your life. This leads you gently forward from the 'here-and-now' towards new possibilities. Take a couple of minutes for this part. Dream up the wider parts of your Self a little bit more.
- **Second Part:** This part is a bit more vague, as it is to do with your unrealised potential. You have millions of brain cells that you don't use very much: what would you be like if you were using them? With a bit of a push in a particular direction, and with some determination and specialist training, you could be (or have been) … a musician, an astronaut, a university professor, a lawyer … whatever! You chose differently, which is fine, <u>and</u> the potential for that other choice is still there: latent within you. You could tap some of that potential now, if you wanted to. It is like a bank of reserve batteries, waiting for you to use them. Spend a couple of minutes in this part: tapping into this potential, seeing what is there.
- **Third Part:** This is the place, or the level, where you can go to contact 'That' which is 'greater' than yourself: that which is 'Other'. This is your personal connection to God, the Universe, or where You can be at One with Everything – however you envisage this. There are not good words for this part: it is almost beyond words, beyond language. But most people can connect with something that they can call their Higher Self, or their Guardian Angel, or that part of Them that touches the 'Other', or God, or Allah, or whomsoever you pray to: 'That' which is greater than your Self. I am sure that you know what I mean. Spend a couple of minutes just 'being' Here with the 'Other':

you don't have to pray, or confess, or do anything – just 'be' in or with the Presence.

The whole exercise has taken only about 15-20 minutes. See if you can find the time to do something like this regularly, 3-4 times a week perhaps, as part of your relaxation time, or as a quite meditation in your lunch break, or (as I said) on the bus or train to work. As the weeks unfold, the feelings of your sense of your Self will increase and deepen. There are many facets to a developed Sense of Self (see below) and that particular list might help you to explore other aspects of yourself. And that is what this is all about!

(see also Appendix 2)

EXERCISE 9

DESCENDING INTO THE DARK
An Exercise: A Meditation

This is a form of a guided meditation. It is essentially for you to do for yourself, probably by yourself. Please allow yourself to experience and to express any emotions that you might feel as you are progressing through it. The free expression of emotions (cries, groans, tears, laughter, howls, or whatever) is an important aspect of this exercise. You may therefore need to create a 'safe space', do it when no-one is around, or put a "Do Not Disturb" sign on the door. It could also read "I am having a Spiritual Emergence experience."

The exercise should take at least 20 minutes minimum and it is probably best done lying on a mattress or squab, so that if you roll or thrash around, you won't get hurt. You might want to get someone to read this through and record it onto a tape, with pauses after each paragraph, and where indicated, if you want to do this totally by yourself. Otherwise, it is good to do this exercise reciprocally with a friend; each taking a full half-hour or so for the exercise; then changing roles from reader to 'do-er'; and then discussing it all afterwards. It beats watching most TV shows.

Descend into the Dark by whatever means comes to your mind. A cave, an entrance to the underworld, a river suddenly running underground, a fall into a bottomless pit, the sudden loss of sunlight, or grace, whatever. This is a journey downwards, with no knowing that you will ever return. Many have gone: few, if any, have returned – unchanged that is. The general prognosis is not good. So, go in with some fear and dread.

Acknowledging Mistakes that you have made. Spend a few moments and remember a few of the "large" mistakes that you have made: the ones where you really 'fucked up'. Of course, things worked out one way and another, eventually, but with these lulus – if you could go back and re-do your life – you would redo these ones. Take yourself, step by step, through the experience to the point of mistake. Don't try to avoid, forgive, or excuse. At best, let this be a real leaning experience. At worst, *"Mea culpa, mea culpa, mea maxima culpa."* There is no "Sorry" here.

Acknowledge all pain and distress that you might also have caused to any other people. Spend a while and go back through your life and acknowledge that you may (frequently) have caused others pain and distress. Allow yourself now to feel their pain. Walk in their shoes, feeling about you as they might have done. No time for hubris, here. Allow yourself to really feel their pain – about you.

Allow All your Fears and Demons to come, and to affect you, but not to deviate you too much from your purpose – to descend further. They will constantly be getting "at" you from now on. All sorts – every single one you have ever had – they are all here now; and they are all "at" you – in your face. You are big enough and strong enough, perhaps, to stare them out and carry on: maybe you have to wrestle with them and defeat them, just. The cumulative toll is enormous. You have lots of fears and demons: legions. They are all here now.

Make yourself one promise: *"If I get out of here, I will (at least) do ....x....."* Make it a restitutive action, because, through proper action, we can be possibly be redeemed. This is the time to decide upon an actual action – a penance. Allow the thought to come from within: this is not a 'should' or an 'ought to' situation, what others might determine: it is what you want to do, from deep within yourself, to make restitution, or some sort of amends, or to give some service – not necessarily connected to anyone or to any previous situation – but for the benefit of the world.

Now Descend Further into the Dark: Lack of acknowledgement of any of this material will prevent you from progressing further on your path. Do you really want to stick here – forever? Some people do. Take a few breaths and complete the things you thought about earlier, but didn't want to face. Then, move on.

You Encounter a Major Obstacle– a deep dark river; a chasm; a bottomless pit; a wall of rock; steel doors; a real "nasty" like a Balrog, or the Sphinx. There seems no way past. It's an impossible situation, and yet you cannot stay here – tormented as you are. You may fail, and then that will be it! There is a way through, round, over: a way of getting to beyond this obstacle - and yet you have to find it – Now! It will take every bit of your skill and ingenuity; every bit of courage; every resource – stuff you never thought that you had. You just have to do it.

You get your 'wound' – your just desserts: In overcoming the major obstacle, you receive a wound. You get badly wounded, hurt, or damaged – in exactly the way that goes in the deepest and hurts the most. You suffer, uniquely for you. If you were proud of your athletic prowess; now you are lame. If you were admired for your beauty, you are now scarred. If you won prizes; now you've lost that potential, your edge. This is a real wound, the Real Wound, a Wound to the Soul – the one that is going to be with you forevermore. No quick fix and plastic surgery for this one. In some obscure ways, this is also why you took this road; this wounding was almost inevitable. Before you now realize you were naïve, or you were hiding your wounds. Your previous wounds were scratches. This is real. This is the price that you must pay for this journey, for anything really worthwhile. And yet there is still no guarantee of any gain – only pain. So, you continue on, but now you are wounded.

Long Pause

You Get Lost– hopelessly lost. There is no path; no light; a maze; endless dark corridors. You are all turned around; no way to go; no way to get back. You have no water, no food, no light, and you are wounded. The despair and the inaction arising from this, from being lost here, now seems interminable; is interminable. There is no sense of time. If you collapse, you will die here. There may be reminders (bones) that you come across of others who have failed. So, you carry on – somehow, wherever. You are lost, you are hurt, and you still have to carry on. But the spark of life in you is now fading.

A Light Glows Faintly – yet it grows as you move towards it: Hope arises; but fear arises also. You have no idea what this faint gleam is and yet it is something. Go towards it slowly, very slowly. It could be worse than what was before.

You are Suddenly in the Presence of Something – This "something" is huge, vast and awesome. You don't know what it is. It is almost alien, or something other dimensional. You cannot fight it; run from it; hide from it; trick it; or escape it in any way. Its power is phenomenal and, at this moment, currently benign. It is not threatening: it is Absolute. You can only submit to it – completely, finally, ultimately. This is It! This is the End! There is nowhere else to go. You surrender.

You are now Judged: You are seen totally. This "Something" can look right through you, to your very soul. It sees everything there is about you to see; it knows everything about you to know. Everything that has ever happened to you – ever, this life, past lives, the lot – is seen, and known, and it is all, now, judged. You see everything laid out: absolutely everything. You have no idea of the place, the space, the ways, the mores, the vision, or the perspective from which this judgment comes. Its parameters are nothing like yours, or anyone else's. This "Something" is almost alien in its removed-ness from your life; except that "It" is so knowing, so familiar, so intimate with every detail of your life, and with you, that it is not alien. And so, you are now Judged.

Long Pause

You receive the Judgment. It was total, complete, exact, absolute, terrible, and it was also almost a relief. It was like the Last Judgment. This is absolute and for all time. You will now take with you whatever you were 'given' by this Judge.

Any rules or guidance that you were given, you must now obey implicitly. Any penance or task to perform, you must perform it completely. This Judgment lasts – for the rest of your life, and for all time. This is now part of You. You will wear this, or carry this now and forever.

You Begin the Return: After a long time, somehow, and by some path, you very slowly begin to move upwards. And you return, slowly, more gently than the descent, to the upper levels. Level after level passes before you. It is not an easy road. It may be very different from before. And there is a growing certainty that this road, this ascent, will lead you back, is leading you back, back to the world above, back here, back in to this room, back to the present now. And now you are back, and here, in the now, and you are also changed.

Work out what the Changes are. You may still be shamed, or wounded. You did make a promise. You overcame almost insurmountable difficulties. You got lost. You despaired. You survived. You were judged. That will stay with you – and ... All this has changed you. So, you are now different – what, how? Even if you fell asleep, all these things still happened on one level. Spend a while exploring what this difference, this change, actually is. Write or memorise an account of your journey of your Descent into the Dark.

Pause for 5- 10 minutes

Now, the exercise is over. Please spend some more time, maybe another ten minutes or so, doing things quietly and gently – but in silence. Get yourself a cup of tea, have a pee, etc. Finish up your writing. Maybe draw or paint something, an impression or image. At some point, find a friend and discuss this experience with them, or talk about this to someone in a supportive setting (co-counselling, therapy, etc.) This helps to concretize the experience. Be sure to keep the Promise as well!

EXERCISE 10

IMAGINE YOUR FAMILY 'SYSTEM' AS A CHESSBOARD

There is considerable 'evidence' that our original family 'system' can be dysfunctional in later life: we do not choose our family, we are born into it and then have to cope with whatever we experience. These experiences can be damaging. Obviously, some families are excellent, loving and supportive. People from such families are somewhat 'blessed'. Even given such a positive start, such people may face difficulties in later life – for which they are not prepared. People from more dysfunctional families have to 'cope' with such difficulties, yet they often feel that 'they' are the problem, not the family. This exercise is designed to give a somewhat different perspective.

So, here is another exercise: Imagine your Family 'System' (or 'Structure') as a large Chessboard in the park. In this imaginary exercise, there is a King (Father = F), a Queen (Mother = M) and at least two Pawns: Siblings: Brother (B) & Sister (S). (You can expand this exercise as far as you like, until the analogy breaks down.)

In your imagery, there are also elastic bands (two-way arrows) that link each member to each other member: indicating a two-way relationship: from A to B and from B to A.

In a family of 4, there are 12 relationships (3 x 4=12): F⇔M; F⇔B; F⇔S; B⇔S; M⇔S; M⇔B. However, in a family of 5, there would be 20 (5 x 4) different relationships; in a family of 6 (possibly including grandparents), there would be 30 (6 x 5) different relationships; and so on.

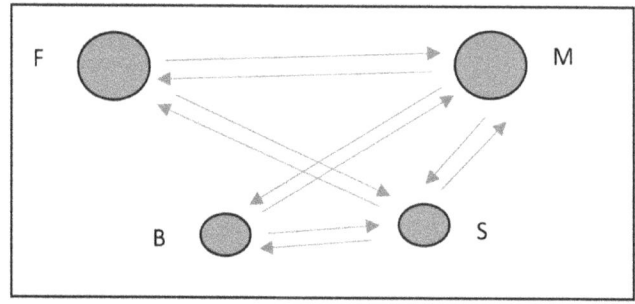

There are, of course, further complications, not gone into detail here in that, between any two people, there are probably more than just two relationships: for example, traditional Psychoanalysis theorises that an individual has three levels of functioning: the Superego (governed by moral and social dynamics), the Ego (more the Self, or who you think you are), and the more instinctual, primitive or inherited Id state; Transactional Analysis psychotherapy posits relationships between Personal Ego States, Adult Ego States and Child Ego States; and Psychosynthesis psychotherapy posits a lower unconscious, a middle unconscious and a higher unconscious, along with a collective unconscious, a conscious self and a higher self. However, in this example, we will stick with just two relationships: A to B and B to A; or Me to You and You to Me.

In your family of origin, please identify the truly 'significant' people: adults and children – and then try to place them appropriately: who is close to whom; and who is further away from whom. The two-way relationships are signified by imagining elastic bands between them.

Please include any close grandparents, step-parents, uncles, aunts, siblings, or friends and neighbours, who go to make up (or are a significant part of) your immediate family 'system', when you were growing up.

These other people can be signified by bishops, knights, rooks (castles), or other pawns. If we now place all these family members as if they were chess pieces on a large Chessboard (as in the park), consider who is close to, or who seems a long way away from, whom. Please take some time and thought over these placements, as they might become significant later on.

Now, there will be periods in your life when these 'familiar – familial' relationships are relatively 'fixed' (or stable) over the years, but also – at some point in time – the relationships – the distancing and the positions – may change, sometimes even drastically: your parents might have gotten divorced, and/or re-married, or one of you siblings might die, or move away, or go to university, or whatever; grandparents may die; some people in the close family may move to different parts of the country; and you may discover that you are much closer to some of these people, etc.

When these sorts of changes happen, these people (signified by these chess-pieces on the board in the park) often experience actual (psychic) changes in the tensions between them: the tension of these elastic bands.

They will then get 'pulled' one way or another: they will feel nearer (or closer) to their other family members. They will experience these as 'changes' in the relationships: *"You seem so distant nowadays"*; *"Golly how you have grown. I wouldn't have recognised you."* You may also feel quite 'different' to some of these family members than the way you did before the changes, some time ago. Explore these dynamics for a while: maybe even with a therapist, or (better still) someone else who was present and might have had a very different perspective on these events: *Oh, you seemed to be coping"* or *"I tried telling X that you seemed to me to be very unhappy, but they said 'Oh, there's no problem. He will get over it!'* and this different perspective can be quite shocking in itself: *"I never knew you felt that!"* or *"You seemed so distant: I wish I had known"*.

However, these changes usually result from 'natural', 'normal' family tensions: all pulling one way or another. Yet some people take these changes in tensions personally – these changes start to 'complicate' their 'natural' relationships. This may be illustrative of what has happened to you – and to everyone else on the planet – throughout time!

Now, put yourself first into one of these positions; then into another; and so on; allowing yourself to 'feel' these changes, these different tensions – from these different perspectives.

So, now, in this exercise, imagine that you are walking around this family system for a few moments: taking a stroll in the park! Look at these dynamic tensions from the outside, rather than just from the different inside positions: it can be a very different perspective.

However, this is what happens to all of us, in different ways and at different times. We experience our family 'systems' or 'structures' in different ways from our original (single, personal) perspective – and then that changes: and then it changes again, and how! So, how do we now see these changes and how did we cope with these changes then. There are no rules, no strategies, no guarantees!

There is also no blame. This is just what happened. Person A moved away; or grew close; or was suddenly 'gone' from our lives. Person B then became more significant; or more distant. This is just what happened – then. We might have wanted something different; but this is what we got. We experienced this – or that – as a loss, a tragedy, or as a blessing, a gift. But, how do we see it now? In retrospect, with hindsight. Does it change?

Take some time over this exercise. Come back to it occasionally. Maybe use an actual chessboard and labels for the different people. Move them around until you feel that this configuration is significant. Did it stay this way? Or did it change?

In this way you can re-examine and possibly even 'liberate' yourself from – get out of – these 'family' systems and dynamics.

You can become more of who you are now!

The point of all these exercises is to help you to discover more about yourself and your 'images', or your 'psychic' self. Take care when you do these exercises: it is probably better to do them with someone whom you trust.

We are often much more than who we think we are.

EXERCISE 11

BETTER MENTAL HEALTH: GUIDED REFLECTIONS

There is overwhelming evidence that almost any form of regular meditation, mindfulness practice, contemplation, or whatever – improves and maintains your mental health.

Possessing a human mind and body is an almost unimaginable gift. Yet, at the same time, this stressful overload also means that – over time – we can become subject to anxiety, fear and uncertainty. Becoming distracted or looking away (as we often do) our body still ages, time still passes, our problems don't go away. Finances, jobs, health, and relationships can shift our attention away from ourselves in a moment, like being blown away the wind. How can we hope to make sense of all of this without being overwhelmed and saddened?

You will need to set some proper time aside to do this exercise. Make some space and time that is quiet and undisturbed. With all of life's chaos and distractions, it can be quite a challenge to switch off, to focus and reflect inwardly. Practice this exercise regularly.

But, while all of this is part of our everyday human experience, we need the regular practice of reflection in order to help us to better understand and accept the nature and mystery of our being.

Think of the following reflections as – something like – a trusty companion, a touchstone to carry with you on your journey; part of your regular everyday practice. Read these reflections more than once. Immerse yourself in these concepts in this practice. Like being a river flowing into the ocean, let them carry you towards greater openness; allow your spaciousness of heart and mind open our soul.

1. **Joy abounds mostly in the small nooks and crannies of life.** Find joy in ordinary moments, like: Taking a step and feeling your body move; eating and digesting an apple; watching a hummingbird mid-flight; taking your next breath. You can – of course – wait for some big, dramatic moment or accomplishment to punctuate your life. Or you

can be receptive to the ordinary and unforeseen joys right before you. Reflect on some of these concepts.
- Reviewing the past week, what ordinary moments and what extra-ordinary moments, can you remember and savour?
- How can you more readily recognize these ordinary and extra-ordinary moments that invite pleasure and joy?
- Find one ordinary thing that nourishes you with joy. How might you share this experience with others?

2. **Your body is the elegant integrator of your inner-outer world experiences.** Bliss lives in each bodily sensation. Grow silent and listen. Feel each heartbeat as it tingles in your fingertips. Feel each breath as it caresses your lungs. See each vibrant image and colour as it glints in your eye. Tap into your personal inner-outer, and know the bliss of the Here-and-Now. Reflect on these aspects within your body. Reflect on all of this.
   - How does your body mediate your inner and outer experiences?
   - How can you slow down enough to find peace and acceptance for whatever the body is sensing right now?
   - Regularly, tune into your body's entire orchestra of experiences, movements, and sensations. How does a greater level of embodiment change things for you?

3. **There's a silver lining in everything.** Yes, there are things you hate, that disrupt your life, and that grate upon your nerves. But how solid and permanent are these? With each phenomenon you witness, there is also a silver lining that materializes with the passage of time. Loosen up, and look back into your past. Try to reflect on what you might have learnt from that bad experience. Then, you will find the grace of silver linings. It is the silver linings that make life rich and meaningful. Reflect on these.
   - What loss in your life has made space for other doors to open for you?

- What is an example from your life of something that initially you thought was bad, but which turned out to have a positive consequence?
- Today, what's it like to actively find a silver lining for a challenge that's occurring in your life right now?

4. **What is your Purpose in this Life?** We are all here to learn, and – through our various incarnations, though all our various lifetimes – we gradually learn, grow and strengthen; we gradually become wiser, and more filled with Light and Love. The effectiveness of these life-long lessons depend on us being able to maintain our connection to the Light, to Spirit, or to G*d (by whatever Name you use). We need to keep maintaining this connection, on a day-to-day, moment-to-moment basis.
    - At various times in our life, we have made choices – for good, or that were not so good. These latter choices we **must** learn from, otherwise they are just painful and destructive.
    - In this life, what sense do you have of your purpose?
    - What experiences in your life might have been connected to your life purpose? How can you learn from these?

EXERCISE 12

BETTER MENTAL HEALTH: YOGA &/OR TAI CHI

Yoga is a form of mind-body exercise, which has become an increasingly widespread therapy used to maintain wellness, and alleviate a range of health problems and ailments. Yoga should be considered as a complementary therapy, or as an alternative (to medical/pharmaceutical) therapy in the treatment of stress, anxiety, depression, and other mood disorders. It has been shown (in numerous research studies) to create a greater sense of well-being, increase feelings of relaxation, improve self-confidence and body image, improve efficiency, promote better interpersonal relationships, increase attentiveness, lower irritability, and encourage an optimistic outlook on life.

A purely medical approach is far less effective in healing the emotional, intellectual, and personality layers of the human entity. The disciplines of these alternative practices offer individuals a timeless and holistic model of health and healing and, although it may not result in the complete elimination of physical diseases and/ or adverse conditions from the body, they offer a holistic path towards healing. There exists an indisputable connection between a person's overall physical and mental health and their inner peace and well-being that disciplines like Yoga and Tai Chi are designed to achieve. They suspend the fluctuations of the mind and, by acting more consciously, we live better and suffer less.

Health professionals and researchers are only just beginning to understand how disciplines, such as Yoga and/or Tai Chi, can promote personal growth, health and well-being. There has been so much focus in the past on illness, that a focus on wellness is rare. By acknowledging the unity of mind, body and spirit, mind-body fitness programs (i.e. Yoga, Tai Chi, Qi-Gong, etc.) can assist people in their pursuit of peace, calmness, greater wholeness, and integration in their lives. Health care professionals, health educators, and the like, need to be much more aware of the potential of these 'alternative' disciplines (such as Yoga & Tai Chi) as an important component of a personal wellness plan.

It is quite likely that there are classes locally, near you: you should try one of these out and see if it is right for you. With Qi-Gong, you can probably find various exercises on the Internet. It will probably take quite a while (at least a couple of months of regular attendance) before you begin to feel the real benefits of these disciplines.

While no concrete guidelines exist regarding the frequency of practice, the more you practice, the more you benefit. Both Yoga & Tai Chi are personalized practices, and as such, frequency and duration are personal questions with individual answers. Practice should happen with wisdom and should be modified to meet individual needs and goals. Individuals should practice as often as possible, especially in the beginning stages. The length of any induction phase will vary, depending on an individual's initial level of fitness and their health status. The more difficult practices are not for someone in the beginning stages, where the main benefits are basic health and what their body/mind needs.

BASIC SPIRITUAL PRINCIPLES

Since there are not many Mystery Schools still around nowadays and good gurus are really hard to find or live in India; and, nice as they are, 'The Celestine Prophesies' are just fictional, so I have put together some basic Spiritual Principles to help you on your journey. You do not have to accept all, or indeed any of these: but some of them may help you a bit. These spiritual principles have been developed and gleaned from many different traditions. Most of the source books are included in the Reading List.

No Expectations: Be Fully Present Now! Feel who you are, where you are, what you are; now! Expectations can really do you over. You create them and then they can disappoint you. You are disappointing yourself. Breathe in; breathe out. If you are here and now, fully present, doing whatever - the washing up, driving, making love, filing papers - then do it fully. Put all your being into what you are doing now. Get ecstatic about it even, or just notice that you are doing it without a lot of enjoyment. Cultivate an interested observer rather than a judge. "Oh, that's interesting!" "Oh, now it has changed." Do not expect anything. Clear the board. Do not assume anything. Try to clear all preconceptions. Stay exactly and precisely with what is here, and what is now. That is all there is!

You Can't Trust Anything! There has been a human society for 6,000 years (at least), which has been pretty well male-dominated, hierarchical, aggressive, polluting, materialistic, racist, and rationalistic. These pervasive principles have denigrated nearly everything and everything else. There has also been an increasing separation from the body, sensuality, sexuality, emotions, and pure pleasure without guilt etc. for the last 6,000 years (at least). We are also quite quickly devastating the planet. Spirituality has been rationalised, denied, marginalized, separated from the individual, stolen from us, made into a Church or religion, confined to the priesthood, gurus, or mystified in some way, for at least 4,000 years. Thus, we have all been fundamentally lied to, enslaved, and cheated – all the way down the line. Our dreams and our goals are therefore very distorted. You think you want something, so think again. You are a fully paid-up member of the society that is causing the problems: you can't trust what you want, or indeed anything else.

Go Within! The only smidgeon of truth that you may be able to find is deep, deep inside you. And it is simple. You'll know it when you find it. You won't find it just by using your head, or just your body. You won't find it outside of you. Anything outside of you might be able to show you a Way, but it won't be the Way. "God" lies within and you are connected to "God" through your spirit. The Way to Spirit and to a sense of "That Which is Greater than Thyself" lies through the body, through the Feelings, through Inner Contemplation. Truth lies within and it takes an effort to get there; to get through all the stuff in the way, the stuff of your own history and the crap that society feeds you. So, practice "Inner Listening" – just listen. There is, at first, a lot of crap, and garbage in the way: the dross of everyday life: things to do, laundry lists, etc. Then there is all the "gabble" of the feelings - "if only...", "I should have...", just let this go as well, don't get caught in it, and go in deeper. You'll get there eventually: you just have to go within and keep listening.

Spirituality v. Religion: There is a substantial difference between spirituality and religion. Spirituality is a matter for the individual. The Dalai Lama says: *"I believe that each individual should embark upon a spiritual path that is best suited to his or her mental disposition, natural inclination, temperament, belief, family and cultural background."* Religions are historical channels for some of these peoples' spiritual paths; they are meant to nourish the human spirit, guide an individual's path in certain ethical behaviours, and make an effective contribution to the development of humanity. They have done all of these. They have also been a source of many conflicts and divisions, wars and suffering. So, closer bonds of understanding and respect between different religions are needed.

Trust Your Process: This is a difficult one, especially if your process has been somewhat traumatic. Let me use the analogy of puberty and adolescence. When one's teenage body first begins to change, adolescent spots, puppy fat, dizzy spells, the menarche (onset of a girl's periods), are all aspects of this process of physical maturation. As soon as these are explained simply and clearly, one does not see these things any longer as an aberration, illness or pathology, but as something that is well within the normal course of events and as something that will also pass. Thus, you learn to trust the process (of puberty & adolescence) and not to panic at the onset of those various symptoms. A spiritual process is somewhat similar. One has to allow and learn to accept the sometimes (also) very frightening and bizarre symptoms, and try to stay in touch with what the underlying developmental process of one's emerging spirit is. This can be very difficult, as our society does not have proper concepts, language or structures for this process. The analogy of a 'Path' or 'Journey' is often useful.

Know Thyself! The greatest oracle of the ancient Mediterranean world was at Delphi. For maybe 1500 years or more, people travelled long distances and braved great hazards just in order to come to Delphi to hear the 'voice of God': as the God Apollo spoke through the medium of the oracle. This was known, accepted, and as matter of fact as we nowadays turn on the radio or TV to listen to the news or a speech made in Parliament – not that there is any real comparison, except that they are both as obscure as each other, for the Oracle spoke in riddles and metaphors. However, to get to the point, the single most important thing that they could think of to carve in stone above the cave leading to the Oracle was *"Know Thyself!"*. That was it! Do that, and you are ready to hear the Voice of God.

Spiritual Practice or Meditation is Very, Very Important: Some form of regular spiritual practice or meditation is fundamentally necessary to anyone who is trying to facilitate their emerging spiritual process. This is pretty universally held across all belief systems, religions, cultures and philosophies, and what can be often linked with "Knowing Thyself", is that the way to do this is through some form of regular spiritual practice and/or inner meditation. This is essential for the training and development of your mental state, your attitudes and psychological & emotional well-being. Rituals, movement forms, silence, prayers, chants, special times and places, and special words can all be a means to this end, but they are not the end in themselves. The desired goal is the state of mind or being (see below) that only really occurs through such a regular spiritual practice or meditation.

Cultural Aspects: Different cultures have different perspectives on these issues:

"The man who sat on the ground in his tipi meditating on life and its meaning, accepting the kinship of all creatures and acknowledging the unity with the universe of things was infusing into his being the true essence of civilisation. And when native man left off this form of development, his humanization was retarded in growth."
Chief Luther Standing Bear
(from McLuhan's *Touch the Earth*)

This quotation indicates that meditation is not just an Eastern form: it is common to many cultures, and also within the established Christian churches, Orthodox, Catholic and Protestant churches, in the West, though it's practice there is more often linked to a particular text or passage to be studied. It doesn't have to be done half-naked with one's body in a contorted position, nor in any special way. I used to meditate a lot walking: just sitting still does my head in and I'm not very good at that form of meditation. What I do know is that the lack of any form of meditation *really* does my head in. What must be done is to meditate regularly; once or twice a day.

The goals of all these various inner spiritual practices and meditations are usually: a calmness of mind; greater objectivity; increased compassion towards & caring for others; more tolerance; a forgiveness for others' & one's own transgressions; a connection with that which is greater than ourselves; an inner stability; an increased ability to withstand life's suffering; a reduction of anxiety; the elimination of anger and hatred; a sustenance for one's faith; an ongoing developmental personal improvement & change; a variety of different perceptions; an increasing depth of realizations and understanding; improved mental health; and a sense of peace and deep happiness. Not bad, if you can achieve it! So, get stuck in on a regular basis.

Less is More: The spiritual principle embodied in this statement here is that a little movement, or taking just one step, or focussing on the immediate detail, or not trying to do anything too big, actually gives you more, or helps you go further, or is more significant. We can get sometimes get lost in the confusion of bigger picture: so focus just on the single brick in front of you. Chew just one mouthful; don't try to eat the whole plate at once. Deal with this little bit now; get to know this bit, just this bit, a little better, and then the rest will take on a new and different perspective. Focus on the next step, and then you will know better what your next step is, and you can then focus on that: keeping looking at the goal and you may miss out on a simple turn in the road. Lao Tse says: *"In the universe, great acts are made up of small deeds. The sage does not attempt anything very big. And thus achieves greatness."* He also writes (in the Tao Te Ching), *"Less and less do you need to force things, until finally you arrive at non-action. When nothing is done, nothing is left undone."* 'Nothing is done' because the doer and the deed have become part of the universal flow. Doing is less than being. There are many different interpretations.

Attitude is Important: Amy Mindell in *"Metaskills: The Spiritual Art of Therapy"* writes well about this very well. What we do, and where we do it, is often not so significant as *how* we do it. But before we acquire the right 'how', our attitude to the Path is important. Are we following this Path in order to achieve greatness and glory? I hope not. Or are we following with a degree of humility and pleasure? Do we meet challenges aggressively, or masochistically? Or do we say, "How interesting!" and maybe even greet difficulties with humour, "Hah-ha, this One again! Back for more work!" Of the people you meet, what attitudes attract you? This may be significant for you, now. The person who you are attracted to may not be your Teacher, but try and spend some time in their company, and acquire something of their 'attractive' attitude. Much of the 'teaching' at the spiritual community of Findhorn (where I lived for 17 years) was to understand, on a basic level, that just (cleaning the toilets) is not enough; they should be cleaned with Love. This also happens a lot in the preparation of food. We also tried to take major decisions this way, paying great attention to 'how' the decision is made, and becoming less attached to the actual outcome.

Your Path will contain both Curiosity and Confusion: You won't get anywhere without Curiosity. This is an innate principle that drives us humans forward. You have it within you, and it may have been dulled or repressed: *"Don't ask Questions!"* was a frequent parental admonition. So, you can cultivate Curiosity now, as well as Enquiry, Inquisitiveness, Learning, and Concern. Ask "How?" and "Why?" Go into 'Explorer-mode' – logical, developmental enquiry. You won't ever get a fully satisfactory answer without some of this, but you will at least be searching. Without Curiosity, you should have stayed at home.

On the other hand, Confusion can tell you that you are getting closer to an important answer. *"What is this? I don't understand,"* means that you are probably on the brink of something new. You are coming to an 'edge' between the known and the unknown, at least in yourself. You cannot ever pass through this Veil into New Knowledge without meeting Confusion, however you can sometimes also get lost in Confusion, so it is not an infallible guide. This may mean that you are trying too hard. Use some of the other Basic Spiritual Principles as well.

The Path contains Opposing Polarities: Sometimes it is necessary to discover that directly opposite views are both true: something is good **and** bad; right **and** wrong; etc. This seems paradoxical. However, it is often not "either... or...", it is more of "both... and..." What you have to do in these situations is to hold these seemingly conflicting opposites as both true, at the same time, even though they seem totally contradictory. Do this, and then you will get to the Greater Truth behind this.

This maxim is essentially Taoist in perspective, and again the *Tao Te Ching* informs us well on this point. In Western terms, you hold both these opposites as true in a state of 'Creative Tension'. There is truth 'here' and there is truth 'there', even though 'here' and 'there' seem opposed to each other. Eventually, a third, deeper truth will manifest itself beyond these two two-dimensional truths that seemed to have existed and contradicted themselves before. This is the real Truth we are after.

This Too Will Pass: There is an ancient Sufi teaching story attributed to the famous Sufi, Attar of Nishapur, an inspirer of Rumi. Once there was a ruler who wanted a magic charm so that when he was happy, he didn't get too elated and out of touch with the sorrows of the world; and when he was sad, he wouldn't get too depressed, and so he could become joyful again. All his magicians failed in making such a charm, and then a wandering Sufi philosopher, Nasruddin, heard of the king's problem and proposed an easy solution. *"Make a ring,"* he advised, *"and on it have these words enscribed: 'This Too Will Pass.'"*

We all need to be constantly reminded of the impermanence of everything, and especially of our feelings. It is a very important spiritual principle, found in many traditions. The Buddhist concept of the world as "Maya" or illusion echoes this principle. We can find similar sentiments in Ecclesiastes: *"Vanity of vanities, saith the Preacher, vanity of vanities; all is vanity."*

You are Alone and You are Not Alone: Everyone is struggling, the same as you, but probably in a different place and on a different path. You will meet lots of wonderful 'helpers' on the Way: friends, partners, lovers, teachers, and enemies. And they will leave you after a while, inevitably. You will need to walk alone at times. These people also have their own Path to follow. They grow and change as well as you. It is very rare (except in fiction or fable) that two people will be together forever. Rumi takes a slightly different perspective and writes: *"The minute I heard my first love story I started looking for you, not knowing how blind that was. Lovers don't finally meet somewhere. They're in each other all along."*

The Path contains Inevitable Pain: There is no easy road, and the Path to Truth and to Spirit inevitably contains pain. You cannot stay naïve and innocent: you have to grow and learn. It is very painful leaving the state of Innocence. Unfortunately, you have to suffer this; there is no other way. Scott Peck, in *The Road Less Travelled* writes: "Life is Difficult." Expect that this is so, and it is less difficult than if you expect otherwise. Along that road, you are essentially alone, which can be also painful and lonely. This solitude is necessary to become an individual.

You will also need to make mistakes, and these mistakes are painful. You have to make mistakes as, only by so doing, do you learn what is 'right' and 'wrong' for you. After a while, you will get better at it and things will get less painful. But the learning never stops, and there is never no pain. Pain is part of life and pain is part of this path – inevitably. Get used to it; it is your best teacher, as you may have a tendency to learn much faster when you are in pain, than in more pleasurable situations, when you get to enjoy (and prolong) the lesson. However, the Path is not only one of pain. There are many joys, and moments of stillness and even occasional ecstasy as well.

There are many Different Levels: Both within yourself and outside of yourself, nothing is simple. You can feel things on many different levels; and you can operate on many different levels. What seems true here, may not be true at a different level, or it will be true in a different way. This is both confusing and useful. What is true on one level may not be totally true on another. If you get stuck on one level, you can always switch to another level. This is practiced a lot in Arnold Mindell's Process Work.

There is no simple truth, yet when you discover the 'Truth' it is always beautifully elegant; it has an aesthetic simplicity. And you will know it is True because it is simple and beautiful and because it works on all levels. Does this seem contradictory? It is all right: it is!

There is a difference between Techniques and Principles: As you go along the Path, and as you discover your own truths or aspects of the truths, you will need to develop your own techniques. These techniques will develop fairly naturally for you out of the interaction between your experiences and these principles. Uesiba, the founder of Aikido, says that the techniques are not set in stone, but must transform from moment to moment. The survival techniques that we learn as children frequently become inappropriate when we become adults. Don't confuse techniques with principles. Ultimately, you will have to drop the techniques anyway, and just live according to whatever principles you have discovered. (Incidentally, these principles are only a few of the very basic ones and they may not all be right for you.)

In order to be Strong, you will need Fluidity: Strength does not lie in Rigidity. Try wearing a suit of armour in battle all day and then try making love, or cuddling your children whilst it is still on: it just doesn't work. A truly strong person is one who can take their armour off, and still survive. Strength is adjusting to what is happening in the moment: rigidity can work against you. What worked 'then', probably doesn't work 'now'. And the 'now' changes – all the time. Change with it. Nothing natural is fixed; everything changes. Become like a Tai Chi or an Aikido Master. Discover what the flow or the direction of change is, and then go with it. It is also a lot easier this way. Sometimes the Path is more like a river, and you need to be alert and fluid with it, as it changes every moment. Spontaneity is very important. With these tools, the journey become more effortless and you will become stronger, through flexibility.

Don't Push the River: This is another principle to do with the process of change and being on the spiritual path. On the one hand it refers to the principle of trying not to force events: *"Go with the Flow"* is an aspect of this, and, in this light, it is somewhat similar to *"Less is More"*. But there is another aspect too. Your spiritual path can seem as if you are suddenly in a powerful and stormy river being carried along seemingly out of control. Many people spend a lot of time and effort trying to swim upstream back to where they were before in their lives, when 'everything was all right'. We hanker after our previous lives, the stability and even the 'known' dysfunctions (as we desperately fear the 'unknown') and we try to put everything back into "Pandora's Box". However, our process, the River, is carrying us somewhere else: it is transforming us. If you swim with the current, you are just as wet, but it is a whole lot easier; you are less frustrated and looking back to the past; you are seeing where this journey will take you; and you may find that you can even be able to swim to the bank on occasions and rest for a bit. There is another danger: "Pushing the River" might also mean trying to force change. You need to allow the speed (or slowness) of the process of change: it is complex. Sometimes, we want it all to be over; sometimes we want it to end up in a certain place: Don't Push the River!

The Time for the Next Step is Now: This principle relates to the metaphor of the spiritual path as a journey by land. If you are already thinking about the next step, and know what it is, take it now. Procrastination is not just the Thief of Time, but it is also the Delayer, the Ball and Chain, the Drain of Spontaneity. The next step is always just in front of you. At any moment you can take it and change, but which moment are you going to choose? What people sometimes forget is that you can also take a step backward if you discover fairly immediately that that next step isn't the exact right one for them. Take it and find out. Now! If it's not right for you, step back and try another step. This does not mean also that the next step for you might be to take some time out. This is a conscious choice; is a next step; and may be absolutely right for a while. You are still on the Journey, but just taking some time out from the Journey.

There is no 'Fixed End': Incidentally this journey has no final goal, no Celestial City waiting for you; no Promised Land beyond the River; no Pot of Gold at the end of the Rainbow; no Happily Ever After; no Land of Promise (TirTairngire) or Land of Eternal Youth (Tir nan Og). These are all metaphors for the state of Enlightenment that one can reach whilst one is on the Journey – and part of that state of enlightenment is when you realise that the goal IS the Journey itself and perhaps to 'Travel Well' is the best of all the Ultimate Goals that any of us can achieve.

The Myths and Legends are really our Road Maps: Joseph Campbell is one of our modern 'heroes' as he realized, and demonstrated, that all the old myths and legends, the 'fairy stories' in every culture, are all teaching stories: that is why they are so powerful, and have lasted for so long. The Mabinogion, the Upanishads, the Vedas, Greek Myths, Grimm's Fairy Tales, the Celtic Book of the Dead, the Tales of King Arthur, American Indian Legends: these are the wisdom of the ages. These tell us how to live. They tell us of the mistakes that we can (and will almost inevitably) make; and how to overcome these. The Bible, the Koran, the Torah, and the teachings of Confucius and Buddha, instead tell us how we should live: however, they also include a morality, a direction. That is one of the differences between religion and spirituality.

Live Your Dreams: The dreams and ideals that you have may be aspects of the inner workings of your mind. If you are really and truly on the spiritual path, then you may need to live them out, not just to see if they are real or not, but also in order to be fully and uniquely you. However, there is more to this Principle than that. The Australian aboriginals live in "Dreamtime" and here they are informed by the spirits of the land and animals: they think that the reason the white men are crazy is that they don't live in dreamtime and are cut off from these spirits. In Celtic mythology, you find something similar: John & Caitlin Matthews write: *"This Otherworld of wonders is a still living dimension to which all mortals can relate. It transcends but also intersects the reality we call 'everyday life'. It is the source from which inspiration comes. It is accessible through that burning glass of the soul – the imagination – which is nothing less than our doorway to the Otherworld, through which come the dreams, visions and ideas which transform ordinary reality."* Albert Einstein developed the Theory of Relativity after having had a dream, and there are many similar stories throughout human history.

Responsibility for... and Responsibility to... are very different: You are responsible for yourself and for yourself alone. Every single one of your thoughts, actions and inactions are fully and totally your responsibility. No-one else is involved; no one else takes the credit, or picks up the mess. Get it! However, you are also responsible to every other living thing, seen and unseen, on this planet as well as to (at least seven) future generations: now – there's a thought-form! A butterfly flaps its wings in a Brazilian forest and a hurricane devastates Britain? Your thoughts, emotions and actions can (possibly) affect everyone else around you. They may have legitimate questions about what you are doing, and how you are doing it. You are also totally responsible <u>for</u> yourself <u>and</u> to others. Get it?

There Are No Mistakes: There are no wrong decisions, no mistakes - just lessons or experiments which either did not work out, in which case you learnt something, or they did work out, in which case you also learnt something. Carlos Casteneda in his 'Don Juan' books says (something like) this: *"A magician never regrets an action; because when he regrets it, it means that not only has he not taken a good decision, but it means he also didn't spend enough time thinking about it first."* Truly seeing that there are no mistakes means that a lot of unnecessary guilt and regret is removed – forever. That does not mean that we should never regret anything: only that most of the guilt and regret that we experience needs to be re-evaluated. Causing pain to others by our actions (or inactions) needs to be regretted: that is how we learn kindness: being unkind and arrogant needs to be regretted in order to learn compassion; and so on.

Switching texts and metaphors for a moment; after the age of innocence ended, and all the evils and tribulations (those things to be overcome) were released out of Pandora's Box (a metaphor) and let loose into the world, remember the last thing that was in the Box? Hope was the last thing.

There Is 'No Right Way': Imagine a mountain rising up from a plain towards the sky and a ring of people standing all around the mountain. They all point to the path immediately in front of them and say, *"This is the Right Way up the Mountain"*. Of course, they are all right, <u>and</u> they are also all wrong. Some even start to fight about it. There is no single 'Right Way': it is "the" that is the problem. Religions can get like this. If you go into the metaphor a little deeper, the Right Way for You can sometimes change. What was 'Right' then, may not be so 'Right' now, and you may need to cast around a little to find the new 'Right Way' for 'You'. It is up to us to find the 'Right Way' for ourselves now, in this moment, with these issues. Sometimes, relationships are the answer; sometimes solitude; sometimes therapy; sometimes work; sometimes a teacher; sometimes an established religion; it varies constantly. There are also no "Stairways to Heaven"; no "Fast Tracks"; no "Celestial Escalators" and the religious rules usually just tell us what not to do. We all have to climb the mountain, one step after another, finding our own route, doing it 'Our Way'.

There Is No Absolute Truth: There are also no Absolute Truths, for there is nearly always a qualifying statement. That *"One and One equals Two"* is only true for certain number systems: in Binary, the answer is One Zero. *"God is Love"* depends upon your belief system. *"Thou shalt not kill"* might depend on whether the person is trying to kill you, your loved ones, or not. This statement, *"There is no Absolute Truth"* should also be challenged in the same way.

Love is All Powerful: Nearly every religion and philosophy advocates focusing on this main quality. Christian Science believes that there are only two synonyms for God: Love and Truth, and that everything else is illusion or 'Error' (bad thinking). The Bible says: *"Faith, Hope and Charity (Love) are the three great virtues. But the greatest of these is Charity (Love)."* Scott Peck in *The Road Less Travelled* speaks of a psychological definition of Love as being a *"a prioritisation of and commitment to the other person's spiritual path"*. Rumi constantly speaks about the 'Beloved' as the principle that is behind or beyond the 'Loved One': *"Whose idea was this, to have the lover visible and the Beloved invisible!"* Peter Caddy, one of the founders of the Findhorn Foundation, said: *"Work is Love in Action"*. The Japanese temple builders in Hokkaido are dismissed if they ever get angry when they are working: only Love and Peace can be 'built' into the temples. Find out what moves you deeply: and that is Love. Find out what makes your heart sing: and that is Love.

The "Perilous Question": This phrase is embedded into the legend of the Grail Quest. When Parsifal, the Innocent Knight, arrived at the Grail Castle, in his naivety and innocence, he did not ask the obvious question when he noticed the contrast between, on one hand, the Abundance of the Grail and, on the other, the fact that the castle was in a Wasteland and the King of the Castle was wounded, with a wound which did not heal. He had been told by his mother not to ask questions. Anyway, the point is about the Perilous Question: *"How can this Wound be Healed?"* He didn't ask this question. So next morning, he found himself outside the Grail Castle, in The Wasteland, and it took him 20 years in the School of Hard Knocks to find his way back.

So, take a risk. Ask yourself this question: *"How can this Wound be Healed."* and you will probably get an answer. However, most of us don't want to ask the question, as it means acknowledging the "wound" and the answer might take us over a particular edge; it might expose us to our part in the problem; our addictions that are in the way; our shame, guilt or fear. And many, many of us don't even want to acknowledge that we are wounded in the first place, that the problem really exists, as we would prefer to pretend that we are whole, or that we can just stay anaesthetised, etc. So ... you now have a simple way of cutting through all the confusions and denials. If you ask the question that actually acknowledges that there is a wound that needs healing; or there something wrong that needs righting, and the question acknowledges the possibility of healing as well; you will get an answer; if not immediately – then very soon. Then, it is up to you to act on that knowledge: that is the perilous part, but it is also the most productive

Personal Angels: Here, we use some Christian imagery. You have your personal Angel & Daemon with you – always! Your personal 'Guardian Angel' is always present, always totally there for you, pushing you forward, helping you grow, doing what is best for you, whenever you want them, working purely for your best interests – and sometimes also helping you when you get stuck. They can give you a little nudge, or kick, even if you might be enjoying being stuck, or stuck with one of your personal addictions. Sometimes, the 'nudge' gets a bit stronger if you have not been paying attention.

By the way, you also carry a personal Daemon with you – all the time - who can take on any shape, any form: who can 'embody' anything that which is needed to be as your next challenge. If you are having a problem with someone, it may be that your Daemon has taken that form for a while; has chosen that person to help you grow. Talk to them regularly. Discuss with them what and how you need to do next. Get to know these two. They are your Companions on the Journey and this is all part of the package of being Human. Learn to live with it!

Angels: We can also sometimes embody other people's angels, as they do ours – usually only for a short time or at an extreme moment. This is perhaps imagery again; perhaps not. Sometimes, other people can act in place of our angel; or when you have a sudden surge of compassion for someone, their angel has just entered into you. Little miracles can also and will happen, time and time again, and again, and again; and we don't really know why or how. We have no idea. This is the work of (our) Angels. From a different perspective, if you are in the flow of things, then you can see or sense the need in others. Compassion can move you to do just that 'right' thing that they need at that particular moment. If you are open and clear about your needs, someone will be there for you. You will be met! If you allow yourself to be so moved by another, then you can be their angel for a moment. There is a balance to the Universe!

Your Enemy is your next Teacher: There is nothing special about loving someone that you like: it's easy, and hardly requires any effort. Whereas ... the person that you hate, or that really gets you going; now that is much harder and you will really learn something about yourself as you consider (and try) loving them. *"Loving Them! You must be crazy! They are trying to kill me!"* This is only perhaps because you are their next Teacher. These things can work both ways. You two may have been thrown together for a purpose, a mutually beneficial one, but different for each. But, we *really* don't want to learn these lessons. These 'Enemies', these 'Teachers', are just embodying something that we don't happen to like about ourselves. Your 'enemy' may also be bold enough to tell you a truth about yourself that your friends have not dared to tell you yet. Maybe, you will only hear this from your 'enemy', because it is a truth that 'hurts'. Don't get too polarised: your 'enemy' today can become your 'friend' tomorrow.

Death: You will almost certainly have to 'die' at least once. This is not just a philosophical principle; it will seem like an actual experience.

On the spiritual path, we need to pass through the 'Valley of the Shadow'(of Death), the 'Dark Veil', the 'Fires of Hell', or whatever. Jung spoke about *The Death of the Ego*. In order for something new to grow, in order to transcend ourselves and our mortal fears, in order to 'kill off' the ego, there is always a price: something old must die. And it will feel like a part of you that is dying. All things have to die. Spring does not follow autumn; there is something called 'Winter' in between. Things will then seem dead; there will be nothing for a while. The next step is not always obvious, and it is not immediate. New seeds take time to geminate. Death and Re-birth is always a part of this Journey. You can also look positively at this. This is a time of rest and regeneration: a fallow period before the next stage of growth. It is also an opportunity to integrate and clear out the old, to spring clean.

This Work is making the Abnormal Normal: What society sees (and thus part of us also see) as being abnormal, or what is denied, or what it condemns or marginalizes, is actually part of a normal, healthy, individualistic, spiritual, developmental process. The problems that arise often lie more with the attitudes of those outside of the process, rather than with anything within the process itself: with other people, rather than with you: or to do with other (social) attitudes and not what you really feel. And the more that we do this type of work, and the more open we are about it being a normal and healthy process, the easier we will feel with it, and then the easier other people can accept it as well. This way we can make changes. The first change that has to happen will (and must) come from deep within ourselves and whether we will be able to make that change will depend upon whether we view these processes as 'normal' or 'abnormal'. If we allow ourselves to be affected by other people's views, then we will not change or grow in the way that works for us.

Be Very Careful About What You Invoke, and Be Very Precise: When you are on the Path, anything & everything that you wish for, will come to you somehow: anything and everything. It is the principle of "Manifestation" and it works! However, because our thoughts are often confused and imprecise, a distortion occasionally happens, and we sometimes ask for that which we do not really want, or we don't usually want what we actually receive, even though we asked for it, or invited it. We are not talking about specifics like winning the National Lottery. We are talking about invoking certain principles: and one of these might be "Abundance". But you must be precise. When you invoke something like "Change", it means that you'll almost certainly get some sort of Change; but what sort of Change, and Change into What? The archetype for this Principle is the story of King Midas, who invoked the power to turn everything that he touched into gold: this was fine, until he wanted to eat, or his daughter gave him a hug. Anyway, now you can take things back as soon as you have said them, and it is best to be as clear and precise as possible. That way you will get what you *really* asked for.

"No Way!" There are Some Things You Must Never Do: they are totally inappropriate, or just plain wrong: So, Don't Do Them: Stop Others from Doing Them, as well. And You Know What They Are. They are those things that feel Wrong, Unnatural, Unkind, Petty, Mean, or Cruel. They do not come out from a place of Love; they come from Fear, or Greed, or Pride, or Envy, or Anger, or Hate. And you know what they are just as soon as you do or say them. So, STOP them happening around you: champion the truth instead! However, in different circumstances, actions around these feelings will differ. What is an Absolutely Wrong action 'here', is (maybe) a Right Action over 'there'. You will still know whether the actions are Wrong or Right, but the point here is that 'Wrongness' does sometimes change with circumstance. However, it is also up to you to stop these things happening.

The Way is Perilous. Rumi says: *"The Way has been marked out. If you depart from it, you will perish. If you try to interfere with the signs on the road, you will be an evil-doer. Go Higher – Behold the Human Spirit."* Of course, there are many dangers on this journey; meeting one's Daemon; the Valley of the Shadow; the Dark Night of the Soul; the Slough of Despond and Vanity Fair, etc. The Way is often narrow and it is definitely the 'Road Less Travelled'. But do not let this stop you! The dangers and the perils are necessary ones: they are uniquely designed for you to overcome and develop your true potential. And, of course, at any one time you can fail. Then try again. You will succeed eventually, even if it is in another lifetime.

There is such a thing as "Sacred Irreverence": It is sometimes absolutely necessary, to the point of being almost sacrilegious, to be irreverent about things which people seem to be holding "sacred" or "holy". The ability to step beyond these confines and to (almost) profane that which people seem to be putting on a pedestal, is an advanced spiritual technique. This is the concept of the "Holy Fool." If you are ready to accept this concept, then if the majority are increasingly accepting that (say) "X" is the new gospel - irrespective of whether it is the latest "neuroscience," political reality ("Axis of Evil"), or a new method of "channelling" – then it is also very good, if not necessary, to also be able to laugh at "X" and pick holes in the doctrine. There has to be a healthy mixture of clear sight, laughter and irreverence in any religion, path, or sect: for, without it, we can become lost in pride and spiritual arrogance, narrow mindedness or bigotry; or just be straight-laced or even boring.

Write, Write, Write: As you follow the Spiritual Path, and all it's many twists & turns, dead ends & pitfalls, mistakes, and insights: write them all down. Keep a Journal and write down your lessons & observations. If you do, you will find that you are, in some way, re-writing all the great spiritual literature – the Koran, the Tao Te Ching, the Upanishads, Science & Health, the Course of Miracles, etc. – in your own words. The Truths are all basically the same: they have different flavours and backgrounds; different images and histories; different perspectives; as will "The Book of You". But the essential truths are similar and it's good to see them written down, by you!

Ritual has an Important Role to Play: When you know what needs to be done, either from insight, or from experience, or from a bit of both; try making it and shaping it into a little ritual. This gives it a form, and a pattern. It also 'embodies' it a little. It gives it some significance. Within this ritual, you can also change and develop things, or adapt them to differing situations: be fluid. But the ritual itself develops a momentum of its own which helps to carry the process along, and (where necessary) helps to repeat it, or to memorise it, or helps to fix it.

There are Three Forms of Knowledge. This also comes from the Sufi, Ibn El-Arabi, who said that: *"There are three forms of knowledge. The first is intellectual knowledge, which is in fact only information and the collection of facts, and the use of these to arrive at further intellectual concepts. The second form is the knowledge of states, which includes both emotional feelings and also various altered states of consciousness. Third comes real knowledge, the knowledge of reality, where people can perceive what is right, what is true, beyond the boundaries of thought and sense. Those who attain the truth are those who know how to connect themselves with the reality that lies beyond the other forms of knowledge."*

You Have Three Brains: The Japanese (used to) believe that you have 3 brains: one in the Head; one in the Heart; and one in the 'Hara' – the centre of your being the belly, what the Chinese call the 'Dan'Tien'. The head is for Intellectual Knowledge; the Heart is for Emotional Knowledge; the Hara is for the basic 'gut feelings' type of knowledge.

A Mountain is Not a Mountain, and then It Is: A Chinese Zen master once said: *"Before a man studies Zen, to him mountains are mountains, and rivers are rivers; after he gets an insight into the truth of Zen through the instructions of a good master, mountains to him are not mountains, and rivers are not rivers; but after this, when he really attains to the abode of rest, mountains are once more mountains, and rivers are rivers."* We often need to see things differently. That does not mean that they will stay different forever. Here's another Zen saying: *"Before I got Enlightenment, I chopped wood and carried water. After Enlightenment, I chopped Wood and carried Water."*

Prayer has a Power beyond Anything you can Imagine: We can always pray: We always have this opportunity and prayer is also a power. Caroline Myss tells a story of someone, a woman, who had a "near death" or out-of-body experience after a car accident. She experienced floating above her body and the wrecked car, and seeing all the other cars back up behind the accident. Then she felt an incredible power or energy or radiance coming from one of these cars in the queue. She floated over and there was a woman in this car and the power came from her. As she wondered what this power was, she got carried back to her body and later woke up in hospital. However, she had remembered the woman's car number and her brother or husband was a policeman, and so she managed to get this woman's telephone number. She rang her up later and described the day and the location and the accident and then asked her what she was doing. The woman in the car said: *"I was praying for the people in the car accident, for you."*

Perfection: *"Excellence isn't good enough: Perfection is what is required!"* This is a difficult one. When people were building the Universal Hall at Findhorn, this was their motto. They were trying to go beyond the norm, or beyond the unusual even. They were trying to build perfection, because this is what is worthy of a sacred place. Some window shelves were sanded, then oiled, then sanded and oiled, etc. until they shone like glass and were as hard. Some pieces of stone were manhandled in and out of the wall for six weeks until they were exactly shaped and fitted perfectly. When you are doing something of value, treat it as sacred work, don't just get it "right," nor just try for "excellence," go for the "perfect." This is the best that we humans can do to bridge something towards the sacred or the divine. You can apply this principle in any work that you do, and beware – if you are not doing it with spiritual principles in mind and grounded in spiritual practice, you will eventually burn out. *"No-one's perfect."* True, but we can try to achieve perfection in everything that we do. We may fail, but the spiritual energy that we put out in trying, says something, teaches us something and leaves its mark. The counter-story about the Universal Hall at Findhorn is that some people also did some things in that building, at that time, more according to their own "guidance" or "attunement" and without any proper supervision. Oy Vey! The faces of the Building Inspectors were sometimes white when they saw electrics that were put in – by "attunement" – where live cables were held in place by copper nails put in the plastic between the two wires! So, we can also get caught up in the 'glamour' of building something 'sacred' and then our sense of discretion goes out of the window. We need discretion, or discrimination, as spiritual tools as well as striving towards perfection. Lessons exist everywhere!

We Don't Know What Is Going On, Nor What Will Happen: Most of the time there will be Great Uncertainty. This is OK. Strange things will happen; that is O.K. too. Get into "Explorer Mode." We cannot hope to know all the different aspects and all the different levels of this new country that we are travelling through. We are only just beginning to discover some of the very Basic Technologies. Dreams will give us some answers. People who we meet will show us the next step, or affirm the last one. Synchronicities will tell us that we are on the right track. Insights might tell us something that we need to know just up ahead. But that is about it. Any more than this and you are not in any new territory, this is old stuff, and it isn't your spiritual path.

You have a Task to Perform: Many spiritual beliefs centre around the belief that you are here for a particular purpose. Rumi says: *"You have a duty to perform. Do anything else, do any number of things, occupy your time fully, and yet, if you do not do this task, all your time will have been wasted."* In this particular belief system, the purpose of our lives is to discover what that task is, and then to perform it, as perfectly as we are able. In so doing, not only do we serve the greater whole, but we also learn all the lessons that we chose to learn, or realized that we needed to learn, before we started in on this life. Nothing else is ultimately good enough or satisfying enough. This is the purpose of our lives. So, how to discover this task? It is often there in front of you: you just have to open your eyes. Stay aligned with your 'guidance'; meditate regularly; practice doing little things first. The task has not gone away: you will find it.

Relationships take on a very different quality: When you are on the Spiritual Path, friendships become more important, and much deeper. People you meet, you "know" in a different way. In partnerships, 'apartness' can be as significant as 'togetherness', both amplifying the 'closeness'; which is very different from "marriage at a distance". In relationships, time doesn't matter so much; quality matters more. Ten minutes of quality time once in ten years can be as, or more, significant to the friendship than seeing someone once every ten days, if there is no real contact. Friendships can transcend 'normal' social relationships; whether one sleeps (has sex with) with someone else is sometimes less significant than the things one talks about together, or the quality of silence between the two of you. Understanding and accepting someone else is a part of the spiritual path, and being understood and accepted as well.

Deep Democracy: means that all the people in a group are equally important; all the different aspects or perspectives are integral to the whole; all the differing views need to be voiced – and heard; all the other parts that are usually marginalized or disavowed need to be owned and incorporated. If we exclude something, however small, we may find that our path or process recycles again and again, until that part is dealt with and we "get it" fully into our systems. There are no short cuts to this: the Path includes everything!

The Inner Change is More Important than the Outer Change: People (especially men) often try to change their job, their partner, their hobbies, their car, or something, rather than make the Inner Changes that are necessary. How do we change from seeing the 'glass half empty' to seeing it half full: this requires an inner change. Many times, it is not what we do (outer change) but how we do it (inner change) that is important.

Once you Feel 'It' in Yourself, See 'It' Also in Others: It makes no sense to just feel all this stuff for yourself. It's like staring only at a wall or a mirror. So, look for 'It' and see 'It' in others as well. Be like Rumi – *"Love the Friend"*. The person in front of you needs what you have got; and you also need what they have got. That is why you have met together on this part of the Journey. They are there for You and You are here for Them. Divine Symmetry – it's Wonderful. Share It – and It Grows. Magic!

And None of This is Anything That You Didn't Know Already!

There are thousands of Spiritual Principles. This is just a small selection. It is not complete. Please add your favourite ones to this list:

....
....
....
....
....

I would be happy to receive your additions by e-mail: see end-pages.

RECOVERY & INTEGRATION

What follows now is much more what happens **after** someone has been identified as having a Spiritual Emergency, and/or also what happens **after** the crisis is over. They will probably have, by now, with some help, got through the actual emergency situation: with or without a Crisis Group, having a psychotic episode, a major illness, or whatever. However, there may have been some trauma experienced which will need to be dealt with – hopefully sooner than later.

They will be beginning to look forward towards a process of healing, recovery and integration. This process will probably take a minimum of 3 to 6 months - maybe even much longer. Compare this to something physical like after a major car crash or having had glandular fever or ME: that's just how long it can take to recover.

If the person's recovery seems almost instantaneous, and may even be accompanied by a surge of insight or energy, perhaps 'be warned' – the person may be getting into something different, or a different stage in their own process, and therefore their transformative process may not be complete. They may possibly be re-cycling; or avoiding something fearful (or deeper) with an adrenaline rush.

The most important and crucial factor in all of this is an understanding of the person's deeper underlying process – by the person and by those around them. If this truly has been a Spiritual Emergence process, then what is that aspect of the human "Spirit" that has been emerging? There are science-fiction stories of people who go through a transition and obtain certain paranormal powers, but until the transition is completed, no-one knows what those powers properly are. Leaving the science-fiction component aside, it is up to the person to discover what their new benefits (rather than powers) are over a period of time after the transition – and then discover how to use these properly, how to integrate them into a new persona.

The concept of special "powers" is – of course – a total glamorisation, hopefully to be avoided, but the basic principle is the same. The 'understanding' required for recovery is both an objective viewpoint, without glamorization, and where the person is capable of reflective introspection – as well as a profound subjective re-orientation towards themselves and the outside world. Psychotherapy can be very useful, if not essential, here. So can quiet, alone times, Zen spaces, retreats, journals, etc.

> **What is absolutely necessary** is for the person to be in touch with – and stay in touch with –their own process. The ways they do this will – of course – vary considerably, but regular meditation or mindfulness practice (20 mins p.d.), journaling, personal reflection, psychotherapy, art therapy, walking, etc. can all help. These processes go in cycles, and it is vitally important to give oneself the proper amount of space and time and inner reflection for the present cycle to complete itself before the next cycle starts. There is often a fairly quick 'surge' of energy at the start of a new cycle, then some sort of peak, and then a much slower 'downward' phase of relaxation and integration. This 'downward' part of the cycle is necessary – essential – to proper integration. Otherwise, the next cycle starts off with unintegrated material from the previous cycle.

Depending on your own particular belief system, religion, or cosmology (which may have changed (or been changed) during the Spiritual Emergence process), your contact with "Spirit" should have increased and your life may have begun to take a certain (different) or spiritual direction. It is now your job to discover what this direction is and to follow it to the best of your ability. Again, try to avoid any glamorization, grandiosity, or followers – most frequently it involves a combination of dedicated regular practice; some additional specialist) training; and then an extended period of service.

For many, it is relatively simple – once their crisis is over. The society they live in might basically support their process; their attempts to change themselves are largely understood; their process is in an accepted context; their symptoms are not too extraordinary, and their priest or psychotherapist can help them get through. Others have had a near-death experience, or a major illness, and have then devoted the rest of their working life to raising money for Body Scan machines, or something similar. For others, they have been to hell and back, or off this planet (and maybe I *am* talking about alien abductions). They need to talk to others, to ground their experiences, to accept the changes. This can be hard if the process has taken them beyond the normal bounds of that society. But you are still human: look instead at the result. There are no set guidelines.

Please remember some of the "caveats" that might apply to you (see below in Section 3). You may well have some obligations from your old life, as well as a new set of directions in your new life. It is not an "either … or …" situation: it is more of a "both … and …" situation. There are probably other people around you who love you dearly: they can and want to help and support you; but they need to understand a bit of what is going on with you, and why you may want to change your life, or how your perspective on life has changed. You will also still need to pay the rent or a mortgage, and possibly put something into a pension fund as well: therefore, do not, repeat **not**, throw everything "old" out of the window, as you embrace the "new". It can be an exhilarating experience – and here is the first "caveat" – which might then impoverishe and impede you later. Keep the 'day job' if you can, until you really know what it is that you want to do next.

Post-Traumatic Growth

This is a relatively new concept that has emerged from Personal Construct Therapy, Schema Therapy and some other 'constructivist' perspectives. While experiencing trauma is usually unpleasant, there is not – necessarily – a pathological outcome: trauma does not – necessarily – involve experiencing PTSD. Whilst trauma usually means experiencing something outside of the 'usual' (day-to-day) range of human experience that may evoke significant symptoms of distress in most people (I am paraphrasing DSM-III & DSM-IV here) – the 'usual' human response to experiencing or witnessing or confronting such an event is intense fear, helplessness or horror. However, the result is not – necessarily – negative: people often experience a form of 'growth' as a result. The traumatic event(s) may have significantly challenged or even invalidated important components of our previous assumptions about ourselves and the world. I am slight hesitant to use here Saul's 'conversion' on the road to Damascus as an example, as my views of how his writings altered the basic Christian message are somewhat negative; but there are many examples of how a 'traumatic' event has led to a 'conversion' to: a more beneficial belief system (not necessarily religious); or a different – healthier – life style; or into a better relationship.

From this perspective, trauma is seen as a highly stressful and challenging, but *life-altering*. event. There is a recently released film, *'Living'* with Bill Nighy, about a civil servant who changes his perceptions and life-style completely, knowing he has only a few months to live. [56]

Such a life-changing event needs to be significant enough to challenge the basic assumptions that we have been holding: about the world around us and our life's purpose or *raison d'être*; or about our future and how to move towards that future, and therefore such a 'disruption' can produce massive anxieties and even psychic pain that are very difficult to manage. There doesn't have to be a single event: there can – and often are – a series of events that accumulate to result in such a traumatic 'change'. But – and this is the point – the end result is not necessarily negative.

This relatively new mainstream perspective on traumatic growth thus steps away from more traditional perspective of PTSD. The emphasis then changes away from how to 'recover' from PTSD, or increase 'resilience' to trauma, and focusses instead on the longer-term changes that come about after reflection and integration.

A word here about the concept of 'growth': what is meant here are positive changes in one's cognitive, emotional and psychic life

---

[56] Based on Akira Kurosawa's 1952 film 'Ikiru'.

that are likely to have behavioural and psychological implications; the changes can be profound and may be truly transformative. *"Personal development, change, increasing maturity, and growth are normative and occur throughout various developmental periods. This type of change is not PTG."* (Tedeschi & Calhoun, 2012).

Post-Traumatic Growth can initiate, or result in, significant changes in the person's perspective of themselves and the world. These changes may even be self-initiated: such as a solo navigation of the world, or space-travel, or mountain-climbing, or artic-exploration. Even if this sort of activity is not in itself definitively traumatic, even though it often involves significant periods of time in relative isolation from other people and 'normal' events, the result is still profound.

If we take an overview of how the traumatic events of the 20th century's two World Wars (plus the interim results of a major influenza pandemic, a massive world-wide depression, the rise of nation states (vs. empires), the growth of technology, and the huge population growth and shifts) have altered – if not totally destroyed – in about 50 years (one generation) – most people's perspectives of themselves, and their world, we can, perhaps, consider how our 'world' has changed … possibly for the better (?) – and how we have all had to adapt to a large number of (previously) 'alien' concepts about ourselves, others and the planet we all live on.

Re-Programming the Self

What is being described in the whole of this second section is – essentially – a necessary re-programming of the Self. One way or another, from an internally-generated process, or as a result of the impact of external events on us, we are being forced to acknowledge that our 'old programme' – the way we were brought up, or the patterns of life that had seemed relatively sufficient – suddenly (and possibly traumatically) became dysfunctional. They did not work any longer. This does not mean that we had done something wrong; nor that there was anything wrong with us: it means that our previous world-view and 'how-it-works', or how-our-life-works, just doesn't work any longer, and this change process may even have profoundly negative implications – unless we can 'go-with-the-flow', adapt and transform.

Much of the next section on recovery and support issues can also apply to people who have had a psychotic episode, or indeed to people recovering from any major trauma or illness. Rather like recovering alcoholics or drug addicts, we may have to go through the whole process over and over again; the process of rejecting the old dysfunctional pattern, each day, every morning, every minute: at least 60-24-7. This involves – in essence – a new regimen: a solid spiritual practice; a high degree of self-discipline; acute discrimination; routine and regularity; active 'listening in'; non-judgmental self-awareness; much greater awareness of the Self; access to support structures when needed; and compassion for oneself and others. Nothing less, nothing else will ultimately manage to change us radically. You might have thought it was all over? But, this is for the rest of your life. Sorry about that!

Cosmology

Our belief systems and cosmology may well have changed. Depending on the type of Spiritual Emergence experience, we will also need to integrate these changes. It is **not** a good idea to be so enthused with the 'revelation' that you try to explain it to everyone else that you meet and then convert them, like the third Rabbi (Introduction: page 6). They may have their own process and it may be, and probably is, very different from yours. What is needed now is for you to work out all the little details and all the twiddly-bits of your own new cosmology. Does (say) a new-found 'Compassion for All Life' involve converting to vegetarianism, becoming a vegan, not wearing leather shoes, protesting against the transport of cattle for slaughter, or scientific research on animals – all very legitimate; or does it involve loving and celebrating the gift of life that we receive *from* all other life forms: carrots, cabbages, animals (pork, lamb, beef, chicken, fish, etc.) and so forth. No-one can tell you which bits of these 'cosmologies' (belief systems) you are going to need, or don't need. This is all about developing **your** new belief system: your new cosmology.

Read & Talk

Many others have travelled similar paths; much of this has been written elsewhere. Find out what worked for others; and what didn't. Don't try to re-invent the wheel; just refine it for your own usage. Reading diverse sets of other people's experiences can / will enrich your own experiences and put them into a wider context.

It is also beneficial to share your thoughts, doubts, fears, and inspirations with others. This is very different from trying to convert them. Try to find a suitable forum where you can listen, and be listened to. This process of discussion and debate can also help you find out what is right (or wrong) for you, and – by doing them, trying them out and sometimes even making mistakes and trying out something else – you are practicing ways of integration and growth, parallel to others. You are also expressing 'stuff' for which we may not – yet – have a very good set of intellectual or linguistic concepts.

John Rowan, from the UK, and Ken Wilbur, in the USA, in their writings have both tried to formulate concepts for these transformational processes. But just reading about these is usually not good enough, we also have to put them into practice and 'test' them out with those around us.

However, here is another caveat – *'Not talking about such things can even drive you crazy'*.

THE SPIRIT OF THE BODY &
THE BODY OF THE SPIRIT

The Spirit of the Body: Sometimes a new topic or page just inserts itself into a book: and this is one of these. There is absolutely no question in my mind whatsoever, that – despite many people's attempts over the years – from the Theosophists, to the aesthetics – to transcend earthly 'stuff' and deny the physical aspects of existence (their bodies) in an attempt to transcend towards the more spiritual aspect of their being – the path to spirit actually lies through their body, not away from it.

The Buddhist practice of Mindfulness involves first becoming aware of your breathing, and then everything that is happening within your body. Many people starting on the Path, start first by exercising more, getting into Yoga, purifying their bodies, stop drinking alcohol or eating meat or processed foods, drinking more water, etc. This is an excellent start: but then they try to transcend their bodies; they feel their bodies are holding them back – sorry!

Yes, you can and maybe will transcend your body, but probably not in this lifetime. When you die, you will leave your body. Until then, it is totally necessary and potentially very functional. But the mistake that many people on the Spiritual Path of Awakening often make is to try to (somehow) do without their body – to transcend their body: however, it is a necessary part of the journey as we can reach spirit *through* our bodies.

Much of this work has been taken from workshops that I used to run with my wife that we called "The Spirit of the Body". As Body Psychotherapists, we do not deny the body – as many aspects of our culture do – and we actually celebrate it. This is not hedonistic: this is actually a path that can lead to the spirit.

Much of our true wisdom lies within ourselves, and we will only find it deep within – our bodies. The further in we go, the more wonderful and intricate it gets – and the bigger it gets as well. Our 'inner space' is so much larger than the space around us. You may have gathered something of this already. When we meditate, we do not leave our bodies; we go 'inside'. Then the Journey starts.

Michael Heller (a Body Psychotherapist colleague) edited a book of papers from the EABP Conference at Travemünde, 1999. This conference was entitled: *The Flesh of the Soul: The Body we Work with*. He writes of being a Body Psychotherapist:

> *Looking at the skin's texture is already a way of contacting the tissues of a human soul. Experiencing this throbbing aliveness with our own aliveness, as it passes from one body to another, requires a capacity to feel how souls communicate, and respect for the needs of the flesh itself.* [57]

The Body of the Spirit

But this section is also entitled "... *The Body of the Spirit.*" We sometimes forget that our spirit needs a body with which to grow, to experience, to manifest many things, to achieve its goals, and in order to feel love and joy, hate and fear ... this is the 'stuff' of life! If we transcend our bodies, we are saying that we don't want to live or grow any longer: is this really part of the Path? What if we fully celebrate having a body, being a body? Is this not an expression of our spirit? In order to 'make our heart sing', we have to have a beating, throbbing, pulsing heart. In order to walk with angels, we need legs and feet. In order to dance the Great Dance, we need bodies ...

There are many transcendent feelings and moments when it seems as if we leave our bodies, but – attractive as continued transcendence is – it is also a bit like going back into the womb, an impossibility. Our experience of transcendence is identified by the ending of that

---

[57] Heller, M. (ed.) (2001) *The Flesh of the Soul: The Body we work with.* Berne: Peter Lang (p. 17).

experience, of returning to our bodies with that transcendent feeling, of 'glowing' from that experience. We cannot abandon our bodies: they are much too important.

They are also remarkable manifestations of miraculous functioning: just open a book on physiology. The complexity of our bodies is absolutely astounding. The amazingly intricate and incredible number of physical, biological, chemical, electrical, hormonal, interchanges that are going on – at different levels, in different places, all the time, is simply mind-boggling. This is very rich, even mysterious or miraculous, and – more significantly – this is You!

You are also so much more than just this Body: but this is a very significant aspect of You, and You cannot exist for a moment or two without it. We are tied to this wonderful, rich, jelly-like soup hung around a framework of bones until the "Golden Bowl" is shattered and the "Silver Cord" is cut: until we die. Except we don't die, our Spirit goes on, and there is a blessed release from the (by now) often aching and painful body.

In olden times, the village storyteller (often also a wise herbalist, sometimes branded as a witch) knew the 'Death Story' – a story that can be told to bring one's Death on. Death was not seen (just) as something to be feared: it was also seen as a beautiful release, and, in these old stories, Death is sometimes portrayed as a beautiful, young Prince (or even sometimes a beautiful, but incredibly strong, Child). In the 'Spirit of the Body' workshops, I sometimes tell the Death Story, not because I want to kill someone, but because we are there to release something, to let something old and now-not-needed go: this is a sort of release (like death). Then, we can move on to the next level of existence: for the rest of our life.

Transformation can be like death, and something has to die. This is not necessarily our bodies, but our 'old stuff', the 'stuff' that was once useful and now is not needed: it is now dysfunctional and can even hold us back. This 'stuff' can die – and a lot of work that we do on the Path is to let this 'stuff' go. It is not just the 'death of the ego', but we also have to transcend our parental scripts; the survival patterns (now habits) that we developed to survive our childhood; the 'identity' that we carry around, thinking "this" is who we are – No: this is who you have become. Who you really are is something much greater and deeper than 'this'.

We still have a lot of work to do – on ourselves and with others. We really need our bodies in order to do this work, are going to need our bodies, and we need to relate to our bodies differently, and we need to work *with* our bodies, to celebrate them, treat them well, let them guide us, and *be* ourselves differently, so as to do this Work and follow our Path.

As a conclusion to this particular section, I am coming more and more to the opinion that it is not just that *Our Bodies Keep the Score*, as Bessel van der Kolk writes; or that *Our Bodies Remember* (Babette Rothschild). Yes, all that is absolutely and definitively true, but – what is becoming increasingly clear – is that *Our Bodies Know the Way*. They actually guide our processes from within; they send us dreams and images that influence our direction; they inform our processes. [58]

The logical / intuitive conclusion is that we need to get into our bodies much more, and then we will be "guided": our process comes from within. We will never be without this sense of direction: we will 'know' through our gut feelings. Of course! Naturally! How not!

---

[58] Arnold Mindel's books, *Dreambody, Working With The Dreaming Body*, and *The Shaman's Body* are particularly relevant here.

CRUCIAL SUPPORT ISSUES

This section is mainly for the families and friends of people who have had a Spiritual Emergency. They often need quite a special set of conditions to assist their support, integration and recovery, and you, the family and friends, can play a big role here. Try to imagine it as if they had just had a triple-bypass operation followed by double pneumonia, but all on a psychological level, or to their psychic body, rather than to their physical body. Hard, I know, but this is how you may be able to help.

They will probably need a very safe emotional & psychic environment. They may very well need some help to make their current environment much safer and more congenial to their present situation.[59] They will usually need a caring, safe, comfortable home-like environment (though not necessarily 'at home' as that may have been where some of the problems were), or a simple 'Zen' space.

They may need time off work, or to take a leave of absence, or a sabbatical. This may well involve getting a 'sick note' from an informed and sympathetic doctor. Their employer should also be consulted, or

---

[59] This is where I differ a bit from Grof and some other spiritual teachers. He wanted to create a residential crisis centre where the person is free "to go through their process" – but I happen to think, and my experience leads me to conclude, that this is just maintaining the separation of the unacknowledged issues about spiritual emergence from the mainstream of society. Therefore, I recommend to try and educate and improve the environment around the person in crisis and to strengthen their boundaries so that they can go through what they need to in the environment of their choice. This also has a knock-on effect in that it affects and educates that person's social environment as well, which is not necessarily a bad thing!

informed. Someone else (like you) may be needed to help to negotiate with such people, with you in a purely advocacy or supportive role.

The person may need to feel free to come and go at odd times of the day or night (sleep patterns are often disturbed); and perhaps without having to explain why, or where they are going. This can be difficult for other people in the same residential environment, especially if there has been some fear or anxiety created previously about where they were, or what they were doing, or whether they were OK or not. Specific agreements will need to be made, and then revised appropriately from time to time about these points to make sure the arrangements work for <u>everyone</u>.

They will often need a 'Zen'-type retreat space – sometimes a quiet, simple, maybe even austere, room where they are not disturbed or distracted. They may need to spend quite a lot of time there, seemingly doing nothing, or writing painting, or just listening to music (sometimes quite loud). Actually, they are probably integrating a lot and re-shaping and forming concepts and structures. It is a little like a physical healing process after an accident where the cells of the body need to re-grow and the stress and trauma symptoms need to be discharged. The synaptic connections of the mind need time to re-connect themselves after a psychic crisis.

The person may <u>not</u> want to involve themselves with lots of other people: they may seem quite reclusive. Close and friends and family are usually welcomed as a normalising factor, on an arranged basis, unless there are unresolved issues between them, in which case some family therapy may be appropriate. Some simple form of explanation or formulation about what has happened may be needed to be devised in order to avoid too many questions, or long heavy silences. The person who was in crisis may prefer only to see a very few people; often the ones whom they can talk to about these matters, or who are not particularly bothered or upset. This is part of their 'normalisation' process.

They will probably also need quite a different support group. Sometimes, people will join a group of like-minded people, because they talk the same language and may have had similar experiences. Grass-roots support groups are very important and significant for people in a number of fields: AA, MIND, Crisis, etc. This is as true for people with a particular form of illness, or people who have been bereaved, as for someone with a mental illness, or who has had a Spiritual Emergence or Emergency process.

Quite often a course of psychotherapy with a psychotherapist, who should be reasonably familiar with transpersonal perspectives and some of these concepts, is an excellent way to work through what has happened. It may take a little time, and a few attempts, to find the right person, but it will be worth it. Such a course of psychotherapy would normally be between three to six months minimum, but may extend much further. There is often quite a lot to work out and continuing therapy after the initial period does not indicate that the person still has problems. After any initial referral (and waiting times are often at least three months), this on-going therapy will probably (almost certainly) not be paid for by the NHS. However, you might be able to get some of this therapy paid for within the terms of a private health insurance scheme (like BUPA or PPP), though a referral from a psychiatrist is likely to be necessary.

The person may also need appropriate medical or psychiatric treatment still. This is usually <u>not</u> a case of medicating the person up to the eyeballs in order to stop their psychic process. Medication can "deep freeze" a person's process and destroy some of the more subtle and sensitive experiences of a person's psychic existence (i.e. Largactil (Chlorpromazine) has often been described as a "liquid cosh"); psychotropic medication does not necessarily restore the person to their original Self. "Appropriate medical or psychiatric treatment" might mean taking, or agreeing to take, some medication but also trying to negotiate carefully with one's doctor or psychiatrist about this, as the experience of taking such medications is often an unpleasant one: they sometimes take a while to work; they sometimes have unpleasant side effects; they can be somewhat addictive; sometimes you have to wind down off them very slowly and in a very structured way; they carry more of a social stigma than (say) Zantac. Medication can be very useful to slow down some of the hyper-manic elements often found with some forms of crisis, or to stop some of the more 'seductive' components of madness (compulsive thoughts, obsessive patterns, addictive behaviours), or any of the more chemically addictive states, until the ego-strength is stronger and better able to cope. Medication might also be targeted, for example to help the person, and everyone else, sleep properly.

People who have gone through such strange experiences usually need a lot of affirmation of their process, reassurance about their symptoms, and support for themselves. This can happen through their therapist helping to affirm their psychological process and help them understand how the events and influences of their life has brought them to this point. It can also come from close supportive friends and family members where the predominant emotions are fairly unconditional love and acceptance: good mothering types, or emotionally stable people to lean on and say back to them, *"You're doing OK!"*

There sometimes needs to be a clear differentiation between what are the person's symptoms and what is their underlying process of spiritual maturation. They may possibly some form of re-parenting <u>and</u> also learning how to manage all this material for themselves. This may also involve some help to give them a sense of true freedom, which is not license.

They will possibly also need some sort of psycho-spiritual re-education. They may need to learn to be able to handle their new experiences or different types of awareness and have learnt to ground these in consensual reality. They may need to learn to listen to their inner voices, and learn how and when to discriminate, and also when and how to follow. They may need to learn how to balance physical & psychic strength. They may need to learn how to help others properly, and when to help themselves. They may need to learn when to cut off, and when to switch on. They may need to learn deep respect for their own process. They may need to read some of the material in classic texts and learn how to apply the principles therein rather than follow the letter. (At the end of this booklet, a partial reading list is provided.) They may need to learn how to interpret their visions, dreams etc. The old concept of the "Mystery School" – if it ever existed - used ideally to teach a lot of this stuff. Some gurus teach it, and trips to India carry their own problems. Some of this material is contained in some psychotherapy education & trainings.

People who are in spiritual emergency don't usually have a teacher, so it has to be a self-learning process. They may need to investigate other belief systems. They may need a guide. A good guide guides from behind. He, or she, will tell them how to achieve something for themselves: they need to discover how to actually do it for themselves. The definition of aid is: *"Do you give someone a fish or do you teach someone how to fish?"* Cults and sects should be avoided. Dogmatism is probably not appropriate either.

Is a crisis really something negative? Many fevers & reactions to illness actually raise the body's state to a level best able to cope with the cause of the illness; however unpleasant that might be. Is a Spiritual Emergency just a way of putting a positive gloss on something fundamentally wrong? Is this all a load of New Age bull-....? As helpers and supporters you must make your own minds up as well. It is not just a matter of re-framing the crisis perspective from something negative into something more positive: it involves something of a new belief system, which, if it is to be used properly, has to be based on solid grounded experience, rather than affirmations, however true they may also be.

However strongly the person may believe in these positive ideas themselves, it is also somewhat insulting or insensitive to try and foist them onto other people who don't believe in them. Other people, the people around you, will need time and patience to change their beliefs, or at least come to terms as to how someone close to them can suddenly hold different beliefs. <u>Example</u>: For as man suddenly to leave his job, his wife and children to go and try to find his guru in India, and then also to expect them to see this as something positive and wonderful is something of a double-whammy. They still have a mortgage to pay; and they will have to cope with feelings of abandonment. Maybe this person *is* running away from something, and hopefully a good guru would tell him so.

This person has changed, possibly quite fundamentally. You, their family and friends, may have to accept this change, or these changes. This acceptance might be very difficult. You may not accept or like the changes. You may want the "old" person back again. Often these changes are not a form of aberration that will necessarily go away with the right medical or psychiatric treatment. You must try to allow this person to be different, perhaps to understand their motivations for change, to recognize their pain and crisis, to listen to and share their fears and new joys, and – by so doing – perhaps also help them to recognize and fully experience this difference. By following these ideas, you will stay in close contact with this person, and you will be able to show your feelings (not necessarily unconditional) of love and support, and possibly be able to help them integrate their experiences.

Maybe with this sort of help, they can find and reformulate their own belief systems and new relationships in line with these new experiences. Priests and ministers are quite well trained in maintaining this sort of differentiation, though usually limited to their own faiths, and clinical psychologists & psychotherapists can also be helpful: psychotherapy is also a form of the "new religion."

When people come to a "plateau" where their crisis is over, the emergency therapy they may have been getting _can_ end at this point … because the crisis is over. At this point, the person may need to pick up the pieces of their own lives, integrate their experience, restore relationships, and begin make the changes in their life indicated by the process so far. However, the person hopefully will also decide to continue working with a therapist, or on themselves, to help them with these tasks, or for reasons to do more with growth or integration, rather than as part of an original crisis intervention. This is not particularly unusual. It does not mean that the person is still 'in need' of therapy; it is more of a choice of this type of skilled support.

There may be the complicated and contentious issue of new relationships, and something needs to be said about this here. It is a potential minefield. Some relationships (partners, families) will not survive such changes: in the same way that if a person is sent to prison, or made redundant, these life events can put such significant stresses onto the extant relationships that the result is that it is significantly damaged or torn apart. This is not the desired outcome, and is exceedingly painful for everyone, and especially so if any children are involved. People sometimes need, or choose, new partners for this new phase of their life, and everyone else has to accept this and learn to cope.

In some instances, a new relationship is formed, often quite quickly, and often intricately involved with this process of change in some way. This can be devastating for the person in the 'old' relationship. It is a 'double-whammy' or even a 'triple-whammy'. One of my friends says, *"How many times do you want to be slapped around the face with a wet fish?"* The partner abandoned experiences that their life partner has not only had a crisis or transformation and changed significantly, but they've also gone off and done it with someone else, and now they, the 'former partners,' are the ones who have to pick up all the pieces and re-build their own life, and maybe the family's as well, and they are now essentially alone, and abandoned. Ugh! They are often now the one's in crisis; through no real fault of their own: maybe this becomes their process.

All that can be said is that this sort of situation is not taken lightly by anyone professionally involved. We certainly do not advocate doing things in this way. This is just how things sometimes happen to turn out. Some relationships are (what is called) co-dependant. If an alcoholic comes off the drink, their long-standing (co-dependent) relationship may not survive as it might have been constructed emotionally around the person being an alcoholic and needing that type of 'support' (positive or negative) for their alcoholism. Now that the person is not a drinker any longer, having had their crisis, the basis for that particular relationship has changed, or been transformed. Their supporter, critic or drinking companion is thus redundant, in some way.

The person in crisis, or who has been through such a crisis, may also want to change their work, or their profession, subsequently. A mid-life crisis for men is sometimes when they realise that the work they have been doing for twenty or so years, is essentially boring for them – now. Maybe it always was and they went along with the perks; or they have just lost interest, or need to explore other aspects of their Self. They really need to change. Fine! There are plenty of new possibilities, but these may mean that some secondary changes are needed as well. Their former lives are sometimes constructed around 'that' place of work, 'that' routine, 'that' regular monthly payment for the mortgage, etc. Sometimes, it is just not so easy to change direction! There is also a risk that they are looking for an external change, when an internal change is actually what is needed.

Understanding from family members can mean that, however much one may disapprove of the result, at least the motive is understood. You remain an ally, rather than an antagonist. Help may be then given to assist the person moving in their new direction; rather than resisting all change and almost creating, or forcing, an unredeemable decision.

The person who has been through a crisis or transformation may need to explore new areas of creativity, new interests, or different forms of activity. These, in themselves, are usually not very threatening. Sometimes the inability to follow these interests turns them into an imperative, and a crisis follows. A Belgian middle-class stockbroker & family man once felt impelled to give everything up and go and paint in a place where the light was right for him. It was a crisis to his family, and he himself later developed syphilis. Yet the world is much richer because of the wonderful paintings of ... Gaugin.

Abstract painting; art therapy; making mandalas; Taizé singing; knitting; training in psychotherapy; writing a journal; wind surfing; studying astrology; listening to baroque music; going to India; hill walking; following a new interest in esoteric philosophy; giving up medicine, writing pop songs and forming a band; adopting different belief systems and spiritual practices; changing their partner, home and job; moving to a different continent; gardening; becoming an ecological activist; raising money for a medical scanner; standing for an elected political position; writing self-help manuals; becoming a Steiner school teacher; training in shamanistic healing; etc. are all activities that various people that I know of have started, or become interested in, after such a Spiritual Emergency process, or having gone through a major illness, or transpersonal crisis. These new activities can be very therapeutic for them, potentially for others as well, and sometimes even financially beneficial as well.

The Spiritual Emergence process can be a little like going through the change from winter to spring, or spring into summer. New seeds germinate and sprout. Please don't try to weed these out too enthusiastically until you know what they are, until maybe a full season has passed. Apply this principle to the person that you know who has had a Spiritual Emergency.

Finally, you are dealing with someone who is now exploring many new aspects of their personality. They might even seem to be something of a different person. Don't worry about it too much: the old person is still there. It is just that these new aspects of their personality or psyche also need to come out and be integrated, and this is possibly what is happening now. These new aspects will tend to predominate for a while, and then a balance will be sought intuitively, or necessarily at a later stage. Try to support the person's process as much as you can.

For partners, members of the family, close relations and friends of someone who has gone through such a crisis, it really helps to be as open as possible; to be as honest as you can; to express your feelings; not to judge too harshly, or quickly, or rigidly; to take time to reflect; to give the person time; to re-educate yourself a little; to share some of their interests and activities (even if you can't share others); to share something of your own journey, your periods of growth, change, or distress; to give what you can; and to wait. If you have been deeply affected or involved, you might want to seek some sort of help and support yourself.

There is also an online (5 webinars) course put out by the Integrative Mental Health University on "How to Support Someone in Spiritual Emergency" with expert + online live meetups every other week for discussion. This course is based in the USA and part of the work developed by Emma Bragdon, one of the pioneers of working with people in spiritual crises and emergencies. It can be helpful on a personal level, as well as a professional level (earning 10.5 CEs), however it costs US$ 495.00, though there may be coupons or discounts available.

———————

PART THREE

THERAPEUTIC COMMUNITIES

Introduction

This third section or part of the book– the newest section – looks at several different therapeutic communities: some in the UK and some in America, and there are also some that exist in other parts of the world. Each one listed was – initially and fairly hopefully – asked to write a few paragraphs about *"How they would view (or screen) people … with particular reference to any psychiatric diagnosis, psychological, existential or psycho-spiritual crisis … and how they might work with them non-medically, psychotherapeutically or differently"*. They were also sent a PDF copy of the 1st edition of this book. However, I did not get any responses. Therefore, the information on their website was copied (and very lightly edited) so as to give a background flavour to the different models of therapeutic communities.

So, we have another caveat: Please, do **not** assume that what is written here is correct: it was accurate at some point in time (2023=2024) when this section was written, but is not necessarily still valid when you read this. Many of these therapeutic communities had to change radically as a result of the CoVid-19 (2020) pandemic. Some are not resuming their previously residential facilities; others may change in different directions. We are all redefining ourselves in many different ways.

Essentially, a therapeutic community is a participative, group-based approach to treat the effects of people with (usually) mental health issues and/or substance abuse. Therapeutic communities are used for both adults and juveniles. Some (not recommended) have even become "boot camps" for delinquent adolescents.

The choice of the communities listed in this section has been done with absolutely no prejudice or preferment, nor are any therapeutic communities specifically recommended, nor has there been any specific selection – other than for basic suitability (relevance). This listing has been developed mainly to show the wide range of differences that can exist between the various therapeutic communities that deal with people with mental health issues. Since this part of the book has been written at one point in time (2023), specific information may well be out of date and the details of these communities may have changed by the time that this is read.

There are – of course – many, many other types of therapeutic communities, some in prisons for prisoners; some (nowadays in increasing numbers) for people with addictions; some for people with learning difficulties and some for sexual / violent offenders. There are also focussed "support groups" (a sort of community) like the 12-Step communities (Alcoholics Anonymous, etc.), which have been reasonably successful over long periods of time. This shows the strength of the therapeutic community model. [60] [61]

In the late 1980's, I was invited to present at a conference in Monterey, CA, with Stan Grof and Arnold Mindell. Grof had developed his concepts of Spiritual Emergence when living in Esalen, Big Sur – almost the archetype of a therapeutic community. My presentation was on what I had put together in a "nuts and bolts" fashion at that time when I was living in another community, the Findhorn Foundation, in Scotland. This was a "spiritual" community, but it could not cope (then) with people in "spiritual emergencies". So, I had – in effect – to 'create' a therapeutic community around the person in crisis. I was deeply indebted to the ideas of Joseph Burke, who I went to for supervision around that time and who gave me one of the concepts outlined in the First Part of the book, in the section on "Forming a Crisis Group" and I write about some of my experiences in doing this in the next section, "Forming a Community around a Person in Crisis".

---

[60] Leon, G.D. (2000). *The Therapeutic Community: Theory, Model and Method.* Springer.

[61] Bunt, G.C. Muehlbach, B. & Moed, C.O. (2008). The Therapeutic Community: An International Perspective. *Substance Abuse, Vol. 299, No. 3, 81-87.*

More recently, as I was writing this third section, my attention was drawn to the career of Dr. Maxwell Jones, a post-war British pioneer of therapeutic communities, who worked – at one point – just down the road from where I now live in the Scottish Borders. [62] I shall therefore start with a little of his history. [63]

Maxwell Jones pioneered techniques of great value in the treatment of those with mental illness or under stress. The main thrust of his work was as an innovator of therapeutic community techniques, but he extended his vision of change to community psychiatry and to education. Jones's early work was as part of the Maudsley Hospital team working in the Effort Syndrome Unit, which investigated the relationship between chest pains and stress in military personnel during the Second World War. Later his work was extended to the treatment of ex-prisoners of war at the Belmont Hospital, Sutton, and then into the setting up there of the Henderson Unit for those with psychopathic disorders.

There are four principles that have emerged as defining the work of a therapeutic community: **1)** democracy; **2)** reality confrontation; **3)** permissiveness; and **4)** communality, and these are seen – not as absolutes – but rather as principles in tension with each other.

For example, the reality of professional accountability cannot be ignored: although it is vital that all community members have a significant voice in decisions that affect their lives, it is important to be realistic and clear about the limits of democratic decision-making and the responsibility of professionals to provide a safe frame for therapeutic work. Likewise, permissiveness would usually be limited to the verbal expression of feelings and would be strongly confronted if it led to other members of the community being emotionally hurt or damaged or feeling excluded. Racist comments, for example, would not be allowed to go unchallenged in modern therapeutic communities. The essence of this work involved his harnessing the forces within the peer group of those requiring help to produce emotional learning and behavioural change. Community meetings of patients and staff

---

[62] Dingleton Hospital, Melrose: www.healthandcare.scot/default.asp?page=story & story=3028

[63] Dr Maxwell Jones: Obituary (www.johnwhitwell.co.uk/miscellaneous/obituary-dr-maxwell-jones)

were used to work with those who, because of their emotional distress, their poor interpersonal relationships, their illness, were incapable of functioning effectively. Each was helped to become more aware of the thinking and feelings of others and more aware of the effect of their own contribution. Patterns of malfunctioning were identified with help towards change. [64]

Maxwell Jones was, perhaps, as influential in traditional psychiatry as R.D. Laing was later to radical psychiatry. Maxwell-Jones was, by all accounts, a charming, slightly eccentric, charismatic character – as one has to be to change one's working world – he somehow avoided being constrained as a result of his upbringing and formal education, and this helped him to be creative. [65] [66]

As the 'therapeutic community concept developed, Haigh [67] described five essential qualities and presents them in a progressive sequence, linking the various developmental stages (helping to restore a damaged psyche), the qualities in the culture, and the structures that establish and maintain them. These are: **Attachment** (leading to belonging); **Containment** (leading to safety); **Communication** (leading to openness); **Involvement** (leading to living-learning); and **Agency** (leading to empowerment).

In the USA, there are – apparently – a total of about 29,000 residential facilities (or residential centres or rehabs), which provide live-in recovery programs for those struggling – mostly with alcohol, drug use, or other behavioural health challenges. Phoenix Houses, that help people with substance abuse, situated in California, New Hampshire, Florida, Metro, D.C. Rhode Island, Texas, Virginia, Vermont, Massachusetts, New York, and the UK, etc., are a good example.

---

[64] Campling, P. (2018). Therapeutic Communities. *Advances in Psychiatric Treatment, 7 (5), 365-372.*
[65] www.cambridge.org/core/services/aop-cambridge-core/content/view/4941C60A0028B6313C5CA1474E070D21/S0140078900000213a.pdf/in-conversation-with-maxwell-jones.pdf
[66] www.journals.sagepub.com/doi/full/10.1177/0957154X221140734
[67] Haigh, R. (1999). The quintessence of a therapeutic community. In: P. Campling & R. Haigh (Eds.), *Therapeutic Communities: Past, Present and Future*, (pp. 246–257). London: Jessica Kingsley.

It is also fairly clear that – in general – people with severe mental illnesses have had much better outcomes after being in therapeutic communities, as compared with those who received more standard care in psychiatric hospitals. We can even, perhaps, actually take this as a fundamental principle: people get better if treated well, as a person, rather than as someone who is mentally ill, sick or crazy.

Incidentally, the 12-Step programmes (like Alcoholics Anonymous, Narcotics Anonymous, etc.), which also have a strong spiritual component, have also been reasonably successful. [68] Together, they form a different sort of community: a supportive community of fellow sufferers.

There is a UK listing of therapeutic communities under 'The Consortium for Therapeutic Communities' (www.therapeuticcommunities.org). Some residential communities deal with a particular clientele: e.g. residential & foster care for children; people with complex needs, or who have a history of substance abuse; etc. Those therapeutic communities in the UK, that are known to deal with people in severe mental health issues or crisis or spiritual emergencies, have been selected: with apologies to any that might have been overlooked.

One of the more famous therapeutic communities, Kingsley Hall, founded by R.D. Laing in 1965, and later conceptually developed by the Philadelphia Association as an alternative community for people affected by mental health crisis, using non-restraining, non-drug therapies, has been one of the most radical experiments in psychiatry.

Based on the notion that psychosis, a state of reality akin to living in a waking dream, is not an illness simply to be eliminated through the electric shocks favoured in the Western tradition of the time but, as in other cultures, a state of trance which could even be valued as mystical or Shamanistic, it sought to allow schizophrenic people the space to explore their madness and internal chaos. [69] Residents (in the

---

68 Although AA has been criticized by some sources for having a low success rate, addiction specialists cite overall success rates between 8% and 12%, however there is quite a higher 'return rate'. A New York Times article stated that AA claims that between 65% – 75% of its members achieve abstinence.
69 Huxley, F. (1989). Liberating Shaman of Kingsley Hall: (Obituary: R.D. Laing). *The Guardian, 25th Aug. 1989.*

grip of psychosis) were often treated with kindness and respect, with sincere efforts to alleviate their suffering.

There have been many 'spin-offs' to Kingsley Hall in the UK and in other countries, perhaps the closest being the **Arbours Association**, founded by Morton Schatzman, author of *Soul Murder* (1974), and Joseph Berke (both colleagues of R.D. Laing).

Another 'spin-off' is the **Philadelphia Association** (www.philadephia-association.com), also started by R.D. Laing, that runs community houses in London for people, who are suffering from mental health issues and need space away from the pressures and demands of modern-day life.

The people living in these communities do not, repeat not, need the disruption, shame and stigma of being considered as a "psychiatric patient", nor being put away into a mental hospital, or being seen as "crazy". Surprisingly, they can live with similar others in these houses for extended periods, often without medication, using the time spent with each other to reflect on their experiences and re-build a sense of themselves in community with others: *"More fulfilling lives become possible as a consequence."*

I would now like to include a little personal history here:

When I was living at the Findhorn Foundation (1986-2003), I also became involved in a local charity that supported people with mental health issues in the community. It was called the Moray Association for Mental Health. In the early 1990s, it was asked to 'take over' some of the activities that had been part of the Mental Health Service, as the Health Board was going to be closing down the local mental health hospital, Bilbohall Hospital, in Elgin. They were building a new facility for the 3 psychogeriatric wards; keeping an admissions ward in the main hospital; and they wanted to get rid of (didn't have space for) the day services and the industrial work unit (which had 2 staff members on permanent contract).

Being reasonably *au fait* with organisations, I helped create a charitable company, limited by guarantee, the Moray Association for Mental Health Co. Ltd., based in Elgin. By the time, I stepped down as one of the Directors, after 7 years, it had built up to having a turnover of about £230,000; running 6 or 7 projects – the Workshop, a Day Centre, a Stay-at-Home Project, an Employment Project; an Outreach

Project, a Befriending Scheme; and employed 20+ staff, many of whom had formerly been 'clients' (people in the hospital). It has, of course, since moved on a bit since then. The original charity ran social events and fund-raising activities. I feel quite proud of that achievement, although it had – at times – some serious difficulties.

Anyway, there now follows several examples of mental health (note 'health' not 'illness') therapeutic residential communities, where people can stay to 'recover' or 're-find' themselves after a crisis, spiritual emergency, or spiritual emergence process.

THE ARBOURS ASSOCIATION, NORTH LONDON[70]

The Arbours Association offers help with a range of emotional problems including those relating to critical life events. These critical events may be bereavement, anxiety, depression, marital breakdown, redundancy, abuse, eating disorders, gender, race and sexual issues. Their aim is to encourage people to come to them as a first rather than a last resort.

Their houses were situated in quiet residential areas of north London. They were comfortably furnished and could accommodate up to eight residents in single rooms with communal rooms shared by everyone. When possible, they tried to ensure an even balance between male and female residents and attempted to provide as wide a range and diversity of cultural and ethnic backgrounds as possible.

Unfortunately, the Arbours Association is no longer offering Therapeutic Communities as part of its ongoing service. The Arbours therapeutic communities closed its doors in May 2020 (as a result of the CoVid pandemic).

Their aim is to maintain a nurturing, non-institutional, home-like atmosphere where respect for the freedom and unique potential of each individual was honoured. They saw their task was to help residents face and work on the difficulties that may be impeding their growth, and to motivate them in the direction of achieving a more satisfying way of life so that they could live as viable members of society. The umbrella of therapeutic and practical support provided by Arbours fostered a climate providing necessary freedom for residents to find their own

---

70 Adapted from the Arbours Association website: www.arboursassociation.org

identity and take responsibility for their lives. The long-term aim was for each resident to overcome his or her emotional and psychological dependency and to gain a more independent way of living.

Referrals to the communities came from individuals, psychiatrists, GPs, social workers, psychologists, and psychotherapists, and from statutory and voluntary agencies. Each potential resident had an interview with an experienced psychotherapist who assessed the applicant's psychological and emotional needs, and suitability as a community resident. This provided an opportunity for the potential resident to raise any questions they had and to receive information about the communities.

The next stages in the assessment procedure were interviews with each of the house clinical coordinators and an informal meeting with the present residents. If all went well, the potential resident was invited to spend a weekend in the community. The whole procedure lasted from four to six weeks. User participation was a vital component of our therapeutic approach. They expected each person to contribute to the running of the house, and to help with cooking, cleaning, shopping, financial management and maintenance, as well as with choosing new members and with attending on-going discussions of house policies.

Throughout their stay in the community, residents were required to attend:

1. The twice-weekly group meetings, which were led by the house clinical coordinators, where the residents could explore and clarify both personal and inter-personal issues. The group could also offer an experience of belonging that was often lacking in individuals who had been isolated by their problems.
2. Two individual psychotherapy sessions a week with a trained and experienced psychotherapist where residents could explore the meaning of their problems and difficulties in a trusting one-to-one relationship.
3. Art and movement therapy groups (one of each a week) where residents could explore their experiences and feelings in a medium other than words: through painting, drawing, sculpture and movement.

In addition, the residents were living in a therapeutic milieu in which they could learn, with the support of the clinical coordinators, the community facilitators and their peers, to take responsibility for themselves and others and to learn relational, social and domestic skills. Any difficulties experienced in meeting these responsibilities were discussed in the regular house meetings.

Their experience showed that it took time for a person's psychological repertoire to unfold. Therapeutic programmes could not, therefore, be static. Residents' progress was assessed on an ongoing basis, and changes were effected at times to meet their needs. In addition, formal internal reviews of residents' needs and progress took place approximately every six months.

The community provided outings and day activities and residents were encouraged to explore and create links with the outside community, working towards eventually making use of courses and other activities.

The Arbours Association has always been concerned about the alienating aspects of "staff-patient" relationships often found in institutional settings. In order to counter-balance such alienation, they developed a careful programme of staff support that proved to be both therapeutic and effective. During the past fifty years, their experience has been that this supportive therapeutic programme has made it easier for residents to resolve their difficulties.

Two clinical coordinators, both experienced psychotherapists, had overall practical and therapeutic responsibility for the house. They were on call for advice and support and led house meetings every week. Residents saw their own individual psychotherapists twice a week and attended art and movement therapy groups once weekly.

In addition to the above, they established a policy of having in the house, residential community facilitators who shared living in the community. In addition, their trainee psychotherapists and volunteers conducted visiting placements. The Arbours office provided assistance with DWP (Department of Work and Pensions) and Local Authority payments, and advice about rights, training courses, benefits and any other issues throughout the resident's stay.

The office staff visited the community regularly to impart useful information and offered practical help, particularly with problems related to social security and with maximising income. The office staff were also available to provide help with move-on accommodation and any other practical issues.

The families, partners and other individuals in the resident's social network may have been in need of emotional psychological support. Where appropriate, we were able to see residents with their partners or family. It was however at times more therapeutic for families and partners to receive individual psychotherapy, which they provided directly by means of a referral.

When moving-on was indicated, appropriate support was provided and residents were able to discuss their anxieties and practical difficulties of moving on with the house clinical coordinators and in the house meetings. Residents were encouraged to take courses, train and find employment before leaving the community.

THE WINDHORSE COMMUNITY[71]

Windhorse Integrative Mental Health is a non-profit organization, based in USA, committed to providing mindfulness-informed, compassionate, team-based care to individuals experiencing life-disrupting psychiatric distress.

There are houses in **Northampton, MA** (www.windhorseimh.org/northampton-ma); **San Luis Obispo, CA** (www.windhorseimh.org/san-luis-obispo-ca): and **Portland, OR** (www.windhorseimh.org/portland-or), offering uses mindfulness-informed clinical teams and therapeutic households to support our clients' recovery journey. Through this strong web of support, clients experience the same dignity and respect as their peers whose lives have not been disrupted by a mental health challenge – they are actively engaged in their community, creating a life of meaning and independence.

Healing through Relationship: Their philosophy stems from the view that each person, regardless of their present state of mind, possesses fundamental goodness and sanity. Windhorse is an innovative program that offers holistic, compassionate care for adults recovering from extreme mind states. Their clients live with dignity in a home environment in the larger community and are supported by mindfulness-informed clinical teams and therapeutic households. The integrative team – with the client at the center – enhances cohesion and awareness, avoiding the fragmentation often found in mental health care. Their teams help clients find their voice and shape their own direction. With the client sharing in decision-making on

---

71   This information was adapted from the Windhorse Community website: www.windhorsecommunityservices.com

a dynamic team, rather than being institutionalized or pathologized, they are encouraged to discover a life of meaning that fits their unique path. They work with people in teams to create a tailored approach for each individual, but the therapeutic relationship is the foundation of the Windhorse approach. By offering genuine relationship, they invite people to relax into who they are authentically and to reconnect gradually to the world around them. These connections can offer a much-needed bridge to others and potentially heal the devastating loneliness that afflicts so many people. The team can become like respectful friends, who also have a therapeutic role. Instead of *"I'm well, you're sick and I'm going to fix you,"* there's a sense that *"We are in this together"*. This intimacy of mutual caring fosters bonds of human kinship similar to an extended family.

Restorative Environments: Their approach, known as "Environmental Therapy" recognize how environments impact us on every level—mentally, physically, spiritually and emotionally. While clients spend time outdoors, 'environmental' doesn't necessarily mean being in the natural world. They value the importance of every environment and every aspect of daily life. This includes the household, the local community, the grocery store, the coffee shop—wherever they find ourselves throughout the day. In addition to paying attention to physical environments, they recognize the power and influence of interpersonal environments such as friendships or the relationship between parent and child. Over time, they work with each environment to support its unique healing qualities. Creating and nurturing healing environments make it possible for clients to draw on their own inner strength and create a life worth living.

Windhorse Integrative Mental Health was founded in Northampton, Massachusetts in 1993 by Jeffrey and Molly Fortuna who worked extensively with Dr. Podvoll. Our program is based on the Windhorse approach, which was first developed in 1981 by Dr. Edward M. Podvoll, M.D., the founding director of Naropa University's Contemplative Psychotherapy program. Prior to his work in academia, he was the psychiatric director at several respected psychiatric hospitals, including Chestnut Lodge and Austen Riggs. Dr. Podvoll and his collaborators drew inspiration from the power of healing relationships emphasized in the psychoanalytic tradition, as well as contemplative teaching and practices from Buddhism, to create what is known as the Windhorse approach. The core concepts and values of the Windhorse approach are described in DR. Podvell's book: *Recovering Sanity* (Shambala, 2003).

Initially applied to a single client who was discharging from a psychiatric hospital in Boulder, Colorado, the approach has since been used throughout the world to help hundreds of individuals achieve sustainable recovery. To learn more about how Windhorse has grown globally, please visit the (www.windhorseguild.org/legacy-project)

After moving to the Berkshires, they met Connie Packard, the mother of the person who would become the non-profit's first official client. From Ms. Packard's home, the three pulled together groups of compassionate and versatile individuals that would act as care teams for other clients. Over time, more Naropa-trained clinicians began migrating to Western Massachusetts to work at the Windhorse non-profit, and it grew in both size and client capacity.

After almost two decades of helping clients experience profound recovery, the organization began exploring the idea of expanding its services to other areas of the country. Windhorse ultimately landed on the West Coast as a response to the dearth of residential programs that existed in this geographic area. With strong financial backing from a satisfied parent and passionate advocate for their work, the San Luis Obispo, California location was opened in 2010, followed closely by the Portland, Oregon location in 2016.

"Windhorse Integrative Mental Health would not be what it is today without a few essential community members. Deeply indebted, they would like to thank the late Dr. Edward Podvoll for creating and disseminating the Windhorse approach, Jeffrey and Molly Fortuna for founding our non-profit organization, Connie Packard and Sally Clay (parent and peer advocate respectively) for bringing the power of Trialogue (peers, professionals, family members being equally heard) into our work, former Board Member Cheryl Stevens for introducing to us the Peer Support model (www.samhsa.gov/brss-tacs/recovery-support-tools/peers), and Marlow Hotchkiss with the Ojai Foundation (www.ojaifoundation. org/project/council-training) for teaching us the way of Council (listening and speaking from the heart). We thank you."

Mission Statement: Windhorse Integrative Mental Health, Inc. is a coalition of professionals, consumers, and family members committed to providing a comprehensive range of services to individuals and their families struggling with life-disrupting extreme states of mind. Our treatment approach is based upon the recognition that significant recovery from major mental disturbances is possible when catalyzed by authentic therapeutic relationships in home settings. To promote recovery, each individual treatment program is designed to attend to the physical, social, mental, and spiritual aspects of the whole person.

We primarily serve persons suffering from life-disrupting mental states, along with their significant family members. Windhorse Integrative Mental Health, Inc. intends to disseminate knowledge gained in the course of this work through publications, training, and educational programs in the field of compassionate whole-person care. As a therapeutic community, we are committed to the development and well-being of all members, as well as those groups with whom we collaborate. The clients receive:

A tremendous amount of one-on-one support:

- 40+ hours per week of one-on-one time with clinicians
- 1 therapeutic housemate per client, living together in a 2-bedroom house or apartment
  - Mindfulness-informed therapeutic team tailored to meet the needs of the client, typically consisting of 5-7 members

Highly individualized care:

- No 'one-size-fits-all' method to treating diagnoses; clients are met wherever they may be on their recovery journey
- Dynamic levels of support that are increased or decreased depending on a client's current and changing needs
- Client-centered and client-guided model: clients collaborate with their team to design their own treatment journey
- Groups and activities are not mandatory; clients can choose when and how they interact with the larger Windhorse community

Integrative, whole-person treatment approach:

- All aspects of life are integrated into the treatment plan
- Client families are intrinsic members of the team
- An emphasis on holistic health, from home life and diet to education and relationships

Interdependence meets independence:

- The client is an active member and decision-maker of the care team, even when it comes to decisions about psychiatric medication.
- Focus on interpersonal connection and mutual recovery rather than isolation and pathology.
- Authentic relationships are formed within Windhorse as a foundation for creating meaningful connections in the greater community outside of Windhorse.

We know you have treatment options, and making the decision can be difficult.

Terms used to describe Windhorse have become ubiquitous in today's culture: "mindfulness," "community-based," "team-based," "relational," "individualized," "alternative." *What do these words really mean? How do esone choose between so many different programs?*

We encourage you to dig deeper and ask specific questions to learn about what makes a treatment program unique and exceptional. Depending on the program, they may not necessarily look like what you'd imagine in practice.

When you do, ask the following questions:

- What does individualized care really look like?
- How is a program alternative?
- What is a compassionate, relational approach to care?
- Is the program truly integrated—do clients live in and interact with the larger community?

- How much one-on-one time do I have with staff?
- What does a treatment day or week look like?
- What does transition to a lower level of support look and feel like?

The Legacy Project

The founding of the "Windhorse Project" in Boulder, Colorado, in 1981 was a seminal event in the field of clinical work with persons suffering with serious mental disorders. The first Windhorse therapeutic community (1981–1987) was the culmination of the career of Edward Podvoll, MD. He was a pioneer who joined his classical psychoanalytic training with intensive contemplative experience during the last thirty years of his life. Dr. Podvoll inspired generations of therapists through four life phases: as the senior staff psychiatrist at Chestnut Lodge and Austen Riggs Center (1966–1977), his teaching at Naropa University (1978–1990), his work with Windhorse (1981–2003) that culminated in the publication of his *Recovering Sanity* (Shambhala Publications, 2003), and his twelve-year meditation retreat in a Buddhist monastery (1990–2002). During 2003, the last year of his life, he returned to live with us in Boulder, CO, where he continued to teach with the poignant intimacy of a man facing death.

Jeffrey Fortuna writes: *"I am the current director of the Legacy Project. Several of his colleagues and I had worked alongside Dr. Podvoll from 1978 through his death. We inherited his extensive intellectual legacy. This legacy consists of the copyright to Recovering Sanity, 600 audio tapes of his lectures and clinical consultations, an extensive collection of his manuscripts, lecture and author notes, clinical logs, and correspondence. In addition to this core material, we continue to archive twenty-six years of recorded teaching and writing by other Windhorse therapists and clients, and many other valued mentors. This is an extensive and valuable archive that we intend to preserve and share with future generations of persons, organizations, and universities interested in exploring the psychology of, and recovery from, extreme states of human experience."*

Activity

In 2013, with the support of a generous foundation grant to the Windhorse Guild, we formed a small working Legacy Group. Our intention was to research the process of how the Windhorse tradition is transmitted person-to-person, by our personal engagement in that process. "Research" for us means to bring the spirit of open inquiry to direct experience grounded in study of the Legacy. We continue to engage in that dynamic process of Windhorse transmission through archival research, clinical studies, group dialogue, writing papers, and teacher training. All these activities are illuminated by the mentoring relationship, which is the co-learning process at the heart of transmission. We actively engage with the other maturing teachers working in the international Windhorse community. Rousing the shared energy of our community dedication, we strive to embody the living quality of the Windhorse tradition. Dr. Podvoll left us these relevant instructions:

"No community can survive without the presence of teachers or elders who can transmit the wisdom of the community and train others to become teachers. In this way, the practices of the community can stay alive and have a continuity beyond the teachers. Just as the presence of a knowledgeable team leader catalyzes an individual therapeutic home, such leadership responsibility is crucial in larger treatment communities." — "Recovering Sanity," 2003, p. 312

We have discovered that the best teachers are the best students. We recognize we are all students openly sharing the Legacy journey into the future.

Intention

The Legacy Project is guided by an educational vision to preserve the Legacy, make it widely accessible, and guide its evolution. We intend to serve the learning needs of the international network of Windhorse centers and practitioners. We also hope to contribute to the larger dialogue of the world-wide recovery movement. We will do this with training teachers, making study materials available widely, and conducting trainings in the field of recovery from mental disorders.

Our scope widens beyond Windhorse to preserve and publish the lasting contributions of elder psychotherapists, teachers, and recovered persons on our website.

By way of sharing the profound impact that this body of work has had on those already close to it, we have compiled submissions to the question, "What Does the Windhorse Legacy Mean to Me?" from a number of authors represented in this library as well as practitioners of the Windhorse approach. As you explore the archive, we hope you will add your own responses to that question in the comment field that appears at the end of each article.

Together we can bring hope and inspiration to everyone working with extreme mental states. It is clearly time for the goodness of human sanity to cross cultural and theoretical borders.

Windhorse Community Services: WCS was founded in 1990 and operates in Boulder, Colorado. It is a privately-owned organization based on the Windhorse principle of whole person, environmental therapy. We are dedicated to cultivating a committed therapeutic community of clients, families, and clinicians through a culture of continuous mutual learning. We serve individuals in recovery from mental health challenges and related conditions. WCS has worked with clients with a wide range of diagnoses and conditions, including schizophrenia and other psychotic disorders, affective disorders, substance abuse, eating disorders, personality disorders, closed-head injuries, obsessive-compulsive disorders, pervasive developmental disorders, autism, challenges of aging, and terminal illnesses. Many of our clients do not easily fit into standard treatment options and seek very individualized support.

A wonderful companion to this Legacy Project is The Windhorse Journal — a creation of Windhorse Community Services. The Windhorse Journal's mission is to inspire compassionate approaches to recovering sanity. Their aim is to create an evolving forum dedicated to exploring contemplative psychotherapy and the creation of therapeutic environments for the well-being of all persons involved. They envision this to be a rich dialogue among people with lived experience, family members, psychology professionals, and anyone interested in whole person-mental health and the diverse expressions of human sanity.

Windhorse Elder Care: Founded in Boulder, Colorado, in May 2000, the mission of WEC is to provide mindful, holistic care and case management services to our clients and their families as well as education to our local communities. WEC serves clients age 65 and up and adults of any age with physical or end-of-life needs: www.windhorsecare.com

International Communities

Austria: Founded in 1994, Windhorse Society is an organization for supporting mental health and for holistic therapy for psychotic states. They operate within the Austrian health care system and are financially supported by the City of Vienna. WS is a continually learning community, building bridges between tradition and innovation based on the practices of mindfulness and compassion: www.windhorse.at

Freiburg: Founded in 2012, Windhorse Freiburg provides social attendance for people living with mental disorders in psychotic phases of life: www.windhorse-freiburg.de

Frankenthal: Windhorse Frankenthal was founded 1999 as the first German Windhorse association for supporting mental health and offering holistic therapy for psychosis and altered states of consciousness. Since the beginning, music and sound-therapy has been included in our therapeutic work, as well as the experience of peers working in our teams as basic attendants. We are part of the social-psychiatric network of the region and are connected with other Windhorse communities to share experience and knowledge: www.windhorse.de

Torino, Italy: Accordo Associazione Scientifico—Culturale di Coterapia was founded in 2008 and operates in Torino and province, but is open to other places, both national or international. Accordo has cultural, scientific, professional aims in the fields of psychic, physical, existential, and social care. In recent years, their collaboration with other Windhorsecenters in the world has increased and has oriented Accordo's activities: www.www.accordo.to.it

LOTHLORIEN THERAPEUTIC COMMUNITY[72]

A positive approach to mental health

Lothlorien is a therapeutic community for people with mental health problems, situated in a quiet rural setting in South West Scotland, UK. Lothlorien was originally started in 1974 by the Haughton family, who built the 13 bedroomed log house, one of the largest in its kind in Britain, from locally hewn larch and pine trees. It has been run since 1989 by the Rokpa Trust, an international charity founded by Dr. Akong Tulku Rinpoche of Samye Ling Tibetan Centre in Dumfriesshire. Buddhist values of compassion and tolerance are the basis of our approach, but Lothlorien is not a religious community and is potentially open to everyone.

The community consists of 8 residents with mental health problems and 5 voluntary co-workers, living in the main house and a further 5 people living in the move-on house, Roan Lodge, which opened in April 2003. There are 4 staff, known as the Core Group, who come in on weekdays. The community has 17 acres of land, including vegetable gardens, woodland and pasture land. The main house has wheelchair access and a disabled toilet on the ground floor.

Here are some comments from residents:

"Lothlorien provides care and support in a very loving environment." "I feel blessed to be here." "Lothlorien is a wonderfully supportive and egalitarian community. I have already benefited from living here. It

---

[72] Adapted from the Lothlorien website: www.lothlorien.tc

has helped me to come out of a very dark period of my life." "Staff are spot on." "It's not them and us." (referring to residents and staff)

Lothlorien and Roan Lodge have received 'Excellent' grades from the Care Inspectorate., which inspected Lothlorien and Roan Lodge in 2017 and awarded 'Excellent' grading in all categories.

- Quality of Care and Support: *6 Excellent*
- Quality of Staffing: *6 Excellent*
- Quality of Management and Leadership: *6 Excellent*

From the inspection report:

"We found the care and support provided by this structured and therapeutic community to be exceptional. ... We found the service to have fully embraced the concepts of person centred, needs based and participative care and support and witnessed this being practiced and lived out on a daily basis. Community members with whom we spoke and those who had completed questionnaires felt that they benefitted greatly from the therapeutic environment adopted by the service and in particular by the staff working there. Outcomes were negotiated and were realistic taking cogniscence of the individual needs and wishes of community members. Our discussions and examination of records and documents regarding the methodology, practice and procedures adopted demonstrated a commitment by the service to improving the physical and mental health of the individual by making use of the therapeutic environment provided thus achieving the best possible results for those residing there. We found several examples of how people's lives had been 'turned around' as a result of their time at Lothlorien."

Further information:

Lothlorien Community is based on the therapeutic community model, which includes principles of collective responsibility and empowerment. Central to the life of the community is the daily meeting, where we plan work and other activities, and attempt to address issues of living together as a group in an open way. Each community member is encouraged to share equally in decision making about community affairs.

At Lothlorien, we have a strong belief in everyone's potential for well-being, even in the midst of pain and distress. We believe that people need not be imprisoned by their past. We avoid diagnosing or labelling, and attempt to break down the distinction which frequently exists between those seen as 'well' and those seen as 'unwell.' As a therapeutic community, we aim to help people to develop their strengths and work towards recovery through the shared experience of community life. All the members of the community play their part in creating a mutually supportive atmosphere and the experience of being part of a therapeutic community allows everyone involved to learn about themselves and how they relate to others.

The ordinary practical tasks of community life, such as gardening, cooking and cleaning, have a grounding effect and the rhythm of daily life provides a structure which helps restore a sense of balance to people's lives. Relaxation, artwork, massage and Qi Gong are also part of the programme. Over the winter months, we have a weekly basketry class, using willow grown at Lothlorien.

The members of the Core Group have backgrounds in either social work, psychotherapy or counselling. They work in the community from 9am to 5 pm from Monday to Friday. They are available on call in the evening and at the weekend. The Core Group's main function is to facilitate the therapeutic aims of Lothlorien. Other responsibilities include offering individual support to residents in order to help them gain maximum benefit from their stay, reviewing new applications and overseeing the financial management of the project.

Lothlorien is an innovative alternative approach to mental health, but it is also respected as a valued provision within the mainstream and there are good links with the local statutory mental health services. Residents normally link with a G.P. and with the Community Mental Health Team at the local health centre in Castle Douglas for the duration of their stay here.

We are registered with Social Care & Social Work Improvement Scotland (SCSWIS) as a housing support service.

Lothlorien is a member of the Association of Therapeutic Communities.[73]

Daily Routine

There is a planned routine of work and activities at Lothlorien between Monday and Friday and everyone is expected to join in.

After breakfast everyone participates in household chores. At 9.45 am the daily community meeting is held. The main work periods are 10.30 to 12.30 and 2.00 - 4.00. There are a wide variety of jobs to be done both indoors and out.

We have seen that people with mental health problems benefit enormously from participation in the ordinary tasks of daily life at Lothlorien. The structured work programme is pitched at a level which takes into account the difficulties that many people have in sustaining long periods of work, either because of their medication or due to the mental health issues with which they are dealing. However, living as part of a therapeutic community encourages and motivates everyone to participate in the essential daily tasks that ensure that the community functions well.

The nature of the work carried out in the community can have a very positive influence on mental wellbeing by having a grounding and healing effect. People can learn to restore a sense of balance to their lives by having a direct, conscious involvement with the ordinary activities of daily community life, such as working in the garden, growing vegetables, cooking, chopping wood for the wood-burning stoves and looking after the house and the environment.

Lunch is at 12.30 and the main meal of the day at 5.30 pm. Everyone takes a turn at cooking. For those who are less skilled in this area or who may find it difficult to cook for large numbers, assistance and advice are always readily available from others. The food is mostly vegetarian with much of it being grown in the vegetable garden. However, meat-eaters are catered for, usually by having some meat dishes over the weekend.

---

73 www.therapeuticcommunities.org

The evenings and weekends are unstructured and a time to relax with other community members or take some time on your own. At weekends some people go away to visit friends or family, others enjoy relaxing around the house or going for walks. Although we are in an isolated spot, the community members regularly organise outings, and there are opportunities to get into town regularly.

Gardening at Lothlorien *by John Allison, who has been the Garden Coordinator at Lothlorien since 2003.*

The garden is a central part of living at Lothlorien. On a basic level, it's the main focus of the working day: everyone does what they can; and those people who are able put in two to four hours, five days a week. That work is productive: for at least four months of the year we're self-sufficient in vegetables. Lots more are stored for eating the rest of the year – sacks of spuds, a sandbox of carrots, freezer-bags of blackcurrants and beans and peas. Even in midwinter there's usually something – leek, cabbage, parsnip – being harvested.

We are 'organic' in as much as we use no chemical biocides and no artificial fertilizers. While we make as much compost as we can from our own resources, we also bring in animal manures from outside; these are not always to full organic standards, but using them allows us to grow more produce of much higher quality than the shop-bought food that would otherwise take its place. So, we're as 'organic' as we practically can be. The principle is to 'grow the soil to grow the crop', and, alongside a rich and bio-diverse soil ecosystem, that results in healthy plants vigorous enough to shrug off most garden diseases. We use physical barriers to deter slug and rabbit – but if a few get past to eat their fill, there's usually enough left for us as well.

The growing area under vegetables runs to about 1500 square metres. The community decides what crops they want, and the eight-course rotation is a compromise between that and what our soil and climate will support. We benefit enormously from two 10-metre polytunnels which allow us a regular tomato crop, extend the growing season (those early strawberries!) and provide a drier and warmer workplace when the weather is less kind. Our lean-to glasshouse, now once again being renovated, is home to two vines as well as providing luxurious peaches and nectarines with, in early Spring, the most beautiful blossoms.

The orchard of 17 apples, struggling with canker, yields somewhat fitfully: we're near the climate/soil limit of what they'll tolerate. There are also a half-dozen plum trees, gooseberries, raspberries and enormously prolific blackcurrant bushes.

On some of the wetter parts of the plot we grow several varieties of willow, which make for attractive living fences as well as providing raw material for winter basket-making sessions. And in 1999 Lothlorien teamed up with South-West Community Woodlands, a local voluntary group, to plant four acres of native hardwoods on selected parts of our ground out with the garden itself. We help in the management of these, keeping weeds down and replanting gaps as necessary. Seeing these new woodlands grow and enrich the landscape is deeply satisfying.

Mostly around the house, but also amongst the vegetables, we grow a range of annual and perennial flowers: a small but very important part of our gardening.

My role as gardener is to help people make the best use for themselves of the garden. For some it will be a place constructively to burn off pent-up energies; others may find a sense of purpose in the meticulousness of 'pricking out' seedlings or hand-pollinating the peach blossom. I try to make sure there's something for everybody. Without pressure, there's always more to learn, more to experience – there is for me. Often the simple act of getting our hands into the earth, knowing we're working toward a tangible, taste able result, can take us out of the repetitious patterns of thought we so easily talk ourselves into.

I aim to ensure there's a range of jobs available, to suit the range of people; and where needed I can provide the know-how to carry out those jobs. I also look after work safety matters, aiming for people to feel safe though not nannied. I hope to keep the garden an attractive place to work and to be in; and at the end of the day I hope to ensure that folk feel their work is recognised and appreciated.

Most importantly, the structures around the garden – the work-hours, the organic methods, the crop rotation and the rest – are there principally to help it function, a means to an end. It's a place where you can weed carrots and talk to those around you, or watch the robin risk getting closer while you mulch the flower-bed, or lose yourself in the blue of the sky or the hiss of rain on the lily pond in a quiet moment alone; a place to find some recovery.

Tara Rokpa Relaxation

Lothlorien's approach to mental health is based on Tara Rokpa Therapy which was developed by Dr Akong Rinpoche, the founder of Rokpa Trust. This form of therapy brings together Buddhist understandings of the human mind with relevant western psychotherapies. As the growing popularity of mindfulness-based approaches demonstrates, many healthcare professionals and others are showing an interest in eastern ways of working with the mind.

At Lothlorien we cultivate the principle that the human mind carries its own dignity and healing capacity which cannot be permanently damaged or destroyed. We believe that it is possible to get to know this innate capacity which we all have, and is most obviously expressed in moments of relaxed openness. In times of difficulty, however, the more usual response of the body and mind is to tighten and to solidly identify with our experience, hence seeing little choice or ways out of our difficulties.

When the mind is more relaxed, creative solutions are easier to find, especially when one is able to access the natural open quality of mind. No-one is a stranger to momentary experiences of calmness, stillness and tranquillity. However, for more calm states of mind to become a stable part of our day to day experiencing relaxation and awareness practices are generally thought to be helpful. The therapeutic sessions which are offered at Lothlorien have their foundations in this approach.

Roan Lodge

Roan Lodge is situated opposite the main house at Lothlorien and was opened in April 2003. It provides accommodation for 5 people and offers a balance between communal and individual living. Each person has a large bedsit room and there is a shared kitchen and living room. The group shares responsibility for shopping and upkeep of the house and sometimes eats together. Decisions on the day to day running of the household are taken at the weekly household meeting.

Roan Lodge is intended to be a safe and secure environment, where the benefits gained from participating in the structured lifestyle at Lothlorien can be consolidated. The overall focus is on developing greater independence and autonomy than is possible within the main house at Lothlorien. This is achieved through pursuing outside interests such as voluntary work or training as well as working in the communal vegetable garden and taking joint responsibility for running the household. The Core Group facilitates the group in running the house and offers individual support to residents. There is, however, an expectation that residents at Roan Lodge will have a lesser need of emotional support than when they were at Lothlorien.

Roan Lodge offers medium term accommodation, normally with a maximum stay of up to 5 years. Roan Lodge will only consider people who have had previous contact with Lothlorien. If others wish to apply to Roan Lodge, they would first need to spend some time in Lothlorien before being considered for Roan Lodge.

Article on Lothlorien

By Brendan Hickey, manager at Lothlorien 1992-2013, published in Therapeutic Communities magazine in 2008 (www.lothlorien.tc/articles.html).

Who can benefit?

Lothlorien welcomes applications from people who are experiencing mental health or psychological problems and who feel that living as part of a therapeutic community would be of benefit in helping to address the issues which affect their lives.

In choosing new community members, we will consider people who are:

- open to personal development and change in their lives
- able to take responsibility for themselves and to live with others with an attitude of respect and co-operation
- willing to join in the daily programme to the best of their ability
- competent in basic living skills and are able to attend to their own personal care, as we do not provide support in this area

- able to share the same living space without causing distress or harm to others
- prepared to link in with the statutory mental health services and comply with any agreed treatment plans
- able to manage their own medication

Applications will not be considered from those with a history of risk to others such as aggression, violence, verbal abuse, serious harm caused, sexually inappropriate behaviours, convictions for violent and sexual offences, threats to harm others, arson/fire setting, incidents involving the Police, stalking and harassment, risk to children. We are unable to accept applications from those whose primary problem is drug or alcohol abuse. We cannot normally be an alternative to acute hospital admission for those in crisis.

We are unable to offer respite stays, except to former members of the community.

The minimum age for joining the community is 21. The maximum stay is normally two years in the main house and up to five years at Roan Lodge. We expect community members to commit themselves to a minimum stay of 6 months when they join the community after completing their two-week trial visit.

Volunteering at Lothlorien

Spending a period of time as a voluntary co-worker at Lothlorien Community is an exciting opportunity in a challenging but rewarding environment. Lothlorien has developed an innovative alternative to mainstream approaches by providing the opportunity for people with mental health problems to develop their potential through living alongside people who are relatively well, in an atmosphere of friendship, acceptance and mutual support. We aim to break down the distinction which frequently exists between those seen as 'well' and those seen as 'unwell.' Co-workers play a key role in this process by helping to create a culture of mutual support which facilitates residents in developing their strengths and allows them to see themselves as having something to offer as well as having something to gain from community life.

Four co-workers live at Lothlorien and along with all community members, participate in a wide variety of daily tasks from domestic chores such as cooking and cleaning to working in the vegetable gardens and grounds. It is not essential that co-workers have any special practical skills; however, those who do are encouraged to use them in ways that benefit the community.

Although distinctions between co-workers and residents are minimised, the co-workers have a key role to play in the community in helping to create a positive atmosphere. It is hoped that through the co-workers' energy and example, everyone will be encouraged to participate to the best of their ability. As their role is essentially that of befriender, co-workers can also be involved supporting people at times of distress.

We have a strong commitment to supporting co-workers to get the most out of the experience at Lothlorien through weekly group supervision and regular individual supervision. There are also opportunities for training such as Nonviolent communication, Mental Health First Aid, Fire Warden or First Aid courses. Core Group members are available on call outside of their working hours and will come in if there is an emergency or if there is something important to attend to.

What you can gain?

Volunteering at Lothlorien offers a valuable opportunity for personal growth. It provides practical experience for those who want to apply for entry into professional training in areas such as social work or counselling. It can also provide useful post-qualifying experience after completing a professional qualification.

Many co-workers come having already had professional experience in the social care field but are drawn to Lothlorien in order to experience an alternative way of supporting people through living in a community and working together from a set of shared values. Some people also come to learn about the therapeutic use of horticulture.

Others may want to take a new direction in life or want time out from their normal career. Prior to applying, it is helpful to have had some experience, either paid or voluntary, in the social care field and practice in compassionate communication. It can also be helpful to have some experience of meditation, mindfulness, contemplation, or other areas of personal development which leads to an increased self-awareness and ability to be present with others in a genuine and calm way.

Training which you will complete as part of your role will include:

- SVQ level 3 award in social services and health care. This will support you to become a skilled healthcare professional within the care sector, and will include a specialist knowledge of mental health care.
- SIPC level 1 (Infection Control)
- Adult Protection and Support
- Non- Violent Communication Skills level 1
- Suicide Prevention

What we are looking for. In selecting co-workers, we are looking for people who are: concerned for others; able to take an active interest in the welfare of others; open-minded; willing to respect everyone in the community for who they are enthusiastic; have a positive attitude; mature; robust enough to handle what can be an emotionally demanding role; responsible; can support the community's values, as well as its structures and routines; open to learning; being prepared to look at one's own values and ways of relating to others; able to work in a team; it is vital that co-workers are committed to working as part of a mutually supportive team.

We ask that all applicants: have a full clean driving licence; have savings for any expenses other than food and board for the duration of their time at Lothlorien; familiarise themselves with the Nonviolent Communication method.

Terms and Conditions

We require a minimum commitment of 6 months, although ideally we would like co-workers to stay for at least one year to ensure continuity and stability within the community. The maximum stay is 2 years. We welcome applications from people of all ages over 21. We like to have a mixture of ages in the co-worker team and we have had people ranging from their early 20s to late 60s.

Co-workers receive free room and board. We can also cover some of the expenses related to study time away from the community. The commitment expected from co-workers is not like that of a 9 to 5 job and it is expected, while recognizing that everyone needs time on his/her own, that co-workers will spend time with the community in leisure as well as work times.

Due to the demanding nature of the role, it is required that co-workers take time away from Lothlorien. All co-workers are required to go through enhanced criminal records disclosure through the Central Registered Body for Scotland.

How to Apply

If you are interested in joining the community, please send a completed application form to the Manager. Vacancies normally arise about every 3 months, although we often have more applicants than vacancies. If you are selected for interview, the first step is to come for a day visit. You can stay overnight if you are coming a long distance. The day visit will enable both you and the Community to see if Lothlorien is the right place for you.

If the day visit goes well, the next step is to come for a week's trial visit, during which time there will be a formal interview. The whole community is involved in the decision regarding the selection of new co-workers.

SOTERIA NETWORK[74]

We promote humane, non-coercive mental health services

We are a network of people in the UK promoting the development of drug-free and minimum medication therapeutic environments for people experiencing 'psychosis' or extreme states. We are part of an international movement of service users, survivors, activists, carers and professionals fighting for more humane, non-coercive mental health services.

People who hear voices, have visions or experience reality in different ways to those around them — and become overwhelmed by their experiences — are often referred to as experiencing 'psychosis'. We believe that people can and do recover from difficulties which tend to be categorised under the term psychosis. This recovery can be with, without and sometimes despite psychiatric intervention.

Soteria Network UK was formed in 2004 in Bradford following a national speaking tour by the late Loren Mosher. The network was inspired by his pioneering work in the founding of the Soteria Project in 1970 and the first Soteria House in San Diego, California. The name Soteria was adopted to clearly indicate the values and principles the Network aspires to, and which remain as valid and relevant in the 21st century as in the 1970s and 80s.

Soteria House began life as an experimental research project designed to see whether people experiencing a 'first episode' acute psychosis and who might otherwise be diagnosed with schizophrenia and treated with medication in hospital, might fare just as well in a

---

[74] Adapted from the Soteria website: www.soterianetwork.org.uk, and from Wikipedia.

house with minimum medication, but with maximum support. Soteria was an ordinary house, in a real sense part of the suburban community, with a sense of homeliness and community within. Soteria employed a 'phenomenological' approach, one which attempts to see and accept the experiences of the person as they are, while developing over time a shared understanding of the meaningfulness of the person's experiences within their social context.

At its first conference held in Bradford in 2009, Soteria Network UK brought together people with the aspiration, commitment and resolve to set up the first UK Soteria house; this ran successfully for over a year, overcoming many challenges, and it's hoped to relaunch it when further funding and the 'right' premises are achieved.

The Soteria philosophy inspires many people who want to develop a more compassionate and effective approach to people in mental distress, enabling them to come through it in a non-coercive, non-oppressive way.

Thus, in addition to the aspiration to set up Soteria houses, Soteria Network aims to support approaches to helping people in mental health crises and distress based on 'being with' rather than 'doing to'. These can include: the creation of networks of support for people in their own homes; responding to individuals and carers seeking alternatives to coercion; linking with community organisations that offer non-judgemental, non-labelling safe space; setting up or co-creating 'coming off medication' groups; informing and supporting mental health professionals wishing to avoid medicalisation. We also participate in conferences, contribute to research and write articles. One such article appeared in the Schizophrenia Bulletin. [75]

The Soteria model is a milieu-therapeutic approach developed to treat acute schizophrenia, usually implemented in Soteria houses.[76] Based on are covery model, the common elements of the

---

75 A Systematic Review of the Soteria Paradigm for the Treatment of People Diagnosed with Schizophrenia, by Tim Calton, Michael Ferriter, Nick Huband and Helen Spandler. *Schizophrenia Bulletin, 2008, 34(1),181-92.*

76 Ciompi, L. & Hoffmann, H. (2004). Soteria Bern: an innovative milieu therapeutic approach to acute schizophrenia based on the concept of affect-logic. *World Psychiatry, 3 (3), 140–146.*

Soteria approach include the use of primarily non-medical staff, limited to the abstinence of anti psychotic medication, and the preservation of residents' personal power, social networks, and communal responsibilities.

Soteria houses provide a community space for people experiencing mental distress or crisis, and are open with no restraint facilities. Loren Mosher, who founded the first Soteria house, believes his work has shown that it is possible to treat acute psychosis without restraint methods. Soteria houses are often seen as gentler alternatives to the psychiatric hospital system, which is perceived as authoritarian, hostile, or violent, and over reliant on the use of psychiatric (particularly antipsychotic) drugs. Soteria houses are sometimes used as "early intervention" or "crisis resolution" services. The Soteria model was and remains controversial, in large part due to its perceived rejection of the widely accepted bio-psycho-social model and lack of quality research into its efficacy.

Theoretical model

Former patients declared that they needed "love and food and understanding, not drugs", and the Soteria Project was meant to compare results of the methods. Most psychiatric hospital wards function according to the medical model. In this model, doctors possess decision-making powers and have final authority; primary therapeutic value is attached to used extensively drugs; patients are considered as having an illness, with concomitant disability and dysfunction which should be "treated" and "cured"; labelling and its consequences, namely stigmatization and objectification, are almost inevitable. At Soteria houses, in contrast, the primary focus is on development, learning, and growth.

History

The original Soteria Research Project was founded by psychiatrist Loren Mosherin San Jose, California, in 1971. A replication facility ("Emanon") opened in 1974 in another suburban San Francisco Bay Area city. Mosher was influenced by the philosophy of moral treatment, previous experimental therapeutic communities (such as the Fairweather Lodges), the work of Harry Stack Sullivan and R.D. Laing. The name *Soteria* comes from the Greek Σωτηρία for "salvation" or "deliverance".

Mosher's first Soteria house specifically selected unmarried patients between the ages of 18 and 30 who had recently been diagnosed with schizophrenia according to DSM-2criteria. Staff members at the house were encouraged to treat residents as peers and to share household chores. The program was designed to create a quiet, calming environment that respected and tolerated individual differences and autonomy. There was also an ethos of shared responsibility in running the house and in playing a part in the mutually-supportive community, where the distinction between experts and non-experts was downplayed (similar to therapeutic communities). Though the model calls for no use of Psychiatric medication, in practice they were not completely rejected and were used in some circumstances. The Soteria staff, compared to staff in other psychiatric services, were found to possess significantly more intuition, introversion, flexibility, and tolerance of altered states of consciousness.

Many professionals around the world admired the approach, aspiring to create mental health services based on a social model as opposed to a medical model. However, the Soteria Research Project was also the subject of much controversy. One of the main critiques was that the project was withholding evidence-based treatment, as it was based on invalid anti-medication and anti-disease models, which went against the widely accepted bio-psycho-social model of disease. Some also questioned the reported efficacy of the treatment, noting that Mosher's definition of patient recovery was staying off of drugs, with no assessment of their symptoms.

The US Soteria Project closed as a clinical program in 1983 due to lack of financial support, although it became the subject of research evaluation with competing claims and analysis. Second-generation US successors to the original Soteria house called "Crossing Place" are still active, although more focused on medication management.[77]

---

[77] Crossing Place: www.woodleyhouse.org

Writing in 1999, Mosher described the core of Soteria as *"the 24 hour a day application of interpersonal phenomenological interventions by a non-professional staff, usually without neuroleptic drug treatment, in the context of a small, homelike, quiet, supportive, protective, and tolerant social environment."* More recent adaptions sometimes employed professional staff.

Soteria-based houses are currently run in Sweden, Finland, Germany, Switzerland, Hungary, the United States, as well as other countries. A first European near-replication of the original Soteria house was implemented in Bern, Switzerland, on May 1, 1984. However, the Bern approach differs from Mosher's original project in that it does not adopt the same anti-medical stance, using a consensual low-dose anti-psychotic treatment and including psychiatric staff. The following criteria was required for patients to be admitted: Aged 17–35; a recent onset of schizophreni form or schizophrenic psychosis defined by using DSM-III-R criteria, not more than one year before admission; at least two of the following six symptoms within the previous four weeks: severely deviant social behaviours, schizophrenic disorders of affect, catatonia, thought disorders, hallucinations, delusions.

Research at Soteria Berne found that the majority of acute schizophrenia patients could be treated as successfully by this paradigm as by standard hospital proceedings, but with significantly lower doses of anti-psychotics and at similar daily costs. Some advantages of the Soteria model may be found at the subjective-emotional, familial, and social level.

In the context of increasing interest in the Soteria model in the United Kingdom, several European countries, North America, and Australasia, a review of controlled trials was conducted in order to evaluate the efficacy of the approach in the treatment of people diagnosed with schizophrenia. The results indicated that the Soteria paradigm yields similar – and in certain cases better – results than standard treatment. However, the review was based on a limited number of studies of questionable quality, and more research is needed in order to form a better consensus.

12-STEP COMMUNITIES

12-Step Communities – and treatment centres that use the 12-Step model – are based on the original idea of Alcoholics Anonymous, which is a widely used treatment tool to help people understand the journey into, during, and after recovery from many sorts of addictions, compulsions and addictive behaviours.

The basic premise of this model is that people can help one another achieve and maintain abstinence from substances of abuse, but that proper healing cannot come about unless people with addictions surrender to a "higher power". This higher power doesn't need to be a traditional Christian version of God – it can be as simple as the community of the 12-step meetings, the universe, or a different version of a higher power that fits your own particular type of spirituality.

The 12-Step movement can be a powerful and helpful force for many people, but some people struggle with what they interpret as a strong religious element of the program, so many addiction treatment programs offer alternatives to 12-Step methodology for those who prefer a more secular foundation for treatment.

A 12-Step program provides a supportive and safe place to learn and share knowledge with others in similar situations and circumstances as they build bonds and strengthen their support system. At meetings, participants share their feelings and experiences with drugs, alcohol, addiction and addictive behaviours. The 12-step model is used by a large number (c. 75%) of addiction treatment centres.

In its original form, the 12-Steps came from a spiritual, Christian inspiration that sought help from a greater power, as well as from peers suffering from the same addiction struggles. In addition to the original Alcoholics Anonymous (**AA**) group, various offshoots now exist, such as Narcotics Anonymous (**NA**), Heroin Anonymous (**HA**), Cocaine Anonymous (**CA**), Gamblers Anonymous (**GA**) and Debtors Anonymous (**DA**). Whilst the regular 'meetings' used to be in person, there are now many meetings online.

The 12 Steps, as outlined in the original *Big Book* and presented by AA, are:

1. Admitting powerlessness over the addiction
2. Believing that a higher power (in whatever form) can help
3. Deciding to turn control over to the higher power
4. Taking a personal inventory
5. Admitting to the higher power, oneself, and another person the wrongs done
6. Being ready to have the higher power correct any shortcomings in one's character
7. Asking the higher power to remove those shortcomings
8. Making a list of wrongs done to others and being willing to make amends for those wrongs
9. Contacting those who have been hurt, unless doing so would harm the person
10. Continuing to take personal inventory and admitting when one is wrong
11. Seeking enlightenment and connection with the higher power via prayer and meditation
12. Carrying the message of the 12 Steps to others in need

There are also support groups for family members of the person in recovery: e.g. Al-Anon for families of alcoholics. Twelve-Step meetings are considered the "fellowship" part of the AA mutual support groups, where people come together and share their experiences.

For many people, these groups may serve as their primary resource for changing their behaviour, but they also often augment formal treatment. Such programs can also be helpful for long-term support and care.

One survey found that there were approximately 64,000 groups in the U.S. and Canada, with more than 1.4 million members. Worldwide, there are approximately 115,000 groups supporting more than 2.1 million members.

By exploring the steps in depth and seeing how others have applied the principles in their lives, you can use them to gain insight into your own experiences, and to gain strength and hope for your own recovery.

The steps and the principles behind them are:

1. **Honesty**: After many years of denial, recovery can begin with one simple admission of being powerless over alcohol or any other drug a person is addicted to. Their friends and family may also use this step to admit their loved one has an addiction.
2. **Faith**: Before a higher power can begin to operate, you must first believe that it can. Someone with an addiction accepts that there is a higher power to help them heal.
3. **Surrender**: Realising that you can change your self-destructive decisions by recognizing that you cannot recover by yourself; but, with help from your higher power, you can.
4. **Soul searching**: The person in recovery must identify their problems and get a clear picture of how their behaviour affected themselves and others around them.
5. **Integrity**: Step 5 provides great opportunity for growth. The person in recovery must admit to their wrongs – at least to their higher power and to another person.
6. **Acceptance**: The key to Step 6 is acceptance – accepting one's character defects exactly as they are and becoming entirely willing to let them go.
7. **Humility**: The spiritual focus of the next Step is humility, or asking one's higher power to do something that cannot be done by self-will or just mere determination.
8. **Willingness**: This step involves making a list of those you one has harmed before coming into recovery. It helps clarify the extent of one's addiction and prepares one for the next step.
9. **Forgiveness**: Making amends may seem challenging, but for those serious about recovery, it can be a great way to start to heal one's significant relationships.
10. **Maintenance**: Nobody likes to admit to being wrong, but this is also a necessary step in order to maintain one's spiritual progress in recovery.

11. **Making contact**: The purpose of Step 11 is to discover the plan your higher power has for your new life – life without the addiction.
12. **Service**: The person in recovery should also carry the message to others and put the principles of the program into practice in every area of their life.

Self-report information collected by AA, NA, and CA suggests that the median length of abstinence among currently-attending members is five years. Around a third of members report remaining abstinent between one and five years. More formal research also supports the findings of support group surveys: for example:

- Attending 12-step recovery programs in addition to specialized substance use treatment is associated with better overall outcomes.
- Greater involvement, particularly when a person first connects with a 12-step program, is also linked to better outcomes.
- Participating in activities and attending meetings helps to reduce the likelihood of are lapse.

While participating in the 12 steps of recovery can be beneficial for many people, one might consider the advantages and disadvantages of these programs before you decide if this approach is right for you.

Benefits

These programs offer a number of benefits, including:

- A free resource for communities to address substance or behaviour use problems
- Readily available
- Community-based
- Encourages members to take an active part in recovery
- Offers online and in-person options

Disadvantages

However, 12-step mutual support groups may not be for everyone. Some challenges or possible disadvantages include:

- Co-occurring mental health or chronic health conditions may make participating in 12-step groups more challenging
- This approach places full accountability for addiction and recovery on the individual
- 12-step groups may be less effective for certain groups, including women, BIPOC and/or LBGTQ+ [78], and other minority groups
- The emphasis on powerlessness can feel disempowering to some people
- Emphasis on a higher power can alienate some people
- Does not address the physical aspects of recovery, such as drug detox and withdrawal

Therefore, while 12-step recovery programs can be helpful and are quite successful, they are not always the best choice for everyone. They are an affordable, available, and convenient resource, especially while people start their journey of recovery from their form of substance use or addictive / compulsive behaviour, but their emphasis on admitting powerlessness and surrendering to a higher power can be a problem for some individuals.

Therefore, they also – to an extent – keep people in fixed position: they assume the addiction will always be present. There is not a fully transcendent component; there are no significant alternative pathways or models of development and thus – in their view – the 'victim' ('addict') stays at risk.

This is – perhaps – a personal critique. However, it has also been made more publicly. This critique does not diminish the "success' of these programmes over many years will thousands, if not millions of people.

---

[78] BIPOC – Black, Indigenous and people of colour; LBGTQ+ stands for lesbian, gay, bisexual, trans-sexual, queer/questioning and many others (including asexual. Non-binary, etc.)

SPIRITUAL CRISIS NETWORK UK [79]

The Spiritual Crisis Network (SCN) interested in studying human experiences that are outside our usual day-to-day experiencing of the world. The term most commonly used in the psychological research for this realm of experience is 'Anomalous Experiences', but many different terms have also been used, such as: 'Exceptional Experiences' - 'Extreme Experiences' - 'Unusual Experiences' - 'Transformational Experiences' - 'Spiritual Experiences' - 'Out of the Ordinary Experiences' (OOEs) - 'Religious Experiences', etc.

An Evaluation of the UK Spiritual Crisis Network

A PhD research study evaluating the work of the SCN was completed in 2021. The results are now available as a summary report [80] and an article for publication in an academic journal is now being prepared. This project was undertaken by Mike Rush, via Canterbury Christ Church University supported by the Professional Development Foundation and the Alef Trust.

SCN Conference, 2022 - Spiritual Crises: Supporting Positive Transformations

The full conference programme, abstracts, and speaker biographies can be downloaded here: Speakers & Abstracts [81]. Video recordings of Steve Taylor's talk and the panel discussion on spiritually

---

79 Adapted from: www.spiritualcrisisnetwork.uk
80 www.spiritualcrisisnetwork.uk/s/SCN-Evaluation-Summary-Report.pdf
81 www.spiritualcrisisnetwork.uk/s/Speakers-Abstracts.pdf

transformative experiences facilitated by Isabel Clarke can be found on the SCN YouTube channel here. [82] The following speakers have also made their PowerPoint slides available below:

- Transformation and Turmoil: When Spiritual Awakening is Sudden and Dramatic - Dr Steve Taylor [83]
- An Evaluation of the UK Spiritual Crisis Network - Mike Rush [84]
- Evidence-based Practices for Integrating Spiritual Emergencies - Dr Marie Grace Brook [85]

Other Research

There are relatively few empirical studies on spiritual crisis (or spiritual emergency). However, despite the dearth of academic studies in this area there are five main themes of research emerging that support the approach that the SCN currently takes. These are summarised below and some of the key articles are cited.

Alternative Approaches

The first theme is comprised of the evaluation studies done on alternative approaches to psychosis and schizophrenia in the 1970s and 1980s. These take a psycho-social approach that minimises the use of medication and encourages the working through of the experience as a problem-solving process in a safe communal space.

- Mosher, L. (1999). Soteria and Other Alternatives to Acute Psychiatric Hospitalization. *The Journal of Nervous and Mental Disease*, 187, 142–149. [86]

---

82 www.youtube.com/playlist?list=PLEyGbrsuW8rCub-3qSfrplCPzOzUMRA2n
83 www.spiritualcrisisnetwork.uk/s/Spiritual-Crisis-network-presentation-ST.pptx
84 www.spiritualcrisisnetwork.uk/s/SCN-Evaluation-SCN.pptx
85 www.spiritualcrisisnetwork.uk/s/MGBrook-2022-Evidence-Based-Practices-for-2022-Integrating-Spiritual-Emergencies-SCN-UK-MGB.pptx
86 www.semanticscholar.org/paper/Soteria-and-other-alternatives-to-acute-psychiatric-Mosher/a077712f538469b1821ac61020e8137c4962147b?p2df

- Mosher, L. & Bola, J. (2004). Soteria-California and its American Successors. *Ethical Human Psychology & Psychiatry*, 6(1), 7–23. [87]
- Mosher, L., Vallone, R., & Menn, A. (1995). The Treatment of Acute Psychosis Without Neuroleptics. *International Journal of Social Psychiatry*, 41(3), 157–173. [88]

Positive Appraisals

The second theme consists of the more recent studies that assess the effects of the appraisal of an experience, by self or others, on its outcome. Positive appraisals tend to result in less distress and reduce the need for clinical intervention.

- Hartley, J. & Daniels, M. (2008). A grounded theory investigation into negative paranormal or spiritual experience, based on the 'diabolical mysticism' of William James. *Transpersonal Psychology Review*, 21(1), 51–72. [89]
- Heriot-Maitland, Charlie, Knight, M., & Peters, E. (2012). A Qualitative Comparison of Psychotic-Like Phenomena in Clinical and Non-Clinical Populations. *British Journal of Clinical Psychology*, 51, 37–53. [90]
- Brett, C., Heriot-Maitland, C., McGuire, P., & Peters, E. (2014). Predictors of Distress Associated with Psychotic-like Anomalous Experiences in Clinical and Non-clinical Populations. *British Journal of Clinical Psychology*, 53, 213–227. [91]

---

[87] www.researchgate.net/profile/John_Bola/publication/233557008_Soteria-California_and_Its_American_Successors_Therapeutic_Ingredients/links/0a85e53741fa38d215000000.pdf
[88] www.madinamerica.com/wp-content/uploads/2011/12/Mosher(2).pdf
[89] www.psychicscience.org/papers/hartleydaniels08.pdf
[90] www.onlinelibrary.wiley.com/doi/abs/10.1111/j.2044-8260.2011.02011.x
[91] www.academia.edu/download/41504353/Predictors_of_distress_associated_with_p20160124-6199-97zzbo.pdf

Narratives and Frameworks

The third theme evidences the importance of a narrative, story, or framework of understanding for the process. These frameworks can be based upon psychological and transpersonal models. Any number of spiritual systems or religious traditions can also provide a context within which to make sense of the experience and different cultural perspectives are important to consider too.

- Hartley, J. (2010). Mapping Our Madness: The Hero's Journey as A Therapeutic Approach. In: *Psychosis and Spirituality: Consolidating the New Paradigm* (pp. 227-238). Wiley-Blackwell.
- Clarke, I., Mottram, K., Taylor, S. & Pegg, H. (2017). Narratives of Transformation in Psychosis. In: *Spirituality and Narrative in Psychiatric Practice: Stories of Mind and Soul* (pp. 108–120). Royal College of Psychiatrists.
- Fischler, R. (2019). *The Crux of the Crisis: An ethnography of UK Spiritual Peer-Support Networks on narratives and experiences of mental health/spiritual crisis as types of knowledges.* MSc Thesis, University of Amsterdam.

Behaviours and Practices

The fourth theme, which is currently the least researched, investigates the effectiveness of particular self-help attitudes, behaviours and practices. There have been no studies that assess the effectiveness of any specific psychotherapeutic interventions for spiritual crisis. However, Brook's (2019) study did examine the effectiveness of 84 behaviours and practices. Those rated most helpful were practising compassion, finding calmer environments, expression of the experience through creativity, and allowing psycho-spiritual issues to surface rather than resisting them.

- Brook, M.G. (2019). Struggles Reported Integrating Intense Spiritual Experiences: Results from a Survey using the Integration of Spiritually Transformative Experiences Inventory. *Psychology of Religion and Spirituality.* [92]

Complementary Strategies

Finally, there appear to be two main strategies for managing a spiritual crisis: a "suppressive" strategy for calming down and regaining some control of the process, and a "facilitative" strategy for exploring the deeper personal meaning and significance of the experience.

- Sedlakova, H. & Rihacek, T. (2019). The Incorporation of a Spiritual Emergency Experience into a Client's Worldview: A Grounded Theory. *Journal of Humanistic Psychology*, 59(6), 877–897. [93]

These five themes form the empirical foundation upon which the SCN bases its approach: providing information and advice via its email support service, organising face-to-face peer-support via its local and online groups, and providing education and awareness raising via its events and conferences.

The SCN Research Group

This is a small group of researchers and others interested in research into spiritual crisis. Researchers from different universities, pursing various post-graduate programmes of study, meet each month online to report on and share their work. Some of this research was presented at SCN conferences at the University of Sunderland in 2013, and at Mundesley Hospital, Gimingham, Norfolk in 2015. The new SCN Research Group met for the first time on 14th November 2020.

SCN Statistics

The SCN monitors some basic statistics in order to evaluate the services it provides.

---

[92] www.psycnet.apa.org/record/2019-14550-001
[93] www.journals.sagepub.com/doi/abs/10.1177/0022167816668114

In 2020 the SCN was contacted by **258** people. **128** of these were asking for support for or advice about their own experiences. **27** were asking on behalf of someone else.

In 2020 the SCN received **58** thank you messages and **0** complaints.

Requests for Support in 2020

Carers can be anyone supporting someone who is experiencing spiritual crisis, including friends, family, or health care professionals.

Types of Request Made to the SCN in 2020

These requests are in addition to the information and support provided by email. The SCN has been running several online peer-support groups during the pandemic in 2020, and has delivered online events in the form of training and awareness sessions. The SCN doesn't currently provide telephone support, referrals to individual therapists, or retreat venues.

Types of Spiritual Crisis Reported to the SCN in 2020

Specific types of spiritual emergency, as defined by Stanislav and Christina Grof and others, were self-reported by people contacting the SCN in 2020. Just over half of the people contacting the SCN did not categorise their experience. Some people reported more than one category of experience. The SCN itself does not impose categories on people's experiences.

Support Services: Online E-mail support service

If you believe yourself or someone else you care for is going through a spiritual crisis, we have a team of trained volunteers who provide e-mail support and advice for those experiencing or going through a spiritual crisis or spiritual emergency. Please contact us and describe what is happening for you, or for someone you are supporting. You can be sure that you will be met by non-judgemental volunteers on the receiving end of your email.

Peer Support Groups

The Spiritual Crisis Network operates a number of local peer-led support groups for individuals who have experienced a spiritual crisis in order to explore experience and receive help, with integrating and understanding their experiences within these small shared peer groups. The groups are held in a safe, non-judgemental space, where you can slowly discover the meaning from your own experience. It is also a great way to meet others who have experienced something similar. We currently have established peer-led support groups in; Bristol, London, Sheffield, Somerset and Glastonbury. We also have an online peer-support group for individuals who do not have a local group in their location.

Community Forum

SCN is in the process of changing its forum platform. Please join, discuss your experiences and support others. Discussions may vary from any topics under the realm of: 'anomalous experiences', 'religious experiences', 'out of the ordinary experiences, (ODEs)', 'spiritual experiences', 'unusual experiences', etc. Topics around mental health and wellbeing are also welcome. All are treated with respect and discretion, creating this safe space together.

Family and Carers: For partners, spouses, family, carers and friends:

Family bonds and relationships are complicated and complex. When a crisis colours these familial connections, an array of challenges immediately come to the fore. If you are related to someone currently experiencing a mental health transition/spiritual crisis and feeling overwhelmed, you may be interested to know that SCN, has an online support group.

Adult relatives caring for children who are undergoing a spiritual crisis and seeking support for themselves are very welcome to join our 'Family and Carer' online support meetings. Due to Children's' Safeguarding legislation, however, we are unable to permit children or young people under the age of 18 to attend. Contact us for information about caring for a minor experiencing a spiritual crisis. This online group meets fortnightly. You are very welcome to join us!

SPIRITUAL EMERGENCE NETWORK USA [94]

The Spiritual Emergence Network (SEN) provides individuals that are experiencing psychospiritual difficulties a specialized mental health referral and support service. In a culture which has not understood issues surrounding spiritual development, the gift of being heard and understood by a knowledgeable and supportive listener can be life-altering. Our referrals are licensed and/or trained mental health care professionals who are preferably in your area (but many also work by phone or encrypted video) who have expertise with many specific psychospiritual issues. SEN offers its referral services and directory listings free of charge! Much of our transpersonal (psychospiritual) directory is online forself-referral. [95] The SEN website is also a spiritual emergence resource guide.

Integrative Mental Health University (IMHU) [96] provides an International Directory [97] of certified Spiritual Emergence Coaches® who know how to support people in spiritual emergence. Training to become a Spiritual Emergence Coach® is available at IMHU as well as many online webinars. These webinars empower individuals with lived experience and their caretakers with knowledge and skills to achieve the positive potential in spiritual emergency. Founder/Executive Director, Emma Bragdon, PhD, has specialized in Spiritual Emergence/Emergency since 1984 and gives many of the presentations.

---

[94] Adapted from: www.spiritualemergence.org
[95] www.spiritualemergence.org/directory
[96] www.imhu.org
[97] www.imhu.org/coaching/directory

Association for Transpersonal Psychology (ATP) [98] is a membership supported international coordinating organization for scientific, social, and clinical transpersonal work that serves the world community. The Association's mission is to promote eco-spiritual transformation through transpersonal inquiry and action. Recognizing the reciprocity inherent between our actions and our world, the Association is dedicated to encouraging and enhancing practices and perspectives that will lead to a conscious, sustainable, co-evolution of culture, nature, and society.

Spiritual Competency Resource Center [99] provides access to online resources that enhance the cultural sensitivity of mental health professionals.

Holos Institute [100] is a non-profit organization offering holistically oriented psychotherapy and educational programs. Their counseling offices are based in both Oakland and San Francisco and offer a range of affordable, high quality psychotherapy services with advanced marriage and family therapist interns who are participating in the Holos ecopsychology training program. They also offer unique group experiences in nature/wilderness therapy and vision quests. In addition to psychotherapy services, Holos serves as a public and professional forum for topics in ecopsychology, holistic, and integrative psychology through ongoing lectures, workshops, and experiential programs.

California Institute of Integral Studies [101] is an accredited institution of higher learning and research that strives to embody spirit, intellect, and wisdom in service to individuals, communities, and the Earth. They also 'housed' the SEN for a while, providing a resource for people to get in touch with professional and supportive help for their process.

---

[98] www.atpweb.org
[99] www.spiritualcompetency.com
[100] www.holosinstitute.net/
[101] www.ciis.edu

Center for Spirituality & Psychotherapy (CSP) [102] was formed in response to the rapidly growing interest in the relationship between spirituality and psychotherapy. It is the first center of this kind within a major psychotherapy and psychoanalytic training institute. It is committed to the study of how psychotherapy can foster the emergence of the spiritual dimension in our lives, and how spiritual practice may enhance our personal lives and the psycho-therapeutic experience. Drawing from all religious and spiritual traditions, psychological perspectives and scientific theory and research, we emphasize how the individual can awaken to the spiritual traditions and practices.

The Hoffman Institute [103] The Hoffman Quadrinity Process is an 8-day retreat that empowers you to resolve previously immovable blocks to healthy relationships, self-knowledge, emotional freedom, and radiant spirituality. It is based on the principle that persistent negative behaviors, moods, and attitudes experienced in adulthood have their roots in the experiences and conditioning of childhood. Until this conditioning – they say – is understood and resolved, it continues to undermine our adult lives.

Emma Bragdon, PhD. [104] wrote the first book published about Spiritual Emergency, *'A Source book for Helping People in Spiritual Emergency'*. It is used in graduate schools internationally to train psychotherapists how to recognize spiritual emergence phenomena so they can offer appropriate support. Another book, *'The Call of Spiritual Emergency'* is full of stories of individuals who have experienced spiritual emergency and the positive outcomes they have had. Emma was licensed as a psychotherapist in 1989. She has extensive training in breath work, energy work, yoga, and intuition. She offers private consultations online and in person. She also trains and certifies Spiritual Emergence Coaches® through IMHU.org. [105]

---

[102] www.psychospiritualtherapy.org
[103] www.hoffmaninstitute.org
[104] www.emmabragdon.com
[105] www.imhu.org/product/spiritual-emergency

Bonnie Greenwell, Ph.D., [106] is a transpersonal therapist and author of *'Energies of Transformation: A Guide to the Kundalini Process'*, a guide for experiencers and therapists based on her dissertation research. Over the past fifteen years, she has lectured, trained therapists, and consulted with hundreds of individuals who have experienced spiritual emergence phenomena. She has training in Ashtanga and Kundalini Yoga, acupressure, and breathwork. She is a founder of the Kundalini Research Network. [107]

Judith Orloff, MD, [108] is accomplishing for psychiatry what physicians like Larry Dossey and Dean Ornish have done for mainstream medicine – she is proving that the links between physical health, mental well-being, and spiritual connectedness cannot be ignored. She has worked as a board-certified psychiatrist and assistant professor of psychiatry at UCLA and is an internationally known writer and lecturer. She is the author of *'Guide to Intuitive Healing and Second Sight'*.

The Center for Spiritual Emergence [109] provides wrap-around, concierge level, in-patient and out-patient services to help people live to their fullest potential by providing a transpersonally-based, systems-oriented, body-centered, and trauma-integrated approach to healing spiritual emergence, spiritual emergencies, and addictions. We address the physical, emotional, mental, social, and spiritual dimensions of our patients' concerns as well as health and wellness as pathways to wholeness.

Spiritual Competency Academy [110] Spiritual crises can often be mistaken for psychiatric disorders, and this can lead to tragically unnecessary hospitalizations and stunting of the growth potential of such experiences. This site helps both clinicians working with spiritual issues and is also a useful self-help resource for persons integrating a spiritual emergency. This site is run by Dr. David Lukoff.

There are some further USA resources mentioned below.

---

[106] www.kundaliniguide.com
[107] www.kundalininet.org
[108] www.drjudithorloff.com
[109] www.centerforspiritualemergence.com
[110] www.spiritualcompetencyacademy.com

MINDFREEDOM INTERNATIONAL

I recently came across a 'synthesis' of mental health information and activism with the above title. They describe themselves as:

Mind Freedom International is a non-profit organization under IRS 501(c)(3). For over two decades and counting, we have been engaging in successful advocacy, peaceful protests, public education, mutual support, lobbying, and organizing without ever giving up our dream of facilitating mental and emotional wellness for all people. We are neither controlled nor funded by any pharmaceutical companies, governments, political parties, or religious organizations. Instead, we are powered solely by contributions from individuals like you and occasional grants from independent foundations. We are also the only organization in the field of mental health that is accredited by the United Nations as a Non-Governmental Organization (NGO) with Consultative Roster Status. [111]

This organisation does not specifically address "spiritual emergencies" but it supports, in a number of different ways, people with mental health issues that are often mis-diagnosed as psychoses and who may be treated by the psychiatric 'system' of hospitalisation and psychotropic medications.

Specifically, there is an excellent series of about 13 short videos – 'Voices for Choices' – on different topics that are very informative and well-worth watching: [112]. They cover topics such as: "What involuntary mental health treatment looks like"; "Alternatives to psychiatric

---

[111] www.mindfreedom.org/about/
[112] MindFreedom International 'Voices for Choices' videos: www.mindfreedom. org/knowledgebase/voices-for-choices-video-series.

hospitals"; "Alternatives to psychiatric drugs"; "Power of peer support"; "Origins of the c/s/x movement"; etc.

In general, they put forward the opinion that the "medical model" for psychiatric patients often does not make sense, is potentially (and sometimes actually) oppressive, and can even be harmful. Two of the videos involve *"Problems with involuntary psychiatric treatment"* and *"How to escape forced psychiatric treatment"*. They describe some of the *"Alternatives to psychiatric hospitals"*, looking as to whether (a) one can keep people out of hospital, (b) seeing these as episodic problems rather than chronic illnesses, and (c) drugs being more as tools rather than as answers in these cases. The recommended 'technique' is rather to 'be with' people, rather than 'do' things to them. They advocate 'respite' and ask the person, *"What would you want that to look like?"*. They also mention the 'Soteria' model (see above) and they favour the "Open Dialogue" approach (as described in the *"Alternatives to psychiatric drugs"* video), with two mental health practitioners, who openly discuss the situation with the 'patient' and close family members and also talk between themselves in front of these, and then again ask for the others' views, thoughts and feelings. They also advocate the *"Power of peer support"* and are somewhat activist, as in *"Getting organised"*.

There are links to various support and advice initiatives and organisations, such as: Medicine-free psychiatric wards in Norway; the Freedom Center; the Coalition to End Forced Psychiatric Drugging; Western Massachusetts Recovery Learning Community (RLC); Pathways Vermont; the ADAPT model [113]; etc.

They have a "Directory of Alternative Providers" and have published a *'Harm Reduction Guide'* for people coming off psychiatric drugs, in conjunction with the Icarus Project [114] and the Freedom

---

[113] Silove, D. (2013). The ADAPT Model: a conceptual framework for mental health and psychosocial programming in post conflict settings. *Intervention, 11 (3), 237-248.*

[114] The Icarus Project (2002-2020) was a network of peer-support groups and media projects with the stated aim of changing the social stigmas regarding mental health. DuBrul, Sascha Altman (2014). The Icarus Project: A Counter Narrative for Psychic Diversity. *Journal of Medical Humanities. 35 (3): 257–271.*

Center [115] (now part of the Western Mass, RLC) [116]. Whilst this latter organisation, now re-branded as the "Wildflower Alliance", only offers peer-to-peer support systems for people based in Western Massachusetts (and online), this can act as a useful model for other local social- and peer-support groups. These types of support organisations are probably the most useful to people who are going through mental health problems, though they should not – necessarily – be used as an alternative to professional support: best to get the best of both worlds.

The Mind Freedom International organisation has also published, with help from the Foundation for Excellence in Mental Health Care, a fairly comprehensive *"Organizing Guide for Psychiatric Survivors"*. This 272-page downloadable booklet is intended to help survivors protect themselves and others from psychiatric harm, as well as to organize for human 'mental health' rights throughout the world. Its 'critique' of the 'mental health' profession, the DSM and the concept of 'diagnosis' is – to say the least – interesting:

> *"... the adoption of disease classifications in the DSM has not led to any innovations in the care and treatment of "mental illness" for nearly fifty years. In fact, researchers are pulling away from using the DSM because of its lack of scientific validity. ... the DSM diagnoses are based on a consensus about clusters of clinical symptoms, not any objective laboratory measure. ... the APA had adopted a 'disease model,' and if you carefully read the DSM III manual, you saw that the authors acknowledged that very few of the diagnoses had been 'validated.' ... The APA's hope and expectation was that future research would validate the disorders, but that hasn't happened. Researchers haven't identified a characteristic pathology for the major mental disorders; no specific genes for the disorders have been found; and there isn't evidence that neatly separates one disorder from the next. The 'disease model,' as a basis for making psychiatric diagnoses, has failed."* (pp. 9-11)

They – quite rightly, in my opinion – go on to say that the whole 'Diagnosis' model can actually create harm: it distances people – and their families, friends and co-workers – from what has been and what

---

[115] Freedom Center: www.freedom-center.org/
[116] Wildflower Alliance: Western Mass, RLC: www.wildfloweralliance.org

is actually happening to the person who is at the centre of it all (I refuse to call them the 'patient'). This person is usually confused and in distress and they need help, support, love, care and understanding: they need a 'diagnosis' like a hole in their head. *Enough!*

Drugs are also **not** the solution – though I have found that they may be useful temporarily as a 'tool' or as an 'aid' to treatment. Rarely do they 'cure'. They are often very powerful; they are not necessarily effective; and they have very many side-effects (please read the small print). In addition to a poor record of recovery, the harmful side-effects of psychiatric drugs have been well documented. At best, individuals can develop *akathisia* (a movement disorder characterized by a feeling of restlessness) or tardive *dyskinesia* (which causes stiff, jerky movements of the face and body). The very long list of other possible side-effects continues with weight gain, vomiting, diarrhoea, confusion, irritability, as well as an increased risk of suicide. Long-term consequences of taking psychiatric drugs are even more devastating — not only can they be addictive (in themselves) and/or self-perpetuating (in that coming off them results in further symptoms), but studies also reveal that they can shorten life expectancy.

Services to help people get off psychiatric drugs are nearly non-existent. For those trying to wean themselves off psychiatric drugs, the Icarus Project and Freedom Center have published the *"Harm Reduction Guide to Coming Off Psychiatric Drugs."* Groups such as at the Sunrise Centers have been running workshops that help people wean off psychiatric drugs. Psychiatric survivor Laura Delano has also founded the Inner Compass Initiative [117] and the Withdrawal Project [118] to connect individuals going through psychiatric drug withdrawal.

So, what does work? Mind Freedom's *"I Got Better"* survey (in 2012, with 400 respondents) asked people what actually helped them. Respondents said they found **a variety of alternatives** more helpful than psychiatric drugs during mental/emotional distress. And **combining multiple treatment tools was far more effective** than relying on one by itself.

---

[117] Inner Compass Initiative:www.theinnercompass.org
[118] Withdrawal Project: www.withdrawal.theinnercompass.org

Going back to the difference between a crisis or emergency, and resolving that, once the person with a mental health difficulty is reasonably 'safe', there is a well-tried and probably more successful option. Dr. Al Galves, a director of Mind Freedom International, spoke about psychotherapy (in one of the videos). Being a psychotherapist myself, I liked this definition:

Psychotherapy is more than just meeting with a therapist and it's much more than just 'talk therapy'. The great benefit of psychotherapy is that you learn skills and knowledge that you can use for the rest of your life, to manage yourself, to manage your thoughts, to use your thoughts, your emotions, your perceptions, your reactions, your behavior – to use it in good ways. In psychotherapy, you learn about yourself; whatever your problems are; whatever behavior you're engaging in that you don't like, if it is creating problems; whatever your state of being is that is making you miserable – you weren't born that way. That's what happened to you as you grew up, and you had to survive, and you had to find a way to survive, and – in the process of surviving and doing the best you can – we all lose parts of ourselves; we all develop limiting beliefs; we all developed fixated responses; and so psychotherapy can help you overcome those. Taking a pill can't. Most psychotherapy sessions last for 50 minutes. Patients know it's a therapy session, so they're going to bring something in that's troubling them, or that they want some help with: probably something to do with relationships, or with their work, or how they're feeling. So, the therapist is listening, and watching what's going on, and paying attention to non-verbal behavior, and – at some point – the therapist will pick up on an issue that seems important. So, the therapist will bring it up and say, "How would it be if we work on that?" The therapist is helping the patient get in touch with something that's bothering him or her; something that they're not feeling good about; that's upsetting – [so as to] get some idea about how to move forward. If you look at the research about psychotherapy, where you ask people who receive psychotherapy, "Was it helpful?", eighty percent of them say, "Yes, it was helpful". And the more they received, the more helpful they thought it was. And it turns out that it doesn't make any difference what approach was used, what makes the difference is the relationship between the patient and the therapist.

So, meet with at least three therapists and tell them that you're meeting with them to see whether you want to work with them. Tell them what you want help with and ask them how they would help you and see which of them makes the most sense to work with."

Addendum

This section (Part 3) of this book is **not** an endorsement of any of the various projects and centres mentioned above. It is intended more as an indication of what is (or has been) available 'out there' in the 'field'.

If you – or someone you know – has been going through a mental health crisis, a chaotic or upsetting experience that may or may not be ultimately transformative, there are places 'out there' that may help. Do **not** just choose one of them – even if it is close or convenient! Explore and discover what might be right for you (or the person near to you). After all, it is **your** (their) process.

Some people need help and support; some need respite and a retreat; some people may need some medical help initially … so, find out what is needed! Be proactive! Be selective! Do the research!

There is a part of the Bible (Genesis) where it describes how God made the Heaven and Earth, and all that dwells upon the Earth, in just six days. And He saw that it was very good. However, it doesn't say how long He thought about it first. Often, the next thing to do is to think, ponder, mediate, explore, on what might work for **you** (or the person close to you). So, what do You need? What might work for You?

I hope that this book has given you a few clues; has given you a potential map of the territory. If so, that is great. However, I also hope it hasn't given you what you might think as **answers**. It may have created lots of questions; that is very good! Answers are for you to find – for you (or for the person close to you).

And there is **not** (never) just one answer: there is a **process** that will lead one toward a potential "better place": a path that might lead out of the tangled briars, towards the peaceful glade, which can then lead towards another path, that might eventually lead one out of the wood.

You are on a journey – and much of this book is an attempt to describe parts of this journey. As mentioned before: the only real goal is to **travel well**.

DEMOCRATIC THERAPEUTIC COMMUNITY (DTC) MODEL [119]

The Democratic Therapeutic Community (DTC) model is a form of group therapy which "emphasises the role of attachment". We aim to create a culture of enquiry, to explore all behaviours, thoughts and emotions. This can be used to form relationships between all members of the DTC, empowering you to take responsibility for yourself and each other.

"This has been synthesised into a simple developmental model of emotional development, where the task of the therapeutic community is to recreate a network of close relationships much like a family, in which deeply ingrained behavioural patterns, negative cognitions and adverse emotions can be re-learned". (Association of Therapeutic Communities).

The therapy comprises of an introduction group (six sessions), the main therapy group (one day per week for 12 months), and a voluntary peer support group for people when they leave therapy.

Eligibility

To be eligible to join the democratic therapeutic community, you must have a diagnosis of borderline personality disorder, or have experienced at least five of the following symptoms:

---

[119] Adapted from NHS Pennine Care: NHS Foundation Trust: www.penninecare.nhs.uk/dtc

- You have engaged in a variety of destructive and impulsive behaviour, including self-harm, excessive use of alcohol, illicit substances or food to cope with difficulties.
- You have demonstrated a pattern of unstable and intense interpersonal relationships, characterised by alternating between extremes of idealisation and devaluation, and/or a persistent unstable sense of self.
- You have a history of complicated, longstanding, emotional and behavioural difficulties, often stemming from traumatic childhood experiences.
- You find existing services unsuitable, difficult to use or not of lasting benefit, which may have led to difficult relationships with professionals.
- You have demonstrated recurrent suicidal behaviours, gestures or threats of self-mutilation behaviour.
- You experience chronic feelings of isolation and emptiness.
- You experience inappropriate, intense anger or difficulties controlling anger and frequent displays of temper.

Expectations

You need to have a care co-ordinator, or have had some exposure to mental health services, either psychological treatment, prior group treatment, or psychiatric care (in or out-patient).

You also need to want to work on changing your behaviour and understanding yourself through the input of others.

You will need to access transport to attend the group on a regular basis.

Our service is not normally open to those with a primary diagnosis of schizophrenia (or other psychotic disorders), bipolar disorder, dementia, those with moderate learning disability, or those who have a history of sexual offences.

Our vision is for a happier and more hopeful life for everyone in our communities.

Our purpose is to maximise people's potential to live more rewarding lives and to create a great place to work.

Our values are kindness, fairness, ingenuity and determination.

We believe that care and compassion underpin everything. This means we:

- Support and care for the people we work with and for.
- Champion great team-work.
- Always respect others.

We treat everyone fairly. This means we:

- Empower and involve others in decisions.
- Are accountable and honest for our actions.
- Work towards a fairer society by being inclusive and challenging stigma.

We are resourceful and innovative. This means we:

- Are creative and solution focused.
- Are curious to continuously improve.
- Enthuse and support people to bring about positive change.

We are courageous and ambitious for what we can achieve together. This means we:

- Aim high.
- Are tenacious and confident.
- Learn from mistakes.

These documents have more information about us and what to expect during sessions:

- General info booklet [120]
- Info booklet for professionals [121]

---

[120] www.penninecare.nhs.uk/application/files/9815/6284/9132/DTC_General_Info_Booklet.pdf

[121] www.penninecare.nhs.uk/application/files/5815/6284/9382/DTC_Professionals_Info_Leaflet.pdf

- About the introduction group [122]
- Introduction group agenda [123]
- Info for professional visitors [124]
- Community group day programme [125]

Spiritual, religious and pastoral services

We understand that there are times when what we most need is compassion, a listening ear and sensitive and confidential support from someone we can trust. Our chaplaincy team delivers spiritual, religious, and emotional support to patients and staff. We support people of any faith, including those who do not have one.

Our seven chaplains are Reverend Giselle Rusted (Christian), Rabbi Chanan Tomlin (Jewish), Imam Olasheni Junaid (Muslim and site lead for Oldham), Reverend Neil Hepworth (site lead for Bury), Reverend Annie McMullen (site lead for Rochdale), John Ling (Humanist) and Reverend Graham Lindley (site lead for Stockport).

We are an inclusive service, respectful of age, gender, race, culture, disability, belief or sexuality. We offer support specific to your situation and sit alongside you whenever you need a friendly face to talk to.

We offer a number of compassionate pastoral care services. Here are some of the ways we can help:

- We are available for confidential one to one chats at times of difficulty and uncertainty. Where we can support your spiritual care and well-being.
- We provide opportunities for dedicated prayer and offer communion.

---

[122] www.penninecare.nhs.uk/application/files/5815/6284/9132/DTC_introduction_group_booklet.pdf

[123] www.penninecare.nhs.uk/application/files/1215/6284/9132/DTC_Introduction_Group_Standing_Agenda.pdf

[124] www.penninecare.nhs.uk/application/files/4815/6284/9132/DTC_Information_for_professional_day_visitors.pdf

[125] www.penninecare.nhs.uk/application/files/1315/6284/9131/DTC_Day_Programme_Taste_and_Orb_2018.pdf

- We safeguard and support the religious and spiritual lives of all our patients and staff.
- Emotional support for those people with no religion who have anxiety and stress, who are confused and troubled and just need to talk
- We provide religious resources for patients and staff on all of our sites.

We provide listening and support for concerns and issues of staff, service users and their carers, meeting individuals where they are in their faith beliefs or no beliefs. Focusing on their emotional, pastoral needs delivering comfort and peace. We will also signpost to other individuals in the trust who can assist. The space we provide is private and confidential.

You can contact the chaplaincy team by emailing: pcn-tr.chaplaincy@nhs.net

There is also an International Network of Democratic Therapeutic Communities: www.indtc.org/en/home

SOME CAVEATS – WARNINGS

Deliverance:

In some cases, especially where there is a strong Christian or religious background, there is a natural tendency to seek help with problems from the 'ministry' of the church. Some churches are better at dealing with these types of situations than others. The Church of England's Ministry of Deliverance has very good and clear guidelines. These are – that the ministry of deliverance should be done:

* in collaboration with the resources of medicine,
* in the context of prayer and sacrament,
* with the minimum of publicity, and
* by experienced persons authorized by the diocesan bishop, and then
* followed up by continuing pastoral care.

There is practice of keeping careful and confidential records, (within the constraints of the Data Protection Act). Clergy and lay people involved in this ministry (should have) all had suitable experience, training, support and supervision. A multidisciplinary approach is to be desired, and it is recommended that those authorized for this ministry should have access to consult and work with other clergy, and with doctors, psychologists and psychiatrists. Services involving deliverance ministry should be simple and use appropriate pastoral and sacramental ministry whilst always ensuring that the welfare of the person being ministered to is of paramount concern. The Episcopalian

Church follows similar guidelines. However, the situation can be different – even with established religions. [126]

Anything less than this is, or more than this, is probably best to stay away from. Some other churches (perhaps the more apostolic or Pentecostal ones) seem to go a little overboard on "deliverance" – the trendy name for exorcism – and the results are not always particularly helpful to, or pleasant for, the person concerned. Deliverance then becomes something that the church needs to do in order to retain the 'purity' of one of its members and thus also itself, rather than a way of helping the person in difficulties that might take them outside of the remit or experience of the other church members. In this way, one can get into quite heavy 'trips'. [127]

Kundalini

This, as mentioned, is a very powerful bodily-based spiritual energy that, when opened or aroused, seems to rise up the body clearing out the different energy centres (chakras) in its path. As with anything, this energy can: **(i)** sometimes be powerful and thus dangerous, and **(ii)** sometimes be abused. Read up on it!

Firstly, it is recommended that any work with kundalini be only done in conjunction with someone like a qualified & experienced Body Psychotherapist and also after a general medical check-up to ensure that your body is reasonably fit and strong enough to take the force or duration of these energies passing through you. As regards the second point, there have been a number of cases of totally inappropriate methodology extending even to blatant sexual abuse from people claiming to be able to liberate your kundalini energy, using their own sexual energy or through forms of sexual contact with them. These people probably need more help – and a lot of therapy – than you do. Please try to avoid them!

As with anything, whatever you do in this area needs to be properly integrated and well 'grounded', ideally with some professional

---

[126] Chavez, W.S. (2021). Modern Practice, Archaic Ritual: Catholic Exorcism in America. *Religions, 12(10), 811.* (www.mdpi.com/2077-1444/12/10/811)

[127] See: Janette Winterson's (1991) book, *Oranges Are Not The Only Fruit.*

therapeutic help. An active Kundalini is <u>not</u> necessarily the answer to your prayers (and your sex life): an active spiritual life and a fully open body may possibly be. That is the direction your process is trying to take you.

Psychiatry:

Traditional psychiatry sees mental problems more as an illness only treatable by **(i)** medication; and occasionally **(ii)** some talking therapy. This is an almost total dualist medicalisation of the person's psychological, emotional, or spiritual situation. Whilst mental illness may sometimes be present, and a psychiatric opinion should sometimes be sought (as has been indicated), the basic tenets of psychiatry do not, per se, acknowledge spirituality in any useful form, even though DSM-IV (psychiatry's diagnostic manual) does now mention a spiritual problem or crisis (see: Appendix 1 by David Lukoff). Some psychiatrists are however much more sympathetic as individuals and may be much more open to these sorts of concepts: *"it all depends on who you talk to"*. Treatment of a spiritual experience as a psychotic episode (involving drugs or other treatments) can be necessary very occasionally, for relatively short time periods, and yet, if prolonged – can also detract from, or even stop, the spiritual component of the experience. It's a fine line, to be trod carefully.

Holotropic Breathwork: (a very personal disclaimer)

Whilst I have mentioned the work of Stan & Christina Grof a number of times, and whilst I have the highest respect for all their pioneering work, their theoretical thinking, their experiences, and their writings within the field of working with people in Spiritual Emergencies, I cannot personally recommend their current spiritual or therapeutic methodology called, and promoted as, Holotropic Breathwork ©.

This is because: both personally and professionally, I have experienced people taking part in these Holotropic Breathwork workshops without (what I consider to be) sufficient prior screening and especially without significant integration work afterwards.

I, myself, did several sections of the Holotropic Breathwork training in the late 1980's & early 1990's, whilst living at the Findhorn Foundation, and I have had personal contact with the Grofs and their 'therapists', subsequently, when professional standards in their training organisation were being established.

I fully admit that these workshops can be a wonderful way to contact aspects of your psyche, usually unavailable or disowned, and yet, some people just don't have the sufficient ego-strength to manage this type of opening easily. Whilst the workshop facilitators are reasonably well-trained in the workshop technique itself, they are not (in my opinion) always sufficiently able to work with someone who may go into deep crisis, become borderline psychotic, or be on the point of a Spiritual Emergency – unless they have had considerable other specialist psychotherapeutic training. Many of them do: but there are certainly some who don't have such expertise.

I also firmly believe that insufficient integration work is undertaken both in the usual workshop format (other than drawing a mandala, and talking with your workshop partner), where insufficient time is given for this within the workshop structure and there is no proper follow-up afterwards.

Back in the mid-1990s, I wrote-up a two-page handout to be given to participants advising them and warning them of some of these aspects to consider. These were handed out for a while by some Holotropic Breathwork practitioners, especially those connected with the Findhorn Foundation. Incidentally, the Foundation has long ceased promoting Holotropic Breathwork workshops.

I have communicated these personal reservations to the Grofs, in person (face-to-face) and also in writing to their Holotropic Breathwork organisation.

Alternative Therapies:

Whilst I have long been an advocate of many forms of Complementary Medicine and Alternative Therapies, there is still a serious "caveat" that I (and others) have about certain therapies, which needs to be stated clearly.

Many alternative health and complementary medicine practitioners are reasonably well trained in their own particular therapy. However, and here is the warning, they are not necessarily all very well-trained in proper professional practice, good ethics, record-keeping, knowledge of limitations and contra-indications, when or who to refer, and specialist conditions. Neither have all these therapies or techniques been properly researched; nor have they all undertaken controlled efficacy studies. So, please do not put your full trust in them! They can sometimes be very useful, but can also sometimes be useless, and much depends on the skill of the individual practitioner. Some of the less well-trained complementary medicine or alternative therapy practitioners apply their particular therapy fairly indiscriminately.

Some of them can even be harmful at certain stages of your own personal process: for example, if you have already been somewhat traumatized by a "rebirth' type of spiritual experience, serious integration is usually called for, not more 'Re-birthing'. If you are a recovering alcoholic, stay away from flower essences and herbal remedies that use brandy as a base for the remedy. Very sensitive people can respond to acupuncture unfavourably, if the needles are not put in … in the correct place, but not at the correct 'level' (depth). There are many other similar examples.

Cults, Sects and Revitalization Movements

Whilst it may be wonderful to be accepted as part of a like-minded group, or experience a charismatic leader, who may seem to have many of the answers that you are looking for, or it may be wonderful to do work that will help bring (back) the better values of society, there are a number of spiritual and religious cults and sects and revitalization movements that, in the longer term, are not so promising or productive.

There are several quite well-known horror stories about extreme cults and sects, and much fear and paranoia has been generated, mainly by the media. There is also some truth to these stories. So, please use your discrimination and talk to others involved, <u>before</u> you get too involved, or so deeply involved with the group that it is difficult or impossible to come out!

Ensure that you can leave the geographical location easily, and come back if you want to: do so for a few times. **Ensure** that there is open contact with other members of your family, and even invite them along to visit you. **Avoid** those groups that put pressure on you to donate your worldly wealth, even in stages (ask to see their published accounts); adopt a different style of dress; or live with them all together. **Avoid** those with any sexual rites or practices. **Avoid** those where the 'sessions' are over-long or exhausting. **Avoid** those where there does not seem to be much integration into the local or wider community; or where there already is some controversy or scandal. **Avoid** those with a single male leader who is 'revered', or overly charismatic, or hypnotic. **Avoid** those that are newly founded, or only have a few people involved. **Avoid** the ones that promise a new millennium, paradise, personal transformation, or whatever, by a particular date, or on a particular happening, or through a particular person, or in a particular way. **Avoid** splits or subgroups dedicated to reviving a particular tradition, or set of (occult) practices. **Avoid** those which justify the otherwise unacceptable opposite: e.g. acts of violence to promote a better world.

This is not to say that every sect, or cult, or revitalization movement, or revolutionary group, or group of 'eco-warriors', is bad, or that anyone with features listed above are essentially harmful. But, they may not be right for you – yet! Some newly founded religions, spiritual groups, cults or movements in the guise of therapies have really helped people: but some can be very detrimental and harming. Please, therefore, discriminate very carefully! [128]

General Health:

It has been fairly conclusively demonstrated that a few simple preventative measures can considerably benefit one's general mental and physical health, boost the immune system, prevent illness and

---

[128] All this would mean that you would probably have avoided the early Christians, thus also avoiding possible persecution & martyrdom; so, discriminate towards my advice as well! Many cult leaders have had a personal apotheosis as well, however their character structure may not be sufficiently sound so that they misuse their personal charisma. (see *Prophets, Cults & Madness* by Stevens & Price)

infection, quicken recovery rates, assist dealing with problems, and prevent any reoccurrence of further problems or illness. These measures include:

- **Regular relaxation and/or meditation** –twenty minutes twice a day minimum; healthy sleep pattern;
- **Regular light exercise** –getting 'sweaty' for a minimum of about twenty minutes and up to about forty-five minutes, three times a week; varied types of exercise; ideally outdoors;
- **A positive self-attitude and balanced outlook** – glass half-full, not half empty; rational *and* emotional; 'sufficient' resources; 'appropriate' attitudes; more monist (non-dualist), holistic, egalitarian beliefs;
- **A balanced healthy diet** – "Five A Day" (portions of fruit & vegetables); organic (where possible); low fat; low carbohydrates; smaller portions; regular meals; at least 2 litres of water per day; no smoking (active or passive); moderate alcohol; no drugs or E-numbers; reduced sugar, caffeine; occasional multivitamins;
- **Relaxed attitudes to life & work** – 35-hour week (maximum); regular holidays & mini-breaks; times 'off' & occasional duvet-days; stress-free & safe workplaces; absence of discrimination or hostility; either an absence of, or a relaxed attitude to, significant 'life events';
- **Varied social contact** –a 'group' of friends; intimate contact with someone; some touch, laughter, and silence; the opportunity to trust, share confidences, listen, and be listened to;
- **Appropriate emotional expression** – feeling able to, and expressing, the whole range of emotions and reactions to life events, which includes some form of personal expression, artistic expression, or method of expressing something important within you;
- **Contact with nature & different environments** –just what is says; experience of different locations, cultures, and that wonderful restorer of all, Mother Nature.

The "caveat' here is when these activities are <u>not</u> happening – when you are not promoting your own general health on a fairly regular basis, then things can start to go downhill as ultimately the absence of these will probably <u>not</u> be that healthy for you or for your spiritual life.

THE RAINBOW

And God said, "This is the token of the covenant which I make between me and you and every living creature that is with you, for perpetual generations: I do set my bow in the cloud, and it shall be for a token of a covenant between me and the earth."

(Genesis 9:12-13)

After the storm comes the rainbow. And what is a rainbow? It is often used as an image of something new and beautiful. In this book, I have been talking about transformation, and you may well have been transformed. Of course, there is no one outcome of that – or any – transformation that can be described; and – of that which has been described – much of the outcome has been in the process of the journey itself. For myself, personally, there have been a number of "spiritual emergencies" that I have been through, both (looking back) before I visited the Findhorn Foundation, during the time I lived there for 17 years; and also in the 20+ years since I left there. But thankfully this phenomenon is found much wider than just at Findhorn and many different people from many different faiths and in many different countries have had many different types of their own personal apotheoses.

Piero Ferrucci wrote a book called *Inevitable Grace - Breakthroughs in the Lives of Great Men and Women: Guides to your Self-Realization*, where he studied the recorded lives of more than 500 such people, 'great' people that he describes as all having exceptional capacities. He writes:

> *My purpose was to identify their moments and periods of greatest happiness - the states of grace they felt to be supremely significant and beautiful. I made some very encouraging findings. The attitudes and techniques adopted ... have an identical form in different ages and civilizations. This means that ... they transcend the confines of history and diversity of cultures. These ... are simple and natural ways of being. We see them at work in ourselves, too, and in the people around us. We all have them, although in an embryonic, dormant, or repressed form and it is quite likely that we could all develop them.*

Some of the findings and conclusions of his amazing study give us a potentially clear blueprint for this transformational process. His point, my point, is that spirituality, whether it stays with us throughout adolescence into adulthood, or whether it reoccurs later in our life, is a perfectly natural phenomenon. It is part of the "package of being human" – a phrase used by Carolyn Myss, a New Age writer and lecturer.

Without this spiritual component, we are somewhat less than human, as Chief Luther Standing Bear succinctly puts it (see Quotations below). However, the phenomena of spirituality and the different pathways that it can take, or it can take us in, are very varied, as we have seen.

Ferrucci divides, or makes a synopsis from, the different lives of these different people of the various 'ways' of what he describes as 'Transformation' into seven different modalities. Here follows a brief description of each of the various 'Ways of Being' extracted from his book:

- **The Way of Beauty** is based on aesthetic enjoyment, inspiration, and creativity. In it we find the artists of various types.
- **The Way of Action** leads to the Self through disinterested service and tireless involvement in the world. It is the path of benefactors and philanthropists.
- **The Way of Illumination** is founded on the practice of meditation and is taken by the great contemplatives, philosophers, yogis, and sages of all times.

- **The Way of Dance and Ritual** covers physical, externalized, and communal approaches to the expansion of consciousness. It is comprised of dancers, performers of rituals, and actors.
- **The Way of Science** leads to attainment of the sublime through research, observation, and speculation. Here we find scientists and inventors.
- **The Way of Devotion** is practices by mystics and saints of all religions. Prayer is the main vehicle, relationship with God its central theme.
- **The Way of the Will** is the path of all who dare: explorers who venture into the unknown, inspired political leaders who confront hostile social forces, and also some athletes who challenge the limits of human capacities.

Whilst each of these ways is very varied, and by no means uniform, there are some notable similarities that happen during the process of transformation (according to Ferrucci):

> *"As one proceeds along a Way to the Self, one comes into contact with an entirely new realm that transcends the confines of individuality - the transpersonal level. Encountering this world can be an ecstatic experience, but it can also upset the mental balance of someone who is not prepared for it. Immature individuals may use transpersonal glimpses as an excuse for covering up their own weaknesses and avoiding the difficulties of life."*

He is saying that some people have difficulties, not perhaps just because of their 'immaturity', but because of the nature of what they are trying to transform. He is also stating that all, - Yes! all - of these 500 people whose lives have been recorded in detail because they are considered, in some way, "great": that they have all had a transformative, transpersonal experience.

These are not people selected at random. They are not people who were selected just because they had a transformational experience, and we've never heard of them before. These people constitute – in Ferruci's eyes – the "cream" of society, the "Top 500" if you like: they are considered as "great". And they ALL had types of transformational experiences. And they ALL survived these transformational experiences. And, perhaps, just perhaps, they are "great" simply because they ALL had – and survived – these transformational experiences.

Perhaps, even, it was the actual transformational experience that turned them in to becoming a 'great' person. Wow, now there's a thought!

TRANSFORMATION & ENLIGHTENMENT

Transformation is what it is all about: but what is Transformation? What is being transformed; what are you being transformed into? Does the caterpillar have any idea about becoming a butterfly?

Joseph Campbell felt that old myths, legends and fairy stories gave us clues: many of them are like road maps for this sort of transformational journey. Eastern philosophies speak of achieving 'satori' or 'samadhi' or becoming at one with the Tao. The Buddha spoke of losing all attachments. For Rumi, it was being totally conscious of the 'Beloved', in people, in nature and ourselves. These are all metaphors for something that we don't have a proper language for, or for what we have a million different metaphors.

There is a state of being where we are totally at peace with ourselves; of having an expanded consciousness and the capacity for discernment; of having a spiritual marriage between the masculine and feminine within ourselves; of being relatively detached from all human desires; of dedicating the rest of one's life towards the welfare of others, or towards enlightenment on the spiritual path.

However, for many, 'transformation' is not the end of the journey, the Celestial City, or some almost unachievable state of grace, or unconditional love. It is the realization that the journey itself is very real and worth enjoying. So, the goal is therefore – simply – to "travel well". Do that, and you are well set on the path of transformation.

In the West, most of the images of transformational journeys – and there are as many as there are paths up a mountain – involve various defined stages. The tenets of Jungian psychology (or 'Analytical Psychotherapy') have many of these stages outlined, and include some of the archetypal concepts have been mentioned in this book: the descent into the dark; facing one's shadow; etc. The writings of Robert Johnson are a very good introduction to some these concepts (See Book List). Johnson identifies three traditional levels of consciousness:

- *simple* consciousness *"Not often seen in our modern technological world"*;
- *complex* consciousness, where most of us are variously stuck; and then –
- *enlightened* consciousness: *"Known only to a very few individuals, which is the culmination of human evolution and can be attained only by highly motivated people after much work and training."*

Here, I take issue with him. I do not think that it is a once-and-for-all state; that you either have it, or you don't; nor is it that rare, or unusual, or extraordinary. It is just a part of our basic human potential.

I think – and this is also my experience with clients – that enlightenment frequently happens in different moments and various stages, and to many of us, and quite often. It is not a single event. We can have a transcendent moment, which passes, but this experience then motivates us forward. We can get somewhere wonderful, at least for a little while, and then we might lose it again; and hopefully, we learn from that loss. We have flashes and insights, which pass, but they help to shape our vision; and there is a steady forward progression.

These glimpses of 'transcendence' – or the 'divine' – are what help us to keep going; and they are important as they can also help modify what we need; teach us lessons; and show us the way towards our own personal state of transformation. They are like 'learning cycles'.

This can be as individual – as well as being universal – as we all are. For some, like Thoreau, it is the journey back to the simple level of consciousness finding happiness in a rich inner world; but to drop our usual consciousness, with our psychic energy under ego control, back into the instinctual is as difficult as raising our psychic energy and placing it under the control of our Higher Self.

Ken Wilbur

Ken Wilber believes that many claims about non-rational states make a mistake that he calls the "pre/trans fallacy". According to Wilber, the non-rational stages of consciousness (what Wilber calls "pre-rational" and "trans-rational" stages) can easily be confused with one another. In Wilber's view, one can reduce trans-rational spiritual realization to pre-rational regression, or one can elevate pre-rational states to the trans-rational domain.

For example, Wilber claims that Freud and Jung also commit this fallacy. Freud considered mystical realization to be aregression to infantile oceanic states. Wilber alleges that Freud thus commits a fallacy of reduction. Wilber thinks that Jung commits the converse form of the same mistake by considering pre-rational myths to reflect divine realizations. Likewise, pre-rational states may be misidentified as post-rational states. Wilber characterizes himself as having fallen victim to the pre/trans fallacy in his early work. Personally, I find Wilbur's concepts are essentially correct, but perhaps a bit too intellectual.

Tibetan Buddhism

Tibetan Buddhism has, for eons, been dedicated to the process of enlightenment and spiritual growth. Chögyam Trungpa, a re-incarnated Tibetan lama, who escaped the Chinese occupation of Tibet, was one of the leading and most original teachers of the Tibetan traditions of Kagyu and Nyingmato and able to reach the West and who helped to found the Buddhist centre of 'Samye-Ling' in Scotland, 'Vajradhatu', in Halifax, Canada, 'Gampo Abbey' in Cape Breton, Nova Scotia and 'Naropa University' in Boulder, Colorado. He coined the phrase "crazy wisdom" for this sort of path towards enlightenment. He was an adherent of the *Ri-mé* ("non-sectarian") ecumenical movement within Tibetan Buddhism, which aspired to bring together and make available all the valuable teachings of the different schools, free of sectarian rivalry. He was a complex character and, in the last few years of his life, might have "lost his way" somewhat until he died in 1987. However, his earlier writings (like *Born in Tibet*, *Meditation in* Action, and *Cutting through Spiritual Materialism*, are full of inspiration).

Therefore, in viewing his work, there is – as always – a balance has to be sought between the 'message' and the 'man'.

Like many other gurus, he / they – as we all do – carry a shadow side and, possibly because of the height of their achievements, they have potentially quite a long way to fall. This takes us into the arena of **Charisma** – almost a separate subject in itself.

Most gurus, spiritual teachers, or community leaders are quite charismatic: as they have to be in order to attract followers. However, charisma [129] – whether it be of the divinely conferred sort or the personality sort – is not (never) enough. The 'guru'-type person is also human and is thus fallible – and fallible people can and do fall. So, such can be said of people like: Bhagwan Shree Rajneesh, Kristnamurti, Mother Meera, Swami Muktananda, Gurmeet Ram Rahim Singh, Chandraswami, Yogi Bhajan, and especially the more obvious leaders of cults or sects like, Jim Jones, David Koresh, Sun Myung Moon, David Berg & Karen (Mama Maria) Zerby, L. Ron Hubbard, Shoko Asahara, Jeffrey Lundgren, and many other gurus and so-called spiritual teachers, or leaders of sects and cults. The list is unfortunately quite long. [130]There are traditionally several different sorts of charisma:

(1) Olivia Fox Cabane in *The Charisma Myth* differentiates 4 sorts: 'Focus Charisma' – someone with a high presence who makes others feel important and heard (viz: Bill Gates, Oprah Winfrey); 'Visionary Charisma' – someone who inspires others to follow (viz: Steve Jobs, many cult leaders, some politicians); 'Kindness Charisma' – someone who creates a deep, warm emotional connection with others (viz: Nelson Mandela, Desmond Tutu); and 'Authority Charisma' – someone with high power and status but not necessarily high in affability (viz: Stalin, Mussolini, Hitler, Rasputin).

---

[129] **Charisma** – a form of grace, charm or authority. [It] is a certain quality of an individual personality by virtue of which he is set apart from ordinary men and treated as endowed with supernatural, superhuman, or at least specifically exceptional powers or qualities. These as such are not accessible to the ordinary person, but are regarded as of divine origin or as exemplary, and on the basis of them the individual concerned is treated as a leader. (Max Weber)

[130] en.wikipedia.org/wiki/Category:Cult_leaders

(2) John Spacey (www.simplicable.com/talent/charisma) lists 8 types: Personal magnetism, Personal presence, Social risk taking, Countersignalling, Kind, Fearsome, Authority, Personality Cult.

(3) The Catholic Church lists 25 'supernatural' Charisms: Administration, Celibacy, Craftsmanship, Discernment of Spirits, Encouragement, Evangelism, Faith, Giving, Healing, Helps, Hospitality, Intercessory Prayer, Knowledge, Leadership, Mercy, Missionary, Music, Pastoring, Prophecy, Service, Teaching, Voluntary Poverty, Wisdom, Writing, Public Tongues, and the Interpretation of Tongues.

The key component is that some people have more personal power than others – and specifically how they choose to use or abuse this power.

Having a Guru

A guru is a Sanskrit term for a mentor, guide, expert or master in a particular area of knowledge (usually spiritual). The literal translation is a "dispeller of darkness (or ignorance)". The term is most often used in the Buddhist, Jain, Hindu or Sikh traditions. A guru is supposed to guide the spiritual progress of their students and their teachings are supposedly tailored to what they see is required for the student to learn.

The implication here is that this happens as a direct communication from the 'Teacher', so that their students may have to give up their former life – at least for a while – and go and live near to the Teacher (guru). Many modern gurus have also written extensive discourses on their teachings.

Most gurus are very charismatic people. However, take care of those who are very pushy or those telling you not to think, or question them, or just to follow them implicitly (and only them) – essentially preventing you using your own judgement.

You might want to read *The Guru Papers: Masks of Authoritarian Power* by Joel Kramer & Diana Alstead (1993, North Atlantic Books) for further examples and also of why people tend to give themselves over to gurus: often it is to fill an inner emptiness, a void, inside of themselves.

Gabor Mate (2018) calls this being in the realm or void of the "hungry ghosts". The void, or the hunger, could be due to trauma, or having experienced some kind of loss, or not having been supported or encouraged in childhood, or low self-esteem. It is like an addiction for belonging, support, connection and external validation, or the need to surrender to something greater than yourself.

A guru may seem to be special – given their deep spiritual knowledge – but that does not mean they are immune to normal human responses and needs: they may indeed be special, but they are also human. There is now a greater public acknowledgement that a guru – any guru – can stray away from the spiritual ideals that they espouse and act in unethical or even abusive ways towards others – especially their students. Such behaviour and abuse of power is increasingly and rightfully being condemned when it occurs.

In times when many people feel lost or confused, it can be seductive to give away your power to just one person, hoping that they will give you all that you need and fill the emptiness and the longing inside. However, this can also be very dangerous. Many people are too vulnerable or lost to trust their gut feelings and their own instincts, even when these are speaking to them loudly. When looking for a guru, **do your research first**.

The easiest way to detect a bad guru is if they speak too highly of themselves. If they claim that they are enlightened or a guru, that's usually a red flag. People, who are enlightened, would never call themselves "enlightened".

The filmmaker, Vikram Gandhi, who grew up in New Jersey in a Hindu household, wanted to prove the absurdity of blind faith, so he started his own fake spiritual movement and called himself "Kumare". He spoke of this: *"Kumare was very real to those around him and the experience to me was actually very real as well. When you're living a - sort of a double life in a way and you realize the fictional, or quote, 'fictional' version of you is so charismatic and so lovable to others, you wonder why you're not that person all the time?"*

While the project may have started off as an elaborate prank, Kumare did in fact have something that he was trying to teach: *"My philosophy is the middle philosophy, that is that all that you are seeing inside of me as a guru, you have inside yourself. That which you find divine in myself, you have inside. Therefore, you do not need a guru, you just simply need to find the guru inside yourself."*

So, if you want a true guru — a living master who is enlightened — then look for silence in their vibes. A quiet presence, depth in the gaze, kindness, and on and on we can cite, but if you were to visit ten gurus, you will probably be able to quickly sort them out according to your intuitive take. You can – all too easily go wrong – but not necessarily *that* wrong. Any guru out there should be fairly adept at teaching the basics: they will also use different sorts of 'wrapping paper'.

If you are already philosophically fairly 'hip', then picking a guru will be a more refined process. No matter what, if one is "picking a guru", one is actually seeking help towards spiritual evolution, and that desire or intentionis always fulfilled. God (or whom-so-ever) will have you learn from a lot of barefoot kids or maybe one special master — but hopefully you will become educated and thus enlightened. Maybe, also inspired by these 'outer' teachers to look within: for that is where true wisdom lies – for you, within you. Every real-life guru will – at some point – become inferior to your inner guru.

Marie Asbury (*Soaring Soul Wellness*) says: *"To me, a guru is anyone I learn from. It could be a toddler throwing a fit, teaching me empathy; or it could be my friend, reflecting back to me in a way that brings an 'Aha' moment. But a person claiming to be a guru hints at my red flag alert."*

So, as in the title of the book, *"If You Meet Buddha on the Road, Kill Him!"*– subtitled *"The Pilgrimage of Psychotherapy Patients"* by Sheldon B. Kopp (Bantam, 1976), echoes something of this essential truth.

Here is an excerpt:

1. Pilgrims and Disciples [131]

> *Difficulty at the beginning works supreme success.*
> *Furthering through perseverance.*
> *Nothing should be undertaken,*
> *It furthers one to appoint helpers.*
>
> I Ching

---

[131] www.amazon.co.uk/You-Meet-Buddha-Road-Kill/dp/0553278320

In every age, men have set out on pilgrimages, on spiritual journeys, on personal quests. Driven by pain, drawn by longing, lifted by hope, singly and in groups they come in search of relief, enlightenment, peace, power, joy or they know not what. Wishing to learn, and confusing being taught with learning, they often seek out helpers, healers, and guides, spiritual teachers whose disciples they would become.

The emotionally troubled man of today, the contemporary pilgrim, wants to be the disciple of the psychotherapist If he does seek the guidance of such a contemporary guru, he will find himself beginning on a latter-day spiritual pilgrimage of his own.

This should not surprise us. Crises marked by anxiety, doubt, and despair have always been those periods of personal unrest that occur at the times when a man is sufficiently unsettled to have an opportunity for personal growth. We must always see our own feelings of uneasiness as being our chance for "making the growth choice rather than the fear choice." So, too, the patient's longing for growth is the central force of his pilgrimage.

The psychotherapist needs only to be aware of this force, in his patient, and to keep it within his vision. Then he may enjoy his work, and need never bog down in boredom. His task is simply to watch, as the person in front of him wrestles with well-nigh paralyzing conflict, for the emergence of what he knows is there: man's inherent longing for relatedness and for meaning. The therapist is an observer and a catalyst. He has no power to "cure" the patient, for cure is entirely out of his hands. He can add nothing to the patient's inherent capacity to get well, and whenever he tries to do so he meets stubborn resistance which slows up the progress of treatment. The patient is already fully equipped for getting well... Since he [the therapist] is not "responsible" for the cure, he is free to enjoy the spectacle of it taking place.

Of course, like everyone else (including the therapist), the patient is too often inclined to act out of fear, rather than out of his longing for growth. If not, pilgrimages would always begin out of an overflow of joy, rather than (as is more often the case) being conceived in pain and turmoil. People seek the guidance of a psychotherapist when their usual, self-limited, risk-avoiding ways of operating are not paying off, when there is distress and disruption in their lives. Otherwise, we are all too ready to live with the familiar, so long as it seems to work, no matter how colorless the rewards.

And so, it is not astonishing that, though the patient enters therapy insisting that he wants to change, more often than not, what he really wants is to remain the same and to get the therapist to make him feel better. His goal is to become a more effective neurotic, so that he may have what he wants without risking getting into anything new. He prefers the security of known misery to the misery of unfamiliar insecurity.

Given this all too human failing, the beginning pilgrim-patient may approach the therapist like a small child going to a good parent whom he insists must take care of him. It is as if he comes to the office saying, "My world is broken, and you have to fix it."

Because of this, my only goals as I begin the work are to take care of myself and to have fun. The patient must provide the motive power of our interaction. It is as if I stand in the doorway of my office, waiting. The patient enters and makes a lunge at me, a desperate attempt to pull me into the fantasy of taking care of him. I step aside. The patient falls to the floor, disappointed and bewildered. Now he has a chance to get up and to try something new. If I am sufficiently skillful at this psychotherapeutic judo, and if he is sufficiently courageous and persistent, he may learn to become curious about himself, to come to know me as I am, and to begin to work out his own problems. He may transform his stubbornness into purposeful determination, his bid for safety into a reaching out for adventure.

You may then ask, "Of what sustained value is the presence of the therapist to such a seeker?" He can be useful in many ways. The therapist, first of all, provides another struggling human being to be encountered by the then self-centered patient, who can see no other problems than his own. The therapist can interpret, advise, provide the emotional acceptance and support that nurtures personal growth, and above all, he can listen. I do not mean that he can simply hear the other, but that he will listen actively and purposefully, responding with the instrument of his trade, that is, with the personal vulnerability of his own trembling self. This listening is that which will facilitate the patient's telling of his tale, the telling that can set him free.

The therapist provides a "dreamlike atmosphere…, and in it…[the patient] has nothing to rely upon except…[his] own so fallible subjective judgment." I have pirated this description. It was written by Carl Jung to describe the usefulness of the I Ching, the three-thousand-year-old Chinese Book of Changes, some lines from which I have used to begin this chapter.

At first, the patient tries to use the therapist, as many over the centuries have tried to use the I Ching, the oldest book of divination. The Book of Changes is made up of images from the mythology and social and religious institutions of the time of its origin. Orientals have too often searched these images for oracular guidance, just as some Christians have opened the Bible to verses picked at random in hope of getting specific advice about how to solve problems. So, too, the psychotherapy patient may begin by trying to get the therapist to tell him what he is to do to be happy and how he is to live without being fully responsible for his own life.

However, the I Ching, the Holy Bible, the contemporary psychotherapist and other gurus, all are poor oracles. They are instead far more significant as well-springs of wisdom about the ambiguity, the insolubility, and the inevitability of the human situation. Their value lies just in their offering imagery that is fixed without being stereotyped, images "to meditate upon, and to discover one's identity in." To these well-springs, the seeker must bring himself, and then listen for the echo returned by the books of wisdom or by his guru. Coming to knowledge of the self is insisted upon throughout the pilgrimage. The helper provides "one long admonition to careful scrutiny of one's own character, attitude, and motives."

The seeker comes in hope of finding something definite, something permanent, something unchanging upon which to depend. He is offered instead the reflection that life is just what it seems to be, a changing, ambiguous, ephemeral mixed bag. It may often be discouraging, but it is ultimately worth it, because that's all there is. The pilgrim-patient wants a definite way of living, and is shown that:

> *The way that can be spoken of*
> *Is not the constant way*
> *The name that can be named*
> *Is not the constant name.*

He may only get to keep that which he is willing to let go of. The cool water of the running stream may be scooped up with open, overflowing palms. It cannot be grasped up to the mouth with clenching fists, no matter what thirst motivates our desperate grab.

Starting out as he does in the urgency of his mission, it is difficult for the pilgrim to learn this patient yielding. This is to be seen in the old Zen story of the three young pupils whose Master instructs them that they must spend a time in complete silence if they are to be enlightened. "Remember, not a word from any of you," he admonishes. Immediately, the first pupil says, "I shall not speak at all." "How stupid you are," says the second. "Why did you talk?" "I am the only one who has not spoken," concludes the third pupil.

The pilgrim, whether psychotherapy patient or earlier wayfarer, is at war with himself, in a struggle with his own nature. All of the truly important battles are waged within the self. It is as if we are all tempted to view ourselves as men on horseback. The horse represents a lusty animal-way of living, untrammeled by reason, unguided by purpose. The rider represents independent, impartial thought, a sort of pure cold intelligence. Too often the pilgrim lives as though his goal is to become the horseman who would break the horse's spirit so that he can control him, so that he may ride safely and comfortably wherever he wishes to go. If he does not wish to struggle for discipline, it is because he believes that his only options will be either to live the lusty, undirected life of the riderless horse, or to tread the detached, unadventure some way of the horseless rider. If neither of these, then he must be the rider struggling to gain control of his rebellious mount. He does not see that there will be no struggle, once he recognizes himself as a centaur.

Enlightenment

The process of enlightenment can also be very enigmatic, like the old Zen koan:

> *What did you do before Enlightenment?*
> *I chopped wood and carried water.*
> *What do you do after Enlightenment?*
> *I chopped wood and carried water.*

QUOTATIONS

Our deepest fear is not that we are inadequate.
Our deepest fear is that we are powerful beyond measure.
It is our light, not our darkness, that frightens us.
We ask ourselves,
"Who am I to be brilliant, gorgeous, talented and fabulous?"
Actually, who are you not to be?
You are a child of God. Your playing small doesn't serve the world.
There is nothing enlightened about shrinking so that
other people won't feel insecure around you.
We are all meant to shine, as children do.
We were born to make manifest the glory of God that is within us.
It is not just in some of us: it's in everyone.
As we let our own light shine, we unconsciously
give other people permission to do the same.
As we're liberated from our own fear,
Our presence automatically liberates others.

Nelson Mandela, 1994 Inaugural Speech
Quoting Marianne Williamson in:
A Return to Love: A reflection on the principles of 'A Course in Miracles'. (1992)

There is Nothing Ahead

Lovers think they're looking for each other,
but there's only one search: Wandering
this world is wandering that, both inside one
transparent sky. In here
there is no dogma and no heresy.

The miracle of Jesus is himself, not what he said or did
about the future. Forget the future.
I'd worship someone who could do that!

On the way you may want to look back, or not,
but if you can say *There's nothing ahead,*
there will be nothing ahead.

Stretch your arms and take hold of the cloth of your clothes
with both hands. The cure for pain is in the pain.
Good and bad are both mixed. If you don't have both,
you don't belong with us.
When one of us gets lost, is not here, he must be inside us.
There's no place like that anywhere in the world.

Jelaluddin Rumi: 425:
from 'Open Secret: Versions of Rumi'
translated by John Moyne & Coleman Barks (Threshold) 1984

Plan for Life: by Mother Theresa

People are often unreasonable, illogical and self-centred.
Forgive them anyway.
If you are kind, people may accuse you of selfish, ulterior motives.
Be kind anyway.
If you are successful, you will win some false friends and some true enemies.
Succeed anyway.

If you are honest and frank, people may cheat you.
Be honest and frank anyway.
What you spend years building, someone may destroy overnight.
Build anyway.
If you find serenity and happiness, people may be jealous.
Be happy anyway.
The good you do today, people will often forget tomorrow.
Do good anyway.
Give the world the best you have, and it may never be enough.
But give the world the best you've got anyway.
You see, in the final analysis, it is all between you and God:
it was never between you and them anyway.

When the dreambody manifests itself as an energetic charge shooting through the spine, we could call it by its ancient name, the Kundalini. When it is experienced as the essence of life, it is Mercury. When one visualizes its energy as streaming through the body, it is the twelve meridian system. If one sees it and acts on this vision, we have Gestalt identification. If one feels it as a cramp in breathing, it is called character armor. If one senses and changes, we might speak of biofeedback. If it appears as a force pushing one in the stomach to do a new task, it is personal power. Obviously, we need a unified approach to the body.

Understanding and accepting the dreambody as process, however, requires factual knowledge about its behavior and the courage to go to one's limits in order to let the dreambody come into awareness. For the dreambody itself hovers between body sensation and mythical visualization.

Arnie Mindell, *Dreambody*

I have lived
On the lip of insanity,
Wanting to know reasons,
Knocking on a door. It opens.
I have been knocking from the inside!

Jelaluddin Rumi

If you will practice being fictional for a while, you will understand that fictional characters are sometimes more real than people with bodies and heartbeats.

The mark of our ignorance is the depths of our beliefs in everything.

What the caterpillar is absolutely convinced is the end of the world; the butterfly sees differently.

Richard Bach: Illusions - Memoirs of a Reluctant Messiah

I am not a mechanism,
an assembly of various sections.
And it is not because the mechanism
is working wrongly, that I am ill.
I am ill because of wounds to the soul,
to the deep emotional self
And the wounds to the soul
take a long, long time,
Only time can help
and patience,
And a certain difficult repentance
long, difficult repentance,
Realisation of life's mistake,
and the freeing oneself

> From the endless repetition
> of the mistake
> Which mankind at large
> has chosen to sanctify.

D.H. Lawrence, *More Pansies*

The body's a mirror of heaven:
It's energies make angels jealous.
Our purity astounds seraphim,
Devils shiver at our nerve.

Jelaluddin Rumi

BRAIN DAMAGE

The lunatic is on the grass
The lunatic is on the grass
Remembering games and daisy chains and laughs
Got to keep the loonies on the path.

The lunatic is in the hall
The lunatics are in my hall
The paper holds their folded faces to the floor
And every day the paperboy brings more.

And if the dam breaks open many years too soon
And if there is no room upon the hill
And if your head explodes with dark forboding tunes
I'll see you on the dark side of the moon.

The lunatic is in my head
The lunatic is in my head
You raise the blade.

You make the change
You rearrange me till I'm sane
You lock the door & throw away the key
There's someone in my head but it's not me.

And if the cloud bursts, thunder in your ear
You shout and no one seems to hear
And if the band you're in starts playing different tunes
I'll see you on the dark side of the moon

Roger Waters - Pink Floyd

Traditional Wisdom

Knowing others is wisdom; Whosoever knows others is clever
Knowing the self is enlightenment. Whosoever knows himself is wise
Mastering others requires force; Whosoever conquers others has force
Mastering the self needs strength. Whosoever conquers himself is strong

Two interpretations of the same piece: Lao Tsu, Tao Te Ching XXXIII

The man who sat on the ground in his tipi meditating on life and its meaning, accepting the kinship of all creatures and acknowledging the unity with the universe of things was infusing into his being the true essence of civilisation.

And when native man left off this form of development, his humanization was retarded in growth.

Chief Luther Standing Bear

The Four Manifestations of Beauty

With any form of Beauty, including living one's life, there are four levels of Ability. This is true of painting, literature, music, dance, acting, calligraphy, - whatever.

The first is the level of Competence. It is the ability to do something over and over again, with the same force, the same, strokes, the same rhythm, the same trueness. This level of ability is absolutely necessary. However this type of Beauty is also Ordinary.

The second level is Magnificent. This goes beyond normal skill. Its Beauty is unique to the Artist, and instantly recognisable. The artist at this level is able to capture different qualities at the same time, and hold them true together. The Observer feels things stirring within them.

The third level is Divine. A person seeing this form of Beauty has no words; they cannot describe how this is done. The Watcher remains separate, and they are deeply touched, even transformed a little, maybe never the same. It is Inspirational, and yet it can never be copied. The Artist can also never again recapture the specialness of that moment of creation, for that moment was Unique. The greater Divinity shines through in the Beauty.

The fourth level is greater than this. It is within each mortal's nature to find it. It is rarely ever attained. We can sense it only if we do not try to sense it. It occurs without motivation or desire or knowledge of what may result. It is the simplicity of being totally within, and just showing this. It is the natural wonder where everything relates to everything else. There are no separations: between the Artist and the Observer, Man and Nature, Self and the World. The Art seems to creates itself. It is unquestionably Beautiful. Often there is no Observer. It just Happens. The World changes a little. This level of Beauty is called Effortless.

Adapted from *The Bonesetter's Daughter* by Amy Tan (Flamingo) 2001: p 211-212

Sometimes an angel appears in the form of a friend who says exactly the words we need to hear that day. Or you will unwittingly act as an angel to someone else, tossing off a message so casually that, although it says another person's life, you hardly remember the moment at all.

Sophy Burnham: in Angels All Around Us

The Story of Life in 5 Short Chapters

Chapter 1.
I walk down a road.
There is a hole.
I fall in.
It takes me a very long time to get out.

Chapter 2.
I walk down the same road.
There is a hole.
I fall in again.
Oh no! Not again! I can't believe this!
Eventually I get out again.

Chapter 3.
I walk down the road.
I see the hole.
I fall in again.
It takes me much less time to get out.

Chapter 4.
I walk down the same road.
I see the hole.
I walk round it.
I don't fall in.

Chapter 5.
I walk down a different road.
No holes.

Ascribed to Portia Nelson

Deliberate meditation is the light of consciousness; let go, and then it is the light of essence. A hair's breath's difference is that of a thousand miles, so discernment is necessary.

If consciousness is not stopped, spirit does not come alive; if mind is not emptied, the elixir does not crystallize.

When the mind is clean, that is elixir; when the mind is empty, that is medicine. When it doesn't stick to anything at all, it is said that the mind is clean; when it doesn't keep anything in it, it is said that the mind is empty.

If emptiness is seen as empty, emptiness is still not empty. When empty and mindless of emptiness, this is called true emptiness.

The Secret of the Golden Flower: trans. Thomas Cleary: X, 14-16

'Have you ever tried to enter the long black branches'

Have you ever tried to enter the long black branches of other lives --
tried to imagine what the crisp fringes, full of honey, hanging
from the branches of the young locust trees, in early summer, feel like?

Do you think this world is only an entertainment for you?

Never to enter the sea and notice how the water divides
with perfect courtesy, to let you in!

Never to lie down on the grass, as though you were the grass!
never to leap to the air as you open your wings over the dark acorn of
your heart!

No wonder we hear, in your mournful voice, the complaint
that something is missing from your life!

Who can open the door - who does not reach for the latch?

Who can travel the miles - who does not put one foot
in front of the other, all attentive to what presents itself continually?

Who will behold the inner chamber - who has not observed,
with admiration, even with rapture, the outer stone?

Well, there is time left --
fields everywhere invite you into them.

And who will care, who will chide you if you wander away
from wherever you are, to look for your soul?

Quickly then, get up, put on your coat, leave your desk!

Mary Oliver, *West Wind*, (Mariner) 1997

In the special dream state, the special dream body is created
from the mind and from the vital energy within the body.
This special dream body is able to dissociate entirely
from the gross physical body and travel elsewhere.
One way of developing this special dream body is first of
all to recognize the dream as a dream when it is over. Then,
you find you can make efforts to gain control over it.
We practise various meditations in dream states. The virtue
of such practices is that during such states, it is possible to

separate the gross levels of consciousness from the gross physical state and arrive at a subtler level of mind and body.

His Holiness the Dalai Lama

What lies before us and what lies behind us are small matters compared to what lies within us. And when we bring what is within us out into the world, miracles happen.

Ralph Waldo Emerson

This is your body, your greatest gift,
pregnant with wisdom you do not hear,
grief you thought was forgotten,
and joy you have never known.
Body work is soul work.
Imagination is the bridge between body and soul.

Marion Woodman

S.E. RESOURCE LIST

UK Residential Centres

*Not all of these residential centres will welcome you with open arms, without prior knowledge, nor may they be suitable for you. Please get this: You **must** contact them first, before you go there, and have a proper discussion about your needs and their resources. Many require a preliminary visit. One part of any discussion may well be about finances.*

Arbours Association, London: www.arbourscentre.org.uk. *Psychoanalytically-oriented psychotherapy training centre with also a residential crisis centre attached, used to working with people in crisis without using medication and in a therapy-oriented community setting. Private, therefore fee-paying.*

Lothlorien (Rokpa Trust), Corsock, Castle Douglas, Kirkcubrightshire. *A rural residential centre in Galloway, Scotland, for people who have mental health problems that is run under the auspices of Samye Ling, a Tibetan Buddhist community. Open to those from every belief system. Visits are needed prior to joining and a 6-month to 2-year commitment is looked for.*

Association of Therapeutic Communities
*This organisation has a directory of residential and day-care settings that are all institutional members of the Association of Therapeutic Communities. More mainstream and traditionally for the chronic mentally ill or recovering alcoholic & drug addicts.*www.therapeuticcommunities.org

Other UK Resources

Asylum Magazine
An international magazine for democratic psychiatry, psychology, education and community development. Incorporating the newsletter of Psychology Politics and Resistance (PPR): www.asylumonline.net

The Centre for Citizenship and Community Mental Health
The University of Bradford, and Bradford District Care Trust have established the Centre for Citizenship and Community Mental Health (CCCMH). There is also now one at the University of Lancashire.

Critical Psychiatry Network
The 'Bradford Group' of psychiatrists first met in Bradford in January 1999. The group provides a network to develop a critique of the contemporary psychiatric system. Currently the group consists of over 350 psychiatrists, two thirds of whom are based in the UK, the rest spread around the world.

Members of the Network exchange ideas and information and have regular meetings and peer support sessions. The Network has held annual conferences since 2013. There is currently an active trainee forum and informal mentorship scheme in the UK and an open reading & discussion group in Toronto, Canada. More information: www.criticalpsychiatry.co.uk

Spiritual Crisis Network UK
A nice and helpful site: lots of information, resources, and contacts – UK based: www.spiritualcrisisnetwork.uk

MIND
Website of a British mental health support organisation for all with mental health issues: www.mind.org.uk

SANE
Website of a British mental health support organisation for all with mental health issues: www.sane.org.uk

Anonymous Blog
An anonymous blog with lots of information, articles, viewpoints and links.
www.spiritualemergency.blogspot.com

Research Centre
The website of the Alister Hardy Religious Experience Research Centre & Society, Dept of Theology & Religious Studies, University of Lampeter, Wales. www.alisterhardyreligiousexperience.co.uk

Hearing Voices Network
This is a mental health services user network, although it does not focus specifically on spiritual emergence experiences: www.hearing-voices.org

European Resources

Soteria, Bern
A long-standing Soteria project in Berne, Switzerland. Information: www.soteria.ch

Weglaufhaus (Runaway House) Berlin, Germany
The Berlin Runaway House is a modern consumer-run initiative whose philosophical roots trace back to a program originating in the Netherlands prior to the era of deinstitutionalization: www.weglaufhaus.de

Peter Lehmann Publishing
The Peter Lehmann publishing house is orientated toward the interests of (ex-) users and survivors of psychiatry whose main concerns are self-determination and freedom from bodily harm. Published books include: 'Coming Off Psychiatric Drugs', and 'Alternatives Beyond Psychiatry': www.peter-lehmann-publishing.com

European Network of (ex-) Users and Survivors of Psychiatry (ENUSP)
This is a European website with information of interest for ex-users of psychiatric services: www.enusp.org/

USA Residential Centres

The Gesundheit! Institute, West Virginia, USA
Founded by Patch Adams, it provides alternative health care centre (including people in crisis), an outpatient clinic, and a school for aspiring activists. Clown, as you work, clown as you heal! www.patchadams.org

Esalen: Big Sur, CA.
*This is 'the' place where much of all this started. In the 1960s and 1970s, this was **the** Mind-Body-Spirit centre. It is still going!* www.esalen.org

Windhorse Community
There are various Windhorse community houses for people with mental health issues. See: www.windhorsecommunityservices.com/services/clinical-servicesand Windhorse Integrative Mental Health: www.windhorseimh.org for these alternative mental health treatment programs. Read the book, 'Recovering Sanity' by Podvoll and see if one of them is for you.

Soteria
There are several Soteria projects world-wide, based on the work of Loren Mosher, a US psychiatrist. These provide a space for people experiencing mental health crises. They exist in the USA, UK, Sweden, Finland, Switzerland, Germany & Hungary. Information: www.imhcn.org/bibliography/recent-innovations-and-good-practices/soteria-programme/#intro

Other USA Resources

Association of Transpersonal Psychology: www.atpweb.org
There are other residential centers and these people know of them. The ATP grew out of Grof's work at Esalen; has been publishing a journal for 40 years; and has many resources. The nature of these centres – like many alternatives to psychiatric care – is that they tend to come and go. There may also be smaller centres existing in Czechoslovakia, the Netherlands, Germany, and Japan.

National Association for Rights Protection and Advocacy

NARPA brings together mental health professionals and administrators, people with psychiatric histories, academics, advocates, and attorneys who share a common goal of promoting equal citizenship of people diagnosed as mentally disabled: www.narpa.org/

Freedom Center

The Freedom Center was founded in 2001 in Northampton MA by Will Hall and Oryx Cohen. Freedom Center has a long-term vision of creating a safe house modelled on Soteria. It is now transforming: www.freedom-center.org

Family Outreach and Response Program

The Family Outreach and Response Program (FOR) is a community, non-profit, charitable agency that was developed as an alternative family support program. It is also in a process of transformation: www.familymentalhealthrecovery.org

The Community Consortium: Toronto, Canada

The Community Consortium is a not-for-profit, tax-exempt charitable organization made up of people with psychiatric histories and their allies: see www.community-consortium.org.

Integrative Mental Health University

IMHU offers professional level courses to provide practitioners with real knowledge and practical advice that can be incorporated in their current practice: www.imhu.org

International Websites

International Network of Treatment Alternatives for Recovery (INTAR)

A group of like-minded mental health workers, survivors and relatives concerned about the lack of alternative treatments in the Western World: www.intar.org

MindFreedom International
MindFreedom International unites 100 grassroots groups and thousands of members to win campaigns for human rights of people diagnosed with psychiatric disabilities: www.mindfreedom.org

ISPS
An international organization promoting psychotherapy and psychological treatments for persons with psychotic conditions: www.isps.org

Spiritual Emergence Network: *San Francisco, CA*
Information and Referral Service: www.senatciis.org

Spiritual Emergency Network (Netherlands)
web.inter.nl.net/users/itant/sen.html

Spirituality and Mental Health Ontario, Canada
www.spiritualityandmentalhealth.org/home.htm

Spiritual Emergency Resource Center
www.internetguides.com/se/index.html

EUTOTAS on Spiritual Emergency
www.eurotas.org/committee3.htm

Spiritual Crisis (Sacred Transformations) Site
www.well.com/user/bobby/index.html

From Spiritual Emergency to Spiritual Problem: Article
www.sonoma.edu/psychology/os2db/lukoff1.html

Spiritual Emergence Resource Centre
www.internetguides.com/se/experiences/exp-lukoff-5.html

Spiritual Emergencies - Diagnosis and Treatment (online course)
Approved 8CE credits for Psychologists: www.internetguides.com/sepromo.html

Spiritual Directors
Spiritual directors available to meet with individuals through the Internet, e-mail: www.shalomplace.com/direction/directors.html

Support Groups
Through this website it is possible to join a discussion group which also acts as something of a support group. www.scispirit.com/psychosis_spirituality

Spiritual Conference
This was a website of resource materials being developed following a NHS conference held in Dundee in August 2004: now not accessible. www.mentalhealth-wellbeing-spirituality-conference.info

Spiritual Competency Resources Center
This is the website of David Lukoff, President of the Association for Transpersonal Psychology, USA. He is co-author of the diagnostic manual DSM-IV category 'Religious or Spiritual Problem' and an authority on spiritual emergency: www.spiritualcompetency.com

Spiritual Recovery Blog
Lots of resources on this site: spiritualrecoveries.blogspot.com

David Lukoff: *On-Line Learning*: www.spiritual-emergency.com/articles.htm

International Spiritual Emergence Resource
Website to help facilitate radical shifts in consciousness and alleviate distress due to profound spiritual transformation and spiritual emergency www.kaia.ca/ISER_Home.php

The Doctor Who Heard Voices
Website of the "Doctor who heard voices", video about what voices are like, and other resources for more peaceful and helpful approaches to mental health problems: www.rufusmay.com

Hazel Courteney

Hazel Courteney is the author of two books on spiritual emergency (See book list.) www.hazelcourtenay.com

Dion Fortune

UK occultist, ceremonial magician, mystic, author and novelist of the early 20th century. All her many books (except one on Tofu), both fiction and non-fiction deal with aspects of the occult: www.angelfire.com/az/garethknight/aboutdf.html

UK Psychotherapists

Although it is not usual to recommend individual therapists, here are some lists of organisations of UK psychotherapists, who do different types of counselling and psychotherapy. Some of them may be able to help you with your spiritual emergence process. You may want to choose those who specifically mention "spirituality" or "transpersonal" as a category of their work:

The British Psychological Society BPS
www.bps.org.uk/e-services/find-a-psychologist/directory.cfm

The UK Council for Psychotherapists UKCP
www.psychotherapy.org.uk/find_a_therapist.html

The British Association for Counselling and Psychotherapy BACP
www.bacp.co.uk/seeking_therapist/index.html

The British Confederation of Psychotherapists BCP– *quite psycho-analytical*: www.bcp.org.uk/finding_a_therapist.html

Association of Accredited Psycho-spiritual Practitioners, The closest thing to a Spiritual Emergence Network that exists in the UK; an informal set-up which uses UKCP accredited psychotherapists from the Psychosynthesis & Education Trust, the Institute for Psychosynthesis, and the Karuna Institute.

Rokpa Trust: The Lothlorien community is run by the Rokpa Trust, an international charitable organisation founded by Dr.Akong Tulku Rinpoche of the Samye Ling Tibetan Centre (www.samyeling.org) in south-west Scotland: www.rokpa.org

Trellis – Scottish charity that promotes the use of horticulture to improve health, well-being and life opportunities for all: www.trellisscotland.org.uk

Mindfulness Association – A non-profit organisation which offers trainings in Mindfulness, Compassion and Insight: www.mindfulnessassociation.net

Nonviolent Communication: A UK-based NVC 'library' for people who want support in developing Nonviolent Communication (NVC) consciousness: www.nvc-uk.com.

Scottish Recovery Network- Promoting recovery from long-term mental health problems in Scotland: www.scottishrecovery.net

Videos

"Spiritual Emergency" A documentary film on DVD by Kaia Nightingale (Spiritual Emergence Service, Canada) - *a 40-minute documentary validating unusual experiences during spiritual emergence, alerting health professionals to the different signs. It illustrates the predicament of people who find themselves in spiritual crisis. There is often very little help available. With information and support, people can move through profound transformation, emerging with new skills and abilities. Available from: www.kaia.ca/Documentary_SpiritualEmergency.php*

"Evolving Minds" An exploration of the alternatives to psychiatry and the links between psychosis and spirituality. Produced by Mel Gunasena and Undercurrents: www.undercurrents.org/minds

"**Hard to Believe**" a film about spirituality and mental health produced by MIND in Croydon, admin@mindincroydon.org.uk & www.mindincroydon.org.uk

Articles

Isabel Clarke (ed) The Journal of Critical Psychology, Counselling & Psychotherapy Special Issue: 'Taking Spirituality Seriously', Vol 2, No 4, Winter 2002. www.therapeuticcommunities.org

Deborah Cornah, The impact of spirituality on mental health. A literature review, *Mental Health Foundation, June 2006*

David Lukoff, "From Spiritual Emergency to Spiritual Problem: the transpersonal roots of the new DSM IV category", *Journal of Humanistic Psychology 1998 Vol. 38, pp. 21-50*

Courtenay Young, When Their World Changed - One Humanistic Perspective of Transpersonal Psychotherapy. In: E. Whitton (2003) *Humanistic Psychotherapy*. London: Whurr.

Courtenay Young, A Spiritual Psychotherapist. In: J. Corrigal, (2000) *UKCP Conference Proceedings.*

Courtenay Young, Psychotherapy & Spirituality. In: C. Featherstone & L. Forsyth (Eds) *Medical Marriage: A new partnership between orthodox & complementary medicine.* Findhorn: Findhorn Press. Courtenay Young, Soul Awakening in Community: Emergence or Emergency? *One Earth magazine: Findhorn Foundation; Issue 20, Winter 1995/6.*

Courtenay Young, Strange Changes in Psychotherapy: The Psychotherapeutic Process of Life Changes, Spiritual Emergence or a Soul Awakening? *International Journal of Psychotherapy, Vol. 13, No. 3, pp. 50-61.*

All of Courtenay Young's articles are available from his website: www.courtenay-young.com

Books

Janet Adler (1995). *Arching Backwards: The mystical initiation of a contemporary woman.* Inner Traditions International

Emma Bragdon (1988). *A Sourcebook for Helping People with Spiritual Problems.* (first published as *A Sourcebook for Helping People in Spiritual Emergency*) LighteningUp Press

Mariana Caplan (1999). *Halfway up the Mountain- The error of premature claims to enlightenment.* Hohm Press

Isabel Clarke (2008). *Madness, Mystery and the Survival of God.* O Books

Isabel Clarke (Ed) (2001). *Psychosis and Spirituality: Exploring the new frontier,* (With contributions from: Peter Chadwick; Gordon Claridge; Chris Clarke; Isabel Clarke; Neil Douglas-Klotz; Peter Fenwick; Richard House; Mike Jackson; David Kingdon; Nigel Mills; Emmanuelle Peters; Shanaya Rathod; Ron Siddle; Nathalie Tobert.) Whurr

Hazel Courteney (2002). *Divine Intervention.* CICO Books

Hazel Courteney (2005). *The Evidence for the Sixth Sense.* Cico Books

Ram Dass (1978). *Journey of Awakening: A Meditator's Guidebook.* New Age Bantam Books

Ram Dass (1971). *Be Here Now.* Lama Foundation.

Jennifer Elam (2002). *Dancing with God Through the Storm: Mysticism and Mental Illness.* Way Opens Press

Bonnie Greenwell (1995). *Energies of Transformation: A guide to the Kundalini Process.* Shakti River Press

Stanislav & Christina Grof (Eds) (1989). *Spiritual Emergency: When Personal Transformation Becomes a Crisis.* (With contributions from: R.D Laing, Roberto Assagioli, John Weir Perry, Ram Dass, Lee Sanella, Jack Kornfield, Paul Rebillot, Holgar Kalweit, Anne Armstrong, Keith Thompson and others.) Penguin Putnam

Stanislav & Christina Grof (1990). *The Stormy Search for the Self, A guide to personal growth through transformational crisis.* Penguin Putnam.

Hilary Hart (2004). *The Unknown She: Eight faces of an emerging consciousness.* Golden Sufi Center

Gabor Mate (2008, 2018). *In the Realm of Hungry Ghosts Close encounters with addiction.* North Atlantic Books.

Loren R. Mosher and Voyce Hendrix, with Deborah C. Fort (2004). *Soteria: Through Madness to Deliverance,* by Xlibris. USA.

Read, J., Bentall, R., Mosher, L. & Dillon, J. (Ed.) *Models of Madness – Psychological, Social and Biological Approaches to Psychosis (*2nd Ed.) Routledge.

Jack Kornfield (2000*). After the Ecstasy, Now the Laundry: How the heart grows wise on the spiritual path.* Bantam Books

John Lilly (1973). *The Centre of the Cyclone.* Marion Boyars

John Weir Perry, *The Self in Psychotic Process,*

John Weir Perry (1974). *The Far Side of Madness.* Prentice-Hall

John Weir Perry (1999). *Trials of the Visionary Mind.* State University of New York Press.

Edward M. Podvoll (2003). *Recovering Sanity: A compassionate approach to understanding and treating psychosis.* Shambala.

Lee Sannella (1992). *The Kundalini Experience: Psychosis or Transcendence?* Integral Publishing.

Morton Schatzman (1974). *Soul Murder: Persecution in the family.* New York: Signet Books.

Lauren Slater (1996). *Welcome to my Country: a therapist's memoir of madness.* Hamish Hamilton.

Irina Tweedie (1986). *Daughter of Fire: A diary of a spiritual training with a Sufi master.* Golden Sufi Centre.

Roger Walsh & Frances Vaughan (eds) (1993). *Paths Beyond Ego: The transpersonal vision.* Tarcher/Putnam.

Frances Vaughan (1995). *Shadows of the Sacred: Seeing through spiritual illusions.* Quest Books.

Books & Articles

Ammerman, N. (2014). Spiritual but not religious? Beyond binary choices in the study of religion. *Journal for the Scientific Study of Religion, 52,* 258–78.

Ankrah, L. (2002). Spiritual emergency and counselling: An exploratory study. *Counselling and Psychotherapy Research, 2(1), 55–60.*

Arnaud, K. & Cormier, D. (2017). Psychosis or Spiritual Emergency: The Potential of Developmental Psychopathology for Differential Diagnosis. University of Alberta, Edmonton, Alberta, Canada. *International Journal of Transpersonal Studies, 36, 44-59.*

Atunes, R. & Oliveira, A. (2018). *Spiritual Intelligence Self-Assessment Inventory.* www.link.springer.com/article/10.1007/s10943-021-01350-2

Barnett, J. (2016). Reflections, are religion and spirituality of relevance in psychotherapy? *Spirituality in Clinical Practice, 3,* 5-9.

Benning, T. & Rominger, R. (2016). Patients' disclosures of near-death experiences and other anomalous death-related phenomena: Perspective from a general psychiatric clinic. *Journal of Near-Death Studies, 34,* 195-223.

Bragdon, E. (2013). *The Call of Spiritual Emergency.* Lightening Up Press.

Bray, P. (2010). A broader framework for exploring the influence of spiritual experience in the wake of stressful life events: Examining connections between posttraumatic growth and psychospiritual transformation. *Mental Health, Religion & Culture, 13,* 293–308.

Brook, M. (2019). Struggles reported integrating intense spiritual experiences: Results from a survey using the integration of spiritually transformative experiences inventory. *American Psychological Association, 1,* 1-18.

Cooper, E., Rock, A., Harris, K. & Clark, G. (2015). The factor analytic structure and personality correlates of 'spiritual emergency.' *The Journal of Transpersonal Psychology, 47,* 242-262.

Dwight, J. (2011). Transpersonal Psychology: Mapping Spiritual Experience. *Religions, 2,* 649-658.

Frame, M.W. (2003). *Integrating religion and spirituality into counseling: A comprehensive approach.* Brooks/Cole.

Fortune, D. (1962, 2000). *Aspects of Occultism.* Aquarian Press / RedWheel.

Goretzki, M., Thalbourne, M. & Storm, L. (2009). The questionnaire measurement of spiritual emergency. *The Journal of Transpersonal Psychology, 41, 81-97.*

Greenwell, B. (2018). *When Spirit Leaps, Navigating the Process of Spiritual Awakening.* New Harbinger Publications, Inc.

Grof, S. & Grof, C. (1989). *Spiritual Emergency: When Personal Transformation Becomes A Crisis.* Tarcher-Perigee/Penguin Random House.

Grof, S. & Grof, C. (1990). *The Stormy Search For The Self: A Guide To Personal Growth Through Transformative Crisis.* Tarcher-Perigee/Penguin Random House.

Hodge, D. (2018). Spiritual Competence: What it is, why it is necessary, and how to develop it. *Journal of Ethnic & Cultural Diversity in Social Work, 27, 124-139.*

Koenig, H. (2012). Religion, spirituality, and health: The research and clinical implications. *International Scholarly Research Network, 1-33.*

Lukoff, D. (2005). Spiritual and transpersonal approaches to psychotic disorders. In: S. Mijares & G.S. Khalsa (Eds.), *The psychospiritual clinician's handbook: Alternative methods for understanding and treating mental disorders,* (pp. 233-258). The Haworth Reference Press.

Muhamad, H., Roodenburg, J. & Moore, D. (2014). The expressions of spirituality inventory: Evidence for the cross-cultural validity in a Malaysian context. *The Journal of Transpersonal Psychology, 46, 58-71.*

Newnes, C., Holmes, C. & Dunn. C. (Eds.) (1999). *This is Madness: A Critical Look at Psychiatry and the Future of Mental Health Services.* PCCS Books.

Oxhandler, H., Parrish, D, Torres, L. & Achenbaum, A. (2015). The integration of clients' religion and spirituality in social work practice: A national survey. *National Association of Social Workers, 60, 228-237.*

Oxhandler, H., & Pargament, K. (2018). Measuring religious and spiritual competence across helping professions: Previous efforts and future directions. *Spirituality in Clinical Practice, 5, 120-132.*

Paper, J.D. (2004). *The mystic experience: A descriptive and comparative analysis.* State University of New York Press.

Pargament, K. (2007). *Spirituality Integrated Psychotherapy: Understanding and Addressing the Sacred.* Guilford Press.

Pargament, K., & Mahoney, A. (2009). Spirituality: The search for the sacred. In: S.J. Lopez & C.R. Snyder (Eds.), *Handbook of Positive Psychology*, (pp. 611-619). Oxford University Press.

Parker, J. (2019). Spiritual and religious multicultural practice competencies: A partial replication study with school psychologists. *National Association of School Psychologists, 13, 53-73.*

Pearce, M., Oxhandler, H., Pargament, K., Vieten, C. & Wong, S. (2019). A novel training program for mental health providers in religious and spiritual competencies. *American Psychological Association, 6, 73-82.*

Persinger, M. (1983). Religious and mystical experiences as artifacts of temporal lobe function: A general hypothesis. *Perceptual and Motor Skills. 21, 1255-1262.*

Phillips, R., Lukoff, D. & Stone, M. (2009). Integrating the spirit within Psychosis: Alternative conceptualizations of psychotic disorders. *The Journal of Transpersonal Psychology, 41, 1-21.*

Piotrowski, J. & Zemojtel-Piotrowska, M. (2020). Spiritual Transcendence and Helping Behavior: Helping Toward Ingroups and Outgroups. *Psychology of Religion and Spirituality, 1941-1022.*

Pomerleau, J., Pargament, K., Ironson, G., Krause, N. & Hill, P. (2019). Religious and spiritual struggles as a mediator of the link between stressful life events and psychological adjustment in a nationwide sample. *Psychology of Religion and Spirituality, 1-9.*

Porter, G. (1995). Exploring the meaning of spirituality and its implications for counselors. *Counseling and Values, 40, 69-79.*

Psaila, C. (2014). Mental health practitioners' understanding and experience of spirituality and religion. *Journal for the Study of Spirituality, 4, 189–203.*

Raab, D. (2014). Creative Transcendence: Memoir writing for transformation and empowerment. *The Journal of Transpersonal Psychology, 46, 187-207.*

Rambo, L. (1993). *Understanding religious conversion.* Yale University Press.

Roberts, A. (2000). An overview of crisis theory and crisis intervention. In: A.R. Roberts (Ed.), *Crisis Intervention Handbook: Assessment, treatment, and research* (2nd ed.), pp. 3-30). Oxford University Press.

Robertson, L. (2008). *The Spiritual Competency Scale:* A Comparison to the Aserbic Spiritual Competencies. (Doctoral dissertation), University of Florida. Retrieved from ProQuest Digital Dissertations.

Rominger, R. (2013). Integration of spiritually transformative experiences: Models, methods, and research. *Journal of Near-Death Studies, 31, 135-150.*

Rosmarin, D., Forester, B., Shassian, D., Webb, C. & Bjorgvinsson, T. (2015). Interest in spiritually integrated psychotherapy among acute psychiatric patients. *Journal of Consulting and Clinical Psychology, 83, 1149-1153.*

Ross, S. (2017). The making of everyday heroes: women's experiences with transformation and integration. *Journal of Humanistic Psychology, 1-23.*

Roxburgh, E., & Evenden, R. (2016). They daren't tell people': Therapists' experiences of working with clients who report anomalous experiences. *European Journal of Psychotherapy & Counselling, 18, 123-141.*

Rutter, M. & Sroufe, L. (2000). Developmental Psychopathology: Concepts and challenges. *Development and Psychopathology, 12, 265-296.*

Sandage, S., Jankowski, P.J. & Link, D.C. (2010). Quest and spiritual development moderated by spiritual transformation. *Journal of Psychology and Theology, 38, 15–31.*

Sandage, S., & Moe, S. (2013). Spiritual Experience: Conversion and Transformation. In: *APA Handbook of Psychology, Religion, and Spirituality: 1, 407-422.*

Sandage, S. & Shults, L. (2007). Relational spirituality and transformation: A relational integration model. *Journal of Psychology and Christianity, 26, 261–269.*

Saunders, S., Petrik, M., & Miller, M. (2014). Psychology doctoral students' perspectives on addressing spirituality and religious with clients: Associations with personal preferences and training. *Psychology of Religion and Spirituality, 6, 1–8.*

Sedlakova, H. & Rihacek, T. (2016). The incorporation of a spiritual emergency experience into a client's worldview: A grounded theory. *Journal of Humanistic Psychology, 1, 1-21.*

Seeman, M. (2010). Raves, psychosis, and spirit healing. *Transcultural Psychiatry, 47, 491-501.*

Sellers, J. (2018). Transpersonal and transformative potential of out-of-body experiences. *Journal of Exceptional Experiences and Psychology, 6, 1-20.*

Shafranske, E. (2010). Advancing "The boldest model yet": A commentary on psychology, religion, and spirituality. *Psychology of Religion and Spirituality, 2, 124-125.*

Shiah, Y., Chang, F., Tam, W., Chuang, S. & Yeh, L. (2018). I don't believe but I pray: spirituality, instrumentality, or paranormal belief? *Journal of Applied Social Psychology, 43, 1704-1716.*

Sinclair, C. (2016). Transformation and subjectivity in spiritual emergence and emergency: A Discourse analytic study. *The Journal of Transpersonal Psychology, 48, 1-24.*

Smith, T. (2006). The national spiritual transformation study. *Journal for the Scientific Study of Religion, 45, 283-296.*

Smith, S. & Suto, M. (2012). Religious and/or spiritual practices: Extending spiritual freedom to people with Schizophrenia. *Canadian Journal of Occupational Therapy, 79, 1-9.*

Sperry, L. (2012). Spiritually sensitive psychotherapy: An impending paradigm shift in theory and practice. In: L. Miller (Ed.), *The Oxford Handbook of Psychology and Spirituality,* (pp. 223–233). Oxford University Press.

Sperry, L. (2016). Spiritually sensitive clinical practice: Differentiating basic form specialized competencies. *Spirituality in Clinical Practice, 3,* 73-76.

Sundararajan, L. (2011). Spiritual transformation and emotion: A semiotic analysis. *Journal of Spirituality in Mental Health, 13,* 78–90.

Stace, W. (1960). *The Teachings of the Mystics.* New American Library.

Stauner, N., Exline, J., Pargament, K. (2016). Religious and spiritual struggles as concerns for health and well-being. *Religion and Health, 14,* 48-75.

Storm, L. & Goretzki, M. (2016). A defense of the Spiritual Emergence Scale: Emergency vs. emergence. *The Journal of Transpersonal Psychology, 48,* 90-209.

Storm, L. & Goretzki, M. (2021). The psychology and parapsychology of spiritual emergency. *Journal of Scientific Exploration, 35,* 36-64.

Taft, R. (1969). Peak experiences and ego permissiveness: An exploratory factor study of their dimensions in normal persons. *Acta Pscyhologica, 29,* 35-64.

Tankersley, S. (2013). *Psychologist's assessment of spiritual and religious beliefs for persons diagnosed with psychotic disorders.* Walden University, Minneapolis, MN.

Tassel-Matamau, N. & Frewin K. (2020). Psycho-spiritual transformation after an exceptional human experience. *Journal of Spirituality in Mental Health, 21,* 237-258.

Taves, A. (2020). Mystical and other alterations in sense of self: An expanded framework for studying non-ordinary experiences. *Association for Psychological Science, 15,* 669-690.

Taylor, S. (2009). Beyond the pre/trans fallacy: The validity of pre-egoic spiritual experience. *Journal of Transpersonal Psychology, 41,* 22-43.

Taylor, S. (2012a). Transformation through suffering: A study of individuals who have experienced positive psychological transformation following periods of intense turmoil. *Journal of Humanistic Psychology, 52, 30-52.*

Taylor, S. (2012b). Spontaneous awakening experiences: Exploring the phenomenon beyond religion and spirituality. *Journal of Transpersonal Psychology, 44(1), 73-91.*

Taylor, S. (2013a). *A phenomenological investigation into the psychological transformation interpreted as spiritual awakening: Possible causes, characteristics and aftereffects.* (Unpublished doctoral dissertation). Liverpool John Moores University, UK.

Telfener, U. (2017). Becoming through belonging: The spiritual dimension in psychotherapy. *Australian and New Zealand Journal of Family Therapy, 38, 156-167.*

Tempel, J. & Moodley, R. (2020). Spontaneous Mystical Experience Among Atheists: Meaning Making, Psychological Distress, and Wellbeing. *Mental Health, Religion, and Culture, 23, 789-805.*

Thalbourne, M. & Storm, L. (2019). The relationship between paranormal belief and psychopathology with special focus on magical ideation, psychosis, and schizotypy. *Australian Journal of Parapsychology, 19, 181-211.*

Tong, E. (2017). Spirituality and the temporal dynamics of transcendental positive emotions. *Psychology of Religion and Spirituality, 9, 70-81.*

Ulman, C. (1989). *The Transformed Self: The psychology of religious conversion.* Plenum Press.

Underhill, E. (1961). *Mysticism*. E.P. Dutton.

Underwood, L.G. & Teresi, J.A. (2002). The Daily Spiritual Experience Scale: Development, theoretical description, reliability, exploratory factor analysis, and preliminary construct validity using health-related data. *Annals of Behavioral Medicine, 24, 22-33.*

Uwland-Sikkema, N., Visser, A., Westerhof, G. & Garssen, B. (2018). How is spirituality part of people's meaning system? *Psychology of Religion and Spirituality, 10, 157-165.*

Vaillant, G. (2008). *Spiritual Evolution: A scientific defense of faith.* Broadway Press.

van Os, J., Linscott, R., Myin-Germeys, I., Delespaul, P. & Krabbendam, L. (2009). A systematic review and meta-analysis of the psychosis continuum: Evidence for a psychosis proneness–persistence–impairment model of psychotic disorder. *Psychological Medicine, 39, 179-195.*

Vaughan Clark, F. (1977). Transpersonal perspectives in psychotherapy. *Journal of Humanistic Psychology, 17(2), 69-81.*

Vich, M., Fadiman, J., Mojeiko, V., Labate, B. & Goldstein, I. (2009). Perspectives in spirituality. *The International Journal of Transpersonal Studies, 28, 1-139.*

Vieten, C., & Scammell (2015). Spiritual and Religious Competencies in Clinical Practice, Guidelines for Psychotherapists and Mental Health Professionals. *New Harbinger Publications.*

Vieten, C., Scammell, S., Pierce, A., Pilato, R., Ammondson, I., Pargament, K.I. & Lukoff, D. (2016). Competencies for psychologists in the domains of religion and spirituality. *Spirituality in Clinical Practice, 3, 92–114.*

Viggiano, D. & Krippner, S. (2010). The Grof's model of spiritual emergency in retrospect: Has it stood the test of time? *International Journal of Transpersonal Studies, 29, 118-127.*

Wade, J. (2018). After awakening, the laundry: Is nonduality a spiritual experience? *International Journal of Transpersonal Studies, 37, 88-115.*

Washburn, M. (2003). *Embodied spirituality in a sacred world.* State University of New York Press.

Wilber, K. (2004). *Integral Spirituality: A startling new role for religion in the modern and postmodern world.* Shambala Press.

Wilber, K., Engler, J. & Brown, D.P. (1986). *Transformations of Consciousness: Conventional and contemplative perspectives on development.* Shambhala Press.

Wildman, W. (2013). Spiritual Experiences: A quantitative-phenomenological approach. *Journal of Empirical Theology, 26, 139-164.*

Williams, P. (2012). *Rethinking Madness.* Sky's Edge Publishing.

Williamson, W. & Hood, R., Jr. (2011). Spirit baptism: A phenomenological study of religious experience. *Mental Health, Religion & Culture, 14, 543–559.*

Williamson, W, & Hood, R., Jr. (2013). Spiritual transformation: A phenomenological study among recovering substance abusers. *Pastoral Psychology, 62, 889–906.*

Wilson, J. (2006d). Trauma and transformation of the self: Restoring meaning and wholeness to personality. In: J.P. Wilson (Ed.), *The Posttraumatic Self,* (pp. 399-424). Routledge.

Wilt, J., Pargament, K. & Exline, J. (2019). The transformative power of the sacred: Social, personality, and religious/spiritual antecedent and consequents of sacred moments during a religious/spiritual struggle. *Psychology of Religion and Spirituality, 3, 233- 246.*

Yaden, D., Hood, R., Haidt, J. & Vago, D. (2015). The varieties of self-transcendent experience. *Review of General Psychology, 21, 143-160.*

Yamada, A., Lukoff, D., Lim, C. & Mancuso, L. (2019) Integrating spirituality and mental health: Perspectives of adults receiving public mental health services in California. *Psychology of Religion and Spirituality, 12, 276-287.*

Yamane, D. (2000). Narrative and religious experience. *Sociology of Religion, 61, 171–189.*

Zukerman, G., Korn, L. & Fostick, L. (2017). Religious coping and posttraumatic stress symptoms following trauma: The moderating effects of gender. *Psychology of Religions and Spirituality, 9, 328-336.*

SPIRITUAL EMERGENCY BOOK LIST

The Call of Spiritual Emergency: From Personal Crisis to Personal Transformation: Emma Bragdon. *Excellent basic Grof-based book. Clear. Factual. Very useful for clients.* (Harper & Row, 2012).

The Stormy Search for Self: A guide to personal growth through transformational crisis: Stan Grof & Christina Grof. *The Grof's talking about SE. More depth. Good scope. OK for clients.* (Tarcher, 1992).

Spiritual Emergency: When personal transformation becomes a crisis: Stanislav Grof (Ed.). *Basic Grof writings about SE. Some good, some intellectual. Covers the field.* (Tarcher, 1989).

The Adventure of Self-Discovery: Dimensions of consciousness and new perspectives in psychotherapy and inner exploration: Stanislav Grof. *First part describes some of the new areas of consciousness and very well and gives a good model of the psyche. Not so good on Holotropic Breathwork.* (State U. of NY, 1988).

The Kundalini Experience: Psychosis or Transcendence: Lee Sannella. *Good explanations of a wide field, also quite technical. Not so good for clients in an SE –type situation.* (Integral, 1987)

Owning your Own Shadow: Understanding the Dark Side of the Psyche: Robert Johnson. *Writes well. Deals with how to work on self. Not many others do.* (HarperCollins, 1994).

Meeting the Shadow: The hidden power of the dark side of human nature: C. Zweig & J. Abrams (Eds). *Good wide collection of snippets about this type of work.* (Tarcher, 1990)

City Shadows: Psychological Interventions in Psychiatry: Arnold Mindell. *Good on work with psychotics; street people work emerged from this.* (Arkana, 2009)

Dreambody; Working with the Dreaming Body; The Dreambody in Relationships; River's Way; Working on yourself alone; The Year I; The Shaman's Body. Arnold Mindell. *A series of books giving the basics of Process Oriented Psychology – one of the more useful forms of psychotherapy in this area.* (Arkana).

The Shaman's Body; The Leader as a Martial Artist. Arnold Mindell. *Two other more recent books by A. Mindell – all good, but diverse.* (HarperCollins)

Metaskills: The Spiritual Art of Therapy, Mindell, Amy (New Falcon) *Addresses some of the spiritual attitudes that lie behind therapy.*

Fire in the Soul, Joan Borysenko (Warner) *Addresses the perspective that the wounds we suffer and heal from can be gateways to an advantageous spiritual transformation. Good quotations and USA resource list.*

The Arkana Dictionary of New Perspectives, Holroyd, Stuart (Arkana) *Clear, fairly comprehensive guide to the 'new' language of all this New Age, psycho-spiritual, stuff.*

The Far Side of Madness, Perry, John Wier (Spring) *Good early work (1974) - nice stories, cases. Focuses on renewal.*

The Language of Madness, Cooper, David (Allan Lane) *Radical perspective. R.D. Laing-ian (1978). Good for therapists.*

The Seduction of Madness, Podvell, Edward (Century) *Good for 4 in-depth cases. Very good concepts of self-cure and on the positive value of psychosis.*

Recovering Sanity: A compassionate approach to understanding and treating psychosis, Podvell, Edward (Shambala) *An up-dated and 'added to' 2003 version of the above.*

Butterfly Man, Berke, Joseph (Hutchinson) *Good descriptions of process. Community as a path / refuge.*

Creating Sanctuary: Toward the Evolution of Sane Societies, Bloom, Sandra Routledge) *Towards creating a sane society and ending family violence.*

Where Two Worlds Touch: Spiritual Rites of Passage, Karpinski, Gloria (Ballentine) *Bit simplistic. Spiritual rites of passage made easy. A bit New Age-y.*

The Courage to Heal (Sexual Abuse): Bass, Ellen & Davis, Laura (Harper & Row) *Excellent self-help book for clients with sexual abuse.*

The Crisis Intervention Manual, Christiensen, Kurt, (Empathy)

Crisis Intervention Handbook: Assessment Treatment & Research (4th Ed.), Yeager, Kenneth & Roberts, Albert, (Eds) (Oxford UP)

Living through Personal Crisis, Stearns, A.K. (Sheldon)

People in Crisis: Strategic Therapeutic Interventions, Everstein, D.S. & Everstein, L. (Brunner Routledge)

Techniques of Brief Psychotherapy, Flegenheimer, W.V. (Aronson) *Five books, quite traditional, on crisis intervention, brief psychotherapy, etc.*

A Road Less Travelled, Scott Peck, M. (Rider) *Good book especially for client on process of psychotherapy, and what is love, what is spirituality. Best seller.*

The People of the Lie, Scott Peck, M. (Rider) *A psychological analysis of evil. Very good.*

The Madness of Adam & Eve: How schizophrenia shaped humanity, Horrobin, David (Bantam) *A very interesting book looking at the evolutionary aspects of schizophrenia. Technical.*

Prophets, Cults and Madness, Stevens, A. & Price, J. (Duckworth) *An excellent fairly modern book from 2 well-established authors and psychiatrists which analyses those elements (both positive and negative) that contribute to the genius of prophets, gurus, cult leaders & messiahs, and also the factors that might push these people into madness and/or differentiate them from those who are definitely psychotic. Good bibliography.*

Psychosis & Spirituality: Consolidating the new paradigm (2nd ed.), Clark I. (Ed.) (Whurr) *Writings from various people looking at mainstream crisis work. Good research section..*

He: Understanding Masculine Psychology; She: Understanding Feminine Psychology; We: Understanding the Psychology of Romantic Love; Femininity Lost and Regained; Transformation: Understanding the Three Levels of Masculine Consciousness, Johnson, Robert A. (HarperCollins) *Excellent and very popular little books, each taking a well-known myth or fairy story and showing how this can be used as a guide for greater understanding and for transformation.*

Sex in the Forbidden Zone: When Therapist, Donators, Clergy, Teachers & Other Men in Power Betray Womens' Trust, Rutter, Peter (Mandala)

Out of Bounds: Sexual exploitation in counselling & therapy, Russell, Janice. D. (Sage) *Two good books on therapist abuse, by male & female authors.*

The Hidden Dimension; The Dance of Life; The Silent Language, Hall, Edward T. (Anchor) *Three books about personal space, silence, language and culture from an anthropologist that gives a good new insight on how our society works.*

Tao Te Ching, Lao Tsu (many different translations) *Essential Reading: Classic text: The basis of Taoism.*

The Secret of the Golden Flower, (Trans. Cleary, Thomas) (Harper) *Another classic text that forms the basis of Chinese Buddhist & Taoist thought that have existed for thousands of years. A basic distillation of the inner psychoactive elements that compose a spiritual life.*

The Circuit of Force, Fortune, Dion & Knight, Gareth (Thoth) *This and many other books (including the very good novels on occult fiction by Dion Fortune) are about how to manage one's esoteric energy for (good) occult purposes.*

Psychic Self-Defense, Fortune, Dion, Rider & Co.

Soteria: Through Madness to Deliverance, Mosher, Loren R. (Xlibris) *Excellent book about the development of the Soteria communities.*

Madness Explained: Psychosis and Human Nature, Bentall, Richard (Penguin) *A substantial, authoritative and highly readable work, by the author of 'Doctoring the Mind: Why psychiatric treatments fail'.*

CLIENT'S ACCOUNTS

The Eden Express: A memoir of insanity, Vonnegut, Mark (Bantam, 1975)
An autobiographical account of Mark, son of Kurt, getting stoned & crazy in the late 1960's hippy culture (believing "Mental illness is a myth"

and *"Schizophrenia is a sane response to an insane society"), & then getting back well again.*

I Never Promised You A Rose Garden, Green, Hannah (Joanne Greenburg) (Pan)
Powerful images of schizophrenia and the benefits of a good relationship with a skilled psychotherapist. This 1964 book was made into a 1977 film and a 2004 play.

I'm Dancing As Fast As I Can, Gordon, Barbara (Harper & Row)
Psychosis induced by a Valium withdrawal, exacerbated by a controlling and alcoholic husband, it describes how she eventually gets out of mental hospital. It was made into a 1982 film starring Jill Clayburgh.

Sybil, Schreiber, S. (Penguin)
Very powerful classic study of childhood sexual abuse & multi-personality.

One Flew Over the Cuckoo's Nest, Kesey, Ken (Pan)
Powerful & popular fictional account of how a mental hospital should not be run. It was made into a 1975 film with Jack Nicholson.

Lightening Bird, Watson, Lyall (Coronet)
Good case study of an epileptic in South Africa.

Dibs - In Search of Self: Personality development in play therapy, Axline, Virginia (Penguin)
Case of a psychotherapist working with a severely autistic child. Gradually, his extraordinary character and the reason for his silent withdrawal is revealed.

The Bell Jar, Plath, Sylvia.
Plath's semi-autobiographical novel provides insights into her struggles with mental illness.

Madness: A bipolar life by Marya Hornbacher, Hornbacher, Marya
Hornbacher shares her personal experiences with bipolar disorder.

It's Kind of a Funny Story, Vizzini, Ned
While a fictionalized account, this movie is based on Ned Vizzini's experiences in a mental health facility.

Hyperbole and a Half: Unfortunate situations, flawed coping mechanisms, mayhem and other things that happened, Brosh, Allie. (Touchstone Books)

1. **Personal Essays and Blogs:**
   - *Hyperbole and a Half by Allie Brosh* - Brosh uses humor and illustrations to depict her experiences with depression and anxiety.
   - *The Bloggess (Jenny Lawson)* - Lawson writes openly about her experiences with mental health on her blog and in her books.

2. **YouTube Channels and Videos:**
   - *TED Talks* - Many individuals share their personal stories of overcoming mental health challenges in TED Talks. For example, Andrew Solomon's talk on depression and Kevin Breel's talk on his experience with depression.
   - *Mental Health YouTubers* - Channels like "The Mighty," "Kati Morton," and "Jessica Kellgren-Fozard" feature individuals sharing their mental health journeys.

3. **Podcasts:**
   - *The Hilarious World of Depression* - This podcast features comedians discussing their experiences with depression.
   - *Mental Illness Happy Hour* - Hosted by Paul Gilmartin, this podcast includes interviews with individuals sharing their mental health stories.

4. **Online Forums and Support Groups:**
   - *Reddit communities* such as r/depression, r/anxiety, or other specific mental health subreddits where individuals share their experiences.
   - *Psych Central Forums* and other mental health forums where people discuss their journeys and offer support.

5. **Documentary Films:**
   - *"Life, Animated"* - This documentary follows an autistic man's journey using Disney characters as a form of communication.
   - *"It's Kind of a Funny Story"* - While a fictionalized account, the movie is based on Ned Vizzini's experiences in a mental health facility.

Professional Articles

Coursey, R.D., Keller, A.B. & Farrell, E.W. (1995). Individual Psychotherapy and Persons with Serious Mental Illness: The client's perspective. *Schizophrenia Bulletin, 21(2), 283-301.*

Perry, B.L. (2012). Coming untied? Narrative accounts of social network dynamics from first-time mental health clients. *Sociology of Health & Illness, 34(8), 1125-1139.*

Vellenga, B.A. & Christensen, J. (1994). Persistent and Severely Mentally Ill Clients' Perceptions of their Mental Illness. *Issues in Mental Health Nursing, 15(4), 359-371.*

Nakash, O., Cohen, M. & Nagar, M. (2018). "Why Come for Treatment?" Clients' and therapists' accounts of the presenting problems when seeking mental health care. *Qualitative Health Research, 28(6), 916-926.*

Lai, D.W.L., Chan, K.C., Daoust, G.D. & Xie, X.J. (2021). Hopes and wishes of clients with mental illness in Hong Kong. *Community Mental Health Journal, 57, 1556-1565.*

OTHER RELATED BOOKS

Anatomy of the Spirit: Carolyn Myss. *Energy medicine from popular New Age speaker and medical clairvoyant.* (Three Rivers, 1997).

The Call to Adventure: Paul Rebillot. *How to use crisis to change your life –The Hero's Journey ritual explained.* (Bookbaby, 2017).

The Soul's Code: In search of character and calling: James Hillman. *A brilliant book, written by a distinguished psychotherapist that offers a liberating view of childhood troubles and an exciting approach to fate and fatalism, character and desire, family influence and individual freedom, and 'calling.* (Bantam, 1997).

Healing your Emotions: Discover your element type and change your life: Angela Hicks. *Typical New Age self-help book, combining Chinese Five Elements theory combined with Neuro-Linguistic Programming.* (Thorsons, 1999).

The Path of Least Resistance: Learning to Become a Creative Force in Your Own Life: Robert Fritz. *Another typical New Age self-help book looking at how to increase your creativity, from the founder of DMA. Interesting.* (Ballantine, 1989).

The Healing Power of Mind: Meditation for well-being and enlightenment: Tulku Thondup. *A primer in healing meditation, based on Tibetan Buddhist practice. Useful.* (Shambala, 2006).

Toward a Psychology of Awakening: John Welwood. *Buddhism, psychotherapy and the path of personal transformation.* (Shambala, 2002).

***A = Astral Sex - Z = Zen* teabags**: Gerry Thompson. *An illustrated (fun) encyclopedia of new Age jargon + jokes. Humour is important.* (Findhorn Press, 2012).

Return of the Bird Tribes: Ken Carey. *Looks at native American spirituality on contemporary life.* (Harper & Collins, 1992).

Living Magically: Gill Edwards. *Psycho-spiritual metaphysics. Very good. Helps thinking on the path.* (Piatkus, 2009).

The Art of Happiness: HH Dalai Lama. *Tibetan Buddhist oriented text from a remarkable spiritual leader.* (Coronet, 1999).

Foods that Harm; Foods that Heal: Readers Digest: *An A-Z guide to safe and healthy eating. Essential.*

Wisdom of the Body Moving: *An Introduction to Body-Mind Centering.* Linda Hartley. (North Atlantic Books, 1995).

It's Here Now (Are You?): A Spiritual Memoir: Bhagavan Das (Broadway Books, 1998).

A Mythic Life: Learning to Live Our Greater Story: Jean Houston. *A very good book, widening the frame and oriented to self-empowerment.* (Harper Collins: 1997).

The Joy of Burnout: Dina Glouberman *A book looking at the possibilities for a better way of lifestyle after a burnout or breakdown. The sub-title is "How the End of the World can be a New Beginning".* (Skyros Books: 2002).

APPENDIX 1: INTERNET ARTICLE (ADAPTED VERY SLIGHTLY)

SPIRITUAL EMERGENCIES AS DSM-IV SPIRITUAL PROBLEMS; DIAGNOSIS OF SPIRITUAL EMERGENCY; DIAGNOSTIC CRITERIA FOR SPIRITUAL EMERGENCY.

By David Lukoff, Ph.D.

SPIRITUAL EMERGENCIES AS DSM-IV SPIRITUAL PROBLEMS

Spiritual emergencies warrant the DSM-IV diagnosis of Religious or Spiritual Problem (V62.89), even though at times there may be symptoms of a mental disorder present. In this way, Religious or Spiritual Problem is comparable to the category Bereavement for which the DSM-IV notes that even when a person's reaction to a death meets the diagnostic criteria for Major Depressive Episode, the diagnosis of a mental disorder is not given because the symptoms result from a normal reaction to the death of a loved one. Rather, the diagnosis of bereavement, which is in the same section as Religious or Spiritual Problem (Other Conditions that may be the Focus of Clinical Attention) is assigned.

Similarly, in the case of spiritual emergencies, sequellae involving hallucinations, delusions, anger, and interpersonal difficulties occur so frequently that they should be considered normal and expectable reactions to the stressful spiritual awakening. Therefore, they should not be diagnosed or treated as mental disorders, but rather as Religious or Spiritual Problems that can lead to long-term improvement in overall well-being and functioning.

DIAGNOSIS OF SPIRITUAL EMERGENCY

Criteria for making the differential diagnosis between psychopathology and authentic spiritual experiences have been proposed by Agosin (1992), Grof & Grof (1989) and Lukoff (1986). There is considerable overlap among the proposed criteria.

Wilber (1980) argues that confusion in distinguishing intense spiritual experiences from psychosis has been created by failing to make the critical distinction between pre-rational states and authentic transpersonal states. This "pre/trans fallacy" has been perpetuated: *"since both pre-personal and transpersonal are, in their own ways, non-personal, then pre-personal and transpersonal tend to appear similar, even identical, to the untutored eye."* (p. 125).

The diagnostic criteria listed below were originally published in the *Journal of Transpersonal Psychology*, in 1985 in an article entitled *Diagnosis of Mystical Experience with Psychotic Features*. The use of operational criteria is intended to identify cases of spiritual emergency with a high degree of accuracy (validity) and consistency across different diagnosticians (reliability). The specific criteria proposed below represent hypotheses that must be subjected to studies to determine whether they achieve acceptable levels of inter-rater agreement and whether they accurately identify positively transforming experiences.

DIAGNOSTIC CRITERIA FOR SPIRITUAL EMERGENCY

1. Phenomenological overlap with one of the types of spiritual emergency.
2. Prognostic signs are indicative of a positive outcome.
3. The person is not a significant risk for homicidal or suicidal behaviour.

1. Phenomenological overlap with one of the types of spiritual emergency

Criterion 1 is based on the clinician's ability to differentiate between phenomenological characteristics of the types of spiritual emergency. I have proposed five criteria by which phenomenological overlap with a mystical experience can be identified. Assessment of overlap for other types can be based on the phenomenology as described in Lesson 4 on Types of Spiritual Emergencies:

i) Ecstatic mood: The most consistent feature of the mystical experience is elevation of mood. Laski (1968) describes this as a state with "feelings of a new life, another world, joy, salvation, perfection, satisfaction, glory" (cited in Perry (1974), p.84). Buckley (1969) examined the experiences of well-known mystics, leaders, and artists, as well as his own mystical experience, and noted they all shared *"a sense of exultation, of immense joyousness"* (p. 9). James (1961) also points to the *"mystical feeling of enlargement, union and emancipation"* (p. 334), and claims that *"mystical states are more like states of feeling than like states of intellect"* (p. 300).

ii) Sense of newly-gained knowledge: Feelings of enhanced intellectual understanding and the belief that the mysteries of life have been revealed are commonly reported in mystical experiences (Leuba, 1929).

James (1961) describes this phenomenon of newly-gained knowledge ("gnosis"): *"They are states of insight into the depths of truth, unplumbed by the discursive intellect. They are illuminations, revelations, full of significance and importance.* (p. 33). Jacob Boehme, a seventeenth-century shoemaker whose mystical experience ushered in a new vocation as a nature philosopher, reported: *"In one-quarter of an hour, I saw and knew more than if I had been many years together at a university. For I saw and knew the being of all things."* (cited in Perry (1974), p. 92).

iii) Perceptual alterations: Mystical experiences often involve perceptual alterations, ranging from heightened sensations to auditory and visual hallucinations.

Boehme felt himself surrounded by light during his mystical experience. Visual and auditory hallucinations with religious content are also common: e.g., Saint Therese saw angels and Saint Paul heard the voice of Jesus Christ saying *"Paul, Paul, why persecutest thou me?"* (Acts 9: v.4: KJV).

iv) Delusions with specific themes related to mythology: James (1961) and Neuman (1964) have both commented on the diversity of content in mystical experiences across time and cultures. The mystical experience does not have any specific intellectual content whatever of its own. It is capable of forming matrimonial alliances with material furnished by the most diverse philosophies and theologies. (James, 1961, p. 333; see also Fortune, 2000)

Electronic media have greatly increased the repertoire of cultural material available for incorporation into both mystical and psychotic experiences. Individuals who in the past might have claimed to be St. Luke, may now claim to be Luke Skywalker.

However, Perry (1974, p. 9). points out that below the surface level of specific identities and beliefs are thematic similarities in the accounts of patients whose psychotic episodes have good outcomes. There appears to be one kind of episode which can be characterized by its content, by its imagery, enough to merit its recognition as a syndrome. In it, there is a clustering of symbolic contents into a number of major themes strangely alike from one case to another,

Based on Perry's research and other accounts of patients with positive outcomes, the following eight themes were identified as occurring commonly in spiritual emergencies:

1. **Death**: being dead, meeting the dead or meeting Death.
2. **Rebirth**: new identity, new name, resurrection, apotheosis to god, king or messiah
3. **Journey**: Sense of being on a journey or mission.
4. **Encounters** with Spirits: demonic forces and/or helping spirits.
5. **Cosmic Conflict:** good/evil, communists/Americans, light/dark, male/female.
6. **Magical Powers:** telepathy, clairvoyance, ability to read minds, move objects.
7. **New Society:** radical change in society, religion, New Age, utopia, world peace.

8. **Divine Union:** God (as father, mother, child); marriage to God, Christ, Virgin Mary, Krishna or Radha [132].

In contrast, the following statements from schizophrenic patients I (Lukoff) have worked with illustrate that not all delusions have content related to the eight mythic themes described above:

> *My brain has been removed. A transmitter has been implanted into my brain and broadcasts all my thoughts to others. My parents drain my blood every night. The Mafia is poisoning my food and trying to kill me. My thoughts are being stolen and it interferes with my ability to think clearly. The person claiming to be my wife is only impersonating her. She's not my wife.*

Familiarity with the range and variation of content in myth, religion and psychosis is essential for determining which delusions have mythic themes.

v) Absence of conceptual disorganization: Some psychotic patients have cognitive deficits which cause them difficulty with their basic thought processes. For example, a person with schizophrenia complained, "I get lost in the spaces between words in sentences. I can't concentrate, or I get off onto thinking about something else" (in Estroff (1981), p. 223). Systematic comparisons of first-person accounts of mystical experiences and schizophrenia have found that:" *Thought blocking and other disturbances in language and speech do not appear to accompany the mystical experience*" (Buckley, 1969, p. 521).

Therefore, the presence of conceptual disorganization, as evidenced by disruption in thought, incoherence and blocking, would indicate the person is experiencing something other than a spiritual emergency.

---

[132] Radhā (Rādhikā) is the goddess of love, tenderness, compassion, and devotion. In the Vedic and Hindu scriptures, she is mentioned as the avatar of Lakshmi, and also as the Mūlaprakriti, the Supreme Goddess, who is the feminine counterpart and internal potency (wife, lover) of Krishna.

2. Prognostic signs are indicative of a positive outcome

Criterion 2 is based on research-validated good prognostic indicators that help predict positive long-term outcome. The features listed below are based on a survey of the outcome literature (Lukoff, 1986). Good prognostic indicators include:

1) good pre-episode functioning
2) acute onset of symptoms during a period of three months or less
3) stressful precipitant to the psychotic episode
4) a positive exploratory attitude toward the experience.

3. The person is not a significant risk for homicidal or suicidal behavior

Criterion 3 concerns issues which might require treatment in a restricted environment. Psychotic disorders can be the basis for homicidal and suicidal behaviours. Both John Lennon and President Reagan were shot by persons with previously diagnosed psychotic disorders. Arieti & Schreiber (1981) have described the case of a multiple murderer whose auditory hallucinations from God and delusions of being on a religious mission fuelled his bizarre and bloody killings. Assessment of dangerous and suicidality are the legal responsibilities of licensed mental health professionals. This exclusionary criterion should be implemented only if the danger seems imminent. Behaviour which appears bizarre, but presents no risk to self or others, does not warrant use of this criterion. Even with the use of these criteria, it is often difficult to distinguish spiritual emergencies from episodes of mental disorder. Agosin (1992) has pointed out that, *"Both are an attempt at renewal, transformation, and healing"* (p. 52).

References

Agosin, T. (1992). Psychosis, dreams and mysticism in the clinical domain. In: F. Halligan & J. Shea (Eds.), *The Fires of Desire.* New York: Crossroad.

Areti, S. & Schreiber, F.R. (1981). Multiple murders of a schizophrenic patient: a psychodynamic interpretation. *J. of American Academic Psychoanalysis, 9(4), 501-524.*

Buckley, R. (1969). *Cosmic Consciousness.* New York: Dutton.

Estroff, S. (1981). *Making It Crazy.* Berkeley: Univ. California Press.

Fortune, D. (2000). *Aspects of Occultism.* Red Wheel/Weiser.

Grof, S. & Grof, C. (Eds.). (1989). *Spiritual Emergency: When personal transformation becomes a crisis.* Los Angeles: Tarcher.

James, W. (1961). *The Varieties of Religious Experience.* New York: MacMillan.

Leuba, J.H. (1929). *Psychology of Religious Mysticism.* New York: Harcourt & Brace.

Lukoff, D. (1986). The diagnosis of mystical experiences with psychotic features. *Journal of Transpersonal Psychology, 17(2), 155-181.*

Neumann, E. (1964) Mystical Man. In: J. Campbell (Ed), *The Mystic Vision.* Princeton, NJ: Princeton University Press.

Perry, J. (1974). *The Far Side of Madness.* Englewood Cliffs, NJ: Prentice Hall.

Wilber, K. (1980). The pre/trans fallacy. *Re-Vision, 3, 51-72.*

APPENDIX 2:

DIFFERENT FACETS OF THE 'SENSE OF SELF'
(adapted and enlarged from Daniel N. Stern, 1985) [133]

By 'facets' I mean something like the facets of a dodecahedron – a 20-sided geometric solid: every facet giving a different aspect of the self, the whole. However, the core of all these facets is at the centre of this 'solid'.

- **The Embodied Self**

    Has bodily coherence; a sense of being complete; a physical whole with good boundaries; the centre of any integrated action, both moving and still. Loss or injury of this to leads to feelings of: fragmentation of bodily experience, depersonalization, out-of-body experiences, being ethereal or unreal, possible somatoform disorders, etc.

- **The Spatial Self**

    A sense of having space; being on firm ground; having the ability to move; the ability to manipulate objects; physical potency. Loss of this leads to feelings of: passivity; helplessness with respect to objects; powerlessness; not feeling one has a 'proper' place or home.

- **The Self in Time**

    A coherent sense of time; has a personal history and a sense of enduring; a sense of continuity with one's own past or with history; a feeling that one 'goes on being'; that can change whilst remaining

---

[133] Thanks also for this basic structure to Malvern Lumsden, "The Moving Self in Life, Art and Community Mental Health: Twelve Propositions." *Journal of Body, Movement & Dance in Psychotherapy: Vol. 5: No. 3. 2010.*

basically the same. Loss of this leads to feelings of: temporal dissociation, fugue states, amnesia, a sense of 'not being', fear of change, etc.

- **The Core Self**

    A sense of 'self' as opposed to 'other'; being a person (having been treated as a person); having essential self-respect; having a unique identity which is appreciated; *"consisting of self-agency, self-coherence, self-history (continuity), and self-affectivity"* (Stern, 1985, xix); etc. Loss or non-development of this can lead to feelings of: indifference, apathy, disinterest, lack of assertion, over-compliance, etc.

- **The Self as Agent**

    A sense of responsibility and satisfaction for one's own actions; having volition; feeling in control over self-generated actions; initiating actions; self-regulation. Loss of this leads to feelings of: powerlessness, paralysis, no responsibility for own actions, loss of control to external agents, paranoia, etc.

- **The Emotional Self**

    A sense of an effective self; experiencing inner qualities of patterned feelings (affects) that 'belong' with other experiences of self; being aware of different levels of feelings. Loss of this leads to feelings of: the inability to experience ordinary pleasurable emotions; dissociated states; being unemotional, withdrawn or unavailable; etc.

- **The Relational Self**

    A sense of belonging or a feeling of participation with others; wanting to be social, relating to others; being reasonably empathic. Loss of this leads to feelings of: loneliness, alienation, reclusiveness, etc.

- **The (En)gendered Self**

    A sense of self as male or female; pleasure and security in that; the ability to relate to others as men and women. Loss or injury of this leads to feelings of: fear of sexual relationships; gender identity disorders; homophobia or misogyny; psychosexual dysfunction)

- **The Intellectual Self**

    A sense of rationality; the ability (and pleasure) to study, reason and think; an awareness of and interest in different ideas that does not threaten us. Loss or lack of this leads to feelings of: irrationality, chaos, confusion; inability to think straight; feeling threatened by new or different ideas; etc.

- **The Moral Self**

    A sense that one's actions are (or should be) influenced by social rules, collective agreements, consensual rationality or philosophical principles, rather than immediate and personal gains and losses. Loss of this leads to (feelings of): selfishness, narcissism, immorality or amorality, being evil.

- **The Verbal Self**

    A sense of 'ownership' of language and of relationship associated with membership in a particular language (and cultural) community; separates the 'lived' experience from the verbal representation; sees 'self' and 'other' more clearly and can identify differences; etc. Loss of this leads to feelings of: alienation, culture shock, dislocation, rootlessness, etc.

- **The Narrative Self**

    The self is sensed as a set of symbolic narratives; this is your 'story' – you sense of your life; there is a 'red thread' running through your life that helps explain choices and actions. Loss of or injury to this leads to feelings of: being neurotic; seeming like a butterfly (never content with something for long); being eccentric; being 'wacky' or disjointed; or having other problems in work (especially with continuance) and having disruptive family relations.

- **The Creative Self**

    A sense of freedom and efficacy in transforming given forms, of dealing with chaos, and of expressing the wider aspects of yourself; having a definite 'form' of expression (music, art, cooking, etc.); seeing the world through this medium of expression. Loss of this tends to lead to feelings of: despair, staleness, frustration, etc.

- **The Spiritual Self**

    A sense of the transpersonal, of transcendence beyond the confines of the individual self; a sense of the 'Other'; a regularly-practiced belief system that really works for you; the ability to 'transcend' of occasion and connect with other things, dimensions, beings, or insights. Loss of this leads to feelings of: despair, dullness, being mundane, being out-of-touch, etc.

    Each of these facets is complex in itself and carries many different aspects, and insights. This only a rough outline or "working model". This listing is also – given the width of human activity - incomplete: one might envisage an "Artistic Self" or a "Historical Self" or a "Maternal Self" (or lack of it) [134]. Several things should be noted:

    A. These various facets of the Sense of Self develop at different times in one's life and it is therefore likely that later ones (e.g., verbal, cognitive and narrative selves) build upon the development of earlier facets (the embodied self, the affective self, etc.). The foundations of these later Senses of Self are therefore – not necessarily – valid. Some of these Senses of Self can be temporary (i.e., a "Professional Self" usually lasts only about 30-40 years, between the ages of 24 and 60.

    B. Most of these facets are essentially non-verbal and experiential. They develop as a result of early bodily interactions and emotional experiences. They are therefore 'sensed' or 'felt'.

    C. The task of development of the full potential of a person's sense of their Self involves not only the development of each facet, but also their integration into a harmonious whole. This developmental integrational process is the essential inner 'work' of our life and thus gives a template for any therapy to help to heal any early disruptive or dysfunctional experiences that have 'damaged' or prevented one of these facets developing.

---

[134] See: Matthies, L.M., Wallwiener, S., Müller, M., Doster, A., Plewniok, K., Feller, S., Sohn, C., Wallwiener, M. & Reck, C. (2017). Maternal self-confidence during the first four months postpartum and its association with anxiety and early infant regulatory problems. *Infant Behavior & Development, 49, 228-237.*

Further Reading

Eugene T. Gendlin (2003). *Focusing: How to Open Up Your Deeper Feelings and Intuition.* Rider & Co:

Eugene T. Gendlin (1986). *Let Your Body Interpret Your Dreams.* Chiron Publications.

Helen G. Brenner (2004). *I Know I'm in There Somewhere: A Woman's Guide to Finding Her Inner Voice and Living a Life of Authenticity.* Gotham Books.

C.K. Germer (2003). *The Mindful Path to Self-Compassion.* Guilford Press.

Rick Hanson & Richard Mendius (2009). *Buddha's Brain: The Practical Neuroscience of Happiness, Love & Wisdom.* New Harbinger Pubs.

Thich Nhat Hahn (2008). *The Miracle of Mindfulness.* Rider & Co.

Paul Jones (2009). *How to Live in the Here and Now: A Guide to Accelerated Enlightenment, Unlocking the Power of Mindful Awareness.* O Books.

D.N. Stern (1985). *The Interpersonal World of the Infant.* New York: Basic Books.

D.N. Stern (2004). *The Present Moment in Psychotherapy and Everyday Life.* New York & London: Norton.

APPENDIX 3:

DSM-IV CLASSIFICATION

In 1994, Dr. David Lukoff, managed to get 'Spiritual Emergencies' included into a new diagnostic classification in the American Psychiatric Association (APA)'s Diagnostic & Statistical Manual – 4th Edition (DSM-IV) under the category ***Religious or Spiritual problem: Code V62.89.*** *This category can be used when the focus of clinical attention is a religious or spiritual problem. Examples include distressing experiences that involve loss or questioning of faith, problems associated with conversion to a new faith, or questioning of other spiritual values which may not necessarily be related to an organized church or religious institution.*

He wrote about this process in a 1998 article that described the rationale for this new category, the history of the proposal, transpersonal perspectives on spiritual emergency, types of religious and spiritual problems (with case illustrations), differential diagnostic issues, psychotherapeutic approaches, and the likely increase in numbers of persons seeking therapy for spiritual problems. It also presented the preliminary findings from a database of religious and spiritual problems.

The original proposal grew out of the work of the Spiritual Emergence Network (Prevatt & Park, 1989) that supported people having such problems and designed to increase the competence of mental health professionals in sensitivity to such spiritual issues.

A systematic analysis of case reports involving religious or spiritual issues in the Medline bibliographic database from 1980-1996 located 364 abstracts. Another 100 cases that described religious and spiritual problems were located in PsychINFO.

The eventual acceptance of religious and spiritual problems as a new diagnostic category in DSM-IV is a reflection of increasing sensitivity to cultural diversity in the mental health professions and of transpersonal psychology's impact on mainstream clinical practice, backed by sufficient research.

This was affirmed in a later article (Lukoff *et al.*, 2011)

A contemporary article (Randal & Argyle, 1998) describes the use of this diagnosis in Australasia to satisfy a major complaint that mental health services – and especially psychiatrists – ignore or pathologise people with spiritual or religious problems. Maori culture has always recognised an understanding of spiritual aspects as an integral part of mental health, but Western psychiatry has historically ignored or pathologized (over-ruled) such experiences.

Lukoff, D. (1998). From Spiritual Emergency to Spiritual Problem: The Transpersonal Roots of the New DSM-IV Category. *Journal of Humanistic Psychology, 38(2), 21-50.*

Lukoff, D., Lu, F.G. & Yang, C.P. (2011). DSM-IV religious and spiritual problems. In: J.R. Peteet, F.G. Lu & W.E. Narrow (Eds.) *Religious and spiritual issues in psychiatric diagnosis: A research agenda for DSM-V.*, (pp. 171-198). American Psychiatric Association.

Prevatt, J. & Park, R. (1989) The Spiritual Emergence Network (SEN). In: S. Grof & C. Grof (Eds.), *Spiritual Emergency: When personal transformation becomes a crisis*, (pp. 225-232). Los Angeles: Tarcher.

Randal, P. & Argyle, N. (1998). 'Spiritual Emergency' – a useful explanatory model? A literature review and discussion paper. *Journal of Humanistic Psychology, 38(2), 21-50.*

APPENDIX 4:

RESEARCH STUDIES

The Spiritual Emergency Scale (SES; **Goretzki, Thalbourne, & Storm, 2013**) assesses the presence of spiritual emergencies - defined as psychotic-like crises or as "critical and experientially difficult stages of a profound psychological transformation that involves one's entire being" (Grof & Grof, 1991).

The Spiritual Emergency Scale was originally developed out of the 84 items, created by **Goretzki, Thalbourne, and Storm (2009)**, divided among ten subscales which measured different types of spiritual emergency: **(a)** Dark Night of the Soul (7 items); **(b)** Awakening of Kundalini (11 items); **(c)** Shamanic Crisis (10 items); **(d)** Peak Experiences (7 items); **(e)** Psychic Opening (13 items); **(f)** Past-Life Experience (5 items); **(g)** Near-Death Experience (8 items); **(h)** Possession States (8 items); **(i)** Activation of the Central Archetype (9 items); and **(j)** Experiences of Close Encounters with UFOs (6 items).

The authors performed a principal axis factor analysis on these items which yielded a single component labelled "spiritual emergency". Following the factor analysis, the authors selected the 30 items that had the highest correlation with the spiritual emergency factor. The final measure consists of 30 items (e.g., *"Have you ever lost your sense of reference as your outer and inner worlds dissolved?"* and *"Have you ever experienced the spontaneous production of complex visual geometrical images or chants inside your head?"*), which then utilized a "yes/no" response format.

Harris, Rock & Clark (2010) adapted the SES to utilize a Likert response scale and tested the measure in a sample drawn from the general population. This study attempted to validate **Goretzki,**

Thalbourne and Storm's (2009) Spiritual Emergency Subscales (SES), and Experiences of Psychotic Symptoms Scale (EPSS) as measures of SE and psychosis, respectively. It also investigated whether personality traits (i.e., transliminality, dissociation, sensitivity, openness to change, tension and abstractedness) predicted SES and EPSS scores. 224 participants completed an anonymous online questionnaire.

Their second study in 2019 examined the relationship between SE (Y), psychic symptoms, and schizotypy, a construct that addresses psychotic-like personality traits in the general population. A total of 250 participants completed an anonymous online questionnaire.

Storm & Goretzki (2021) then assessed psychological aspects of SE to differentiate it from psychosis and other proposed psi-inhibitives ymptoms – namely, alogia (i.e. poverty of speech), depression, anxiety, and stress. Two groups of participants were formed: controls (mainly psychology students) and SE-experients. Participants either completed the study on a computer in the laboratory or online. Questionnaires on Spiritual Emergency (which includes a subscale on Psychic Opening), positive symptoms of psychosis, alogia, spiritual identity, paranormal beliefs, mysticism, depression, anxiety, and stress, were administered to participants, who then completed the Imagery Cultivation (IC) picture-identification psi task, which uses a shamanic-like journeying protocol (Storm & Rock, 2009a, 2009b).

Another independent study (**Corneille & Luke, 2021**) investigated the phenomenological variances of SE experiences, including the potential differences between Spontaneous Spiritual Awakenings (SSA) and Spontaneous Kundalini Awakenings (SKA), a subset of awakening experiences that the authors postulate may produce a higher likelihood of both physical and negative effects; to explore how these experiences compare to other Altered States of Consciousness (ASC), including those mediated by certain psychedelic substances; and understand their impact on well-being.

A total of 152 participants reporting their most powerful SSA/SKAs completed questionnaires measuring non dual, kundalini, and mystical experience, as well as depth of ASC, and trait absorption and Temporal Lobe Lability (TLL). Spontaneous Kundalini Awakenings were found to be significantly more physical, but not significantly more negative than SSAs, and overall, both sets of experiences were perceived to be overwhelmingly more positive than negative, even in cases where the experience was initially challenging.

There is also a nice research-type article on *"The Grofs' Model of Spiritual Emergency in Retrospect: Has it Stood the Test of Time?"* by **Darlene Viggiano & Stanley Krippner**, both from Saybrook University, which examined whether the Grofs' model was still useful or whether it should be revised. At first, its longevity was questioned because some of the supporting communities (Soteria and Diabasis House [135]) had closed down. However, (according to the AltaVista search engine, 109,000 of the 120,000 matches for the term "spiritual emergency" are very recent, which is supportive. However, PsycNET have only 30 matches, which might indicate the scientific and medical communities need to keep up with public demand. Others seem to favour the term "spiritual diversity" or are included in "cultural competence". They state – in support of the Grofs' model, *"Johnson & Friedman (2008) recognized the need for both culturally sensitive and psychometric methods of differentiating spiritual emergencies from psychotic episodes."*, but surprisingly note that some earlier studies [136] suggest *"that it may be possible for a spiritual emergency approach to be combined with psychopharmacology and to be beneficial even in bona fide cases of schizophrenia."* This point is followed up by a reference to Lukoff *et al.*'s 1996 work, where it is stated, *"Transpersonal psychiatry ... attempts to preserve the transformative potential of psychosis during the acute phase by allowing for the expression of symptoms rather than squelching them is it is practised in mainstream medical-model approaches."* (p. 280). They conclude: *It is statements such as these that indicate the Grofs' model was a pioneering discovery that has come into its own as patients are identified who cannot be diagnosed or treated as effectively with other models."*

Corneille, J.S. & Luke, D. (2021). Spontaneous Spiritual Awakenings: Phenomenology, Altered States, Individual Differences, and Well-Being. *Frontiers in Psychology, 12, 720579.*

---

[135] Cornwall, M. (2022). The Dramatic Results of John Weir Perry's Diabasis House Program. *Mad in America: Science, Society & Social Justice,*

[136] Viggiano, D. (2010). The role of dreams and dream- like experiences in spiritual emergence processes. (Unpublished doctoral dissertation). Saybrook University, San Francisco.

Goretzki, M., Thalbourne, M. A. & Storm, L. (2013). Development of a spiritual emergency scale. *The Journal of Transpersonal Psychology, 45(2), 105–117.*

Harris, K.P., Rock, A.J. & Clark, G. (2015). Spiritual emergency, psychosis and personality: A quantitative investigation. *Journal of Transpersonal Psychology, 2015, Vol. 47, No. 2, 263-285.*

Harris, K.P., Rock, A.J. & Clark, G. (2019). Spiritual Emergence (y), Psychosis, and Personality: Investigating the Role of Schizotypy. *International Journal of Transpersonal Studies, 2019, Vol. 38, No. 2, 1-30.*

Johnnson, C. & Friedman, H. (2008). Enlightened or delusional? Differentiating religious, spiritual, and transpersonal experience from psychopathology. *Journal of Humanistic Psychology, 48(4), 505-527.*

Lukoff, D., Lu, F. G. & Turner, R. (1996). Diagnosis: A transpersonal clinical approach to religious and spiritual problems. In B.W. Scotton, A.B. Chinen & J.R. Battista (Eds.), *Textbook of Transpersonal Psychiatry and Psychology,* (pp. 231-249). New York, NY: Basic Books.

Storm, L.& Goretzki, M. (2021). The Psychology and Parapsychology of Spiritual Emergency *Journal of Scientific Exploration, Vol. 35, No. 1, 36-64.*

Viggiano, D.B. & Krippner, S. (2010). The Grofs' model of spiritual emergency in retrospect: Has it stood the test of time? *International Journal of Transpersonal Studies, 29(1), 118–127.*

ABOUT THE AUTHOR

Courtenay Young is a very experienced Humanistic, Body-Oriented & Transpersonal Psychotherapist, who has worked in various different locations and areas in the mental health field for over 40 years. He trained originally at the Gerda Boyesen Centre for Biodynamic Psychology & Psychotherapy (1979-1983). Since completing his psychotherapy training, he has worked in psychiatric hostels, in community settings, with psychiatric & socially disadvantaged adolescents and with psycho-geriatric patients for Brent Social Services.

For over 17 years, from 1986, Courtenay was – in effect – the resident psychotherapist at the Findhorn Foundation, an international spiritual community located in north-east Scotland. Since 2003 (having left Findhorn), he has been working in the NHS in the Central Belt of Scotland, in and around Edinburgh, as a Counsellor & Psychological Therapist, for Employee Assistance Programmes, as well as in NHS GP surgeries, and in departments of Clinical Psychology in three different NHS trusts in Scotland, as well as having a private psychotherapy practice in Edinburgh and in the Scottish Borders.

He was, at one point in time, the Regional Co-ordinator for Scotland for the Spiritual Emergency Network (UK) and he has written books and articles, given training seminars, conference lectures and workshops on Spiritual Emergence processes and Spiritual Emergencies for psychotherapists in the UK, in Europe and the USA.

He still – occasionally – works individually with people in spiritual crisis and emergencies.

He and his wife, Laura Hope Steckler, an American Clinical Psychologist and Body Psychotherapist, have run weekend and week-long residential workshops at Findhorn, in Germany, and elsewhere, entitled *The Spirit of the Body*: a combination of spiritual emergence work, movement exercises, and body-oriented psychotherapy.

In 2023, aged 75, Courtenay retired from 20 years of clinical practice in the NHS, whilst retaining a small private practice, and is now hoping to travel more and visit psychotherapy training schools and centres in other countries as a visiting tutor. He continues to write books and articles and also to edit books.

Courtenay's first published book was *Help Yourself Towards Mental Health* (Karnac Books, 2010), and the 1st edition of this book, *First Contacts with People in Crisis & Spiritual Emergencies*, was his second book, published by AuthorHouse in 2011.

He has since written many published articles, most of which are available to download from his website: www.courtenay-young.com and has edited and co-edited several other books writing. He is still in the process of writing a much larger book about Spiritual Emergencies and the whole transformational process, possibly to be entitled, *When Their World Changed*.

In 2010, he founded the imprimatur of 'Body Psychotherapy Publications' (www.bodypsychotherapypublications.com), of which he is the director, and he has now published a series of 7 edited books on this theme. Hopefully, more will follow (see end pages).

He was the English-language Editor for the definitive and massive tome: *The Handbook of Body Psychotherapy & Somatic Psychology* (North Atlantic Books, 2015), edited by Gustl Marlock & Halko Weiss with Courtenay Young & Michael Soth, with about 1,000 pages, 90 chapters and 60 contributing authors.

In 2022, he produced *"The 'New' Collected Papers of Biodynamic Psychology, Massage & Psychotherapy (2022)"* as a PDF book, with about 50 articles from about 50 different authors, 1,550 pages, which runs to about 850,000 words and is available from Body Psychotherapy Publications.

He is currently helping to edit and complete two other Body Psychotherapy books for different authors and there are a few more similar books in the pipeline. He has also attended and presented at a great many international psychotherapy conferences.

In parallel – and in the somewhat more 'political' fields of psychotherapy – he has served on many committees for several professional associations. He has served on the Governing Boards of the United Kingdom Council of Psychotherapy (UKCP), the UK Association for Humanistic Psychology Practitioners (UK-AHPP), the European Association of Body Psychotherapy (EABP) and the European Association for Psychotherapy (EAP). He is also a Graduate Member of the British Psychological Society (BPS).

He was the lead writer for the EAP's "Statement of Ethical Principles", and their "Project to Develop the Professional Core Competences of a European Psychotherapist" (www.psychotherapy-comopetency.eu), which completed its first phase in 2013, restarting again in 2023.

He has been an active member of the EAP's Statutes Committee, Ethical Guidelines Committee, European-Wide Accrediting Organisations Committee (EWOC) and Scientific & Research Committee; as well as serving in a number of different political and administrative roles for the European Association of Body Psychotherapy (EABP) between 1992 and 2004. He has served on the Governing Board of the United Kingdom Council for Psychotherapy (UKCP) in 1992, 2007 and is currently (2023=>) a Trustee on the Governing Board of the UKCP.

In 2012, he was made an Honorary Member of the European Association of Body Psychotherapy (EABP), and an Honorary Member of the European Association for Psychotherapy (EAP) in 2023.

He is still currently the Editor of the EAP's International Journal of Psychotherapy (www.ijp.org.uk), although he is trying to step back a bit from this role after having been involved on the Editorial Board since 2009 and having been the Editor since 2011.

Finally, besides everything else that he does (including looking after a large garden and enjoying being with his grandchildren), he is putting together a narrative to be submitted for a Doctorate by Public Works from the Parkmore Institute.

He can be contacted by e-mail: courtenay'@'courtenay-young.com (by removing the 2 inverted commas).

About Body Psychotherapy Publications

Body Psychotherapy Publications is a new venture. It is an imprint dedicated to publishing materials relevant to the training and professional practice of Body Psychotherapy and Somatic Psychology. The goal has been to start a publishing house specifically for publishing body psychotherapy / somatic psychology material: entitled "Body Psychotherapy Publications" and/ or "Somatic Psychology Publications" – probably one title for this side of the Atlantic, and the other for that side, but essentially exactly the same business. The intention is to do at least three things:

1. Reprint significant articles to do with B-P that are now not so easily accessible; and to reprint these articles as an edited book in collections with a common theme: i.e. The Historical Basis of B-P; About the Science of B-P; About Touch in B-P; etc.

2. To provide a possible venue for new B-P authors as sometimes our contributions are not sufficiently well placed within the 'mainstream' and mainstream publishers are really only out to make money; neither of which says anything about the quality of the actual material. This possibility now opens a door for new authors in the field of B-P.

3. Providing a way of getting the very rich and varied B-P articles 'out there', but which are not written in English, to be translated from their language of origin, and then publishe.

Hopefully, in due course, the flow will go the other way, and people will want to translate these volumes into different languages. We wold be very open to that and would be willing to offer copyright permission at very reasonable rates, or to publish our own translated versions.

Whilst – so far – this is virtually a one-person business, it is very early days, and we in Body Psychotherapy Publications are very open to working with other contributors (authors, editors, investors, translators, marketing suggestions, etc.) in a variety of different ways as long as these people are energetic or enthusiastic. Suitable contracts and remuneration will be worked out. The 'company' will be set up on a co-operative, work democratic basis.

bodypsychotherapypublications.com

SPRITUAL AWAKENINGS

BODY PSYCHOTHERAPY PUBLICATIONS

1ST PUBLICATION IN 2011

THE HISTORICAL BASIS OF BODY PSYCHOTHERAPY

Edited by Courtenay Young

Contents

– Roots: 4 extracts on the roots of Body Psychotherapy, by Barbara Goodrich-Dunn & Elliot Greene; Ulfried Geuter; Nick Totton; and David Boadella
– An Overview of the History of Body Psychotherapy, by Bernd Eiden
– Psycho-physical synthesis at the foundations of Body Psychotherapy: the 100-year legacy of Pierre Janet, by David Boadella
– A series of 6 essays on The History & Development of Body Psychotherapy, by Courtenay Young
– On Elsa Lindenberg & Reich, by Courtenay Young
– What is European Body Psychotherapy Now? by Courtenay Young

This book has a paperback cover, is about 23cm x 15cm and has 300 pages.
ISBN: 978-1-908729-00-2 – RRP: £18.00; €22.00; $30.00

Also available as a downloadable PDF file
ISBN: 978-1-908729-01-9 – £15.00; €18.00; $24.00

COURTENAY YOUNG

PUBLISHED IN 2012

ABOUT THE SCIENCE OF BODY PSYCHOTHERAPY

Edited by Courtenay Young

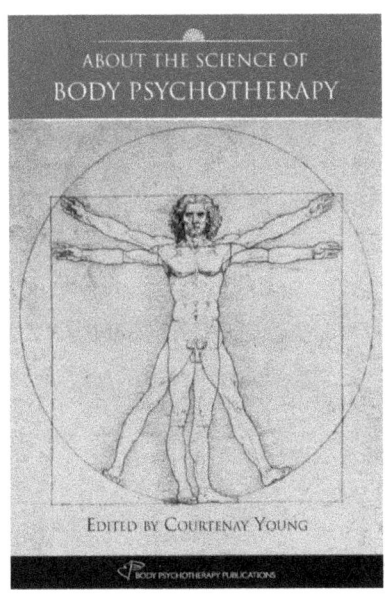

Contents

- Body Psychotherapy Research: An Introduction by Alice Kahn Ladas
- At the border between chaos and order – what psychotherapy and neuroscience have in common, by Roz Carroll
- Research 101 for Body Psychotherapists: Cultivating a Somatically-Informed Mind by Christine Caldwell and Rae Johnson
- Four extended essays on the Science of Body Psychotherapy Today by Courtenay Young
- A Background History
- The Current Situation
- Appropriate Science
- New Science & Research
- (Body) Psychotherapy is a Craft, not a Science, by Courtenay Young
- Efficacy of Bioenergetic Therapies and Stability of the Therapeutic Result: A Retrospective Investigation by Christa D. Ventling
- Body-Oriented Psychotherapy – the state of the art in empirical research and evidence-based practice: a clinical perspective, by Frank Röhricht

This book has a paperback cover, is about 23cm x 15cm and has 342 pages.
ISBN: 978-1-908729-02-6 – RRP: £18.00; €22.00; $30.00

Also available as a downloadable PDF file
ISBN: 978-1-908729-03-3 – Only from the website: £15.00; €18.00; $24.00

SPRITUAL AWAKENINGS

PUBLISHED IN 2012

ABOUT RELATIONAL BODY PSYCHOTHERAPY

Edited by Courtenay Young

Contents

- 2 short interviews about Relational Body Psychotherapy, by Nancy Eichhorn, with Michael Soth and with Robert Hilton
- Relational Therapy, by Nick Totton & Allison Priestman
- Current Body Psychotherapy: an integral- relational approach for the 21st Century, by Michael Soth
- More than Words: Moments of Meaning in Relational Body Psychotherapy, by Angela King
- Relational Living Body Psychotherapy: From Physical Resonances to Embodied Interventions and Experiments, by Julianne Appel-Opper
- Four essays by Asaf Rolef Ben- Shahar
- The Relational Turn and Body Psychotherapy: Part I. From Ballroom Dance to Five Rhythms: An Introduction to Relational Psychoanalysis and Psychotherapy
- The Relational Turn and Body Psychotherapy: Part II: Something Old, Something New, Something Borrowed, Something Blue, by
- The Relational Turn and Body Psychotherapy: Part III: Salsa Lessons and the Emergent Self: Somatic organization, relationality and the place of self in Body Psychotherapy
- T he Relational Turn and Body Psychotherapy: Part IV: Gliding on the Strings that Connect Us: Resonance in Relational Body Psychotherapy
- Intercultural Body-Oriented Psychotherapy: The culture in the Body and the Body in the Culture, by Julienne Appel-Opper
- The Dawn of a New Identity: Aspects of a relational approach to psychotherapy with a transsexual client, by Angela King
- Let There Be Light: Creating Differentiation and Safety with a Highly Dissociative Client Through Relational Body Psychotherapy, by Asaf Rolef Ben-Shahar & Kate Wood

This book has a paperback cover, is about 23cm x 15cm and has 306 pages.
ISBN: 978-1-908729-08-8 – RRP: £18.00; €22.00; $30.00

Also available as a downloadable PDF file

COURTENAY YOUNG

PUBLISHED IN 2014

THE BODY IN RELATIONSHIP
Self – Other – Society

Edited by Courtenay Young

Contents

PRESENTATIONS FOR
THE EABP/ISC CONGRESS
LISBON, SEPTEMBER 2014
This volume contains about 35 edited chapters from a number of different presenters who came to this Congress. They are Body Psychotherapists, from a number of different countries and from different backgrounds and modalities.

Their presentations speak – very clearly – for themselves, both in this book, and at the Congress:
Merete Holm Brantbjerg, Denise Saint Arnault & Sharon O'Halloran, Ursula Schorn, Grace Wanderly de Barros Correia, Enrica Pedrelli & Luciano Rispoli, Elya Steinberg & Gerhard Payrhuber, Wade H. Cockburn, Brasilda Rocha, Shai Epstein, Will Davis, Traudl Szyszkowitz, Miriam Nelken, Frederic Lowen, Luis Gonçalvez Boggio, Christina Bader-Johansson, Boris Suburov, Vera Pivoňková, Fernando Barbosa de Freitas, Olinda Fertinani Nunes, Marion Lausche, Genovino Ferri, Liane Zink, Madlen Algafari, Renata Terruggi & Carlos de Sousa, Gabrielle & Christian Bartuska, Maya Schrier-Kerstan, Volnei Jorge Pinheiro Jr., Panagiotis Stambolis & Sophia Tsoumaki, Nancy Eichhorn, the EABP Science & Research Committee, Anette Torgersen, Mary Jane Piava, Laura Hope Steckler, Carin Ballas, and Dora Theodoropoulou.

This book has a paperback cover, is about 23cm x 15cm and has 374 pages.
ISBN: 978-1-908729-10-1 – RRP: £18.00; €22.00; $30.00

Also available as a downloadable PDF file
ISBN: 978-1-908729-11-8 – Only from the website: £15.00; €18.00; $24.00

SPRITUAL AWAKENINGS

PUBLISHED IN 2018

BODY PSYCHOTHERAPY CASE STUDIES

Edited by Courtenay Young
in conjunction with the EABP Science & Research Committee

Contents

- 3 introductory articles: from the EABP SRC; About Body Psychotherapy & An Introduction to Case Studies
- Bernhard – A Case Study of Soma & Spirit, by Stanley Keleman
- A List of Historic Body Psychotherapy Case Studies
- Three Case Studies, Presentations on the theme of Embodiment from the EABP Scientific Symposium in Athens, 2016: The Role of Embodiment in Therapeutic Process, by Sladjana Djordjevic; Female Emancipation: Achieving stable embodiment in the face of early stress, by Christina Bader Johansson and Doing Effective Body Psychotherapy without Touch, by Courtenay Young
- Sexual Violence and its Consequences, by Herbert Grassmann
- Marina Crossing the Bridge: An adolescent crisis with the symptomatology of an eating disorder, by Christina Bader Johansson
- Three Short Body Psychotherapy Case Studies from Bernhard Schlage: How Deep Tissue Work Can Assist the Release of Post-Traumatic Stress Tension; About the release of effects of Pre-Natal Traumatization through Enactment Techniques and The Release of Pain in the Upper Back by Body Psychotherapy exercises: Defining personal boundaries
- Somatic Experiencing in the treatment of Post Traumatic Stress Disorder with convulsions, by Galit Serebrnick-Hai
- And So It Goes On – A story of one therapy, by Russell Rose
- Yet Another BP Session, by Russell Rose
- Medical Trauma: Interpersonal Neurology and the Autonomic Nervous System, by Jacqueline A. Carleton
- A Woman of Many Colours, by Laura Hope Steckler
- Transcultural Case Study: First Interview with a Chinese Client, by Ulrick Sollmann & Wentian Li
- Guidelines on Writing a Body Psychotherapy Case Study (2014), EABP Science & Research Committee

This book has a paperback cover, is about 23cm x 15cm and has about 250 pages.
ISBN: 978-1-908729-04-0 – RRP: £18.00; €22.00; $30.00

Also available as a downloadable PDF file
ISBN: 987-1-908729-05-7 – Only from the website: £15.00; €18.00; $24.00

TO BE PUBLISHED IN 2019

ABOUT TOUCH IN BODY PSYCHOTHERAPY
Volume I

Edited by Courtenay Young

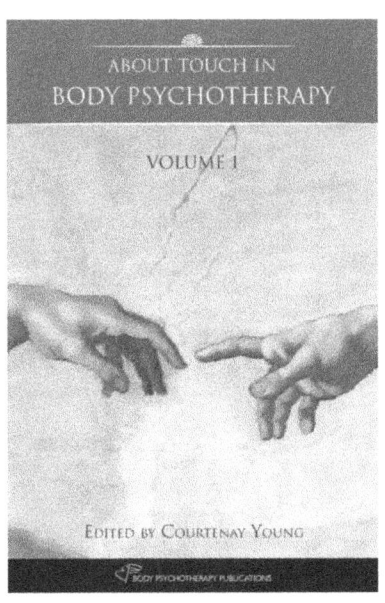

Contents

- Overview: The Use of Touch in Psychotherapy, by Bernd Eiden
- Relating through Physical Touch in Contemporary Psychotherapy, by Gill Westland
- The Power of Touch in Psychotherapy, by Courtenay Young
- The Continuing Evolution of Touch in Psychotherapy, by Anastasia D. McRae
- A Study of Ethical and Clinical Implications for the Appropriate Use of Touch in Psychotherapy, by Kerstin E. White
- Somatic Tracking and the Ethical Use of Touch, by Jaffy Phillips
- Touch and the Therapeutic Relationship 1 & 2, by Andrea Uphoff
- Biodynamic Massage as a therapeutic tool, by Clover Southwell
- Stirring the Depths: Transference, counter-transference and touch, by Tom Warnecke
- A Cup, Grasping my Fingers, by Asaf Rolef Ben-Shahar
- Attuned Touch, by Susan McConnell
- About the Ethics of Professional Touch in Psychotherapy, by Courtenay Young.

This book has a paperback cover, is about 23cm x 15cm and has about 270 pages.
ISBN: 978-1-908729-04-0 – RRP: £18.00; €22.00; $30.00

Also available as a downloadable PDF file
ISBN: 987-1-908729-05-7 – Only from the website: £15.00; €18.00; $24.00

SPRITUAL AWAKENINGS

The 'New' Collected Papers of Biodynamic Psychology, Massage & Psychotherapy: 2022

In Celebration of the 100th Anniversary of Gerda Boyesen's birth

EDITED BY COURTENAY YOUNG

BODY PSYCHOTHERAPY PUBLICATIONS

COURTENAY YOUNG

The 'New' Collected Papers of Biodynamic Psychology, Massage & Psychotherapy: 2022

Contents

Introduction		*Courtenay Young*
<u>Preface</u>		*Mona-Lisa Boyesen & Ebba Boyesen*
§1	**The Collected Papers of Biodynamic Psychology, Volume 1**	
1.1	Experience with Dynamic Relaxation and the Relationship of its Discovery to the Reichian View of Vegeto-therapy	*Gerda Boyesen*
1.2	The Primary Personality and its Relationship to the 'Streamings'	*Gerda Boyesen*
1.3	Psycho-peristalsis, Part 1: The Abdominal Discharge of Nervous Tension	*Mona-Lisa Boyesen*
1.4	Psycho-peristalsis, Part 2: Emotional Repression as a Somatic Compromise: Stages in the Physiology of Neurosis	*Mona-Lisa Boyesen*
1.5	Psycho-peristalsis, Part 3: A Case History of a Manic Depressive	*Gerda Boyesen*
1.6	Psycho-peristalsis, Part 4: Dynamic of the Vaso-motor Cycle: Nuances of Membrane Pathology according to Mental Condition	*Mona-Lisa Boyesen*
1.7	Psycho-peristalsis, Part 5: Function of the Libido Circulation	*Mona-Lisa Boyesen*
1.8	Psycho-peristalsis, Part 6: Bio-physical Aspects of Libido Circulation	*Mona-Lisa Boyesen*
1.9	Psycho-peristalsis, Part 7: From Libido Theory to Cosmic Energy	*Mona-Lisa Boyesen*
1.10	Psycho-peristalsis, Part 8: Self-Regulation and the Streamings	*Mona-Lisa Boyesen*
1.11	Flesh, Energy and Orgonotic Contact	*David Boadella*
1.12	The Essence of Energy Distribution	*Ebba Boyesen*
1.13	The Energy Distribution Treatment	*Clover Southwell*
1.14	The Scope of Energy Distribution	*Robyn Lee (Speyer)*

§2 The Collected Papers of Biodynamic Psychology, Volume 2

2.1	Foundation for Biodynamic Psychology, Part 1: Spontaneous Movements and Visceral Armour	*Mona-Lisa & Gerda Boyesen*
2.2	Foundation for Biodynamic Psychology, Part 2: Cries from the Guts	*Mona-Lisa & Gerda Boyesen*
2.3	Bio-Release, Part 1	*Mona-Lisa Boyesen*
2.4	Bio-Release, Part 2: The Startle Reflex Pattern and Organic Equilibrium	*Mona-Lisa Boyesen*
2.5	Psycho-Orgastic Vibrations: A Standing Exercise in Ecstasy	*Ebah Boyesen*
2.6	The Chemistry of Armour: Adrenaline as an Agent of Neurosis	*Surendra*

§3 Journal of Biodynamic Psychology: Vol. 1; Vol. 2; Vol. 3; & (Vol. 4)

Volume 1: 1980

3.1.1	What is Biodynamic Psychology?	*Gerda Boyesen*
3.1.2	Internal Organismic Pressure	*Clover Southwell*
3.1.3	Prevention of Neurosis: Self-Regulation from Birth On	*Eva Reich*
3.1.4	Biodynamic Theory of Neurosis	*Gerda & Mona-Lisa Boyesen*
3.1.5	The 'Spontaneous' Rhythmical Activity in Smooth Musculature	*Johannes Setekleiv*
3.1.6	Physiological Changes in Psychotherapy	*Paul Holman*
3.1.7	Biodynamic Concepts and Definitions	*I. F. B. P.*

Volume 2: 1981

3.2.1	Firing Zones, Muscle Tone, and the Orgasm Reflex	*David Boadella*
3.2.2	The Essence of Therapy	*Ebah Boyesen*
3.2.3a	The Infant & the Alpha	*Mona-Lisa Boyesen*
3.2.3b	Appendix	*Gerda Boyesen*
3.2.3c	Stimulating the Feeding Rhythm in the New-Born	*Mona-Lisa Boyesen*
3.2.4	A Translucent Turtle Ascends to the Stars	*Gottfried Heuer*
3.2.5	The Use and Abuse of Language in Therapy	*Courtenay Young*
3.2.6	Self-Help for Angina Sufferers	*Peg Nunneley*

3.2.7	Respondability – The Way of the Heart	*Dana Winkler*
	Volume 3: 1982	
3.3.1	The Primary Personality	*Gerda Boyesen*
3.3.2	Biodynamic Massage as a Therapeutic Tool – with special reference to the Biodynamic Concept of Equilibrium	*Clover Southwell*
3.3.3	The Dynamics of Psychosomatics	*Gerda Boyesen*
3.3.4	Transference, Resonance & Interference	*David Boadella*
3.3.5	Masochism and Masochistic Energy – an Insight	*Gerda Boyesen*
3.3.6	Aspects of a Biodynamic Gestalt Therapy	*Rainer Pervöltz*
3.3.7	Communication, Intention and Attention – An Essay	*Peg Nunneley*
	(Volume 4: 'The 1985 Lectures')	
3.4.1	The Aim of Psychotherapy	*Gerda Boyesen*
3.4.2	The Esoteric Function of Breastfeeding	*Gerda Boyesen*
3.4.3	The Prevention of Neurosis	*Gerda Boyesen*
3.4.4	Gerda Boyesen on Wilhelm Reich	*Gerda Boyesen*
3.4.5	Bio-electricity and Psychosomatic Symptoms	*Gerda Boyesen*
3.4.6	The Function of Psycho-peristalsis	*Gerda Boyesen*
3.4.7	The Primary Personality	*Gerda Boyesen*
§4	**Biodynamic Body Psychotherapy in Practice:** A Synopsis of Articles from *"The Biodynamic Philosophy & Treatment of Psychosomatic Conditions: Vol. 1 & 2"*:	
4.1	The Biodynamic approach to causes and treatment of idiopathic lower back pain	*Peg Nunneley*
4.2	The Broken Coccyx, the Kundalini and the Psycho-peristalsis	*Peg Nunneley*
4.3	Biodynamic Concepts and Treatment in the Ideopathic Pathology of Parkinson's Syndrome	*Peg Nunneley*
4.4	Biodynamic Theories and Techniques applied to the Syndrome of Migraine	*Peg Nunneley*
4.5	The Role of Biodynamic Therapies in Depressive States	*Peg Nunneley*
4.6	An Introduction to and Treatment by the Pulsatory Touch Technique	*Peg Nunneley*
4.7	Glossary of Terms used in Biodynamic Psychology & Psychotherapy	

§5 Collective Papers from the 2nd, 3rd & 4th Biodynamic Conferences, London 2nd Biodynamic Conference, London 2014

5.1.1	History and the Model of the Mind in Biodynamic Psychology	Clover Southwell, et al.
5.1.2	Biodynamic Psychotherapy: Where are we now?	Elya Steinberg
5.1.3	The Dynamic in Biodynamic Psychotherapy	Clover Southwell
5.1.4	Revisiting Gerda Boyesen's Theory of Psycho-peristalsis	Carlien van Heel
5.1.5	Biodynamic Psychotherapy's Worldview and the Client as a Self-Healer	Daniel Tanguay
5.1.6	Biodynamic and Mind: Building a Natural Theory of Biodynamics	Siegfried Bach

3rd Biodynamic Conference: London 2015

5.2.1	Introduction to the 3rd Biodynamic Conference: London 2015	Elya Steinberg
5.2.2	'I go to my Temple': Transcript of a video recording	Gerda Boyesen
5.2.3	The Role and Importance of Massage and Therapeutic Attitude in Biodynamic Body Psychotherapy: An interview with Gerda Boyesen	Daniel Tanguay
5.2.4	Biodynamic Psychotherapy and Embodied Spirituality	Anat Ben-Israel
5.2.5	Connecting to the 'Primary Couple Personality' – Couples Therapy with Body Psychotherapy	Gabriel Shiraz
5.2.6	Voodoo Death, Dissociative Identity Disorder (DID) and Biodynamic Psychotherapy	Elya Steinberg
5.2.7	The Eyes, the Windows of the Soul	Gabriele Gad
5.2.8	The Diaphragm as the Gateway to the Unconscious	Carlien van Heel & Albert von Eeghen
5.2.9	The Effect of Parental Attunement in Early Development on Adults: The Pink Infant in the Room	Shlomit Elishar
5.2.10	From Identity to Id-entity: Biodynamic Therapy as Soft Tissue Feminism	Guy Smith
5.2.11	Essence and Extension of Biodynamic Psychotherapy	Ebba Boyesen
5.2.12	Phases of Libido Circulation Development: A Psycho-postural Perspective	Alice Jacobus

4th Biodynamic Conference: London 2017

5.3.1	Biodynamic Typology: Stone, Warrior, Trouble Sunshine, Spiritual Warrior and Beyond	Daniel Tanguay

5.3.2	Feeling What You See and Hear: On Biodynamic Synaesthia	*Guy Smith*
5.3.3	Martial Arts and Biodynamic Body Psychotherapy: The Evolution of the Motoric Ego	*Elya Steinberg with Rüdiger Biedermann*

§6 'Biodynamic Massage': The Journal of the Association of Biodynamic Massage Therapists: Selected Articles

6.1	The History of Biodynamic Massage	*Bernd Eiden*
6.2	An Evolving Model of Supervision for Biodynamic Massage	*Gill Westland*
6.3	On Peristalsis	*Kathrin Stauffer*
6.4	The Psychotherapeutic Force of Biodynamic Massage: Part One: A Change in the Stuff of Who We Actually Are	*Clover Southwell*
6.5	The Psychotherapeutic Force of Biodynamic Massage: Part Two: Working with the Developmental Potential	*Clover Southwell*
6.6	"And let me wring your heart": Hamlet and the Somatic Metaphor	*Roz Carroll*
6.7	Biodynamic Massage: Is the Client Touched or Moved?	*Clover Southwell*
6.8	Biodynamic Massage Therapy, Change and the Nervous System	*Shaun & Lesley McCallion*
6.9	Biodynamic Massage: The Interface with Psychotherapy	*Gill Westland*
6.10	Massage for Shock & Trauma	*Kathrin Stauffer*
6.11	Managing Yourself and Managing the Dis-ease: Using Biodynamic Massage Therapy with Dystonia	*Denise Bailey-McCrohan*
6.12	Connective Tissue, the Connective Spirit and Structure of Tissue	*Lorna McNeur*
6.13	Does it matter if we look at Biodynamic Massage from a psycho-analytical perspective?	*Gill Westland*
6.14	Amplification – where massage and psychotherapy meet	*Lesley McCallion*
6.15	From Wanting to Having – The Vasomotoric Cycle and Receptivity	*Kathrin Stauffer*
6.16	Early Experiences as a Biodynamic Massage Therapist	*Vicki Martin*

6.17	An Exploration of How Touch can be Contactful in Psychotherapy	*Gill Westland*
6.18	A Biodynamic Massage Psychotherapy Client's Experience	*Jane Frances*
6.19	Inflammatory Bowel System, Part 1	*Lindsay Fovargue*
6.20	Inflammatory Bowel System, Part 2	*Lindsay Fovargue*
6.21	Biodynamic Massage in Business	*Pam Billinge*
6.22	Biodynamic Massage – Past, Present & Future	*Susan Frazer*
6.23	A Holistic View of Basic Metabolism	*Kathrin Stauffer*
6.24	Biodynamic Massage and Person-Centred Dementia Care	*Luke Tanner*
6.25	My Experience of Being 'Touched' and 'Held' in Biodynamic Supervision	*Hilary Price*
6.26	Responding to Our Clients Responses	*Clover Southwell*
6.27	Biodynamic Massage and Research	*Peter Mackereth*

§7 The Reichian World of Gerda Boyesen

7.1	The Reichian World of Gerda Boyesen and the Jellyfish Exercises	*Michael Heller*

§8 Other Biodynamic Articles – from various other sources

8.1	The Soul of the Body	*Gerda Boyesen*
8.2	Relating through Physical Touch in Contemporary Body Psychotherapy	*Gill Westland*
8.3	Biodynamic Psychology: Healing through the wisdom of the body	*Ellena Fries*
8.4	Biodynamic Massage as a body therapy and as a tool in Body Psychotherapy	*Monika Schiable*
8.5	The Gerda Boyesen Method: Biodynamic Therapy	*Clover Southwell*
8.6a	Transformative Moments: Short Stories from the Biodynamic Psychotherapy Room, Part 1	*Elya Steinberg*
8.6b	Transformative Moments: Short Stories from the Biodynamic Psychotherapy Room, Part 2	*Elya Steinberg*
8.6c	Transformative Moments: Short Stories from the Biodynamic Psychotherapy Room, Part 3	*Elya Steinberg*

8.6d	Transformative Moments: Short Stories from the Biodynamic Psychotherapy Room, Part 4	*Elya Steinberg*
8.7	Physical Touch in Psychotherapy: Why are we not touching more?	*Gill Westland*
8.8	Biodynamic Psychotherapy – Meeting the Psyche in the Body	*Clover Southwell*
8.9	Massage and Psychotherapy: Mapping a Landscape	*Roz Carroll*
8.10	Biodynamic Massage in Psychotherapy: re-integrating, re-owning and re-associating through the body	*Roz Carroll*
8.11	Levels of Consciousness and of Contact in Biodynamic Psychotherapy	*Clover Southwell*
8.12	Gerda Boyesen: Extracts from various sources	*IOBM website*
8.13	How I Developed Biodynamic Psychology	*Gerda Boyesen*
8.14	Biodynamic Massage Research: Psycho-peristalsis	*Kate Codrington*
8.15	Hearing Peristalsis: theory, interpretation and practice in Biodynamic Psychotherapy	*Theo Raymond*
8.16	Psycho-Peristalsis in the Shared Body	*Shlomit Eliashar & Yael Shahar*
8.17	Biodynamic Psychotherapy and the Intestinal Brain	*Gerda Boyesen*
8.18	The Sexual Boundary in Therapy	*Clover Southwell*
8.19	The Use of the Voice in Biodynamic Psychotherapy	*Gerda Boyesen*
8.20	The Breadth and Scope of Biodynamic Psychotherapy	*Carlien van Heel*
8.21	How Can We Evaluate the Subjective and Objective Aspects of Effectiveness in the Therapeutic Alliance?	*Elya Steinberg*
8.22	The Physiological Working-Out Principle	*Gerda Boyesen*
8.23	The Opening of the Heart and the Genital Embrace	*Gerda Boyesen*
8.24	Schematic Process of a Typical Session in Biodynamic Vegeto-therapy	*Clover Southwell*
8.25	The Biodynamic Use of 'It-level' and 'I-level' Language	*Clover Southwell*
8.26	Body Psychotherapy is a Psychotherapy	*Gerda Boyesen*
8.27	Biodynamic Psychotherapy and the Primary Personality	*Carlien van Heel*
8.28	The Biodynamic Therapeutic Approach	*Clover Southwell*
8.29	Biodynamic Massage: A Truly Therapeutic Massage	*Denise McCrohan*
8.30	The Use of Psychodrama in Biodynamic Psychotherapy: Case Examples from a Domestic Violence Healing workshop	*Denise St. Arnault et al.*

8.31	The Evidence-Base for Biodynamic Psychology (new)	*Courtenay Young*
8.32	The Origins and Characteristics of Biodynamic Psychotherapy	*Siegfried Bach*
8.33	"You made your bed, now you can lie in it": a Biodynamic understanding of healing the social mechanisms keeping women in abusive relationships	*Denise St Arnault et al.*
8.34	Narcissism in the light of Biodynamics	*Siegfried Bach*
8.35	Reflections on Gerda Boyesen's Concept of the Primary Personality	*Carlien van Heel*

§9 Other Short Articles on the Biodynamic Work

9.1	Some Thoughts on Involuntary Muscles	*Tom Warnecke*
9.2	Therapeutic Insights into Infant Massage	*Shlomit Eliashar*
9.3	The Emotional Cycle: Extracts from 'Soul and Flesh'	*Clover Southwell*
9.4	Quotations from Gerda Boyesen's: *The Joy of Healing*	*Siegfried Bach*
9.5	On Energetic Fluids	*Gerda Boyesen*
9.6	The Mother of Body Psychotherapy	*Kate Codrington*
9.7	Working with the Life Force	*Susan Frazer*
9.8	Becoming More Conscious of our Bodily Presence	*Clover Southwell*
9.9	Personal Reflections on Biodynamic Psychology: Its Strengths, Its weaknesses and its working with Ego & Id	*Clover Southwell*
9.10	The Gerda Boyesen Method	*Clover Southwell*
9.11	Biodynamic Psychology: SAGE Encyclopaedia	*Mary Molloy*
9.12	Tribute to Gerda Boyesen on her 70th Birthday	*David Boadella*
9.13	The Liberation of Energy: Interview with Gerda Boyesen Presentation at Gerda's 75th Birthday	*Robyn N. Lee*
9.14	Biodynamic Interviews: Links to Videos	*Rubens Kignel*
9.15	Twelve Healing Elements of the Biodynamic Approach	*I.O.B.M.*

Four Short Articles & One Longer Article on Transference

9.16	Beyond Transference	*Ebba Boyesen*
9.17	Transference and Projection	*Paul Boyesen*
9.18	Transference in Biodynamic Psychology: Gerda Boyesen interview	*Michael Heller*
9.19	Organic Transference / Energetic / Psychic Transference	*Mary Molloy*

9.20	Organic Transference	*Jacob Stattman*

§10 Obituaries & Epilogues

10.1	On the Enjoyment of Healing: An Obituary of Gerda Boyesen	*Peter Freudl*
10.2	The Healer: In memory of Gerda Boyesen	*Richard Burns*
10.3	The Life and Work of Gerda Boyesen	*Carlien van Heel*
10.4	Gerda Boyesen: 1922-2005	*Gill Westland*
10.5	A Tribute to Gerda Boyesen	*Bernd Eiden*
10.6	Epilogue	*Courtenay Young*

Authors in the Volume

Information & Other Books

R.D. Laing: 50 years since *The Divided Self*

Edited by Theodor Itten
& Courtenay Young

Originally published by PCCS Books:
2012 Remaindered (in 2023).

First published in 1960, *The Divided Self* by Scottish psychiatrist R.D. Laing (1927 - 1989) set out to explain psychosis as an ordinary and understandable human experience. Laing's insight was absolutely revolutionary in its humane approach. One commentator described it as 'that particular touch of genius which causes one to say "Yes, I have always known that; why have I never thought of it before?". Collected in these pages are writings critically appraising Laing's life, work, frailties, brilliance, and his wide and varied influences over the last half century. You will find transcripts, memoirs, newly commissioned articles and a few previously published papers. Contributions have come from colleagues, friends and clients, as well as people who never knew him personally, yet deeply appreciate his work. Each is different in tone and character. Each captures something unique about Laing and his work. R.D. Laing was famous for his empathic perception, sagacious intellect and wisdom of the heart, as well as his rebelliousness and falling from grace. In reading this book, you may be made to rethink some of your assumptions. We hope that you will find more than a little inspiration.

Chapters by: Hanspeter Gschwend, Phylliis Chesler, Theodor Itten, Mina Semyon, David Abrahamson, Leon Redler, Voyce Hendrix, Murray Gordon, Bruce Scott, Courtenay Young, Emmy van Deurzen, Andrew Feldmar, Susan Griffen, Chris Oakley, Anthony S. David, Brian Evans, Ron Roberts, Ljiljana Filipović, Brent Potter, A.P. Tom Ormay, Benjamin Sünkel-Laing, Francis Huxley, A.C. Smith & L. Ratna.

Review: Yet another book on R. D. Laing may appear self-indulgent. In fact, several of the contributions to this edited collection do seem to be of this nature. However, the title registers the half-century anniversary of Laing's The Divided Self, first published in 1960, which the authors and editors 'commemorate and celebrate in [their] various ways' (p. vii). The book appraises 'Laing's life, work, frailties, brilliance, and his wide and varied influences' (back cover).

The editors are both on the editorial board of the International Journal of Psychotherapy (IJP), which published a special R. D. Laing issue in 2011. These essays and articles have been reused in this book. I found the collection something of a hotch-potch, including some transcripts of somewhat vacuous interviews that had previously, perhaps understandably, not been published, and some reprinted material from the British Journal of Psychiatry and The Guardian. Of the new material, I thought the best chapter was that by Chris Oakley, entitled 'Where did it all go wrong?' His simple and simplistic answer is 'alcohol'. But the more complex version is that Laing was engulfed by his desire for adulation, becoming the tolerated and celebrated psychiatric superstar, operating on the edge of madness. To be clear, Laing was not mad but became the product of others, who twisted and obfuscated his message, for example undermining him by repeatedly calling him an 'anti-psychiatrist'. Laing's capacity to sabotage may explain his demise but he did provide a vision of the uncertainties and enigmas of personal interaction.

The other chapter that I appreciated was by Emmy van Deurzen, who established an existential therapy school at Regent's College and set up the Society for Existential Analysis. As she says, her form of existential psychotherapy is indebted to Laing's ideas and she came to work with what she thought would be existential therapy at the Arbours and Philadelphia Associations. However much Laing may be associated with existential psychotherapy, she argues that in practice he provided no practical direction for its development, instead turning to psychoanalysis and rebirthing.

The opportunities for new inspiration about R. D. Laing may be limited but there are a few, if far between, in this book.

For copies, go to website:
www.bodypsychotherapypublications.com

SPRITUAL AWAKENINGS

ABOUT BODY PSYCHOTHERAPY & TRAUMA

Edited by Courtenay Young

Extended essays about Body Psychotherapy and clinical work with people who have been traumatised: also included are essays about how to work with one's own trauma; 'vicarious trauma'; transgenerational trauma; PTSD; and other topic (list of contents to be confirmed):

- From Fragmentation to Wholeness: A brief history of the understanding of trauma, by David Boadella
- The Limits of Talk: Bessel van der Kolk wants to transform the treatment of trauma, by Mary Sykes Wylie
- The Assessment and Treatment of Complex PTSD, by Bessel van der Kolk
- Dissolving Trauma, by Courtenay Young
- Crowded Intimacy – Engaging Multiple Enactments in Complex Trauma Work: An Embodied Relational Approach, by Morit Heitzler
- The Polyvagal Theory for Treating Trauma: A tele seminar session with Stephen Porges & Ruth Buczynski
- Outliving Oneself: Trauma, Memory & Personal Identity, and The Aftermath of Violence, by Susan J. Brison
- The Effect of Abuse on the Soul and the Ego, by Al Pesso
- Do cry for me Argentina! The challenges trauma work poses for holistic psychotherapy, by Asaf Rolef Ben-Shahar
- Including the Body in Mainstream Psychotherapy for Traumatized Individuals, by Pat Ogden, Clare Pain, Kekuni Minton & Janina Fisher
- One Method of Processing Traumatic Memory, by Pat Ogden & Kekuni Minton
- Traumasomatics: Access to the present moment: Structural and Neurological Integration in the Light of Mindfulness, by Herbert Grassmann
- The Neurophysiology of Dissociation & Chronic Disease, by Robert C. Scaer
- Healing Trauma through the Body: The way in is the way out, by Ariel Giarretto
- The Importance of Breath in Vicarious Trauma, by Marjory Rand
- Understanding Vicarious Trauma: Self-help for paramedics & emergency service workers, health service workers & therapists, by Courtenay Young.

This book is planned to be published in 2025.
Please check out the BPP website for further information.

FORTHCOMING TITLES

ABOUT TOUCH IN BODY PSYCHOTHERAPY
Volume II

To Touch or Not to Touch? That is the Question

Edited by Courtenay Young

More extended essays about the Use of Touch in Body Psychotherapy:

- The Clinician's Use of Touch in Psychotherapy, by Anastasia D. McRae
- The Effective Use of Body Psychotherapy without Touch, Part 1, by Courtenay Young
- Embodiment: The Effective Use of Body Psychotherapy without Touch, Part 2, by Courtenay Young
- Somatics & Touch, by Lisbeth Marcher, et al
- Why Touch?, by Jerome Liss
- Physical Touch in Psychotherapy: Why are we not touching more?, by Gill Westland
- To Touch or Not to Touch: A Relational Body Psychotherapy Perspective, by Soshi Asheri
- Touch in Therapy and The Standard of Care in Psychotherapy and Counselling: Bringing clarity to illusive relationships, by Ofer Zur
- Touch as a Relational Affirmation, by Angela King and about three other essays.

**This book will (hopefully) be published in 2019 or 2020.
Please check out the BPP website for further information.**

bodypsychotherapypublications.com

SPRITUAL AWAKENINGS

OTHER PLANNED VOLUMES IN THIS SERIES

SOMATIC TRANSFERENCE, COUNTERTRANSFERENCE & RESONANCE

TRANSCULTURAL BODY PSYCHOTHERAPY

ABOUT SEXUALITY & SPIRITUALITY IN BODY PSYCHOTHERAPY

THE NEW FACE OF BODY PSYCHOTHERAPY

Probably a volume (or volumes) on Body Psychotherapy for certain conditions: Depression, Anxiety, Chronic Pain, etc.

Probably a volume on 'Body Psychotherapy & Dance/Movement Psychotherapy'

Possibly a volume on 'Embodied Supervision'

Possibly a volume on 'Transference & Countertransference in Body Psychotherapy'

and …
Maybe a couple of other volumes of other 'Miscellaneous Essays in Body Psychotherapy'

If you would like to become involved in Body Psychotherapy Publications in any way, or if you know of any Body Psychotherapy material – possibly in a different language – that you would like to see published or re-published; or if you would like to suggest a topic for a volume (as above)

Please e-mail: enquiries@bodypsychotherapypublications.com

www.ingramcontent.com/pod-product-compliance
Lightning Source LLC
LaVergne TN
LVHW061538070526
838199LV00077B/6829